Creating
VISUAL
BASIC
5 Add-ins

Creating
VISUAL
BASIC
5 Add-ins

Gene Swartzfager

CORIOLIS GROUP BOOKS

an International Thomson Publishing company I(T)P®

Albany, NY • Belmont, CA • Bonn • Boston • Cincinnati • Detroit • Johannesburg • London
Madrid • Melbourne • Mexico City • New York • Paris • Singapore • Tokyo • Toronto • Washington

PUBLISHER	KEITH WEISKAMP
PROJECT EDITOR	ANN WAGGONER AKEN
PRODUCTION COORDINATOR	NOMI SCHALIT
COVER ARTIST	PERFORMANCE DESIGN
COVER DESIGN	ANTHONY STOCK
INTERIOR DESIGN	NICOLE COLÓN
COMPOSITOR	PROIMAGE
COPYEDITOR	BONNIE TRENGA
PROOFREADER	CHARLOTTE ZUCCARINI
INDEXER	DICK EVANS
CD-ROM DEVELOPMENT	ROBERT CLARFIELD

Visual Developer Creating Visual Basic 5 Add-Ins
ISBN: 157610-167-3
Copyright © 1998 by The Coriolis Group, Inc.

Limits of Liability and Disclaimer of Warranty

Trademarks

The Coriolis Group, Inc.
An International Thomson Publishing Company
14455 N. Hayden Road, Suite 220
Scottsdale, Arizona 85260

602/483-0192
FAX 602/483-0193
http://www.coriolis.com

Printed in the United States of America
10 9 8 7 6 5 4 3 2 1

Dedicated to my father and mother, Albert and Philomena Swartzfager. I learned the value of patience and attention to detail from my mother, as she helped me with my school work as a child. My father, in his daily life, exemplifies the virtues of determination and perseverance. Whatever abilities I have as a writer and teacher flow from them.

ACKNOWLEDGMENTS

Some people discover their calling early in life and never deviate from it. My brother Dennis received a chemistry set for Christmas as a boy and, from that point on, knew in his heart that he was going to be a chemist. Others, like myself, struggle to find themselves. I taught junior high school for two years in my early 20s and enjoyed it very much. However, I was drafted during the Vietnam-era callup, and by the time I returned to civilian life, I had somehow lost my vocation as a teacher. It took me another 20 years to find it again.

I write VB books because it is another way to teach. Over the years, I've been inspired by several fine teachers. My first grade teacher, Sister Helen, lingers fondly in my memory. As I was soon to learn in the second and third grades, not all teachers had her gift for making learning fun and for making students want to come to school. I had several fine teachers in high school and college. Two philosophy teachers, Fathers Paul Berg and Thomas Hinsberg, stick out. Although their styles were different, they shared one very important trait: they loved the subject that they taught and conveyed their enthusiasm to their students.

Later in my life, three teachers have had a great influence on me. My partner and wife, Judy Ford, has over the years been a teacher, principal, superintendent, and director of curriculum. She has taught little kids with runny noses, doctoral candidates in Education, and children of all ages in between. I learn from her every day. Julia Heiman and Stuart Wachter are two mentors of mine who don't know the first thing about VB and are unlikely to ever read any book about computer programming, but they provided the map that helped me to rediscover myself as a teacher and writer.

I want to thank the members of The Coriolis Group's editing and publishing team for their contributions to this book. Two in particular deserve mention. Ann Waggoner Aken, my editor, had just started with Coriolis as I was beginning the book. I know she had other writers to work with during the last six months, but I always felt like I was the only one. Last but not least, thanks must go to Jeff Duntemann, who gave the thumbs-up sign to the idea for this book. Most publishers I talked to about the book basically said, "VB add-ins! What's an add-in?" Jeff's a technology guru and visionary who said, "VB add-ins! Cool stuff! We want to do the book." And so here it is.

CONTENTS

FOREWORD

When Gene Swartzfager called to ask me if I would write the foreword to his new book on creating VB5 add-ins, I said to him "I'll be glad to, but you know that I'm semi-retired these days and pretty worn down from my 25 years as a computer jock." He said that was precisely why I was the right person to write the foreword. "I'm a little confused" was my rejoinder.

Then he explained that because I had been with Ford Motor Company's MIS department all those years, I was the perfect guy to assess the significance of the new add-in software technology. He pointed out that I had started way back in the prehistoric era of computer programming, when IBM's "big iron" mainframes ruled the scene and the only languages that a corporate developer needed to know were Cobol and Assembler. I had survived to see the day, 20-some years later, on Microsoft's campus when the Windows 95 rollout extravaganza occurred. He reminded me that I had even gotten my picture taken that day with Chairman Bill and Jay Leno as part of my job as Ford's manager of the Microsoft Windows 95 Beta Program. I had seen and lived through it all, Gene said, so I was eminently qualified to place VB5 add-ins in their proper historical perspective.

I decided to take everything Gene said as a compliment and break away from surfing the Net for awhile. In my last few years with Ford, I had kept up with Visual Basic's evolution because a lot of the company's "propeller heads" that I managed were using it to write their Windows programs. I installed his book's CD-ROM files on my PC and fired up VB5. I have to admit that I don't write much VB code these days, but I know where the Add-Ins menu is so I spent a couple hours playing with the many different add-ins he wrote.

I'm amazed by what Microsoft's VB development team has done with this add-in technology. If I had only had this kind of tool back when I was sweating out Cobol code, programming would have been a lot more fun, I'd have averaged quite a few more lines of code a day, and I'd probably have fewer gray hairs. VB5 add-ins are a fantastic addition to the language. Gene's many demonstrations of how you can use the Extensibility object library to customize VB's development environment and automate the drudge work of programming are first rate.

Microsoft's role in the evolution of computer programming is still not quite clear. Windows and NT are currently the products with the biggest historical impact. But I see the ActiveX/COM/DCOM software architecture and its promise of component-based development as looming larger in the long run. In another 10 years, this architecture will have made significant inroads on other operating systems (including the Net) besides Windows. The beauty of the architecture lies in its flexibility, elegance, and ease of reuse. The fact that you can write such different kinds of applications as ActiveX add-ins, servers, controls, and documents and reuse them all in essentially the same way is remarkable.

I enthusiastically recommend Gene's book on add-ins to any VB programmer who wants to stay on the "cutting edge." Add-ins have only a cameo role to play in the bigger picture that is ActiveX and reusable software. But, for a VB programmer who wants top billing among his peers, mastering add-in development is a sure road to stardom.

—*Jim Schott*
Manager, Microsoft Windows 95 Beta Program

INTRODUCTION

All speech, written or spoken, is a dead language, until it finds a willing and prepared hearer.

—Robert Louis Stevenson

This book was written for the experienced Visual Basic and Windows developer who wants to take advantage of the new add-in Extensibility object model included with the Professional and Enterprise Editions of Visual Basic 5.0. This add-in object model is contained in the file VB5EXT.OLB; the reference name of VB5EXT.OLB is Microsoft Visual Basic 5.0 Extensibility, and its class library name, when it is viewed in VB's Object Browser, is VBIDE. VB5EXT.OLB enables you to develop what Microsoft refers to as a VB5 add-in.

A VB5 add-in is an ActiveX component that you create programmatically by reusing collections, objects, and members in VB5EXT.OLB. A VB5 add-in, as opposed to a Microsoft Excel, Access, or FoxPro add-in, is a special kind of ActiveX component that is designed to be reused only from within VB5's integrated development environment. The primary reason for developing an add-in (from here on in the book, the terms *add-in* and *VB5 add-in* are assumed to be synonymous) is to enable you to automate something in VB's IDE that is difficult, tedious, or time-consuming to accomplish manually.

I'm not sure why Microsoft used the term *add-in* to describe the kind of ActiveX component you create with the Extensibility object model. However, even if it's only coincidence, it's interesting to note that the initials *AI* can be used both as an abbreviation for add-in and for artificial intelligence. In a very real sense, an add-in is Microsoft's way of enabling a VB developer to add artificial intelligence or intelligent agents to VB's IDE. At the risk of sounding pretentious (or high on the latest designer drug), the implications of the previous statement are potentially mind-boggling! What might it mean in the future to say that the VB programming language's development environment has artificial intelligence?

Often when a complex new software technology is introduced, its possible applications and ramifications are only dimly understood. A common reaction to a new technology is to metaphorically scratch your head and say, "Wow, that's cool! But what's it good for?" That's the question this book, *Visual Developer Creating Visual Basic 5 Add-Ins*, is meant to answer. I wrote this book to:

- Show you how to write your own custom add-ins to automate drudge work and become a more productive VB programmer.

- Serve as the definitive reference work on add-ins and the object model contained in VB5EXT.OLB.

- Convey a sense of the magical feeling that you can get and the fun that you can have when you learn how to make VB's IDE jump through hoops and pull rabbits out of hats.

Whether you are a corporate VB developer at the Fortune 500 or 1000 level, a member of the VB development team of a Microsoft Solutions Provider company, or just a maverick VB hacker with a dream of writing a cool new ActiveX component, you will benefit if you learn how to create add-ins. This *Introduction* lays out the assumptions and conventions used in writing the book, the add-in code that comes with it, and the Windows Help file (ADDINEFS.HLP) that documents VB5EXT.OLB. It also tells you how to install the files that are on the book's CD-ROM and provides other information that will be helpful to know before you dig into the rest of the book.

Prerequisites For Using The Book

To use this book successfully, you must be an experienced VB programmer. An add-in is probably the most complex and difficult-to-test kind of ActiveX component that you can create with VB5. No beginners need apply for add-in development; and this book, although 500 pages long, does not waste any time explaining normal VB programming. It takes for granted that you have extensive knowledge of VB's syntax and language elements up through release 4.0 of the product.

You need to have access to a computer with the Professional or Enterprise Edition of VB5 installed on it. This is because VB5EXT.OLB is not included with VB5's Learning or Control Creation Edition. You also need to have the Windows 95 or the Windows NT (3.51 or higher) operating system on your PC to run the SETUP.EXE installation routine on the book's CD-ROM. This is because VB5, unlike VB4, only comes in a 32-bit version.

All references in this book to add-in language elements and syntax reflect the VB5 release. Although it is true that VB4 included add-in capabilities and an object library (VBEXT32.OLB), VB4's implementation of add-ins was primitive and inadequately documented; frankly, it deserved the obscurity in which it languished.

If you are going to develop VB5 add-ins, it helps to have some knowledge of the object-oriented programming (OOP for short) development paradigm's terminology and of Microsoft's specific ActiveX implementation of it. Ideally, a reader of this book would already have read my previous book titled *Visual Basic 5 Object-Oriented Programming* (ISBN 1-57610-106-1), published by Coriolis Group Books. However, this is not really a prerequisite; I will explain the fundamental OOP terminology and concepts used in add-in development later in this *Introduction*.

What The Book Contains

This book explains, documents, and demonstrates all the major capabilities and features that VB5 supports for add-in development. It consists of an

Introduction, 9 chapters, a *Dictionary* of add-in language elements, and a CD-ROM that contains add-in examples and their source code. The CD-ROM also contains a Windows Help file (ADDINEFS.HLP) that is the most comprehensive and definitive source of reference information on add-ins that currently exists. The book is divided into four parts.

Part I

Part I, titled *An Introduction To Add-Ins,* consists of Chapters 1 and 2. Part I includes the assumptions and conventions used in writing this book, the add-in code that comes with it, and the Windows Help file (ADDINEFS.HLP) that is the best reference for the add-in language elements and syntax. It explains the steps involved in the add-in development cycle and walks you through the process of creating a simple add-in. It also provides an add-in that demonstrates each of the 243 individual language elements of the add-in object model. Finally, it shows you how to customize and enhance the behavior of the various elements of an add-in's internal and external interface (Add-In Manager dialog box, VB Add-In Toolbar, **IDTExtensibility** object, and so on).

Part II

Part II, titled *How To Use Add-In Objects And Members* consists of Chapters 3 through 6. Part II breaks down VB's Extensibility object model into four general categories:

- Manipulating VB's menus, toolbars, and other IDE-level add-in objects

- Handling higher-level add-in objects (projects, references, code modules, designers, and controls)

- Manipulating lower-level objects (properties, members, and code)

- Handling and reacting to add-in related events

In Part II, you will learn how to syntactically combine the various objects, collections, and members of the add-in object model and create utility add-ins that do useful work.

Part III

Part III, titled *Case Studies Of Add-Ins*, consists of Chapters 7 through 9. The case studies in Part III are complex, sophisticated add-ins that artfully combine the elements of the add-in object model to create these useful applications:

- Dialog Box Builder
- VB Programmer's Log
- ActiveX Control Creation Tutor
- Code Librarian

Part III explains how these add-ins were designed and developed, demonstrates how they work, and suggests ways to enhance them.

Part IV

Part IV, titled *Add-In Dictionary*, is an alphabetical listing of all the collections, objects, and members of the add-in object model. You will find the *Dictionary* to be a very useful reference work for three reasons. First, VB5 shipped without any printed documentation. Second, the online information about add-ins and the Extensibility object model that comes with VB is inadequate, confusing, and in some cases erroneous. Third, the *Dictionary* refers to and is supplemented by extensive example code (in the associated ADDINEFS.HLP file) that is guaranteed to run because it all exists in the DEMOSYNT.VBP project on this book's CD-ROM.

The *Dictionary* also has entries for the objects and members contained in the VBAI class library, which is a collection of methods that I wrote for add-in development. The methods in the VBAI class library:

- Enhance the capabilities of the add-in object model
- Simplify some of the tasks commonly encountered in add-in development
- Customize the behavior of the VB Add-In toolbar and of your own add-ins

Installing The Files From The CD-ROM

To install the files that are on the CD-ROM that comes with this book, insert the CD-ROM into your PC's drive and close the drive. The AUTORUN.INF file on the CD-ROM should automatically display the Creating VB5 Add-Ins Setup dialog box shown in Figure I.1. If it does not, from Windows Explorer, double-click on the file SETUP.EXE on the CD-ROM's root directory to display the dialog box.

Select the logical drive on which you want to install the files (C: is the default) and click on Install. The setup routine then creates the structure of subdirectories listed in Table I.1 and copies the files to the appropriate subdirectories. The setup routine also automatically registers all the add-ins and copies the file ADDINEFS.HLP to the Windows \HELP subdirectory so it can be shared by all the book's add-ins. The installation requires about 6 MB of hard drive space. You cannot run the add-ins until they have been installed from the CD-ROM to your PC's hard drive.

After you have run the book's installation routine, you'll see that the Uninstall button on the Setup dialog box is enabled. If something goes wrong with the files you installed from the book's CD-ROM and you need to reinstall them, you should first click on Uninstall. After Uninstall removes the corrupted files and the subdirectory structure, click Install again to rerun the setup routine. Because of the way the Uninstall routine on the book's CD-ROM works, you should not save any files of your own to the \ADDINEFS subdirectory structure lest they be deleted if you uninstall the book's files.

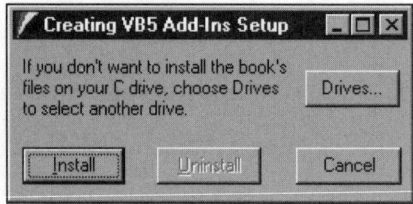

Figure I.1
Creating VB5 Add-Ins Setup.

	TABLE I.1

BOOK'S CD-ROM SUBDIRECTORY STRUCTURE.

Subdirectory Name	Description Of Files
\ADDINEFS\BRWSAPIS	Add-in version of demo copy of 16-bit Windows API Browser Utility
\ADDINEFS\CHAPTER1	Simple add-in discussed in Chapter 1
\ADDINEFS\CHAPTER2	Add-in that individually demonstrates all 243 of the add-in language elements and illustrates all of the interface customization features discussed in Chapter 2
\ADDINEFS\CHAPTER3	Add-in that shows how to control other add-ins, write entries to the Windows registry, and manipulate VB menus and toolbars
\ADDINEFS\CHAPTER4	Add-in that shows how to handle higher-level VB components (projects, references, code modules, designers, and controls)
\ADDINEFS\CHAPTER5	Two add-ins: one that shows how to manipulate lower-level objects (properties, members, and code) and an Add-In Interface Builder add-in
\ADDINEFS\CHAPTER6	Two add-ins: an Events Log add-in that shows how to handle and react to add-in related events raised by VB and a Controls Monitor add-in
\ADDINEFS\CHAPTER7	Two add-ins: Dialog Box Builder add-in and VB Programmer's Log add-in
\ADDINEFS\CHAPTER8	ActiveX Control Creation Tutor add-in
\ADDINEFS\CHAPTER9	Code Librarian add-in
\ADDINEFS\KNOWBASE	Files containing articles about add-ins from Microsoft's Knowledge Base
\ADDINEFS\VBAI	Source files for ActiveX server component that is VBAI class library
\ADDINEFS\WINDINFO	Window Information Utility add-in

 If you want to install and register the add-ins on the CD-ROM under both the Windows 95 and the NT (release 4.0 or later) operating systems, run SETUP.EXE and click Install under each of the operating systems. You can install the files on the same drive or partition for both operating systems and save disk space.

ReadMe Changes And Updates

There are a few changes and updates that didn't make it into the *Dictionary* section of the book. The topics for three add-in language elements (**GetGuid** method, **InsertFile** method and **VBNewProjects** collection) are not in the book, but you can find them in ADDINEFS.HLP.

In general, you should be aware that ADDINEFS.HLP contains the most recent version of the reference materials for VB5's add-in object model. If you notice a difference between the information provided in the Dictionary section of the book and the information in ADDINEFS.HLP for a particular language element, you should rely on the information in the Help file. Any such differences are minor in nature.

Typographic Conventions

The typographic conventions used in this book are listed in Table I.2.

TABLE I.2

TYPOGRAPHIC CONVENTIONS.

Example	Description
`Err.Raise 3`	This font is used for add-in code samples.
. . . .	This font and four dots separated by spaces indicate code that exists in an add-in's procedure but is not listed in the book.
TypeName, VarType	Words in bold with the initial letter capitalized indicate VB keywords or identifiers.
method	A word in italics indicates a word or words being used as a term, a technical term, or a reference to a section or chapter of this book.
Prompt	In syntax, a word in italics indicates the name of an argument in a procedure.
[*HelpFile*]	In syntax, an argument inside square brackets is optional.
Public|Private	In syntax, a pipe character (|) indicates that the parts on either side of the character are mutually exclusive.
ADDINEFS.HLP	Words in all capital letters indicate directory and/or file names.

Programming Conventions

The programming conventions used in the sample code listings in this book are:

- An apostrophe (') followed by a space introduces a code comment:

```
' Constants and variables:
```

- All comments are set off by one blank line before the comment and appear above the lines of code to which they are related. No endline comments are used.

- Control-flow code blocks are indented three spaces from the enclosing code:

```
Function GetDesc(VBE As VBE, ProgID As String) As String

   ' Check for specified failure case:
   If Not IsProgID(VBE, ProgID) Then
      GetDesc = ""
      Exit Function
   End If


   .  .  .  .


End Function
```

- VB5 supports the use of a line-continuation character, a space followed by an underscore (_). Code statements too long for one line are continued on the next line using the line-continuation character. Each continuation line is indented to line up logically with the code in the line above it. An example is:

```
' Center form:
Move (Screen.Width - Width) * 0.5, _
     (Screen.Height - Height) * 0.5
```

- Each variable is explicitly declared. The assumption is that Require Variable Declaration is checked on the Editor tab of VB's Options dialog box (Tools|Options).

- All declarations follow the format

```
Dim Item As String
```

where the declaration's data type is explicitly stated using the **As** keyword. The only exception to this rule is the declaration of a Windows API function. In that case, the suffix approach is used to conserve space and, as much as possible, to minimize the use of the line-continuation character. For example:

```
Declare Function LockWindowUpdate& Lib "USER32" (ByVal hWndLock&)
```

- If a VB intrinsic or enumerated constant exists, it is used. Examples:

```
' Warn user there will be a delay.
Screen.MousePointer = vbHourglass

' Reset default cursor.
Screen.MousePointer = vbDefault
```

- If a constant or constants exist for a Windows API function's arguments or return values, this book uses them. Examples:

```
' Constants for Windows API functions:
Const SWP_NOSIZE = &H1
Const SWP_NOMOVE = &H2
```

- If no VB enumerated or Windows API function constants exist, this book's code declares its own constants and assigns most numeric or string literals and control array index values to these constants. All enumerated constants that the book's code declares are prefixed by the lowercase letters *ai*.

Naming Conventions For Code

Naming conventions are akin to religious beliefs. Every VB programmer can give you several good reasons why his or her naming conventions are better than all the rest. Most programmers do not waste time preaching to the unconverted. Still, you cannot help but feel when you read books on VB or Microsoft Access programming that, if you do not adhere to the prescribed naming conventions, you will be excommunicated from the VB flock. Microsoft's suggested conventions for VB and Visual Basic For Application (VBA) are explained briefly in Visual Basic Books Online (select Help|Books Online) under the topic titled *Constant And Variable Naming Conventions*.

The naming conventions in this book for VB's built-in objects are based on Microsoft's suggested conventions for VB and VBA. However, the rest of the book's naming conventions are based on the assumption that you are going to use VB5 to write encapsulated, object-oriented code that will be compiled into an add-in ActiveX component. When you do this, you want to write procedures which, when viewed from VB's Object Browser dialog box (F2), appear the same, with regard to names/syntax, as VB's and VBA's members appear. To achieve this, this book names:

- A procedure that is a method with a verb. If necessary, the verb is followed by a noun that specifies a related object.

- A procedure that is a property with a noun.

- An argument with a noun or, occasionally, a verb. The name of the argument is not preceded by a three-letter prefix indicating the data type of the variable because the arguments for VB's and VBA's members do not use three-letter prefixes.

Names For Variables

Variables are given descriptive names when they are explicitly declared and are not given any prefix to indicate their data type. This sounds like heresy of the worst sort compared to the commonly-used VB naming conventions, which all use prefixes of some kind. The rationale for not using prefixes is threefold: 1) All the procedures are part of an encapsulated, object-oriented design; 2) 99 percent of all the add-in code variables are declared with procedure-level scope; 3) The code is meant, as much as is possible, to be readable like a natural language.

Today's generation of Windows programming languages and the ActiveX component software protocol Microsoft is promoting make it easy to write highly cohesive, encapsulated procedures/modules/classes. If you adhere to the object-oriented programming paradigm, the procedures comprising the members of a class library or component should be relatively short and should not be coupled with the code of other procedures except through message passing. No public/global variables should be used, and module-level variables, except for those required in conjunction with VB's **Property Get**, **Let** and **Set** procedures, should only be rarely declared (and then closely commented to document their use).

For those VB developers who commit themselves to the OOP paradigm, programmers who continue to clutter their procedures with elaborate and esoteric variable naming conventions and broadly-scoped variables seem very much like those who continue to observe an antiquated religious dogma.

The scope of variables is specified in this way:

- Public or global variables are only used in certain situations and are not prefixed to indicate their scope. First, object variables declared with the **WithEvents** keyword are required by VB to be **Public**. Second, to promote readability, the **VBE** object variable is always named the same as the **VBE** object that is the root object of the VB5EXT.OLB object library. Third, an object variable that is assigned a reference to one of the objects in the book's VBAI class library (**AITBar**, **Cmd**, **Reg** and **Util**) is named the same as the class it instantiates.

- Module-level variables are declared with the prefix *m*. There are two exceptions to this rule. First, the **VBE** object variable is always named the same as the **VBE** object it references. Second, an object variable that references one of the VBAI class library's objects is named the same as the class it instantiates.

- Except for the uses of **Public** variables previously mentioned, all module-level variables are declared with the **Private** statement. Procedure-level variables, declared with the **Dim** or **Static** statement, are of course private by nature.

Names For Form And Control Objects

All form and control objects intrinsic to VB are identified by a lowercase, three-letter prefix specifying the class of the object. These prefixes are listed in Visual Basic Books Online under the topic titled *Object Naming Conventions*.

 I do deviate from this naming convention for controls that are part of a control array. In such cases, I simply use the control's three-letter prefix as its **Name** property. The control's **Index** property value is then specified by an enumerated constant. For example, two **CommandButton** objects for OK and Cancel, which are part of a control array, would be identified in code by cmd(aiCBOK) and cmd(aiCBCancel), with aiCBOK and aiCBCancel being enumerated constants.

Other Conventions

Other conventions used in this book are:

- Unless specified otherwise, the letters *VB* stand for the Professional Edition of Microsoft Visual Basic 5.0.

- The pronoun *you* refers to the VB developer and/or person that is reading the book.

- Menu commands that are to be selected as part of a sequence are separated by a pipe character (|).

- Throughout the book, references are made to the paths on which different files are found (for example, C:\ADDINEFS\CHAPTER2). The root drive or partition in these references is assumed to be C:, but you must remember on which drive you actually installed the files.

- The initials *EFS* are used in the names of the book's Help file and installation subdirectories. They are the three initials of my legal name (Eugene Francis Swartzfager), are arbitrarily used, and have no significance whatsoever (except that my mother is very pleased).

Object-Oriented Terms And Concepts

As I said earlier in this *Introduction,* to best understand the material in this book and ADDINEFS.HLP, it helps to have some knowledge of the object-oriented programming development paradigm's terminology and of Microsoft's specific ActiveX implementation of OOP. I don't have enough space in this book to write a complete section on OOP concepts, but there are about a half dozen terms (*class, object, instantiation, member, method, public interface,* and *messaging*) that are constantly used. These terms are listed and succinctly explained in the following bullet points:

- Class: A class is a template or formal category that defines the possible settings of an object's properties, the methods that govern an object's behavior, and the events to which an object can respond. The formal specification of an object's properties, methods, and events (generically referred to as *members*) is done only once when the class is created. A commonly-used metaphor for a class is that it is like a cookie-cutter. Examples of classes are human being, male, and female. Classes can be organized into hierarchies, with male and female being considered subclasses of human being or girl and woman being considered subclasses of female.

- Object: An object is an example or instance of a particular class. When a class is instantiated, an object or instance of that class is created whose properties are initially set to certain default values. The settings of these properties can change during the life of the object, but only within the range defined by the object's class. An object is like a cookie that emerges from the cookie-cutter. Examples of objects are Tom and Dick (of the male class) or Susie and Mary (of the female class). Tom has properties like HairColor and Age, whose values change over the years.

- Instantiation: Instantiation is the process by which an object is created from a class. In VB, you instantiate an object either by using the **CreateObject** function or the **Dim As New** mode of declaration.

- Member: A member is an element of an object. It is a generic term that is equivalent, in VB's implementation of OOP, to a property, method, or event. At the code level of abstraction, a VB member consists of a procedure. Members can be either **Public** or **Private** in scope, and only **Public** members are displayed in the Object Browser.

- Method: A method is a **Sub** or **Function** procedure that acts on an object and causes it to behave in some manner.

- Public interface: The public interface of a class is the information about the class that is publicly available. A class or object instance of a class is sometimes referred to as a "black box," which hides most of the details of its implementation. What you can know about a class (that is, its public interface) is revealed, in VB's implementation of OOP, via the Object Browser. The major elements of the public interface of a VB class library or ActiveX component are its **Public** classes and the **Public** procedures/arguments/return values of those classes. If a class library or ActiveX component has a Windows Help file associated with it, the information in the Help file can be thought of as an extension of the public interface. A programmer reuses an object by sending messages to elements of its public interface.

- Messaging: Messaging is the process by which objects interact with each other. A message to an object is a request that a method be carried out, a property be set/returned, or an event be raised. To send a message, you specify the name of the object, the name of one of its members, and the parameters specified by the member's arguments (required or optional). Most members of an object also return a message to the reuser of the object, which consists of the return value(s).

 For more detailed information about object-oriented programming with VB, see my book titled *Visual Basic 5 Object-Oriented Programming* (ISBN 1-57610-106-1), published by Coriolis Group Books. Probably the best book about ActiveX component programming with VB (excluding ActiveX add-ins, which are not addressed) is titled *Dan Appleman's Developing ActiveX Components With Visual Basic 5.0* (ISBN 1-56276-510-8), published by Ziff-Davis Press.

Chapter 2's Demo Syntax Add-In

The *Dictionary* section of this book will probably turn out to be its most-used portion. I wrote the *Dictionary* first, and I've constantly referred back to it as I wrote the rest of the book and the book's add-in code. However, I have a confession to make; the *Dictionary* is incomplete. The publisher and I decided that we would not be doing the right thing if we printed all the Example code for the 243 individual language elements in the *Dictionary* itself. Printing the Example code would have required about another 300 pages and would have resulted in charging you, the reader, another $10 to $15 to purchase the book. Instead, what I decided to do was to create one add-in (discussed in Chapter 2) whose sole purpose is to demonstrate and run the Example code for each of the 243 add-in language elements.

 In addition, you can also find the Example code in ADDINEFS.HLP under the Help topic for each language element.

Running The Demo Syntax Add-In

When you run SETUP.EXE on the book's CD-ROM, this Demo Syntax add-in is installed and registered. To run and use it, follow these steps:

- Assuming that you have installed the files from the book's CD-ROM, start VB5.

- Select Add-Ins|Add-In Manager to display the Add-In Manager dialog box.

- Check the item Creating VB5 Add-Ins: Chapter 2 and choose OK to close the dialog box.

- Run the Demo Syntax add-in by clicking its button (marked #2) on the VB Add-In toolbar or by selecting Add-Ins and clicking the menu item Creating VB5 Add-Ins: Chapter 2. The Demo VB5 Add-In Syntax dialog box appears as in Figure I.2.

From here on, running the Example code for a specific language element is a no-brainer. Double-click the item (for example, **Activate** method) or select it and click on Demo. VB performs the action(s) dictated by the Example code and a series of message boxes are displayed by the Example code to explain what is happening. For example, the first message box for the **Activate** method demo is in Figure I.3.

If you click on the message box's Help button, the Help topic in ADDINEFS.HLP containing the Example code is displayed as in Figure I.4.

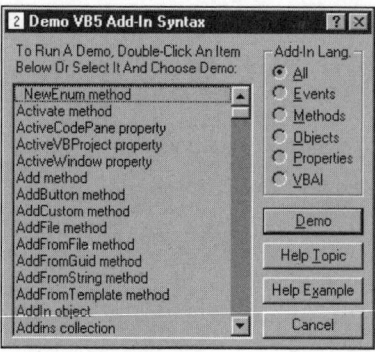

Figure I.2
Demo VB5 Add-In Syntax dialog box.

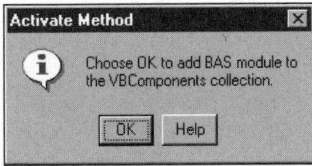

Figure I.3
Message box displayed by Demo Syntax add-in.

If the add-in language element you are demonstrating has more than one usage, clicking a message box's Help button displays the Example code scrolled down to the line in the code where the demonstration is currently executing.

 To get Help for how the Demo VB5 Add-In Syntax dialog box itself works, click the ? button at the top-right corner of the title bar to enable the context-sensitive, What's This Help popup mode. Then click the control (for example, the **ListBox**) on the dialog box for which you want information and a Help popup like the one in Figure I.5 is displayed.

Other Info About Demo Syntax Add-In

You should also be aware of these other points about the Demo VB5 Add-In Syntax add-in:

• When you run it and the Example code for an add-in language element, each demonstration starts from scratch and adds a Standard EXE project to VB's IDE that it names "Demo". This "Demo" project is added before the procedure demonstrating the language element executes (you will see this project added to the Project Explorer window).

• If you run it while another project is open within VB's IDE, it will not interfere with or corrupt the other project in any way.

• Although its major function is to demonstrate each of the add-in language elements, the Demo Syntax add-in is also used to illustrate all the possible interface customization features an add-in can support. It does this by displaying message boxes as the various **IDTExtensibility** object interface methods execute. If you don't want to be bothered with these message boxes, start the add-in from the Add-In toolbar. To learn how to do this, see the section in Chapter 2 titled *The VB Add-In Toolbar Add-In*.

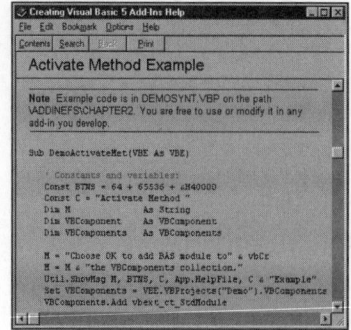

Figure I.4
Add-in language element's Example code.

> Contains list of add-in language elements to be
> demonstrated. Items in list are determined by Add-In
> Lang. option button that is checked.

Figure I.5
Example of popup Help for Demo Syntax add-in.

- You can run the Demo Syntax add-in project (DEMOSYNT.VBP) in debug mode and watch its source code execute step-by-step. To learn how to do this, see the section in Chapter 1 titled *Testing And Debugging An Add-In*.

ADDINEFS.HLP For Add-Ins

The installation routine for this book's CD-ROM places the file ADDINEFS .HLP on the \HELP subdirectory of the Windows or Windows NT path on your PC, so it can be shared by all the add-ins for this book. This Windows Help file, which I wrote while developing the *Dictionary* section of the book, is the definitive reference for VB5 add-ins. You can access ADDINEFS.HLP either by running Chapter 2's Demo VB5 Add-In Syntax add-in or by double-clicking the file from Windows Explorer. Its Contents topic is shown in Figure I.6.

Each of the 243 add-in language elements is documented in this Help file. For example, the topic for the **Activate** method is shown in Figure I.7. ADDINEFS.HLP uses the standard Microsoft-style format for documenting an ActiveX component, with See Also, Example, and Applies To jumps. In addition, the 32 methods of my VBAI class library and the hidden members of the Extensibility object model are also documented in ADDINEFS.HLP.

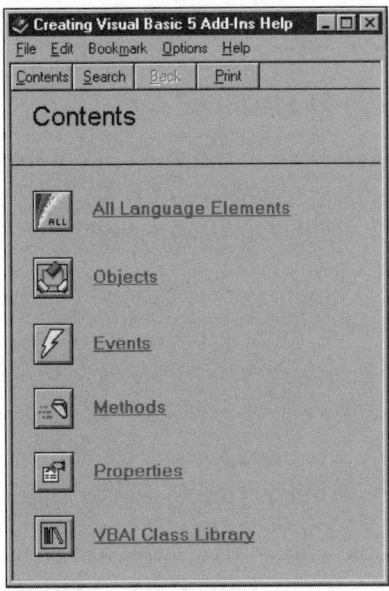

Figure I.6
Contents topic of ADDINEFS.HLP.

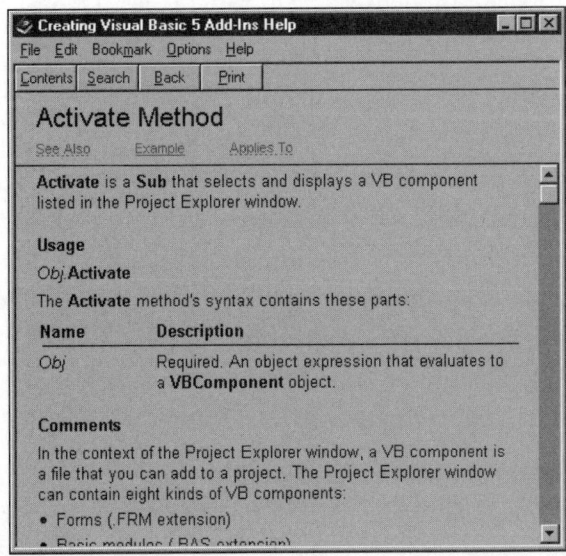

Figure I.7
Help topic in ADDINEFS.HLP for **Activate** method.

Other Sources Of Info About Add-Ins

Besides this book, its ADDINEFS.HLP file, its Demo VB5 Add-In Syntax add-in, and the other add-ins on the book's CD-ROM, the other sources of information about add-ins that I'm aware of are:

- Visual Basic Books Online: From VB's menu, select Help|Books Online. Then, from Visual Basic Books Online, select View|Index and type "add-ins" in the Index box to display a list of all the keywords and topics related to add-ins. The add-in information available in Visual Basic Books Online is better than what was included with VB4; however, it is mostly geared toward a beginner's level and contains no extensive sample code.

- VB's Help file: Topics for the individual add-in language elements are available here, but the information provided is often inadequate, confusing, and in some cases erroneous. For example, there is a **Description** property in the VBIDE add-in class library. If you compare its inadequate Help topic in VB5.HLP to its comprehensive Help topic in ADDINEFS.HLP, you will see why I say that ADDINEFS.HLP is the definitive reference on add-ins.

- VB sample add-in: There is one sample add-in that ships with Visual Basic that is written in VB (the VB TabOrder Window add-in), whose source code is on the VB path \SAMPLES\COMPTOOL\ADDINS\TABORDER. It is not registered when VB is installed, and thus it doesn't appear in the Add-In Manager dialog box. To compile and register it, follow the instructions in Chapter 1 of this book, in the section titled *Compiling, Registering And Running An Add-In* (the sample add-in's project file is TAB-ORDER.VBP). The source code for this add-in is worth your study, even though I find its readability quotient to be pretty low.

Unfortunately, although VB ships with many other Wizard-style add-ins, you will not be able to find the source code for them. Microsoft chose to ship only the compiled DLL ActiveX components for these add-ins, which are found on the VB path \WIZARDS.

- Other sources: The installation routine for this book's CD-ROM placed any articles about VB5 add-ins from the Microsoft Knowledge Base or from www.microsoft.com on the path \ADDINEFS\KNOWBASE. There wasn't much information available.

I would include a bibliography of articles and books about VB5 add-ins if there were any to be cited; however, I have checked all the VB books that have been published since the release of VB5 and not a single one contains any detailed information about or examples of VB5 add-ins.

 In July 1997, a new book by Rod Stephens titled *Advanced Visual Basic Techniques* (ISBN 0-471-18881-6) was published by Wiley Computer Publishing. Although this book contains much good information, do not be fooled by its Table of Contents that lists a Part Two containing four chapters on add-ins; these add-ins were written with the old VB4 Extensibility object model.

Tips On Using VB5's New IDE

VB5's new IDE (integrated development environment) is a classic case of good news, bad news. The good news is that the new menu structure and toolbars (yes, there's more than one toolbar now) are much more similar than in the past to those used by VBA in Microsoft's Office 97. The bad news is that the IDE is very different from the one in either VB3 or VB4. So, if you are just starting with VB5, it's going to take a little getting used to. If you have already been using VB5 for awhile, you can skip the rest of this section.

The major features of VB5's new IDE that I want to highlight are:

- The first time you start VB5, it will display itself in its default MDI (multiple document interface) mode. This new feature does come in handy when you need to open more than one project at a time, a capability that VB5 now supports primarily to facilitate ActiveX component development. However, if you typically work with one project at a time, you may prefer the greater freedom that the old SDI (single document interface) mode permits. To switch from MDI mode to SDI mode, select Tools|Options and click on the Advanced tab of the Options dialog box. You can then check the SDI Development Environment option.

- In order to support its new MDI mode, VB5 also makes the various windows of its IDE dockable (Project Explorer, Properties, Toolbox, and so on).

To get them to float free, you can drag them free; or, select Tools|Options, click the Docking tab, and deselect the name of the window you want to float free.

- The first time you start VB5, it will display its default toolbar configuration, which displays the Standard toolbar only. You will immediately wonder what has happened to the handy debug toolbar buttons. VB5 can now display as many as five different toolbars (Standard, Edit, Debug, Form Editor, and Add-In), and you can create your own custom toolbars. You can also dock them or let them float free. To change the configuration of the toolbars, select View|Toolbars and proceed from there.

- VB5 no longer has VB4's Insert menu. To add a new form, standard module, class module (or just about any kind of file) to a VB5 project, use the new Project menu. You'll find all the Add options there.

- Compared to the old days with VB3, the number of possible Project-level or IDE-level options that VB5 now lets you set is mind-boggling. VB5 splits these options up between two menus. To set project-level options (now referred to as properties of the project), select the Project|Properties menu command and find the setting on one of the four tabs of the Project Properties dialog box. To set IDE-level options, select the Tools|Options and find the setting on one of the six tabs of the Options dialog box.

- As with previous releases, VB5 comes with a Help file, which is now named VB5.HLP (not VB.HLP as it always was in the past). In addition, VB5 has two new Help-related features that, once you get used to them, are great additions to the IDE. One new feature is Visual Basic Books Online. To start it, select Help|Books Online. The other new Help-related feature is VB5's ability to display, as popups in a code module, information about the syntactical element, object, or member for which you are currently writing code. These Auto popups, as they are called, are turned on by default when you install VB5. To turn any one of the three Auto features off (List Members, Quick Info, or Data Tips), select Tools|Options and change their settings on the Editor tab of the Options dialog box.

That's it for your *Introduction* to this book and VB5 add-ins. It's time to get your feet wet and wade into the add-in development pool; you needn't worry, because the water in Chapter 1 is warm and inviting. I'm going to start you off at the shallow end of the pool by showing you how to create, debug, test, compile, and register a simple add-in. However, before you even create a simple add-in, you should learn about the design options that are available to an add-in developer; and that's the topic with which we're going to start Chapter 1.

Part

AN INTRODUCTION
TO ADD-INS

CREATING A SIMPLE VB ADD-IN 1

*If a man will begin with certainties, he shall end in doubts, but if he
will be content to begin with doubts, he shall end in certainties.*

—*Francis Bacon*

In Chapter 1, you're going to learn everything you need to
know to create a simple VB5 add-in from scratch. Although
you may have created add-ins in the past with VB4
or Microsoft Office's Excel or Access, you need to work
your way through this chapter. VB5 add-ins use a different
Extensibility object model than VB4 add-ins. Although add-
ins implemented in VB5 are functionally similar to those
implemented in Excel or Access, creating them is quite a different process.

An add-in is an ActiveX component that you create by writing
code that reuses the public objects and members in VB's
Extensibility object model. The add-in can be either a DLL
(in-process) or EXE (out-of-process) ActiveX component. The
VB Extensibility object model, whose functionality you can
access and reuse in an add-in, is contained in the Microsoft
Visual Basic 5.0 Extensibility class library. You can set a reference to this in the References dialog box. After you do so, the
VB Extensibility object model appears in the Object Browser
as the VBIDE class library.

3

VB add-ins customize and extend the Visual Basic integrated development environment (IDE). They also enable you to automate something in VB's IDE that is difficult, tedious, or time-consuming to accomplish manually. You can also write add-ins to enhance existing features of VB's IDE; for example, you can write an add-in that copies and pastes both VB controls and their underlying code from one **Form** object to another.

VB Books Online refers to an add-in as a "snap-on." Other Windows applications like Adobe Photoshop or 3D Studio Max call them "plug-ins." In this book, we will stick with "add-in." VB Books Online also refers to four kinds of add-ins (add-in, Wizard, utility, and builder). I see no point in adhering to this arbitrary and unnecessary add-in classification scheme, except for the term "Wizard," which is widely used and clearly defined in the development arena. In the context of an add-in, a Wizard is a tool that helps you perform a task by displaying several forms in succession, soliciting input from you on each form, and then creating a file based on your inputs.

To get you off the add-in development bench and into the ball game, Chapter 1 discusses how to:

- Design an add-in's public interface

- Assemble its component modules and members

- Write the procedures for its class modules

- Use generic coding techniques to maximize the performance and readability of its code

- Test and debug it

- Compile, register, and run it

- Troubleshoot problems you may encounter when trying to compile or run it

Designing An Add-In's Public Interface

You need to carefully consider several design issues before you start to create an add-in. Creating an add-in is no different from any other software development project. The initial time and effort you invest analyzing design issues and their tradeoffs will pay off two or three times over when you actually start to write the code. In this chapter, we will outline and discuss in general terms the key design variables you need to consider. Later in the book, we will deal with various possible implementation strategies in more depth. Table 1.1 lists the design issues.

Kinds Of ActiveX Components

Most of the initial design issues relate to the add-in's public interface. Your choices determine how the add-in's ActiveX component runs and behaves, how it communicates with other ActiveX components, and vice-versa. The first two issues you must resolve are: what kind of ActiveX component (in-process DLL vs. out-of-process EXE) you want your add-in to be, and how you are going to create it (from scratch or with VB's Add-in project template).

This book is not intended to be a primer on creating ActiveX components. Excellent books already exist on this subject. Two of the best are *Dan Appleman's Developing ActiveX Components With Visual Basic 5.0*, ISBN 1-56276-510-8 (published by Ziff-Davis Press), and my own title, *Visual Basic 5 Object-Oriented Programming*, ISBN 1-57610-106-1 (published by The Coriolis Group). The focus of this book, *Creating Visual Basic 5 Add-Ins*, is much narrower and is restricted to the issues related to creating the special kind of ActiveX component known as an add-in. When one of these add-in issues relates to a

	TABLE 1.1

ADD-IN DESIGN ISSUES.

Issue	Options
Kind of ActiveX component	DLL (in-process) vs. EXE (out-of-process)
Use VB-provided template	Create from scratch vs. use VB's add-in project template
How add-in should be started	From menu item, VB Add-In toolbar button, custom toolbar button, or none of the above
GUI provided by add-in	**Form** object, Wizard-style succession of **Form** objects, ActiveX document object, or none of the above
Reuse other ActiveX components	Reuse them or not; which ones to reuse
Expose add-in's members	Declare all add-in members as **Private** or **Friend** vs. declare some as **Public**

more general ActiveX issue (for example, the relative advantages of an EXE vs. DLL implementation), we will address it to the degree required and then move on.

An ActiveX software component is a physical encapsulation of one or more services that are made available through its interfaces. A component is defined by the services it provides and how it interacts with other components. All we know about a component externally is its interface; the outside world does not see the internal construction and implementation of the component (sometimes referred to as a *black box*).

An add-in is a special kind of ActiveX component that:

- Interacts with just one other component, VB's IDE

- Implements a unique kind of internal interface, called the **IDTExtensibility** object, that enables it to interact with VB's IDE

Now let's move on to deciding between a DLL add-in and an EXE one. A DLL add-in runs in the same memory process as VB itself, so it runs faster than an equivalent EXE one. This is a major advantage because, as you will learn later in this book, performance is a major issue for add-ins. A DLL add-in also displays forms that automatically receive the focus. And, unlike the case with VB4, VB5-created DLL add-ins can display modeless forms and can execute code asynchronously.

The only real advantage an EXE add-in has over its DLL counterpart is that an EXE add-in's **StartMode** property can be either 0 - **vbSModeStandalone** (component is being run as a standalone application), or 1 - **vbSModeAutomation** (component is being run as an add-in). Once in a blue moon, you might have an add-in whose special nature warrants running it as a standalone application instead of from within VB's IDE. I recommend that all add-ins that you create be DLL components. Microsoft itself obviously believes that this is the best policy because it has compiled almost all of the add-ins that accompany VB as DLLs. The only EXE add-in distributed with VB is the VB API Viewer (referred to as the API Text Viewer in its standalone version).

 Given that the DLL add-in component is the preferred design choice, it seems odd that Microsoft's VB development team decided that the add-in project template icon in the New Project dialog box should open an ActiveX EXE project template. This makes no sense whatsoever and, for this reason alone, I recommend that you create your add-in projects from scratch and not use VB's add-in project template. Besides, if you want to learn how to create VB add-ins, you need to learn to do so from the ground up without taking shortcuts.

Start Options For An Add-In

Next, we must decide how the VB developer who will be reusing your add-in will interact with it. How will the developer start the add-in? Four start options are available:

- Choose a VB menu item
- Click a button on the VB Add-In toolbar
- Click a button on a custom toolbar
- Connect the add-in from the Add-In Manager dialog box (no further action required)

No hard-and-fast rules apply here. When it comes to the first three start options, conventional add-in programming practice and personal preference tend to dictate how you choose. My own recommendations are based primarily on convention. A developer should be able to start any add-in that interacts visually with him or her from both its own menu item on VB's Add-Ins menu and from a toolbar button.

If the add-in functions independently of other add-ins or is not part of an add-in suite, it should have a button on the VB Add-In toolbar that Microsoft distributed with VB. However, if the add-in is part of a suite of utility-type add-ins, it makes sense to create your own custom toolbar and populate it with buttons for the various add-ins. We will look at how to implement these different toolbar interfaces later in the book.

 You can rule out the last of the four start options except for the rare add-in that does not display a form as a GUI but instead runs in the background and does not interact with the developer visually.

Once you decide how the developer will start your add-in, you need to consider what type of interface the add-in itself will present after it is started. Here are the four options:

- A single **Form** object (or at most two)

- A succession of more than two **Form** objects (as in the case of a Wizard add-in)

- An ActiveX document object

- No GUI at all

As with the start options, my recommendations here are based primarily on convention. If an add-in doesn't fall into the Wizard category and requires no more than two modal or modeless forms, create the interface with a plain vanilla form(s). If an add-in's functionality is so complex that it requires the developer to choose from a long series, go with the Wizard GUI metaphor. Wizards are as close to a de facto standard in Windows development as you can find; there is no reason to reinvent this particular wheel because it works very well.

If an add-in needs to create a new VB IDE Tool window (for example, to display a customized programmer's log or journal), then your add-in will have to include and display an ActiveX document object. In this chapter, we will look at the first design option (a single **Form** object). In later chapters, we will provide examples of the second and third options (Wizards and ActiveX document objects).

 Again, you can rule out the last of the four interface options except for the rare add-in that does not display any window as a GUI but instead runs in the background and does not interact with the developer visually.

Interacting With Other ActiveX Components

The design decision you need to make before writing any add-in code is how your add-in interacts programmatically with other ActiveX components. First, how many other ActiveX components will an add-in reference and how many of these other components' public members (that is, methods, properties, and events) will it reuse? At a bare minimum, any VB add-in must reference and reuse some objects from at least these four class libraries:

- Visual Basic For Applications (VBA)

- Visual Basic runtime objects and procedures (VBRUN)

- Visual Basic objects and procedures (VB)

- Microsoft Visual Basic 5.0 Extensibility (VBIDE)

The first three reference the default or intrinsic ActiveX components that comprise VB itself. These default references are included in every VB5 project, cannot be removed, and must be part of any application (add-in or otherwise). The fourth references the VBIDE class library, which contains the Extensibility Object model that enables an add-in to programmatically interact with and exert control over VB's IDE.

In addition to these four, you must decide what other ActiveX components you want your add-in to reference. You make this decision based on whether or not you want to reuse any of the public members a given ActiveX component contains. For example, all VB add-ins that you want a developer to start from a menu item or custom toolbar need to reference the Office class library (Microsoft Office 8.0 Object Library) because Office contains the reusable objects and members required to implement menu items and toolbars in VB5.

Likewise, an add-in may benefit from reusing the functionality contained in other kinds of ActiveX components (such as servers or controls). For example, the VBAI ActiveX server component that comes with this book on the CD-ROM, Creating VB5 Add-Ins: Library Of Reusable Members, is a class library that provides many methods to assist in writing and customizing add-ins. Another example would be an add-in that, at some point in its execution, needs to display a common dialog box. One way to do this is to set a reference in the add-in to the **CommonDialog** ActiveX control (Microsoft Common Dialog Control 5.0), instantiate it on a **Form** object, and write code in the add-in to display and manipulate it.

I can make no valid general recommendation regarding the other ActiveX components that an add-in should reference. All of the add-ins in this book, except the simple one in this chapter, reference at least six other components: the four required ones (VBA, VBRUN, VB, and VBIDE), Office, and VBAI. I believe that, once you become familiar with this book's VBAI class library, you will always want to reference and reuse it in any add-in you write. However, that's your design decision to make. One of the most elegant features of Microsoft's entire ActiveX/COM/DCOM architecture is the ease with which you can reuse other components' functionality and the freedom you enjoy to reuse or not, depending on your needs and programming philosophy.

Once you have determined how many other ActiveX components your add-in will reference and reuse, you need to flip to the other side of the coin. When writing an add-in, you must decide whether or not to declare as **Public** any of the add-in's class members, thus making them available for other ActiveX components or standalone applications to reuse. VB Books Online straightforwardly recommends: "All class procedures should be declared as **Private** to prevent other routines from inadvertently referencing them." I agree, for the majority of cases.

However, you can make an exception in two cases. First is the case of an out-of-process EXE add-in that you want to be able to start in either 0 - **vbSMode Standalone** or 1 - **vbSModeAutomation** mode. For this kind of add-in, it might make sense to expose some of its functionality as public members. Second is the case of methods in an add-in that you would declare with the **Friend** keyword (new to VB5). **Friend** modifies the definition of a method in a class module to make the method callable from modules that are outside the class but part of the add-in containing the class module. Methods declared as **Friend** are not visible to and cannot be reused by other ActiveX components or standalone applications.

Other than these two exceptions, all add-in methods should be declared as **Private** (it should go without saying that no **Public** variables should be used in a class module). There are several good reasons for observing this policy:

- It prevents any confusion or damage from occurring if a developer were to view a **Public** member of an add-in in the Object Browser and then try to reuse it.

- There's no need to worry about version compatibility issues. By definition, if the interface of an ActiveX component does not expose any **Public** members for reuse, version compatibility cannot be violated.

- It eliminates the need to write a Windows Help file to document an add-in's reusable members from the Object Browser. A very complex add-in or Wizard might still benefit from a Help file that explains the add-in's functionality, but that's another issue entirely.

 This last point is an issue to consider if you are pondering whether to use VB to develop the next great "killer" ActiveX control or add-in. Any commercial-quality ActiveX control requires an extensive Windows Help file to document each of its **Public** properties, methods, and events; this is not a trivial task. On the other hand, an add-in that doesn't contain any **Public** members doesn't require such a Help file.

Now it's time to start creating your first add-in. As far as design issues are concerned, let's assume the following:

- You're going to develop a DLL add-in from scratch

- You want to be able to start it from either an Add-Ins menu item or the VB Add-In toolbar

- It will provide one **Form** object as its GUI

- It will reuse two non-default ActiveX components (the VBIDE and Office class libraries)

- None of the add-in's members will be declared as **Public**

The next three sections of this chapter will show you how to:

- Assemble an add-in's VB component modules, members, and procedures

- Test and debug the add-in

- Compile, register, and run the add-in

For those of you who want to work your way step by step through the next three sections, please do. For those of you who prefer just to read them and analyze the code, the add-in project for this chapter is CHAPTER1.VBP and is found on the path \ADDINEFS\CHAPTER1 on the CD-ROM enclosed with this book.

Assembling An Add-In's Modules And Members

To assemble the Chapter 1 add-in's component modules from scratch and not rely on VB's canned add-in project template, follow these steps:

1. From a new instance of VB, select File|New Project and double-click the ActiveX DLL template icon in the New Project dialog box.

2. In the Properties window, select Name for Class1 and set it to Connect.

3. Select Project|Add Class Module and double-click the Class Module template icon (not the Add-In icon) in the Add Class Module dialog box.

4. In the Properties window, select Name for Class1 and set it to VBEvents.

5. In the Properties window, select Instancing for VBEvents and set it to 1 - Private.

6. Select Project|Add Module and double-click the Add-In template icon in the Add Module dialog box.

7. In the Properties window, select Name for Module1 and set it to basGenlPrcs.

8. Select Project|Add Form and double-click the Form template icon (not the Add-In icon) in the Add Form dialog box.

9. In the Properties window, select Name for Form1 and set it to frmChapter1.

At this point, you are using four component modules in Chapter 1's add-in project. Let's look at what needs to be done with these components and what they are used for.

 I actually used a fifth component in Chapter 1's add-in. It is a resource file (CHAPTER1.RES) that provides the icon for the add-in when it is displayed on the VB Add-In toolbar. An add-in does not require a custom icon because the VB Add-In toolbar will automatically display a generic icon when no custom icon exists. We will look at how to create and use a custom icon in Chapter 2.

Connect Class Module

The **Name** property of the initial class module is set to Connect because it is conventional add-in programming practice to give this name to the class that serves as an add-in's connection object and contains the **IDTExtensibility** object interface. You can see this convention at work in Figure 1.1, which lists the entries in a typical VBADDIN.INI file, (note that the part of the entry after the dot delimiter is either Connect or Wizard).

The **Instancing** property of the **Connect** class defaulted to 5 - MultiUse when you opened the new ActiveX DLL project. You should leave this setting unchanged for the class module that serves as the add-in's connection object because it enables one instance of the add-in's connection class to provide multiple copies of the object. This means that multiple instances of VB's IDE can run the same add-in in a memory-efficient fashion.

Now let's add the references and members that the **Connect** class requires. To do so, follow these steps:

1. Select Project|References and uncheck any items in the References dialog box except the three default Visual Basic references (any unnecessary references simply slow down the add-in).

2. Check both the Microsoft Visual Basic 5.0 Extensibility and the Microsoft Office 8.0 Object Library items, and then choose OK.

3. In the Declarations section of the **Connect** class, type the statement "**Implements IDTExtensibility**," and then press Enter.

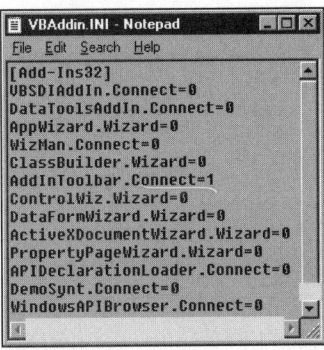

Figure 1.1
Add-in entries in the VBADDIN.INI file.

4. From the Object drop-down box, click the IDTExtensibility item and watch as VB automatically inserts the opening and closing statements of the **OnConnection** member of the **IDTExtensibility** object in the code pane.

5. From the Procedure drop-down box, successively click the OnAddIns Update, OnDisconnection, and OnStartupComplete items. Again, VB inserts the opening and closing statements of the members in the code pane.

At this point, the **Connect** class contains the code and members' declarations, as Listing 1.1 shows.

LISTING 1.1   IDTEXTENSIBILITY OBJECT'S MEMBERS.

```
' IDTExtensibility object (VB 5.0 add-in interface).
Implements IDTExtensibility

Private Sub IDTExtensibility_OnAddInsUpdate _
        (Custom() As Variant)

End Sub

Private Sub IDTExtensibility_OnConnection _
        (ByVal VBInst As Object, _
         ByVal ConnectMode As VBIDE.vbext_ConnectMode, _
         ByVal AddInInst As VBIDE.AddIn, _
         Custom() As Variant)

End Sub

Private Sub IDTExtensibility_OnDisconnection _
        (ByVal RemoveMode As VBIDE.vbext_DisconnectMode, _
         Custom() As Variant)

End Sub

Private Sub IDTExtensibility_OnStartupComplete _
        (Custom() As Variant)

End Sub
```

 Note that I have added line continuation characters and lined up the argument names of the declarations in Listing 1.1 to fit on a book-sized page. I recommend getting in the habit of doing this because it enables you to easily see all the arguments of any procedure's declaration and ensures that, if you eventually document your code, the code listings will fit on 8.5" by 11" paper.

The **IDTExtensibility** object interface contains four methods that VB calls when events related to an add-in occur. While these are methods to the **IDTExtensibility** object interface, to you as a VB developer, they act and behave like events. For example, when an add-in is connected to VB's IDE, the **OnConnection** method is called automatically, similar to an event being raised; when it is disconnected, the **OnDisconnection** method is called automatically. See Table 1.2 for descriptions of an **IDTExtensibility** object's four methods. For more detailed information about them, see their entries in the *Dictionary* section of this book.

TABLE 1.2

METHODS OF THE **IDTE**XTENSIBILITY OBJECT.

Method	Description
OnAddInsUpdate	A **Sub** procedure that occurs automatically when changes to the VBADDIN.INI file are saved by the current instance of VB's IDE through the Add-In Manager dialog box. You use the **OnAddInsUpdate** procedure to call the **Update** method of the **Addins** collection and refresh it.
OnConnection	A **Sub** procedure that occurs automatically when an add-in is connected to the current instance of VB's IDE and is started. An add-in can be connected in three ways: 1. When the developer checks an add-in item in the Add-in Manager dialog box, or when an add-in's code sets another add-in's **Connect** property to **True**; 2. When, upon startup, VB finds that an item in the Add-In Manager dialog box's list is checked and so automatically connects that add-in; 3. When an add-in is connected by another program (for example, the VB Add-In toolbar program), or programmatically by calling the **OnConnection** method from within the add-in. You use the **OnConnection** procedure to create the add-in's menu item and to store the root **VBE** object passed in by VB's IDE as the *VBInst* argument of **OnConnection**.

(continued)

TABLE 1.2

METHODS OF THE IDTEXTENSIBILITY OBJECT (*CONTINUED*).

Method	Description
OnDisconnection	A **Sub** procedure that occurs automatically when an add-in is disconnected from the current instance of VB's IDE and is shut down. An add-in can be disconnected in three ways: when the developer closes the current instance of VB, when the developer unchecks the add-in's item in the Add-In Manager dialog box, or when an add-in's code sets an add-in's **Connect** property to **False**. You use the **OnDisconnection** procedure to remove the add-in's menu item and unload any form(s) displayed by the add-in.
OnStartupComplete	A **Sub** procedure that occurs automatically when the startup of the current instance of VB's IDE is complete and if the add-in's entry in VBADDIN.INI is "1." You can use the **OnStartupComplete** procedure to read a Windows registry entry for the add-in to determine if one of its forms was displayed when VB was last shut down. If so, the procedure's code should redisplay the form.

There are some other miscellaneous points to note about the use of the **Implements** statement (new in VB5) and the **IDTExtensibility** object interface whose methods **Implements** maps to the **Connect** class:

- You can only use the **Implements** statement in the Declarations section of a class module.

- You can only expose an **IDTExtensibility** object with the **Implements** statement after you have set a reference to the VBIDE class library (Microsoft Visual Basic 5.0 Extensibility). If you do not set this reference, VB allows you to type the statement **Implements IDTExtensibility** and press Enter; but, when you try to run or compile the project, a compile error is raised (User-defined type not defined).

- You must be sure to implement all of the methods in the **IDTExtensibility** object interface. This means that all four methods must be present in your class module and each one must contain at least one comment or executable statement to prevent the compiler from removing a method as an empty procedure.

- You can change and shorten the declared types for any of the arguments of the methods that explicitly specify the VBIDE class library. For example, in the **OnConnection** method's declaration, you could shorten the *ConnectMode* argument's type (VBIDE.**vbext_ConnectMode**) and the *AddInInst* argument's type (VBIDE.**AddIn**) to just **vbext_ConnectMode** and **AddIn** respectively. I do not abbreviate them in Chapter 1's add-in but I do later on.

We need to add one other object and its member to the **Connect** class. When you type the statement

```
Public WithEvents CommandBar As CommandBarEvents
```

in the Declarations section of an add-in's class module and press Enter, VB adds a CommandBar item to the list of the Object drop-down box. When you then click CommandBar in the list, VB automatically inserts the opening and closing statements of the **CommandBar_Click** event procedure in the code pane. The **WithEvents** keyword, which must be used with the **Public** statement, specifies that you are declaring an object variable that is to be used to respond to events raised by an ActiveX component. In the case of an add-in, the ActiveX component that raises the events is VB's IDE. **WithEvents** is valid only in class modules. You can declare as many different individual variables as you like using **WithEvents**; however, you can neither create arrays nor use the **New** keyword with **WithEvents**.

A module-level variable declared in an add-in with the **WithEvents** keyword can be one of seven object types (**CommandBarEvents**, **FileControlEvents**, **ReferencesEvents**, **SelectedVBControlsEvents**, **VBComponentsEvents**, **VBControlsEvents**, or **VBProjectsEvents**). In this case, where we want the add-in to respond to the **Click** event of a VB menu item, the variable CommandBar is declared as a **CommandBarEvents** object. The code you write in the **CommandBar_Click** event procedure tells the add-in what to do when the developer clicks the add-in's menu item (for example, display a form for the developer to interact with).

 You can give an object variable declared as a **CommandBarEvents** object any name you want. However, it makes the code more readable to name it CommandBar, which is the same name as that of the **CommandBar** object that has the **Click** event as a member.

VBEvents Class Module

The **Name** property of the add-in's other class module is set to VBEvents because it is designed to contain one or more of the six other event-handling objects the Extensibility object model supports. The class module's **Instancing** property is set to 1 - Private because it is only used internally. In Chapter 1's add-in, the VBEvents class contains one general declaration. When you type the statement

```
Public WithEvents VBControls As VBControlsEvents
```

in the Declarations section of an add-in's class module and press Enter, VB adds a VBControls item to the list of the Object drop-down box. When you then click VBControls in the list, VB automatically inserts the opening and closing statements of the **VBControls_ItemAdded** event procedure in the code pane. It also makes available, in the Procedure drop-down box, the other event procedures that the **VBControlsEvents** object supports, **ItemRemoved** and **ItemRenamed**. In this chapter's add-in, we use only the **ItemAdded** event procedure.

 You can give an object variable declared as a **VBControlsEvents** object any name you want. However, it makes the code more readable to name it VBControls, which is the same name as that of the **VBControls** collection that has the **ItemAdded** event as a member.

The code in the **ItemAdded** event procedure of this chapter's add-in demonstrates how an add-in can automatically adjust the **Height** property of a newly added **CommandButton** or **TextBox** object from VB's default setting of 510 twips to the Windows standard of 315 twips. We will look at this code and the related **ConnectTo** method's code later in this chapter.

GenlPrcs Standard Module

The standard module component you added by double-clicking the Add-In template icon in the Add Module dialog box contains a declaration for the Windows API function **WritePrivateProfileString** and a procedure entitled **AddToINI**, as in Listing 1.2.

LISTING 1.2 ADDTOINI CODE IN GENLPRCS STANDARD MODULE.

```
' DLL declarations:
Public Declare Function WritePrivateProfileString& _
                        Lib "Kernel32" _
                        Alias "WritePrivateProfileStringA" _
                        (ByVal AppName$, ByVal KeyName$, _
                        ByVal keydefault$, ByVal FileName$)


' ****************************************************************
' This sub should be executed from the Immediate window
' in order to get this app added to the VBADDIN.INI file.
' You must change the name in the second argument to
' reflect the correct name of your project.
' ****************************************************************
Sub AddToINI()

    Dim ErrCode As Long
    ErrCode = WritePrivateProfileString("Add-Ins32", _
                                "Chapter1.Connect", _
                                "0", "VBADDIN.INI")

End Sub
```

This add-in template module saves you the trouble of finding and loading the API function declaration with VB's API Text Viewer. The comment in the **AddToINI** procedure says that, to add the required entry for this add-in to VBADDIN.INI, you need to change the name of the second argument of the API call to the programmatic ID of your add-in. An add-in's programmatic ID (for example, Chapter1.Connect) consists of two parts separated by a dot delimiter:

- Preceding the delimiter, the Project Name entry on the General tab of the Project Properties dialog box

- Following the delimiter, the **Name** property setting of the connection class module

You can then execute the **AddToINI Sub** from the Immediate window. You run the **AddToINI** procedure by selecting VB's Immediate window, typing the statement

```
basGenlPrcs.AddToINI
```

in the window, and pressing Enter. The general point to note here is that all VB5 add-ins must have entries both in the VBADDIN.INI file and the Windows registry (which we'll discuss later in this chapter). You can also use this GenlPrcs standard module to hold any other procedures that are called more than once from within an add-in; however, Chapter 1's GenlPrcs standard module does not contain any procedures other than **Sub Main**.

 When you are developing and testing an add-in on your own PC, executing an **AddToINI** procedure in VB's Immediate window is sufficient to add an entry to VBADDIN.INI. However, when you are distributing and registering an add-in on another PC, you will have to make sure SETUP.EXE makes the entry (as the installation routine for this book's add-ins did). Also, you should note that the code in the **AddToINI Sub** uses the **Long** variable ErrCode to catch the value that the API function **WritePrivateProfileString** returns. This error code variable is superfluous because the procedure's code does nothing with it and, even if **WritePrivateProfileString** fails, the **AddToINI** procedure does not result in a runtime error.

The GenlPrcs standard module contains one other general declaration and an empty **Sub Main** procedure, as Listing 1.3 shows.

LISTING 1.3 OTHER CODE IN GENLPRCS STANDARD MODULE.

```
' Public reference to current instance of VB's IDE (I don't
' prefix it to indicate its scope so that its use in various
' add-in syntax object expressions exactly mirrors its use
' in VB's Object Browser and in ADDINEFS.HLP). In many of the
' book's add-ins, VBE is the only variable declared publicly,
' other than those being assigned event-handling objects.
Public VBE As VBE

Sub Main()

End Sub
```

It is a practice of mine to include the **Public VBE** object variable and the **Sub Main** procedure in every add-in I write. They perform the following functions:

- The **Public VBE** object variable holds a reference to the current instance of VB's IDE, which is passed in as an argument of the **OnConnection** method of the **IDTExtensibility** object. You can't write any add-in code without a reference to this **VBE** object, which is the root object that contains all other objects, collections, and members in the Extensibility object model. Because **VBE** is declared as **Public**, it is easily available to all procedures in all modules in the add-in.

- I always use the **Sub Main** procedure as the starting point of any ActiveX component that I write and, thus, set the Startup Object entry of every add-in to **Sub Main**. This entry is made on the General tab of the Project Properties dialog box.

Form Module

Figure 1.2 shows the GUI for Chapter 1's add-in, as it appears at runtime after the developer clicks the add-in's menu item.

At this early stage on your add-in learning curve, I wanted to keep things fairly simple. Chapter 1's add-in demonstrates, in a straightforward and easily understood way, four add-in capabilities:

- VB IDE windows manipulation

- Automatic code generation

- Code pane manipulation

- Automatic reaction to VB IDE events

It is not necessary to look at all the code in frmChapter1 now. Most of the important code is in the **Click** event procedures of the four demo buttons. Later in the chapter, we'll analyze the generic add-in coding techniques that these procedures utilize. The one procedure in frmChapter1 that we will discuss now is the tmrConnectEvts **Timer** object's code, which Listing 1.4 shows.

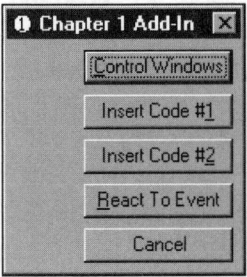

Figure 1.2
The form of Chapter 1's add-in.

LISTING 1.4   CODE IN TIMER OBJECT.

```
Private Sub tmrConnectEvts_Timer()

    ' Variables:
    Dim SelVBComponent      As VBComponent
    Static LastVBComponent  As VBComponent

    ' Assign selected component to variable.
    On Error GoTo EH
    Set SelVBComponent = VBE.SelectedVBComponent

    ' If we don't have new selected component, do nothing:
    If SelVBComponent Is LastVBComponent Then Exit Sub

    ' If new selected component has designer object,
    ' connect it to event-handling object by calling
    ' ConnectTo method in VBEvents class module:
    If SelVBComponent.HasOpenDesigner Then
        Set LastVBComponent = SelVBComponent
        VBEvents.ConnectTo VBE, SelVBComponent
    End If

EH:

End Sub
```

The tmrConnectEvts **Timer** object is turned on when the developer clicks the React To Event demo button. Its code watches for a change in the selected VB component (for example, the developer clicks on a different form or module in VB's IDE). If the newly selected component is a designer that can contain controls, the **Timer** object's code calls the **ConnectTo Friend** method in the VBEvents class module, which connects the component and its controls to the **VBControlsEvents** object to make them responsive to the **ItemAdded** event. Then, each time the developer adds a **CommandButton** or **TextBox** control to a form or other designer, its **Height** property changes from the default setting of 510 twips to the Windows standard of 315 twips.

This short procedure in the **Timer** object, along with the code in the VBEvents class module, illustrates a very practical use for an add-in: You need to make sure that a non-visual add-in procedure runs in the background while VB's IDE is open, and that it automatically enforces standards like control size, naming conventions, and property settings.

Coding An Add-In's Class Module Procedures

The procedures that you write in an add-in's class modules implement the conventional, generic behavior of an add-in. For example, the procedures in a Connect class determine how an add-in behaves when a developer connects it to and disconnects it from VB's IDE, and the procedures in a class like VBEvents specify how an add-in reacts to add-in related events that are raised by VB's IDE. Other kinds of procedures, which are less generic in nature and implement the functionality of a particular add-in, are normally written in one or more BAS or FRM modules.

Connect Class Procedures

After you have implemented the **IDTExtensibility** object interface and its methods in the **Connect** class, you can write code for a simple add-in like that in Listing 1.5.

LISTING 1.5   CODE FOR IDTEXTENSIBILITY OBJECT'S METHODS.

```
Private Sub IDTExtensibility_OnAddInsUpdate _
        (Custom() As Variant)

  ' Refresh Addins collection to reflect entry made to
  ' VBADDIN.INI through VB's Add-In Manager dialog box.
  VBE.Addins.Update

End Sub

Private Sub IDTExtensibility_OnConnection _
        (ByVal VBInst As Object, _
         ByVal ConnectMode As VBIDE.vbext_ConnectMode, _
         ByVal AddInInst As VBIDE.AddIn, _
         Custom() As Variant)

  ' Assign current instance of VB's IDE to public variable.
  Set basGenlPrcs.VBE = VBInst

  ' If VB is automatically connecting add-in on startup or if
  ' developer connects add-in via Add-In Manager dialog box:
  If ConnectMode = vbext_cm_Startup Or _
    ConnectMode = vbext_cm_AfterStartup Then
```

```
                    ' Create add-in's menu item and set its caption:
                    Set mMenuItem = VBE.CommandBars("Menu Bar"). _
                                    Controls("Add-Ins"). _
                                    Controls.Add(msoControlButton)

                    mMenuItem.Caption = "Creating VB5 Add-Ins: Chapter 1..."

                    ' Make menu item responsive to Click event.
                    Set CommandBar = VBE.Events.CommandBarEvents(mMenuItem)

                ' If developer connects add-in by clicking toolbar button:
                ElseIf ConnectMode = vbext_cm_External Then

                    mfrmChapter1.Show

                End If

            End Sub

            Private Sub IDTExtensibility_OnDisconnection _
                    (ByVal RemoveMode As VBIDE.vbext_DisconnectMode, _
                    Custom() As Variant)

                ' If developer is disconnecting add-in's menu item:
                If RemoveMode = vbext_dm_UserClosed Then

                    ' Remove add-in's menu item and unload form:
                    mMenuItem.Delete
                    Unload mfrmChapter1

                End If

            End Sub

            Private Sub IDTExtensibility_OnStartupComplete _
                    (Custom() As Variant)

                ' Add comment to IDTExtensibility object's procedure to
                ' prevent compiler from removing it as empty procedure.

            End Sub
```

The comments included in the code for Listing 1.5 explain the code for the **IDTExtensibility** object's methods. You will see how this code works later in the chapter when we discuss how to test and debug an add-in. The remainder of the code in the **Connect** class that we have not already discussed is in Listing 1.6.

LISTING 1.6 OTHER CODE IN CONNECT COMPONENT.

```
' Module-level variable to assign add-in's form to.
Private mfrmChapter1   As New frmChapter1

' Module-level variable to assign add-in's menu item to.
Private mMenuItem      As Office.CommandBarControl

Private Sub CommandBar_Click _
                    (ByVal CommandBarControl As Object, _
                    Handled As Boolean, _
                    CancelDefault As Boolean)

   mfrmChapter1.Show

End Sub

Private Sub Class_Terminate()

   ' Free system resources associated with objects:
   Set IDTExtensibility = Nothing
   Set mfrmChapter1 = Nothing
   Set mMenuItem = Nothing
   Set CommandBar = Nothing

End Sub
```

As we discussed earlier in the chapter, VB automatically creates the **Command-Bar_Click** event procedure's opening and closing subs when you declare the **CommandBar** object variable using the **Public** and **WithEvents** statements. However, you must write the code for the procedure. In this chapter's add-in, the code consists of one statement that tells the add-in to display its form.

The code in the **Terminate** event procedure explicitly disassociates the module-level object variables from the actual objects they refer to by assigning **Nothing** to the variables. This releases any memory and system resources that the objects use. Although VB's Help file states that memory and system resources are automatically freed when the object variables go out of scope, various articles on this issue in Microsoft's Knowledge Base over the years suggest that it is better to be safe than sorry. Therefore, I always explicitly set module-level object variables to **Nothing** in the **Terminate** event procedure of a module.

VBEvents Class Procedures

The procedures in this add-in's VBEvents class specify how the add-in reacts to an **ItemAdded** event that VB raises whenever a developer adds a **Command-Button** or **TextBox** control from VB's Toolbox to a form or other designer component. The **Height** property of the newly added control is changed from VB's default setting of 510 twips to the Windows standard of 315 twips. Listing 1.7 shows the code in VBEvents.

LISTING 1.7   CODE IN VBEVENTS COMPONENT.

```
' Module-level object variable that responds to add-in's React
' To Event demo (I don't prefix it to indicate its scope so that
' its use in various add-in syntax object expressions exactly
' mirrors its use in VB's Object Browser and in ADDINEFS.HLP).
Public WithEvents VBControls As VBControlsEvents

Private Sub VBControls_ItemAdded(ByVal VBControl As VBIDE.VBControl)

    ' Adjust height of certain controls to Windows standard
    ' when they are added from the Toolbox to a component:
    Select Case VBControl.ClassName
      Case "CommandButton", "TextBox"
         VBControl.Properties("Height") = 315
    End Select

End Sub

Friend Sub ConnectTo(VBE As VBE, VBComponent As VBComponent)

    ' Variables:
    Dim VBForm      As VBForm
    Dim VBProject   As VBProject

    ' Get designer object associated with VBComponent object.
    Set VBForm = VBComponent.Designer

    ' Get active project by working back up object hierarchy
    ' from VBComponent to its parent collection (VBComponents)
    ' to parent object of VBComponents (active VBProject).
    Set VBProject = VBComponent.Collection.Parent

    ' Make VBControls event-source object (declared
    ' at module level) responsive to IDE's events:
    Set VBControls = VBE.Events.VBControlsEvents(VBProject, VBForm)

End Sub
```

```
Private Sub Class_Terminate()

   ' Free system resources associated with objects:
   Set VBControls = Nothing

End Sub
```

In order for the **ItemAdded** event procedure's code to execute when the developer adds a control from the Toolbox to a form or other designer, the **ConnectTo** method's code must first be called to make the **VBControlsEvents** object responsive to VB IDE's events. The developer does this with the **Timer** object's code each time he or she selects a different component. **ConnectTo** is declared as **Friend** so that the method can be called internally from anywhere within the add-in but is not reusable from an external application or component.

 Not every add-in requires an events-handling class module component. I used such a class in Chapter 1's add-in because it helped me to demonstrate a few generic add-in coding techniques that I refer to in the following section.

Gene's Top 10 Generic Add-In Coding Tips

As part of your introduction to add-ins, I want to highlight several generic coding techniques that are an essential part of every add-in developer's toolkit. VB's Extensibility object model and its associated syntax are so rich in features that there are usually different ways to do just about anything. The generic coding techniques that I discuss in this section focus on improving the performance, readability, and maintainability of add-in code. I refer to these techniques as Gene's Top 10 Add-In Coding Tips (with apologies to David Letterman). You can see them all in this chapter's add-in.

Tip 1—Declare VBE As Public In GenlPrcs

As mentioned earlier in the chapter, you can't write any add-in code without first referring to the root or top-level **VBE** object of the Extensibility object model. The easiest way to ensure that you can access the **VBE** object from anywhere within an add-in's code is to declare a **Public** variable to which you assign the **VBE** object, which represents the current instance of VB's IDE passed in as the *VBInst* argument of the **OnConnection** method.

I'm in the habit of declaring this variable with the statement

```
Public VBE As VBE
```

in the general declarations section of the GenlPrcs standard module. You should note that VB has no problem distinguishing between the name of the object variable (**VBE**) and the **VBE** object type that it is declared as. Naming this project-level object variable **VBE** allows you to write code that perfectly mirrors the syntax of the Extensibility object model. For example, in the **cmd Code1_Click** event procedure of Chapter 1's add-in form, the statement

```
VBE.ActiveVBProject.VBComponents.Add(vbext_ct_StdModule)
```

adds a standard module to the current project (equivalent to manually selecting Project|Add Module). The first object reference in the statement (**VBE**) is to the **Public** object variable declared in GenlPrcs.

Tip 2—Use Accessor Properties When Possible

The term *accessor property* is not referenced in VB Books Online. However, if you search for "accessor" in VB's Help file, it returns three topics that use the term. All three are add-in topics that were documented late in the development cycle and are found in the ReadMe category on the Contents tab of the Help file's dialog box.

An accessor property returns an object or collection of the same type as signified by the property name. The statement

```
VBE.ActiveVBProject.VBComponents.Add(vbext_ct_StdModule)
```

uses an accessor property (**ActiveVBProject**) to return a **VBProject** object that represents the project that is currently selected in the Project Explorer window. If the currently selected project is named Project1 and is the only project open in VB, the statements

```
VBE.VBProjects("Project1").VBComponents.Add(vbext_ct_StdModule)
```

and

```
VBE.VBProjects(1).VBComponents.Add(vbext_ct_StdModule)
```

perform the same function as the statement that uses the **ActiveVBProject** accessor property.

Other examples of accessor properties that return an object are **ActiveCode Pane**, **ActiveWindow**, **CodeModule**, **CodePane**, **Designer Window**, **Selected VB-Component**, **VBE**, and **Window**. The seven event-handling objects mentioned earlier in the chapter (for example, **CommandBarEvents**) are all returned by their accessor properties. Examples of accessor properties that return a collection are **Addins**, **CodePanes**, **CommandBars**, **Linked Windows**, **Members**, **Properties**, **References**, **SelectedVBControls** and **VBControls**, and **Windows**.

Accessor properties are faster, easier to write, and easier to maintain than alternative syntaxes. For example, if you don't use the **ActiveVBProject** accessor property, you have to concern yourself with whether the name or the index number of the project has changed. Also, the code itself is slower because it has to drill down through the **VBProjects** collection to the specified **VBProject** object, whereas the **ActiveVBProject** already caches a reference to the **VBProject** object.

Tip 3—Scope Variables Locally When Possible

No single coding practice promotes readability and easier maintenance more than scoping variables locally. Except for the use of the **Public VBE** object variable in Tip 1, you should avoid declaring add-in variables as **Public** as you would avoid the plague. As far as module-level variables are concerned, use them rarely and be sure to document their purpose. The golden rule of the object-oriented programming methodology is to declare variables locally whenever possible. This practice is essential to complying with the OOP design objective of encapsulation.

Tip 4—Name Local Object Variables The Same As Their Types

In the **cmdWindows_Click** event procedure of Chapter 1's add-in form, the statement

```
Dim Window As Window
```

declares a local object variable as the add-in object type **Window** and gives the variable the same name as the object type. VB has no trouble distinguishing between the name of the variable and its type. This naming scheme results in more readable and more easily maintained code. For example, later in this same event procedure, the code

```
For Each Window In VBE.Windows
    Window.Visible = True
Next Window
```

displays every window in VB's IDE. It's hard to imagine clearer and more readable code than this code block. Note too that the first statement in the code block uses the **Windows** accessor property to return the **Windows** collection. I want to emphasize that this tip pertains primarily to local, procedure-scope object variables. Normally, you should give any module-level object variable a more specific name.

Tip 5—Use For Each...Next Instead Of For...Next

The block of code in Tip 4

```
For Each Window In VBE.Windows
    Window.Visible = True
Next Window
```

could also be written as

```
For El = 1 To VBE.Windows.Count
    VBE.Windows(El).Visible = True
Next Window
```

where El is a counter variable. As far as readability and maintenance are concerned, the advantages of the **For Each...Next** statement over the **For...Next** statement should be obvious. It has also been well documented that the performance of **For Each...Next** is slightly better than that of **For...Next**.

Tip 6—Always Shorten Long Object Expressions

In the **cmdCode2_Click** event procedure of Chapter 1's add-in form, the object expression

```
VBE.ActiveVBProject.VBComponents("Module1").CodeModule
```

is referred to in a loop 200 times to demonstrate how performance suffers when such a long object expression is not shortened/cached by assigning it to an object variable declared as the **CodeModule** type.

The golden rule here is to count the number of dot delimiters you use in your code: The more dots you have in your code, the more slowly the code runs. How much slower depends on a number of variables (in-process vs. out-of-process, Native Code vs. P-Code compilation, and so on). The main point here is that an add-in's code, because it is constantly accessing objects that are three to six levels deep in the object hierarchy, needs to use every trick in the book to improve performance. Shortening/caching long object expressions is guaranteed to improve performance.

Tip 7—Use The With Statement When Possible

In the **cmdCode2_Click** event procedure of Chapter 1's add-in form, the code block

```
With CodeModule.CodePane
   For Nbr = 1 To 200
      .TopLine = Nbr
   Next Nbr
End With
```

uses the **With** statement to execute the same statement 200 times on a **CodePane** object. As in Tip 6, using the **With** statement caches the object expression, reduces the number of dot delimiters used in the code, and improves performance. The code block

```
For Nbr = 1 To 200
    CodeModule.CodePane.TopLine = Nbr
Next Nbr
```

does the same thing but runs more slowly.

Tip 8—Access Items In A Collection By String Index When Possible

In Tip 2, I wrote that the statements

```
VBE.VBProjects("Project1").VBComponents.Add(vbext_ct_StdModule)
```

and

```
VBE.VBProjects(1).VBComponents.Add(vbext_ct_StdModule)
```

both add a standard module to a project. You can access items in most add-in collections either by a string index (Project1) or a numeric index (1). Unless you are looping through all the items in a collection, which would require you to access them by numeric index, it makes the code more readable to access the item by string index. The kind of string index that you use varies from one add-in collection to another. See the *Dictionary* entry for the **Item** method for more detailed information about the string index that a given add-in collection uses.

Tip 9—Use Enum Intrinsic Constants

The Extensibility object model contains a large number of intrinsic constants that the **Enum** statement implements. Likewise, you can declare constants in your own add-in code by using the **Enum** statement. In the **cmdWindows_Click** event procedure of Chapter 1's add-in form, the code in the block

```
For Each Window In VBE.Windows
    Kind = Window.Type
```

```
    If Kind <> vbext_wt_Designer And _
       Kind <> vbext_wt_CodeWindow Then
            Window.Close
    End If
Next Window
```

uses the intrinsic constants **vbext_wt_Designer** and **vbext_wt_CodeWindow**. The constants obviously make the code more readable and easier to maintain than if you used their respective numeric values of 1 and 0.

Tip 10—Use Collection And Parent Properties

In the **ConnectTo** method of the VBEvents class module, the statement

```
Set VBProject = VBComponent.Collection.Parent
```

uses a neat technique that the Extensibility object model supports. Most add-in objects or collections have either a **Collection** or **Parent** property that you can use to return the object's or collection's parent object. Sometimes you may write an add-in procedure that gets passed an object reference as an argument (in the case of the **ConnectTo** method, a **VBComponent** object that represents the module the developer has just selected).

You may need to determine to which project the selected module belongs (remember that VB5 supports multiple projects open within one instance of VB's IDE). The easiest and sometimes the only way to do this is by using the **Collection** and/or **Parent** properties. In the statement

```
Set VBProject = VBComponent.Collection.Parent
```

I first use the **Collection** property to access the **VBComponents** collection that contains the selected module. Then I use the **Parent** property of the **VBComponents** collection to access the **VBProject** object that represents the project to which the selected module belongs. I need to determine the project because the following statement

```
' Make VBControls event-source object (declared
' at module level) responsive to IDE's events:
Set VBControls = VBE.Events.VBControlsEvents(VBProject, VBForm)
```

requires a **VBProject** object as one of its arguments. You will see many uses of the **Collection** and **Parent** properties throughout this book. They are useful because they make add-in code shorter and more readable, and sometimes they are the only way that you can achieve your objective.

Testing And Debugging An Add-In

So now it's put-up or shut-up time: time to try and run the add-in and test and debug it internally. VB5 makes it fairly easy to do this; in fact, you can actually test and debug an add-in before you compile and register it in the Windows registry. This is a nice feature because it means that you don't need to clutter up the Windows registry with outmoded entries by repeatedly compiling and registering the add-in each time you change its public interface.

However, you do need to do three things before you can test and debug an add-in. First, save the add-in project and its component files. Second, add an entry for the add-in to VBADDIN.INI. As discussed earlier in the chapter, you do this by executing, in the VB IDE's Immediate window, the **AddToINI Sub** procedure in the GenlPrcs standard module. Third, type the Description entry for the add-in's connection object (that is, the **Connect** class) in VB's Object Browser.

Typing this Description entry in the Object Browser is entirely different from typing the Project Description entry on the General tab of the Project Properties dialog box (which we discuss in the next section). To type the Description entry for the Chapter 1 add-in's **Connect** class in the Object Browser, follow these steps:

1. Press F2 to display the Object Browser and select the Chapter1 item from the Libraries drop-down box at the top-left corner of the Browser.

2. From the Classes list, right-click Connect to display the shortcut menu.

3. From the shortcut menu, select Properties to display the Member Options dialog box.

4. Type the Description entry (as in Figure 1.3) and click OK.

This Description entry for the add-in appears in the Add-In Manager dialog box. It should describe for the VB developer what the add-in does or what application it is associated with.

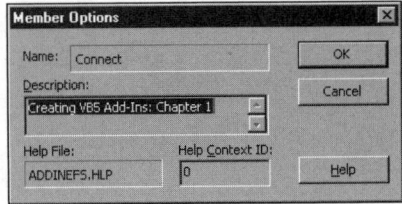

Figure 1.3
The Member Options dialog box for the **Connect** class.

 Strictly speaking, an add-in does not need to have this Description entry; however, if you don't make such an entry, VB displays in the Add-In Manager dialog box the programmatic ID of the add-in's connection object, which is the entry that is added to VBADDIN.INI (in this example, Chapter1.Connect). Ordinarily, the programmatic ID doesn't tell a VB developer as much about an add-in as you would like.

Now we're ready to test and debug the add-in. Follow these steps:

1. Make sure the add-in's project that you are testing is open in an instance of VB.

2. Select Run|Start (F5) to run the add-in you are testing and then minimize VB's main window.

3. Start up a second instance of VB and double-click the Standard EXE icon in the New Project dialog box.

4. Select Add-Ins|Add-In Manager to display the Add-In Manager dialog box.

5. Check the add-in item that you want to connect/test and choose OK (as in Figure 1.4). This causes VB's IDE to call the add-in's **On-Connection** method and, typically, add an item for the add-in to the Add-Ins menu.

6. From the Add-Ins menu, click the menu item for the add-in. This causes VB's IDE to execute the add-in's **CommandBar_Click** event procedure and, typically, display the add-in's initial GUI element.

From this point on, you can test the add-in and run it through its paces in any way that its functionality supports. In the case of Chapter 1's add-in, you can

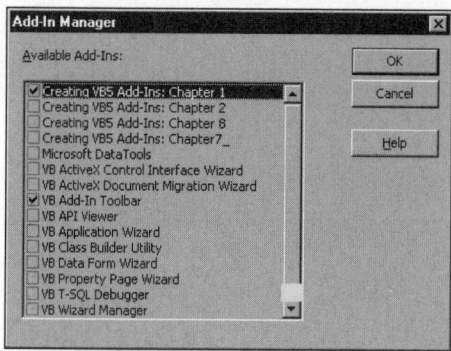

Figure 1.4
The Add-In Manager dialog box.

click any of the four demo buttons and observe what happens to the Standard EXE project in the second instance of VB.

If a runtime error occurs while you are executing the add-in's code, the first instance of VB's IDE that contains the add-in's project displays the normal error message. For example, I deliberately wrote a statement in Chapter 1's add-in that causes a runtime error if it is executed. If you hold down the Shift key and right-click the Cancel button on the add-in's form, VB raises runtime error 438 (Object doesn't support this property or method) and displays the dialog box shown in Figure 1.5. Click Debug on this error dialog box and VB restores the first instance of VB and displays the code pane and statement where the error occurred, as in Figure 1.6. You can either fix the statement (change **VBProject** to **ActiveVBProject**) and press F5 to continue, comment out the statement, or end the add-in's execution (if it's a complex error situation).

You can also set a breakpoint anywhere in the add-in's code and, when that statement executes, single-step through the code. For example, you

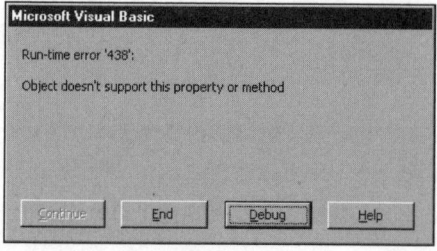

Figure 1.5
Error message while testing Chapter 1's add-in.

Figure 1.6
Code pane and statement where error 438 occurred.

could set a breakpoint on the **IDTExtensibility_OnDisconnection** method's first statement

```
If RemoveMode = vbext_dm_UserClosed Then
```

and then, while the Chapter 1 add-in's form is still visible, select Add-Ins|Add-In Manager. Uncheck the Chapter 1 add-in's item and choose OK to disconnect the add-in. This causes VB's IDE to call the **OnDisconnection** method and code execution pauses at the breakpoint, as in Figure 1.7.

You could then single-step through the remaining code in the **OnDisconnection** method and watch as it removes the add-in's menu item and unloads the add-in's form.

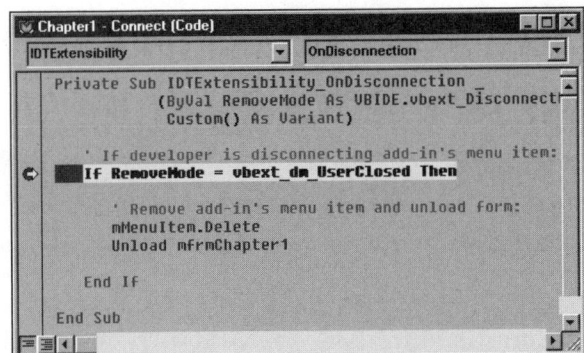

Figure 1.7
The breakpoint in the **OnDisconnection** method.

The important points to remember about testing and debugging an add-in are:

- An add-in is unlike any other kind of ActiveX component that you create with VB; the only way you can test and debug it is by running two separate instances of VB: the first containing the add-in's project in run mode and the second being used to connect the add-in and execute its functionality.

- The first few times you try debugging an add-in, it will be a frustrating experience because it is confusing to see the focus jump back and forth between the two instances of VB.

- A few members of the add-in Extensibility object model do not behave the same way when run in debug mode as they do when run from a compiled add-in. In a couple of cases, like the **Object** property of a **Property** object, the member causes a runtime error when run in debug mode and yet behaves correctly when run from a compiled add-in. I will note any cases of this kind throughout the book.

Of course your add-in also needs to be completely tested in its compiled/distributed version. Ideally, the tester should not be the VB developer who wrote the add-in. To test an add-in's compiled/distributed version, you can check its item in the Add-In Manager dialog box to connect it and then click its menu item to run it; alternatively, you can connect/run it from the VB Add-In toolbar.

Compiling, Registering, And Running An Add-In

After you have tested and debugged the add-in's project, you need to compile and register the add-in. VB makes this very easy to do. At this point, we will assume that you have already:

- Added an entry for the add-in to VBADDIN.INI. You do this by executing, in VB IDE's Immediate window, the **AddToINI Sub** procedure in the GenlPrcs standard module.

- Typed the Description entry for the add-in's connection object (that is, the **Connect** class) in VB's Object Browser.

Now you're ready to compile and register Chapter 1's add-in. To do so, you first need to make the appropriate entries on the four tabs (General, Make, Compile, and Component) of the Project Properties dialog box. To access the Project Properties dialog box, select Project|Properties. We look at the entries for each of the four tabs in the following sections. After you have made these entries, select File|MakeDLL to compile and register the add-in.

General Tab Entries

There are four required entries on the General tab of the Project Properties dialog box: Project Type, Startup Object, Project Name, and Project Description. Project Type is automatically set to the correct entry of ActiveX DLL when you load a new ActiveX DLL project to begin creating an add-in. If you were creating an out-of-process EXE add-in, which is rarely done as explained earlier in this chapter, Project Type would be set to ActiveX EXE.

The Startup Object entry is initially set to (None) when you load a new ActiveX DLL project. You can leave it set to (None), but I recommend that you get in the habit of changing the setting to **Sub Main** for two reasons. First, the **Sub Main** procedure is the conventional startup point for most ActiveX components except an ActiveX control. Second, the **Sub Main** setting allows you to easily assign certain kinds of **Public**, project-level variables that are best declared in the GenlPrcs standard module. Although the Chapter 1 add-in's GenlPrcs standard module does not contain any **Public** variables other than **VBE**, we will look at how to use this technique later in the book.

The Project Name entry, as explained earlier, specifies the first part of the programmatic ID string that identifies the connection class of an add-in. This book's add-ins all use a naming scheme for Project Name that identifies the add-in by chapter number (for example, Chapter1). The Project Name entry can be different from the name of the add-in's VBP project file, and you can set it to any entry other than the **Name** property of a module in the project or the name of an object library that the project references.

The Project Description entry should be the same as the Description entry you made from within the Object Browser for the Connect class. You might ask why you need to make the same entry in two places, and all I can tell you is that this is a quirk in VB's add-in development architecture. The Description entry you made from within the Object Browser appears in the Add-In Manager dialog box's list. The Description entry on the General tab is used in three other places as:

- The add-in's item that appears in the References dialog box's list.

- The add-in's item that appears in the Add/Remove ToolbarItem dialog box's list, which is displayed by the VB Add-In toolbar.

- The tooltip for the add-in's button on the VB Add-In toolbar.

The other entries on the General tab are optional. If you specify a Help File Name entry, just enter the name of the HLP file and don't hard-code the path. Then, if the add-in's SETUP.EXE file installs the Help file either on the same path as the add-in or on the Windows Help path, the Object Browser will automatically find and display the Help file. If you have one Help file that needs to support different add-ins installed on different paths, you should make sure SETUP.EXE installs the HLP file on the Windows Help path. In all of this book's add-ins, ADDINEFS.HLP is the Help File Name entry. The Project Help Context ID entry defaults to 0. To display a Help topic for an add-in from the Object Browser, change this entry to the context ID number of the topic. In all of the book's add-ins, 1 is the Project Help Context ID entry, which specifies the Contents topic of ADDINEFS.HLP.

The entry for Upgrade ActiveX Controls defaults to checked; it's easier to just leave it checked for any add-in, even if it doesn't use an ActiveX control. The Unattended Execution entries should be disabled for any add-in that contains a form or calls VB's **MsgBox** or **InputBox** functions. The Unattended Execution entries would only be used in an add-in that contains no user interface elements and that would benefit from threaded execution.

The entries on the General tab for Chapter 1's add-in appear in Figure 1.8.

Make Tab Entries

VB automatically handles the entries on the Make tab of the Project Properties dialog box for you. For the Version Number entries, VB sets 1, 0, and 0 for the Major, Minor, and Revision numbers respectively, unless you manually change the numbers or check Auto Increment. These Version Number settings are the conventional ones used for the first release of any application. VB sets the Title

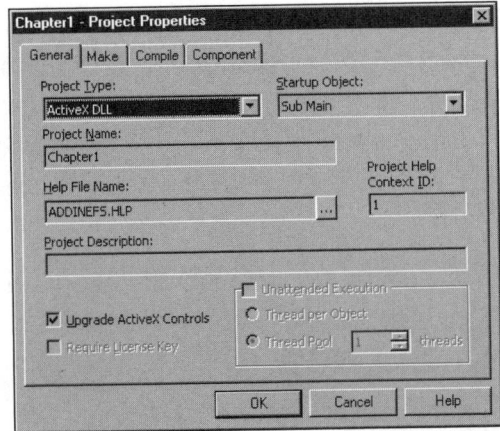

Figure 1.8
General tab settings for Chapter 1's add-in.

entry to the same string as the Project Name entry you made on the General tab; there is no reason to change this Title entry. VB leaves the Version Name entries (Comments, Company Name, File Description, Legal Copyright, Legal Trademarks, and Product Name) empty. If you create an add-in for commercial or company-wide release, you can set these entries if you wish. VB leaves the Command Line Arguments and Conditional Compilation Arguments entries blank. Most add-ins will not need to change these entries.

The one entry on the Make tab that deserves special mention is the Icon drop-down box. The **Name** property of each **Form** object in an add-in's project is listed as an item in this drop-down box; however, its default setting is blank (that is, no item is selected). You should leave the Icon entry set to its default of no item. In a normal EXE application, a VB developer uses this setting to specify the icon that is associated with and displayed for the EXE file. In an in-process DLL ActiveX component, this setting normally has no effect.

However, in the case of a DLL add-in component, setting the Icon entry to anything other than its default of no item confuses the VB Add-In toolbar application. Instead of using the Icon entry to specify the icon on the toolbar button for the add-in, the VB Add-In toolbar ignores it and displays a generic icon from its own library. The only way to specify the icon that the VB Add-In toolbar displays for an add-in is to do it with a resource (.RES) file. This is an undocumented feature of the VB Add-In toolbar application that we explain in Chapter 2.

 If you accidentally set the Icon entry on the Make tab to the name of one of the add-in's forms, you will find that it is impossible to set it back to nothing. This is a frustrating bug in VB that Microsoft ought to fix. If you mistakenly do this, then even using a resource file to set the icon will not override the confused behavior of the VB Add-In toolbar.

The entries on the Make tab for Chapter 1's add-in appear in Figure 1.9.

Compile Tab Entries

The entries on the Compile tab of the Project Properties dialog box for Chapter 1's add-in appear in Figure 1.10.

There are three points to note about the Compile tab entries. First, when you open a new ActiveX DLL or EXE project, VB's default Compile setting is Native Code. While you are developing, testing, and recompiling an add-in over and over, you are better off changing the Compile setting to P-Code, which compiles 5 to 10 times quicker than Native Code. However, when you are done testing and are ready to distribute your add-in, you should switch the Compile setting back to Native Code and recompile it one last time. Based on my informal benchmarks and the add-ins I developed for this book, there is no doubt that add-ins run noticeably faster when compiled to Native Code; therefore, the final version of all the book's add-ins is in Native Code.

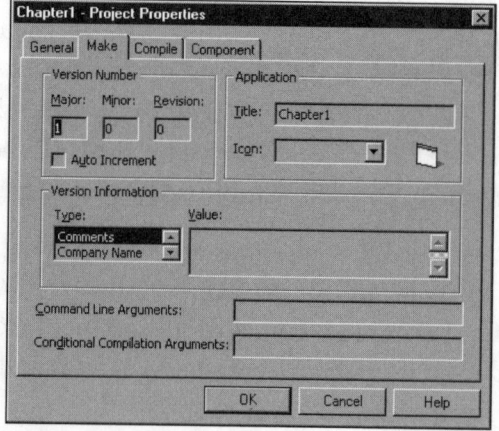

Figure 1.9
Make tab settings for Chapter 1's add-in.

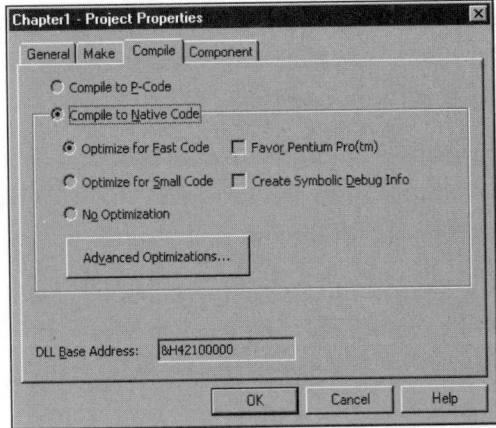

Figure 1.10
Compile tab settings for Chapter 1's add-in.

Second, the individual settings under Compile To Native Code are available if you want to use them. I've used VB's default setting of Optimize For Fast Code, but you can read the information in VB's Help file or Books Online about the other possible settings and do as you please. Unless you know that your add-in will only be run on the Pentium Pro microprocessor (Favor Pentium Pro setting), it's hard to believe that any of the other possible combinations of optimization settings will result in a perceptible improvement in performance.

Third, the DLL Base Address setting warrants your close attention. This setting is explained fairly well in VB Books Online under the topic titled *Setting Base Addresses For In-Process Components*. These are the important points:

- The address can be entered either as a hexadecimal (the default) or unsigned decimal integer.

- VB assigns the default value of &H11000000 or 285,212,672.

- You should never use the default base address value. If you don't change the default value, your DLL add-in might conflict with any other in-process component compiled using the default value. Such a conflict can perceptibly slow performance because, if another DLL component is already using the default address, Windows must relocate the DLL data and code.

- The base address value must be between 16MB (&H10000000 or 16,777,216) and 2GB (&H80000000 or 2,147,483,648).

- The base address value must be a multiple of 64K. This means that the unsigned decimal value must be evenly divided by 65,536, or the hexadecimal value must end with four zeros.

- Microsoft recommends that you choose an address at random from within the valid range. A simple approach for doing this is to randomly generate a number between 10 and 30,000 and then multiply it by 65,536.

Here is the addressing algorithm I used for this book's add-ins: take the default value of &H11000000, change the first character from the left to 4 (the number of brothers in my family), change the second character from the left to 2 (my second book), and change the third character from the left to the chapter number of the add-in. So, Chapter 1's add-in has a DLL Base Address setting of &H42100000, Chapter 2's value is &H42200000, and so on.

 If you are creating an out-of-process EXE add-in, you don't have to worry about the DLL base address setting on the Compile tab because it is disabled.

Component Tab Entries

The settings on the Component tab are all straightforward. The Start Mode entry is always disabled for any in-process DLL component, add-in or otherwise. The Remote Server entry is only available with the Enterprise Edition of VB, and it is never checked for add-ins. I have left the Version Compatibility entry set to No Compatibility because I am distributing the source code for the book's add-ins. If I were distributing only the compiled version of an add-in, I would have selected Binary Compatibility and entered the path and name of the DLL file that is the add-in.

 Although you can't manually change the Start Mode entry on the Component tab for a DLL component, you can access and change it programmatically with an add-in by setting the **StartMode** property of a **VBProject** object. See the *Dictionary* entry for the **StartMode** property for more information. There is no valid reason to do this, but this capability illustrates a generic problem associated with add-in code: The exception-handling built into VB's IDE (for example, disabling the Start Mode entry on the Component tab for an ActiveX DLL project) does not always govern how an add-in's code behaves.

The entries on the Component tab of the Project Properties dialog box for Chapter 1's add-in appear in Figure 1.11.

Windows Registration Entries

After you have made the requisite entries to the Project Properties dialog box, compiling an add-in and registering it in the Windows registry is as simple as selecting File|Make DLL or, in the rare case of an out-of-process add-in, File|Make EXE. The only way you can compile a VB add-in is with VB. However, there are other ways of registering an add-in on another developer's PC. You can use:

- VB's Setup Wizard to create a set of distribution disks and a SETUP.EXE routine, which automatically makes the registration entries.

- The REGSVR32.EXE utility that is on the \TOOLS\REGUTILS path of VB's CD-ROM. REGSVR32.EXE is a Windows program that registers and unregisters in-process DLL ActiveX components. For information on how to use this utility, see README.TXT on the \TOOLS\REGUTILS path.

- The GUIDGEN.EXE utility that is on the \TOOLS\IDGEN path of VB's CD-ROM. It generates a globally unique identifier (GUID). For information on how to use this utility, see README.TXT on the \TOOLS\IDGEN path. You could then manually or programmatically make the necessary entries in the Windows registry, including those requiring a GUID string.

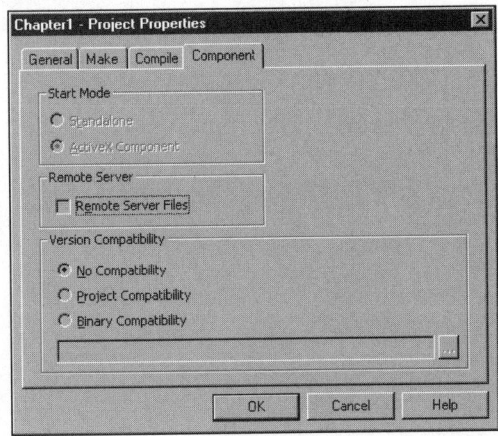

Figure 1.11
Component tab settings for Chapter 1's add-in.

Obviously, the easiest way to register an add-in is to do so when you compile it or by using VB's Setup Wizard. It doesn't matter which approach you use; each add-in results in three sets of entries in the Widows registry. The first set of entries, which is a subkey of the predefined key HKEY_CLASSES_ROOT, lists the programmatic ID and GUID of the add-in. Figure 1.12 shows this first set of entries for Chapter 1's add-in on my PC. The second set of entries, which is a subkey of HKEY_CLASSES_ROOT\CLSID, is based on the GUID string and contains several entries. Figure 1.13 shows this second set of entries for Chapter 1's add-in on my PC. The third set of entries, which is a subkey of HKEY_CLASSES_ROOT\TypeLib, is based on the GUID string and contains several entries related to the add-in's type library. Figure 1.14 shows this third set of entries for Chapter 1's add-in on my PC.

 You can find the same three sets of registration entries for Chapter 1's add-in on your PC. Just open the Registry Editor (type REGEDIT.EXE in the Windows Start button's Run dialog box and press Enter), select Edit|Find to display the Find dialog box, type Chapter1.Connect in the Find What box, and choose Find Next. After the Registry Editor finds the first set of entries, select Edit|Find

Figure 1.12
Add-in's Windows registry entries (1).

Figure 1.13
Add-in's Windows registry entries (2).

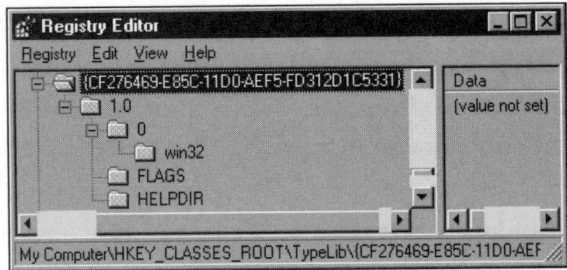

Figure 1.14
Add-in's Windows registry entries (3).

Next (F3) to find the second and third set of entries. These entries will look the same on your PC as they do in the book's figures except for the GUID string, which may be different if I recompiled Chapter 1's add-in since I wrote this chapter.

Running An Add-In

The only way to know for sure that an add-in has been compiled and registered correctly on a PC is to run it. Follow these steps:

1. Start an instance of VB.

2. Select Add-Ins|Add-In Manager to display the Add-In Manager dialog box.

3. Check the add-in item that you want to connect/run and choose OK (for example, Creating VB5 Add-Ins: Chapter 1).

4. From the Add-Ins menu, click the menu item for the add-in or click its button on the VB Add-In toolbar. This typically causes VB's IDE to display the add-in's initial GUI element. From there, you can run/test the add-in's functionality.

When you are done running an add-in, you need to decide whether you want to disconnect it and, in the process, delete its menu item. If you do want to disconnect it, follow these steps:

1. Select Add-Ins|Add-In Manager to display the Add-In Manager dialog box.

2. Uncheck the add-in item that you want to disconnect and choose OK.

VB then calls the **OnDisconnection** method of the add-in's **IDTExtensibility** object. If the add-in has been conventionally programmed, code in the **OnDisconnection** method's procedure deletes its menu item and closes its form (if you have not already done so manually).

Troubleshooting Add-In Problems

I know this chapter must seem like a marathon race that will never end, but you're almost to the finish line. Don't quit now! This last section lists the most common problems that can crop up with regard to VB add-ins and suggests possible solutions. If you get an error when creating or running your add-in, make sure that:

- The add-in was created as an ActiveX DLL or ActiveX EXE project.

- The add-in is correctly registered in both VBADDIN.INI and the Windows registry on the PC on which you are going to use it.

- Microsoft Visual Basic 5.0 Extensibility is selected in the References dialog box for the add-in's project. If this item is not selected, references to add-in objects and their members in the add-in's code cannot be resolved, and you'll get errors when you try to compile the add-in.

- Microsoft Office 8.0 Object Library is selected in the References dialog box if your add-in's code uses command bars (that is, menu items or toolbar buttons).

- The project name written to VBADDIN.INI (the part preceding the dot delimiter) exactly matches the Project Name entry on the General tab of the Project Properties dialog box.

- The **Name** property setting of the add-in's class module that contains the **IDTExtensibility** object interface exactly matches the name written to VBADDIN.INI (the part following the dot delimiter).

- The add-in's class module containing the **IDTExtensibility** object interface has procedures for the **OnAddInsUpdate**, **OnConnection**, **OnDisconnection**, and **OnStartupComplete** methods. All four of these procedures must be present and must contain at least one statement, even if it is only a comment; otherwise the compiler will remove the empty procedures from the class module, and the add-in will not work correctly.

Well, after working your way through Chapter 1, I hope you feel that I achieved my objective, which was to provide in one place all the information essential for you to create a simple VB add-in. Of course, there's much more to learn about creating add-ins, as you'll discover in the course of reading the rest of this book and referring to the entries in the *Dictionary* section. However, early in your add-in learning curve when basic questions or problems crop up, you should be able to find answers to most of them right here in Chapter 1.

Now it's on to Chapter 2, which gets into a lot of very interesting material on how to customize an add-in's interface. Chapter 2 also shows you how to code an add-in to do all kinds of neat tricks that are either undocumented or not directly supported by the Extensibility object model.

CUSTOMIZING AN ADD-IN'S INTERFACE

2

Our masks, always in peril of smearing or cracking, in need of continuous check in the mirror or silverware, keep us in thrall to ourselves, concerned with our surfaces.

—Carolyn Kizer

In Chapter 2, you're going to learn techniques and tricks for creating more complex, commercial-quality add-ins. Chapter 1's add-in represented the plain vanilla version, and it demonstrated only roughly 10% of the possible syntax associated with the various interfaces that an add-in can present or interact with. Think of the add-in that you looked at in Chapter 1 as the tip of the iceberg. The add-in you'll be studying in Chapter 2 represents the other 90% of the iceberg, the part under the water.

Of course, the deeper you go under water, the murkier and darker it gets; watch out because you can run into some pretty strange things down there. This chapter will function as your searchlight and lifeline as you explore the many ways in which you can customize a complex add-in's interface. More specifically, in this chapter you're going to learn how to deal with (or, in some cases, work around):

- Deficiencies/bugs associated with the **Connect** property of an **AddIn** object, which fails to refresh the contents of the Add-In Manager dialog box and VBADDIN.INI.

- The VBAI class library (Creating VB5 Add-Ins: Library Of Reusable Members), which is an ActiveX server component I wrote that was registered on your PC when you ran SETUP.EXE on this book's CD-ROM.

- The quirky behavior and undocumented features of the VB Add-In toolbar, actually a VB add-in itself.

- **IDTExtensibility** object conventions, automatic startups, and customization options.

- Preventing more than one instance of an add-in's form from being displayed by the current instance of VB.

- Displaying a custom message box better suited to add-in work than the one supported by VB's **MsgBox** function.

In addition to illustrating all of the interface customization features that an add-in can support, Chapter 2's add-in also demonstrates all the add-in language syntax that the Extensibility object model supports. Every add-in collection, object, or member in the VBIDE class library (and every item in the *Dictionary* section of this book) is demonstrated in Chapter 2's add-in.

One of the major hurdles you have to overcome when you begin to learn an entirely new formal language is what I call the problem of insufficient context. The *Dictionary* section of this book lists about 250 add-in syntax items. When you first try to use one of these new language elements, you quickly realize that you must understand half a dozen other related language elements (most of which you are also unfamiliar with). If the example provided for a given language element is too complex and context-dependent, you cannot learn effectively.

Chapter 2's add-in deals with this early learning-curve problem of insufficient context by demonstrating each language element with example code that is precisely focused and not overly context-dependent. In addition, the behavior of the add-in itself illustrates all of the interface customization features that this chapter deals with. By the time you're done with Chapter 2, I think you'll agree that you've been exposed to just about every imaginable add-in interface issue.

The Add-In Manager Dialog Box

You learned in Chapter 1 that one typical way a VB developer connects an add-in is to manually check the add-in's item in the Add-In Manager dialog box and choose OK. VB then sets that add-in's entry in VBADDIN.INI to "1" and calls the **OnConnection** method of the add-in. If the add-in has been conventionally programmed, code in the **OnConnection** method creates a VB menu item for it.

Now, let's pose this question: If the developer shuts down VB without having disconnected the add-in (that is, its item is still checked in the Add-In Manager dialog box), what happens the next time an instance of VB is started? Well, VB automatically calls the **OnConnection** methods of all add-ins whose items in VBADDIN.INI are set to "1" and, if the code in the methods dictates it, creates the menu items for those add-ins.

As we mentioned in Chapter 1, it is also possible to connect an add-in programmatically. Each add-in listed in the Add-In Manager dialog box and VBADDIN.INI is represented by an **AddIn** object, which has properties that enable you to programmatically control it from its own or another add-in's code. An **AddIn** object's **Connect** property returns or sets a **Boolean** that specifies the connected state of an add-in. If you set **Connect** to **True**, VB calls the **OnConnection** method of that add-in; if you set **Connect** to **False**, VB calls the add-in's **OnDisconnection** method.

However, there is a bug in the way the **Connect** property works. Setting the **Connect** property of an **AddIn** object to **True** or **False** fails to refresh the status of the add-in's item in the Add-In Manager dialog box and VBADDIN.INI. So if you shut down an instance of VB during whose life an add-in has been programmatically connected, that add-in will not be automatically reconnected the next time you start VB.

While studying VB's Extensibility object model to write this book, I ran across many such bugs and deficiencies among the various add-in language elements. Rather than just lambaste Microsoft over these glitches, I decided to fix the problems whenever possible and incorporate all the fixes in the VBAI class library that comes with this book's CD-ROM. VBAI.DLL is an ActiveX server component that I'll discuss in more detail later in the chapter. In this section, I'll focus just on the **Connect** method of the **Util** object in VBAI, which fixes the **Connect** property's bug.

In order to call the methods in my VBAI class library from an add-in's code and achieve the best performance possible, you should use the ActiveX technique of early binding. To do this, select Project|References, check the VBAI class library item (that is, Creating VB5 Add-Ins: Library Of Reusable Members), and choose OK. You can then connect an add-in (for example, the Windows API Browser demo installed from this book's CD-ROM) by instantiating a **Util** object and calling its **Connect** method with the statements:

```
Dim Util As New VBAI.Util
Util.Connect VBE, "WinAPIBrowser.Connect", True
```

To disconnect the add-in, you would use the statement:

```
Util.Connect VBE, "WinAPIBrowser.Connect", False
```

To demonstrate and compare the effect of the **Connect** property of VBIDE to that of the **Connect** method of VBAI, start Chapter 2's add-in and run the demo code for both the **Connect** property and the **Connect** method. For more detailed information about these or any other language elements in the VBIDE and VBAI class libraries, see the appropriate entry in the *Dictionary* section of this book or ADDINEFS.HLP. The code that comprises the **Connect** method is shown in Listing 2.1.

LISTING 2.1 CONNECT METHOD'S CODE.

```
Function Connect(VBE As VBE, _
                 ProgID As String, _
                 Flag As Boolean) As Boolean

    ' Variables:
    Dim Desc      As String
    Dim Descs()   As String
    Dim Pos       As Integer
    Dim Item      As Variant

    ' Check for specified failure cases:
    If Not IsProgID(VBE, ProgID) Then Exit Function
    If ProgID = "AddInToolbar.Connect" Then Exit Function

    Desc = GetDesc(VBE, ProgID)
    GetDescs VBE, Descs()
    SortDescs Descs()

    For Each Item In Descs
```

```
' Find add-in whose item in Add-In Manager
' dialog box is being checked or unchecked—
If Item = Desc Then

    ' Prevent desktop window from being redrawn.
    LockWindowUpdate GetDesktopWindow

    ' Run Timer thread to find/work on Add-In Manager
    ' dialog box when it is displayed with following
    ' SendKeys statement. Timer thread is required
    ' because dialog box is modal and code execution
    ' here is suspended until thread closes dialog box.
    ' Timer is started in AIMgrItem property procedure.
    frmTimer.AIMgrItem(0) = Pos

    ' Give VB's main window focus and open Add-In Manager
    ' dialog box so Timer thread can do its thing:
    VBE.MainWindow.SetFocus
    SendKeys "%AA", True

    ' Redraw desktop window
    LockWindowUpdate False

    Exit For
End If
Pos = Pos + 1
Next Item

Connect = True

End Function
```

After validating that an add-in with the specified *ProgID* argument exists and deriving its **Description** setting, what the **Connect** method in Listing 2.1 actually does is display the Add-In Manager dialog box, check/uncheck the add-in's item, and close the dialog box. You don't see this happen on the screen because the Windows API functions **LockWindowUpdate** and **GetDesktopWindow** are called at the outset to suspend screen redrawing.

The other tricky technique that the **Connect** method uses is to start a separate thread in a **Timer** object (tmrAIMgrDlgBox) on a hidden **Form** object (frmTimer) in the VBAI class library. It is only after this thread is running that **Connect** opens the Add-In Manager dialog box with a **SendKeys** statement. The thread then finds the dialog box's window, checks/unchecks the add-in's item, and chooses OK.

We use this technique because the Add-In Manager dialog box is displayed
modally and cannot be controlled programmatically except by a separate thread.
When the thread closes the modal dialog box, code execution resumes in the
Connect method, redraws the Windows screen, and returns **True** to the calling
add-in to signify success. The code that comprises the **Timer** object's thread is
shown in Listing 2.2.

LISTING 2.2   THREAD THAT CONTROLS ADD-IN MANAGER DIALOG BOX.

```
Private Sub tmrAIMgrDlgBox_Timer()

    ' Constants for Windows API functions:
    Const GW_CHILD = 5
    Const GW_HWNDNEXT = 2
    Const WM_GETTEXT = &HD

    ' Variables:
    Dim Buff        As String * 256
    Dim Down        As Long
    Dim HWndAIMgr   As Long
    Dim HWndCtl     As Long
    Dim HWndOK      As Long

    ' Try to find VB's Add-In Manager dialog box.
    HWndAIMgr = FindWindow("#32770", "Add-In Manager")

    ' If it exists:
    If HWndAIMgr <> False Then

        ' Get handle of first child window/control.
        HWndCtl = GetWindow(HWndAIMgr, GW_CHILD)

        ' Until all controls have been examined:
        Do Until HWndCtl = False
          DoEvents

            ' Get caption of control.
            SendMsg HWndCtl, WM_GETTEXT, Len(Buff), Buff

            ' If it is OK button, store its handle and exit loop:
            If Left$(Buff, 2) = "OK" Then
              HWndOK = HWndCtl
              Exit Do
            End If
```

```
        HWndCtl = GetWindow(HWndCtl, GW_HWNDNEXT)
    Loop

    ' Use Down arrow key to move to add-in
    ' item to be checked or unchecked:
    If mAIMgrItem <> 0 Then
        For Down = 1 To mAIMgrItem
            SendKeys "{DOWN}", True
        Next Down
    End If

    ' Check/uncheck item with space key.
    SendKeys " ", True

    ' Depending on add-in's run mode, two tricks
    ' are required to close Add-In Manager dialog box:
    ' * When internally debugging add-in, Enter key works.
    ' * When running add-in normally, giving focus to OK
    '   button and then sending space key works.
    If mDebugMode Then
        SendKeys "{ENTER}"
    Else
        SetFocusAPI HWndOK
        SendKeys " ", True
    End If

    ' Clean up:
    tmrAIMgrDlgBox.Interval = 0
    Unload Me

    End If

End Sub
```

As you can imagine from looking at the code in Listings 2.1 and 2.2, designing, writing, and debugging the **Connect** method was not a trivial task. However, this method and the others contained in the VBAI class library provide real value and are a worthwhile addition to the VB add-in developer's toolkit. Even compiled to native code, VBAI.DLL takes up only 70KB. I recommend that you add a reference to it in every add-in that you create. We'll take a closer look at the design and contents of the VBAI class library in the next section of this chapter.

The VBAI Class Library

The VBAI class library (VBAI.DLL) was installed from this book's CD-ROM and is found on the path \ADDINEFS\VBAI. You can view its source code in VBAI.VBP and add to or modify it whenever you want. However, if you do so, be careful not to break its existing public interface, because if you do, you'll need to recompile all of this book's add-ins.

The VBAI class library contains four **Public** classes whose reusable methods are quite useful when writing VB add-ins. The four classes/objects and a description of their general purposes are:

- **AITBar**: Provides methods for an add-in to call to manipulate the VB Add-In toolbar

- **Cmd**: Provides methods for an add-in to call to manipulate VB menus and custom toolbars

- **Reg**: Provides methods for an add-in to call to add, modify, and remove string entries from the Windows registry

- **Util**: Provides methods for an add-in to call to perform miscellaneous tasks

In addition to the **Connect** method of the **Util** object, there are other methods you will encounter in Chapter 2 that relate to customizing an add-in's interface. They are listed in Table 2.1.

The **Cmd** object and its methods rectify a deficiency in the files that are distributed with VB5. VB's menus and toolbars are now all based on the new

	TABLE **2.1**

VBAI CLASS LIBRARY INTERFACE–RELATED METHODS.

Object/Method	Purpose
AITBar/AddButton	Adds the entries for an add-in button to VB's Add-In toolbar Windows registry subkey, immediately adds the button to the toolbar, and returns **True**. Improves upon the **AddToAddInToolbar** method of a **Manager** object of the VB Add-In Toolbar add-in.
AITBar/CopyButtonIcon	Copies the icon from an add-in's toolbar button to an add-in's menu item and returns **True**.

(continued)

	TABLE 2.1

VBAI CLASS LIBRARY INTERFACE–RELATED METHODS (*CONTINUED*).

Object/Method	Purpose
AITBar/DelButton	Turns off the entry for an add-in button in VB's Add-In toolbar Windows registry subkey, immediately removes the button from the toolbar, and returns **True**. Improves upon the **RemoveAddInFromToolbar** method of a **Manager** object of the VB Add-In Toolbar add-in.
AITBar/Hide and **Show**	Displays the VB Add-In toolbar on or removes it from the main window of the current instance of VB's IDE and returns **True**. Is the programmatic equivalent of unchecking/checking the VB Add-In Toolbar item in the Add-In Manager dialog box.
Cmd/AddMenuItem	Adds a menu item for an add-in to a VB menu or popup menu and returns the new menu item as a **CommandBarControl** object of the Office class library.
Util/IsBeingDebugged	Checks whether or not an add-in is being run/debugged in one instance of VB while being connected to another instance of VB and returns **True** or **False** accordingly.
Util/IsFormDisplayed	Finds an add-in's form that is currently displayed, brings the form to the foreground, and returns **True**. If the form is not displayed or is displayed by another instance of VB, **IsFormDisplayed** returns **False**.
Util/ShowMsg	Creates an enhanced modal or modeless message box that can display a Help topic by keyword instead of context number and as a popup instead of a jump. **ShowMsg** returns an integer that is the number of the chosen button.

CommandBar and **CommandBarControl** objects that are a part of the Office class library, which was developed for Microsoft Office 97. Although the Office class library file itself is distributed with VB, you have to purchase Office 97 in order to get the associated Help file that explains how to reuse the Office class library's **Public** members. Yes, there are some examples in VB Books Online that show how to create custom menus, menu items, and toolbars, but these examples are rudimentary at best. Take it from me, if you need to create custom menus or toolbars for an add-in, you'll find it's a lot easier to reuse the methods of the **Cmd** object in my VBAI class library than to struggle with the Office class library syntax.

The methods of the **Reg** object, although not directly related to customizing an add-in's interface, come in quite handy when you need to read/write entries from/to the Windows registry. Any VB developer who has called the Windows API functions provided for Windows registry work knows how frustrating they can be (they don't work the same under Windows vs. Windows NT, they require too much setup work and too many arguments, and so on). In the course of writing this book, I decided to write my own **Reg** object to handle Windows registry work so that I would never experience the frustration again.

 Throughout the rest of the book, a code listing that contains a statement with a reference to an **AlTBar**, **Cmd**, **Reg**, or **Util** object indicates that I'm reusing one of the **Public** members of the VBAI class library.

The VB Add-In Toolbar Add-In

When you first install and start VB5, you will probably notice the cool new, draggable toolbars that it supports. If you select View|Toolbars, you'll see a pop-up menu that lists five toolbar items (Debug, Edit, Form Editor, Standard, and Customize).

What you do not see is any item for a VB Add-In toolbar, because it is not part of VB itself. Rather, it is an add-in that you can only connect and run the first time by selecting Add-Ins|Add-In Manager and checking its item in the Add-In Manager dialog box. After you have done this, the code in the VB Add-In toolbar's add-in adds another item (Add-In Toolbar) to the Toolbars popup menu and displays the toolbar at the bottom of the other visible toolbars as in Figure 2.1.

When you first display the VB Add-In toolbar, it has seven buttons on it. If you click the button on the left (the one with the +/- sign on it), the Add/Remove Toolbar Items dialog box appears as in Figure 2.2.

The six checked items in the Available Add-Ins list of the dialog box correspond to the add-ins represented by the other six buttons. These six add-ins come

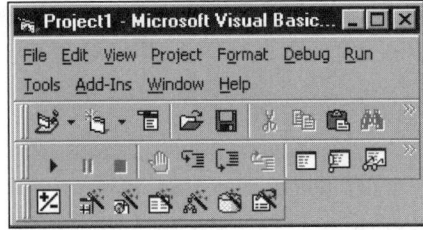

Figure 2.1
Initial docked appearance of VB Add-In toolbar.

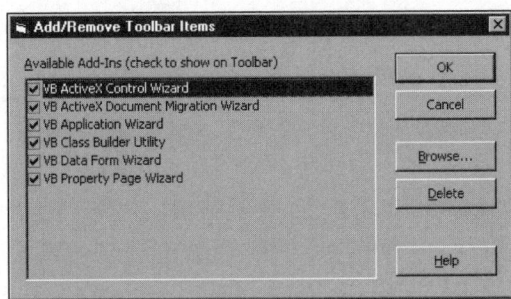

Figure 2.2
VB Add-In toolbar's dialog box.

with VB and are automatically installed and registered when you run VB's SETUP.EXE program. The basic features of the Add/Remove Toolbar Items dialog box are listed in Table 2.2.

	TABLE 2.2

ADD/REMOVE TOOLBAR ITEMS DIALOG BOX FEATURES.

Feature	Description
Add new item to list	Adds an add-in to the Available Add-Ins list by choosing Browse and using the New Add-In dialog box to find the ActiveX DLL or EXE component's file that is the add-in. If you try to add the DLL file for the VB Add-In Toolbar itself (AITOOL.DLL, which is found on VB's \WIZARDS path), an error message is displayed. (The Add-In Toolbar cannot be added to itself.)
Check item in list	Adds a button to the toolbar by checking its add-in item and choosing OK.

(continued)

TABLE 2.2

ADD/REMOVE TOOLBAR ITEMS DIALOG BOX FEATURES (*CONTINUED*).

Feature	Description
Uncheck item in list	Removes a button from the toolbar by unchecking its add-in item and choosing OK.
Delete item from list	Removes an add-in from the Available Add-Ins list by selecting its item and choosing Delete.
Get Help for dialog box	Although there is a Help button on the dialog box, there is no Help file associated with it. If you choose Help, you'll only get the generic Windows Help warning message (Topic does not exist).

Once you have initially displayed the VB Add-In toolbar by checking its item in the Add-In Manager dialog box, you can hide/show the toolbar by checking/unchecking its menu item on the Toolbars popup menu. However, this hide/show setting only affects the current instance of VB. If you start another instance of VB, the VB Add-In toolbar is either displayed or not depending on whether or not its item in the Add-In Manager dialog box's list is checked. This behavior is different from that of the other VB toolbars, which are displayed or not depending on whether or not their popup menu items were checked the last time you exited VB.

Like all the other VB toolbars, you can drag the VB Add-In toolbar by its handle on the left side of the bar and make it float as in Figure 2.3. To redock the toolbar, double-click its title bar. The tooltip displayed for each button on the toolbar is determined by the add-in project's Description entry on the General tab of the Project Properties dialog box.

The Add-In toolbar is a convenient repository for all of the add-ins you normally use as a VB developer, and provides easy access to them. The toolbar saves you the trouble of selecting Add-Ins|Add-In Manager to display the Add-In

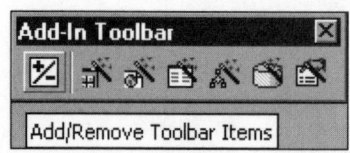

Figure 2.3
VB Add-In toolbar in floating mode.

Manager dialog box, checking the add-in item that you want, clicking OK to connect the add-in to a menu item, and then clicking the menu item to run the add-in. Instead, once you have placed a button for an add-in on the Add-In toolbar, you can connect and run the add-in by simply clicking its button. In addition, the Add-In toolbar automatically restores its most recent set of buttons each time you start an instance of VB.

 A new instance of VB can also automatically restore the menu item for an add-in whose item is checked in the Add-Manager dialog box's list. However, this requires code in the **OnConnection** and **OnStartupComplete** methods of the add-in's **IDTExtensibility** object, whereas the Add-In toolbar restores an add-in's button without relying on any code in the add-in. We will look at how to code the procedures for these methods and restore an add-in's menu item and form status later in this chapter.

Add-In Toolbar's Registry Entries

When you start an instance of VB, the VB Add-In toolbar is displayed or not depending on whether or not its item in the Add-In Manager dialog box's list is checked. However, the buttons that are displayed on the toolbar, the items that are in the Add/Remove Toolbar Items dialog box's list, and the checked/unchecked status of this item are controlled by a set of entries in the Windows registry. These entries are appended to the HKEY_CURRENT_USER\Software \Microsoft\Visual Basic\5.0\AddInToolbar subkey. Immediately after you install VB with SETUP.EXE, the entries appear as in Figure 2.4.

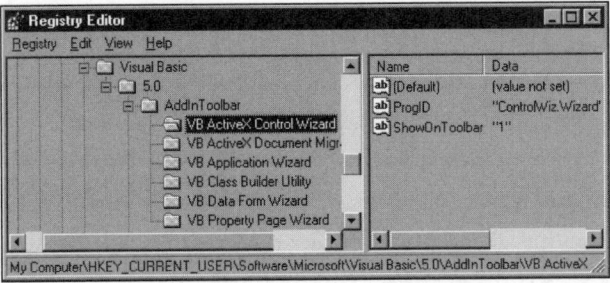

Figure 2.4
Windows registry entries for VB Add-In toolbar.

CHANGING REGISTRY ENTRIES MANUALLY

You can change the VB Add-In toolbar's registry entries manually by using the Add/Remove Toolbar Items dialog box. The actions that you take in the dialog box and their effects on the registry entries are listed in Table 2.3.

CHANGING REGISTRY ENTRIES WITH TOOLBAR METHODS

The Microsoft developer who wrote the VB Add-In Toolbar add-in also exposed two methods that enable you, to some degree, to control the behavior of the Add-In toolbar. These are the **AddToAddInToolbar** and **Remove-AddInFromToolbar** methods. To call either of these methods, you must first instantiate the **Manager** class of the VB Add-In Toolbar ActiveX component. The two ways you can create a **Manager** object are: set a reference to the ActiveX component's item (that is, VB Add-In Toolbar) and declare an object variable **As New Manager** (early binding), or declare an object variable as **Object** and assign it a reference to a **Manager** object with the **CreateObject** function (late binding).

Using the late binding approach, you can add a button to the toolbar for this book's Windows API Browser add-in by instantiating the **Manager** object with

```
Dim Manager As Object
Set Manager = CreateObject("AddInToolbar.Manager")
```

and calling the **AddToAddInToolbar** method with

```
Manager.AddToAddInToolbar "C:\ADDINEFS\BRWSAPIS\APIBRWSE.EXE", _
                          "WinAPIBrowser.Connect", _
                          "Creating VB5 Add-Ins: Windows API Browser", _
                          True, True
```

What the **AddToAddInToolbar** method actually does is write entries to the Windows registry and VBADDIN.INI. It writes a "1" to the ShowOnToolbar entry of the appropriate add-in subkey. If the subkey does not exist, **AddToAddInToolbar** creates it. HKEY_CURRENT_USER\Software \Microsoft\Visual Basic\5.0\AddInToolbar \Windows API Browser is the subkey for this book's Windows API Browser add-in. If the last argument of **AddToAddInToolbar** is set to **True**, the method also writes "1" to VBADDIN.INI for the add-in's entry.

	TABLE 2.3

ACTIONS AFFECTING ADD-IN TOOLBAR REGISTRY ENTRIES.

Dialog Box Action	Effect On Registry
Add new item to list	Adds new item to AddInToolbar subkey with three values (Default, ProgID, and ShowOnToolbar). New item's string is same as add-in's Description entry on General tab of Project Properties dialog box, and ShowOnToolbar value's setting is 0.
Check item in list	Changes setting of ShowOnToolbar value to 1.
Uncheck item in list	Changes setting ShowOnToolbar value to 0.
Delete item from list	Deletes item and its three values from AddInToolbar subkey.

You can remove the button for this book's Windows API Browser add-in from the toolbar by calling the **RemoveAddInFromToolbar** method with

```
Manager.RemoveAddInFromToolbar _
        "Creating VB5 Add-Ins: Windows API Browser"
```

where the argument refers to the add-in's item in the Add-In Manager dialog box's list. You can find more information about these two methods in VB's Help file or in the comprehensive *Dictionary* section of this book.

 When you make changes to the Add-In toolbar with the Add/ Remove Toolbar Items dialog box, the toolbar is refreshed as soon as you close the dialog box. However, when you call the **AddToAddInToolbar** or **RemoveAddInFromToolbar** methods, the Add-In toolbar is not refreshed until the next instance of VB's IDE is started.

CHANGING REGISTRY ENTRIES WITH VBAI CLASS METHODS

To correct for the deficiencies of the **AddToAddInToolbar** and **RemoveAddInFromToolbar** methods, I wrote the **AddButton** and **DelButton** methods of the **AITBar** object in the VBAI class library. These two methods change the Add-In toolbar's registry entries and also immediately refresh their appearance.

The two ways you can create an **AITBar** object are: set a reference to the ActiveX component's item (that is, Creating VB5 Add-Ins: Library Of Reusable Members) and declare an object variable **As New AITBar** (early binding), or declare an object variable as **Object** and assign it a reference to an **AITBar** object with the **CreateObject** function (late binding).

Using the late binding approach, you can add a button to the toolbar for this book's Windows API Browser add-in by instantiating the **AITBar** object with

```
Dim AITBar As Object
Set AITBar = CreateObject("VBAI.AITBar")
```

and calling the **AddButton** method with

```
AITBar.AddButton VBE, "WinAPIBrowser.Connect"
```

where the first parameter (**VBE**) is an object reference to the current instance of VB's IDE and the second parameter is the programmatic ID of the add-in (the entry in VBADDIN.INI) for which a button is to be added.

You can remove the button for this book's Windows API Browser add-in from the toolbar by calling the **DelButton** method with

```
AITBar.DelButton VBE, "WinAPIBrowser.Connect"
```

You should note one major difference between the way the **AddToAddInToolbar** and **RemoveAddInFromToolbar** methods work and the way my **AddButton** and **DelButton** methods work: The VBAI class library methods can only be called from within an add-in. As we mentioned in Chapter 1, the only way to obtain an object reference to the current instance of VB's IDE is from the *VBInst* argument of the **OnConnection** method of an add-in.

 To demonstrate the **AddButton** and **DelButton** methods, start Chapter 2's add-in and run the demo code for both methods. For more detailed information about these two methods (or any methods in the VBAI class library), see their entries in the *Dictionary* section of this book, or ADDINEFS.HLP.

I wrote the **AddButton** method myself, so I'm able to provide a code listing for it. I won't be listing all 33 of the methods in the VBAI class library in the course of this book. However, when a particular method exemplifies a new technique or trick related to add-in development, I will provide the code. The **AddButton** method's code is shown in Listing 2.3. The **DelButton** method is so similar to **AddButton** method that it is not necessary to list its code.

LISTING 2.3   ADDBUTTON METHOD'S CODE.

```
Function AddButton(VBE As VBE, ProgID As String) As Boolean

    ' Variables:
    Dim Desc        As String
    Dim SubKey      As String
    Dim TBarProgID  As String
    Dim HWndSubKey  As Long

    ' Check for specified failure cases:
    TBarProgID = "AddInToolbar.Connect"
    If ProgID = TBarProgID Then Exit Function
    If Not IsProgID(VBE, ProgID) Then Exit Function
    If IsButton(VBE, ProgID) = True Then Exit Function

    ' Get setting of add-in's Description property (default entry
    ' of programmatic ID subkey of add-in's connection class):
    Desc = Util.GetDesc(VBE, ProgID)

    ' Concatenate subkey string:
    SubKey = "Software\Microsoft\Visual Basic\5.0\AddInToolbar\"
    SubKey = SubKey & Desc

    ' Get handle to Add-In toolbar's registry subkey for add-in.
    HWndSubKey = Reg.OpenSubKey(aiKTCurUser, SubKey)

    ' Write entries for ProgID and ShowOnToolbar values:
    Reg.SetValue HWndSubKey, ProgID, "ProgID"
    Reg.SetValue HWndSubKey, "1", "ShowOnToolbar"
    Reg.CloseSubKey HWndSubKey

    ' If displayed, hiding/redisplaying toolbar causes toolbar
    ' application to reread Windows registry and add button:
    If VBE.Addins(TBarProgID).Connect Then
        Hide VBE, ProgID
        Show VBE, ProgID

    ' If not displayed, just displaying toolbar causes toolbar
    ' application to reread Windows registry and add button:
    Else
        Show VBE, ProgID
    End If

    AddButton = True

End Function
```

There are three key points to note about the **AddButton** method. First, it calls the **GetDesc** method of the **Util** object to obtain the setting of the **Description** property of the **AddIn** object for which a button is to be added to the toolbar. I call **GetDesc** rather than read the setting of the **Description** property of the **AddIn** object because **GetDesc** will never fail. The **Description** property approach can fail if you start the add-in from the VB Add-In toolbar.

Second, I call methods of the **Reg** object to change the Windows registry entries for the Add-In toolbar. I'm not going to go into detail in this chapter about how the **Reg** object's methods work. All the information you need to know is in the *Dictionary* section of this book or in ADDINEFS.HLP for each one of the **Reg** object's methods. Third, calls to the **Hide** and **Show** methods of the **AITBar** object enable the **AddButton** method to immediately refresh the Add-In toolbar. We will study these two methods in the next section.

 If you want to determine if a button for an add-in is already displayed on the VB Add-In toolbar, you can call the IsButton method of the AITBar object.

Displaying And Hiding The Add-In Toolbar Programmatically

As I mentioned in the previous section, because the VB Add-In toolbar is itself an add-in, the only way to make sure it is displayed each time a new instance of VB is started is to have manually checked its item in the Add-In Manager dialog box's list. However, it would be nice to be able to programmatically display and hide the Add-In toolbar. To do so, I wrote the **Show** and **Hide** methods of the **AITBar** object. Both methods work the same way, so I'll analyze just the **Show** method's code in Listing 2.4.

LISTING 2.4   SHOW METHOD'S CODE.

```
Function Show(VBE As VBE, ProgID As String) As Boolean

   ' Variables:
   Dim TBarProgID   As String
   Dim Descs()      As String
   Dim Pos          As Integer
   Dim Desc         As Variant
```

```
' Check for specified failure cases:
TBarProgID = "AddInToolbar.Connect"
If ProgID = TBarProgID Then Exit Function
If Not IsProgID(VBE, ProgID) Then Exit Function
If VBE.Addins(TBarProgID).Connect Then Exit Function

GetDescs VBE, Descs()
SortDescs Descs()

' Find toolbar description's position in sorted array:
For Each Desc In Descs
    If Desc = "VB Add-In Toolbar" Then Exit For
    Pos = Pos + 1
Next Desc

' Prevent desktop window from being redrawn.
LockWindowUpdate GetDesktopWindow

' Run Timer thread to:
' * Find Add-In Manager dialog box when it is displayed with
'   following SendKeys statement.
' * Check toolbar's add-in item.
' Timer thread is required because dialog box is modal and
' code execution here is suspended until thread closes dialog
' box. Timer is started in AIMgrItem property procedure.
If Util.IsBeingDebugged(VBE, ProgID) Then
    frmTimer.AIMgrItem(True) = Pos
Else
    frmTimer.AIMgrItem(False) = Pos
End If

' Give VB's main window focus and open Add-In Manager
' dialog box so Timer thread can do its thing:
VBE.MainWindow.SetFocus
SendKeys "%AA", True

' Redraw desktop window.
LockWindowUpdate False
Show = True

End Function
```

It is possible to display the Add-In toolbar by simply setting the **Connect** property of the toolbar's **AddIn** object to **True**. Unfortunately, this does not cause VB to check the toolbar's item in the Add-In Manager dialog box's list. As a result, the next time an instance of VB runs, the toolbar reverts back to its previous status and is not displayed. The **Show** method prevents this from happening.

The technique that makes the **Show** method of the **AITBar** object work is basically the same trick that the **Connect** method of the **Util** object uses. **Show** runs a separate thread in a **Timer** object (tmrAIMgrDlgBox) on a hidden **Form** object (frmTimer) in the VBAI class library. After **Show** opens the Add-In Manager dialog box, the **Timer** object's thread finds the dialog box's window, checks the VB Add-In Toolbar item, and closes the dialog box.

This **Timer** thread executes while drawing of the desktop window is suspended and, as a result, the developer does not see these actions. Although this technique violates the encapsulation of an **AITBar** object, it is necessary because the Add-In Manager dialog box is displayed modally and cannot be closed programmatically except by a separate thread. The only difference between the **Show** and **Hide** methods is that **Show** checks the VB Add-In Toolbar item while **Hide** unchecks it.

If you want to determine whether or not the VB Add-In toolbar is displayed, you can call the **IsDisplayed** method of the **AITBar** object. Or, as I do in the **Show** method's code in Listing 2.4, you can read the **Connect** property of the **AddIn** object that represents the Add-In toolbar with a statement like

```
If VBE.Addins("AddInToolbar.Connect").Connect = True Then
```

and write code accordingly, based on whether **Connect** returns **True** or **False**.

Controlling The Icon On An Add-In Toolbar Button

An undocumented feature of the VB Add-In Toolbar add-in is how it decides which icon to display on the button for a particular add-in. From what I've been able to discover through a little reverse engineering, its behavior varies depending on a couple of variables and how they interact:

- Whether the add-in is an ActiveX EXE or DLL component

- Whether or not, for the add-in's project, there is an icon specified on the Make tab of the Project Properties dialog box

You would also like to know how to use the icon that is on an Add-In toolbar's button on the menu item that is created when you connect the add-in through the Add-In Manager dialog box. For example, the icon for the VB Application Wizard add-in's button is shown in Figure 2.5. When you connect the VB Application Wizard add-in from the Add-In Manager dialog box, its menu item uses the same icon (shown in Figure 2.6).

In the next section, you'll learn how to specify and manipulate these two aspects of the VB Add-In Toolbar's behavior.

SETTING AN ACTIVEX EXE ADD-IN'S ICON

An ActiveX EXE add-in is a simple scenario. In this case, the Add-In toolbar button's icon is set to the one associated with the EXE file (that is, the icon that is displayed in the Windows Explorer). As with all VB applications, you can most easily specify this icon by setting the Icon entry on the Make tab of the Project Properties dialog box. The only EXE add-in on this book's CD-ROM is the Windows API Browser demo. Its project's Icon entry is set as in Figure 2.7. Therefore, if you add it to the VB Add-In toolbar, it is the icon that is displayed on the button (as shown in Figure 2.8).

Figure 2.5
VB Application Wizard's toolbar icon.

Figure 2.6
VB Application Wizard's menu item icon.

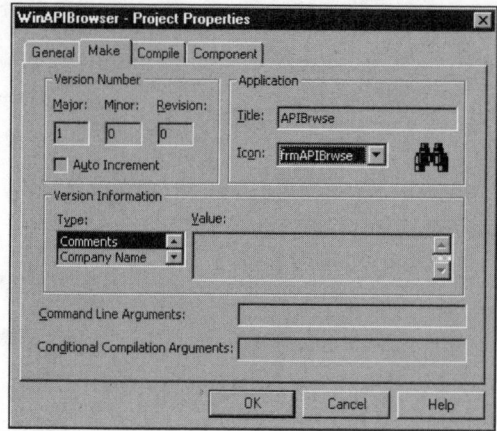

Figure 2.7
Icon entry for ActiveX EXE add-in.

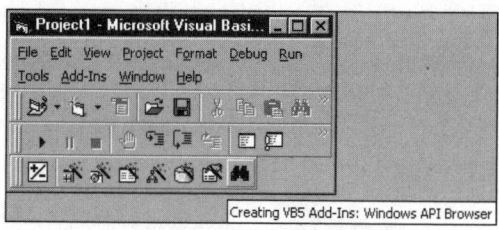

Figure 2.8
Icon displayed for ActiveX EXE add-in's toolbar button.

SETTING AN ACTIVEX DLL ADD-IN'S ICON

Specifying the icon for an ActiveX DLL add-in's toolbar button involves a more complex process. Instead of setting the Icon entry on the Make tab of the Project Properties dialog box to specify the icon, you must do so with a resource (.RES) file.

The entry that you make to specify an icon for a RES file

```
APPICON     ICON     CHAPTER2.ICO
```

contains three parts separated by tabs and is contained in an RC file. An RC file is simply a text file with an .RC file extension. After you have created this RC file and the ICO file specified in the third part of the entry, you create the

RES file by running the Microsoft Resource Compiler (RC.EXE) with a command line like

```
C:\ADDINEFS\CHAPTER2\RC.EXE /r /fo CHAPTER2.RES CHAPTER2.RC
```

Once you have created the RES file, you can include it in an add-in's project by selecting Project|Add File. Then, after you select File|Make DLL, the RES file is part of the compiled DLL add-in. The VB Add-In Toolbar application is coded to look for such an icon resource reference in a DLL add-in and, if it finds it, to use it as the icon on its toolbar button. Each of the add-ins on this book's CD-ROM contains a RES file that specifies the icon to be displayed on the Add-In toolbar. In the interest of consistency and organization, I created icons that display the chapter numbers associated with the add-ins. For example, the icon displayed for Chapter 2's add-in is shown in Figure 2.9.

You can find more information about creating these kinds of files on the VB CD-ROM in the file RESOURCE.TXT, which is located on the path TOOLS \RESOURCE. The associated files for the Microsoft Resource Compiler itself (RC.EXE, RC.HLP, and README.TXT) are also located on that path. This RC.EXE application can be used to create 32-bit resources used in applications under Windows 95 or later and Windows NT 3.51 or later. You can also include strings and bitmaps in a RES file. I'm not going to explain how to create a more elaborate resource file here; a detailed example is presented in Chapter 8.

As we mentioned in Chapter 1, setting the Icon entry on the Make tab of the Project Properties dialog box to anything other than its default of no item for a DLL add-in confuses the VB Add-In toolbar application. If you do that, the Add-In toolbar ignores any icon resource reference and displays a generic icon from its own library.

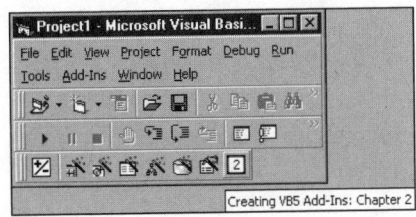

Figure 2.9
Icon displayed for Chapter 2's add-in button.

COPYING AN ADD-IN TOOLBAR BUTTON'S ICON

It is conventional add-in programming practice, as demonstrated in the examples in Figures 2.5 and 2.6, to use the same icon for an add-in's menu item that the VB Add-In toolbar uses for its button. The **Public** members that the Office class library exposes for creating an add-in's menu item and assigning a graphic to it are cumbersome to use and poorly documented. An easier way to do this is to call the **CopyButtonIcon** method of the **AITBar** object in the VBAI class library. The code for **CopyButtonIcon** is shown in Listing 2.5.

LISTING 2.5   COPYBUTTONICON METHOD'S CODE.

```
Function CopyButtonIcon(VBE As VBE, _
                        Desc As String, _
                        Menu As Office.CommandBarControl) _
                        As Boolean

    ' Copy icon from add-in's toolbar button to
    ' clipboard and paste it on add-in's menu item:
    On Error GoTo EH
    VBE.CommandBars("Add-In Toolbar").Controls(Desc).CopyFace
    Menu.PasteFace
    Clipboard.Clear

EH:
    If Err = False Then CopyButtonIcon = True

End Function
```

The **CopyButtonIcon** method takes three required arguments:

- *VBE*: An object expression that evaluates to a **VBE** object of the VBIDE class library. This is always obtained from the *VBInst* argument of the add-in's **OnConnection** method.

- *Desc*: A **String** expression that specifies the setting of the Project Description entry of the add-in whose toolbar button's icon is to be copied. This entry is made on the General tab of the Project Properties dialog box for the add-in's project. If Show ToolTips is checked on the General tab of VB's Options dialog box, *Desc* is displayed when you move the mouse over the button. If *Desc* is set to a value for which no button is displayed, **CopyButtonIcon** fails.

- *Menu*: An object expression that evaluates to a **CommandBarControl** object of the Office class library and that represents the menu item for a connected add-in. You can get *Menu* by first calling the **AddMenuItem** method of a **Cmd** object of the VBAI class library.

Once it has the parameters for its three arguments, **CopyButtonIcon** calls the **CopyFace** method of the Office library's **CommandBarButton** object that represents the add-in's toolbar button. **CopyFace** copies the icon of the button to the Clipboard. Then **CopyButtonIcon** calls the **PasteFace** method of the **CommandBarButton** object that represents the add-in's menu item. **PasteFace** pastes the contents of the Clipboard onto the specified menu item.

Coding The Behavior Of The Add-In Toolbar

It is easy for a developer who is using VB5 for the first time to not even be aware of the existence of the VB Add-In Toolbar application. If you don't know that it is an add-in, you probably won't notice it in the Add-In Manager dialog box's list and thus may never check its item to display the toolbar. One approach that you can take as an add-in developer to ensure that this doesn't happen is to code the **OnConnection** method's procedure of each add-in you write to implement the following algorithm (using members of the VBAI class library):

- Call the **IsButton** method of the **AITBar** object to check if an entry for the add-in exists in VB's Add-In toolbar Windows registry subkey, and is turned on.

- If **IsButton** returns **False**, call the **AddButton** method of the **AITBar** object to create the entry.

- Call the **IsDisplayed** method of the **AITBar** object to check if VB's Add-In toolbar is displayed in the current instance of VB.

- If **IsDisplayed** returns **False**, call the **Show** method of the **AITBar** object to display the toolbar.

- Once the VB Add-In toolbar is displayed with a button/icon for the add-in, create the menu item for the add-in and call the **CopyButtonIcon** method to add that icon to the menu item.

Except for Chapter 1's simple add-in, each of the add-ins on this book's CD-ROM implements the previous algorithm. The code in Chapter 2's add-in that does so is shown in Listing 2.6.

LISTING 2.6   CODE TO DISPLAY AND COPY BUTTON ON ADD-IN TOOLBAR.

```
Private Sub IDTExtensibility_OnConnection _
        (ByVal VBInst As Object, _
        ByVal ConnectMode As vbext_ConnectMode, _
        ByVal AddInInst As AddIn, _
        Custom())

    ' Variables:
    Dim Item       As String
    Dim Ch2ProgID  As String
    Dim Ch2Desc    As String

    ' Assign local variables:
    Item = "Creating VB5 Add-Ins: Chapter &2..."
    Ch2ProgID = "Chapter2.Connect"
    Ch2Desc = Util.GetDesc(VBE, Ch2ProgID)

.   .   .   .

        ' If running in normal mode, display button for add-in
        ' on AddIn toolbar (doesn't work properly in debug mode):
        If Not Util.IsBeingDebugged(VBE, Ch2ProgID) Then
            SetAIToolBar Ch2ProgID
        End If

        ' Create add-in's menu item.
        SetAIMenuItem Item, Ch2Desc

.   .   .   .

End Sub

Private Sub SetAddInToolBar(ProgID As String)

    If Not AITBar.IsButton(VBE, ProgID) Then
        AITBar.AddButton VBE, ProgID
    ElseIf Not AITBar.IsDisplayed(VBE) Then
        AITBar.Show VBE, ProgID
    End If

End Sub
```

```
Private Sub SetAIMenuItem(Caption As String, AIDesc As String)

    ' Variables:
    Dim Mnu As Office.CommandBarControl

    ' Create add-in's menu item and give it same
    ' icon as its button on Add-In toolbar has:
    Set Mnu = VBE.CommandBars("Menu Bar").Controls("Add-Ins")
    Set mMenuItem = Cmd.AddMenuItem(VBE, Mnu, Caption)
    AITBar.CopyButtonIcon VBE, AIDesc, mMenuItem

    ' Make add-in respond to menu item's Click event.
    Set CommandBar = VBE.Events.CommandBarEvents(mMenuItem)

End Sub
```

The code in Listing 2.6 ensures that the Add-In toolbar is displayed with a button/icon for Chapter 2's add-in and that the same icon is placed on the add-in's menu item, as shown in Figure 2.10.

Well, that's about it as far as the VB Add-In Toolbar's functionality is concerned. ("Thank goodness," you're probably saying to yourself at this point.) Actually, there are a couple more items, but we'll deal with them in the following section. What we've done so far in this chapter is examine the ways in which an add-in can relate to and customize these three external interface elements:

- VB's Add-In Manager dialog box

- Other class libraries (VBAI and Office)

- The VB Add-In Toolbar add-in

What we are going to do in the next section is demonstrate how you can customize an add-in's own **IDTExtensibility** object interface.

Figure 2.10
Icons displayed for Chapter 2's add-in.

Customizing The IDTExtensibility Object Interface

As you saw in Chapter 1, the **IDTExtensibility** object interface contains four methods that VB calls when events related to an add-in occur: **OnAddInsUpdate**, **OnConnection**, **OnDisconnection**, and **OnStartupComplete**. The procedures that you write for these four methods determine how an add-in behaves when:

- A developer starts VB, manually connects/disconnects an add-in, or runs an add-in.

- Another add-in programmatically connects/disconnects an add-in or runs it.

There is little to write about the **OnAddInsUpdate** method's procedure. You might want to include the statement

```
VBE.Addins.Update
```

in an add-in if it interacts in some way with other add-ins. In such an add-in, calling the **Update** method of the **Addins** collection refreshes the collection to reflect any additions to add-in related entries in the Windows registry. The other three methods of the **IDTExtensibility** object can be extensively customized and we need to study each of them closely.

The Three Faces Of The OnConnection Method

The ways that an add-in can behave when its **OnConnection** method is called are directly related to the parameter that is passed in to that method's *ConnectMode* argument. The three possible settings for *ConnectMode* are described in Table 2.4. You already saw the code that executes when *ConnectMode* is set to 0 - **vbext_cm_AfterStartup** in Listing 2.6. What we need to look at next are the two other possible scenarios: automatic connection by VB and external connection via the VB Add-In toolbar or programmatically.

AUTOMATIC CONNECTION BY VB

Each time an instance of VB is started, its splash screen is displayed first. Then, before anything else occurs, VB checks the settings in VBADDIN.INI and

TABLE 2.4

SETTINGS OF **ONCONNECTION** METHOD'S *CONNECTMODE* ARGUMENT.

Setting	Description
0 - vbext_cm_AfterStartup	Add-in is connected after the initial Open Project dialog box is shown. This occurs when the developer checks an add-in item in the Add-In Manager dialog box or when an add-in's code sets another add-in's **Connect** property to **True**.
1 - vbext_cm_Startup	Add-in is connected before the initial Open Project dialog box is shown and while VB's splash screen is visible. This occurs when, upon startup, VB finds that an item in the Add-In Manager dialog box's list is checked (that is, its entry in VBADDIN.INI is set to "1") and automatically connects that add-in.
2 - vbext_cm_External	Add-in is connected by another program or programmatically by calling the **OnConnection** method from within the add-in. This normally occurs when the developer clicks the add-in's button on the VB Add-In toolbar.

automatically calls the **OnConnection** method for each add-in that was connected the last time VB was shut down. You can easily demonstrate this behavior by following these steps:

- Start an instance of VB.

- Select Add-Ins|Add-In Manager to display the Add-In Manager dialog box.

- Check the item Creating VB5 Add-Ins: Chapter 2 in the Available Add-Ins list and choose OK.

- Select File|Exit to shut down VB.

- Start another instance of VB.

Immediately after displaying its splash screen, VB calls the **OnConnection** method of Chapter 2's add-in and the message box in Figure 2.11 is displayed above the splash screen. The code in the **OnConnection** method's procedure that displays the message box is shown in Listing 2.7.

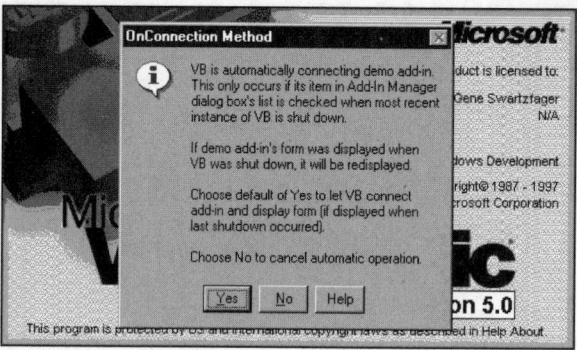

Figure 2.11

Demonstration of **vbext_cm_Startup** *ConnectMode*.

LISTING 2.7   CODE RELATED TO VBEXT_CM_STARTUP *CONNECTMODE*.

```
Private Sub IDTExtensibility_OnConnection _
        (ByVal VBInst As Object, _
        ByVal ConnectMode As vbext_ConnectMode, _
        ByVal AddInInst As AddIn, _
        Custom())


    ' Constants for literals:
    Const BTNS = 64 + 65536 + &H40000
    Const C = "OnConnection Method "

    ' Variables:
    Dim M As String


.   .   .   .


    If ConnectMode = vbext_cm_Startup Then

        M = "VB is automatically connecting demo add-in." & vbCr
        M = M & "This only occurs if its item in Add-In "
        M = M & "Manager" & vbCr
        M = M & "dialog box's list is checked when most "
        M = M & "recent" & vbCr
        M = M & "instance of VB is shut down."
        M = M & vbCr & vbCr
        M = M & "If demo add-in's form was displayed when" & vbCr
        M = M & "VB was shut down, it will be redisplayed."
        M = M & vbCr & vbCr
        M = M & "Choose default of Yes to let VB connect" & vbCr
```

```
M = M & "add-in and display form (if displayed when" & vbCr
M = M & "last shutdown occurred)."
M = M & vbCr & vbCr
M = M & "Choose No to cancel automatic operation."
Button = Util.ShowMsg(M, BTNS + vbYesNo, C, _
                        App.HelpFile, C & "Example")


' If developer chooses No, prevent OnStartupComplete
' method's code from executing by turning on flag:
If Button = vbNo Then mCancelConnection = True


.   .   .   .


End Sub
```

When an add-in is automatically started by VB, the same results are achieved as when a developer connects it through the Add-In Manager dialog box (initialize variables, create its menu item, display the Add-In toolbar, and so on). However, you should note that these tasks are not done by the **OnConnection** method's procedure but rather by code in the **OnStartupComplete** method's procedure (see the section later in this chapter titled *Customizing The OnStartupComplete Method*).

The startup tasks are done in **OnStartupComplete** because you can't be sure that the VB Add-In Toolbar add-in itself has been connected at the **OnConnection** stage in VB's startup cycle. The code in Listing 2.7 demonstrates that you can give the developer the option to cancel the automatic connection of an add-in by turning on the module-level flag **mCancelConnection**, which the code in the **OnStartupComplete** method will read later.

 I display the message box in Figure 2.11 and the other **IDT Extensibility** object-related message boxes shown in this chapter to illustrate what can be done during the execution of the object's methods and the sequence in which the methods occur. If you want to run Chapter 2's add-in just to demonstrate an add-in language element and don't want to be bothered with these message boxes, start the add-in from the Add-In toolbar.

EXTERNAL CONNECTION BY THE TOOLBAR

If the VB Add-In toolbar is displayed and a button for an add-in is on it, clicking that button calls the **OnConnection** method of the add-in. There are three points to note about this kind of connection that are different from the other two kinds (**vbext_cm_AfterStartup** and **vbext_cm_Startup**):

• The *AddInInst* argument of the **OnConnection** method evaluates to **Nothing** because the add-in is not being connected to VB's IDE; instead, it is being connected externally via the Add-In toolbar. From a practical viewpoint, this means that the **AddIn** object representing the externally connected add-in does not get refreshed and so its **Description** and **Guid** properties return zero-length strings instead of their normal settings. Also, the **AddIn** object's **Connect** property returns **False**.

• When the code in the **OnConnection** method is done executing, the **Terminate** event of the add-in's connection object is raised and any code in its event procedure is executed. This too occurs because the add-in is not being connected to VB's IDE.

• The **OnAddInsUpdate** method is not called because no change has been made to VBADDIN.INI through the Add-In Manager dialog box.

In all other respects, an add-in that is connected externally through the VB Add-In Toolbar behaves the same as one that is connected through the Add-In Manager dialog box.

EXTERNAL CONNECTION BY CALLING ONCONNECTION INTERNALLY

You can call the **OnConnection** method from another method of an **IDTExtensibility** object. However, this capability is limited and should be employed sparingly and carefully. To demonstrate how you can do this, code in the **OnDisconnection** method of Chapter 2's add-in displays the message box in Figure 2.12 and asks you to confirm your intention to disconnect the add-in via the Add-In Manager dialog box.

If you choose No, the code in Listing 2.8 programmatically calls the **OnConnection** method, passing to its *ConnectMode* argument parameter 2 - **vbext_cm_External** and to its *Custom()* argument a zero-based array whose only element is set to **True** (that is, **aiCancelDisconnection**). The code in the **OnConnection** method in

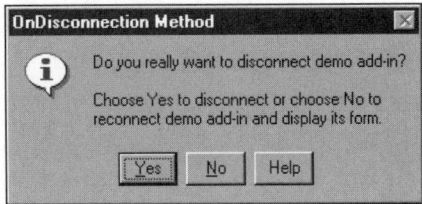

Figure 2.12
Message box confirming intent to disconnect add-in.

Listing 2.9 then reacts to the values of the *ConnectMode* and *Custom()* arguments and displays the message box in Figure 2.13.

The *Custom()* argument of the **OnConnection** method is defined in VB's Help file as an array of **Variant** expressions to hold user-defined data. If you use the **VarType** function on *Custom()*, it returns 8204 (**vbArray + vbVariant**). However, if you try to use the **LBound** function on *Custom()*, it results in trappable error 9 (subscript out of range). This means that when VB calls the **OnConnection** method, it is passing *Custom()* an unsized array. This implies that *Custom()* is not currently being used by VB and is probably provided for future use by Microsoft's VB development team. As Chapter 2's add-in demonstrates, you can call **OnConnection** internally and signal this by passing *Custom()* a sized array containing some flag; however, you should exercise caution when doing so.

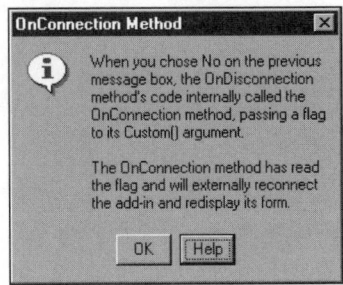

Figure 2.13
Message box signaling internal call of **OnConnection** method.

LISTING 2.8   ONDISCONNECTION METHOD CALLING ONCONNECTION METHOD.

```
Private Sub IDTExtensibility_OnDisconnection _
        (ByVal RemoveMode As vbext_DisconnectMode, _
        Custom())


    ' Constants for literals:
    Const C = "OnDisconnection Method "
    Const BTNS = 64 + 65536 + &H40000

    ' Variables:
    Dim M       As String
    Dim Visible   As Boolean


    .   .   .   .


    ' If developer is disconnecting add-in's menu item:
    ElseIf RemoveMode = vbext_dm_UserClosed Then

        ' Remove add-in's menu item and unload its form:
        mMenuItem.Delete
        Unload mfrmDemoSynt

        ' Rest of procedure shows how to programmatically
        ' call method of IDTExtensibility object:
        M = "Do you really want to disconnect demo add-in?"
        M = M & vbCr & vbCr
        M = M & "Choose Yes to disconnect or choose No to" & vbCr
        M = M & "reconnect demo add-in and display its form."

        If Util.ShowMsg(M, BTNS + vbYesNo, C, App.HelpFile, _
                    C & "Example") = vbNo Then

            Flag(aiCancelDisconnection) = True
            IDTExtensibility_OnConnection VBE, vbext_cm_External, _
                                    mAIDemo, Flag()


        .   .   .   .


        End If

End Sub
```

LISTING 2.9   ONCONNECTION METHOD BEING CALLED INTERNALLY.

```
Private Sub IDTExtensibility_OnConnection _
        (ByVal VBInst As Object, _
         ByVal ConnectMode As vbext_ConnectMode, _
         ByVal AddInInst As AddIn, _
         Custom())

    ' Constants for literals:
    Const BTNS = 64 + 65536 + &H40000
    Const C = "OnConnection Method "

    ' Variables:
    Dim M                        As String
    Dim CalledByOnDisconnection  As Boolean


    .   .   .   .


    ' If add-in is connected by clicking Add-In toolbar
    ' button or OnConnection method is called internally:
    ElseIf ConnectMode = vbext_cm_External Then

        ' Error handler is for normal case when developer clicks
        ' Add-In toolbar and Custom() argument is unsized array
        ' that is passed in by VB's IDE. However, if error does
        ' not occur, then OnConnection method is being called
        ' internally by OnDisconnection method's procedure.
        On Error Resume Next
        If Custom(aiCancelDisconnection) Then
            If Err = False Then CalledByOnDisconnection = True
        End If
        On Error GoTo 0

        If CalledByOnDisconnection Then
            M = "When you chose No on the previous" & vbCr
            M = M & "message box, the OnDisconnection" & vbCr
            M = M & "method's code internally called" & vbCr
            M = M & "the OnConnection method, passing" & vbCr
            M = M & "a flag to its Custom() argument."
            M = M & vbCr & vbCr
            M = M & "The OnConnection method will now" & vbCr
            M = M & "reconnect/redisplay the add-in." & vbCr
            Util.ShowMsg M, BTNS, C, App.HelpFile, C & "Example"

        End If
```

```
DisplayForm

End If
```

Customizing The OnStartupComplete Method

The **OnStartupComplete** method of an add-in occurs automatically when the startup of the current instance of VB's IDE is complete and the add-in's entry in VBADDIN.INI is "1". As I mentioned earlier in this chapter, when **OnConnection** is called automatically by VB, the startup tasks normally done in the **OnConnection** procedure (creating the add-in's menu item and displaying the Add-In toolbar) should be done in the **OnStartupComplete** procedure.

In addition, you should read a Windows registry entry for the add-in to determine if one of the add-in's forms was displayed when VB was last shut down. If so, **OnStartupComplete** should redisplay the form. Such a Windows registry entry is typically set to "1" when the form is displayed and to "0" when the form is unloaded. The conventional way to do this is with a statement like

```
SaveSetting App.Title, "Settings", "DisplayForm", "1"
```

that uses VB's **SaveSetting** statement to save the entry to the Windows registry. **SaveSetting** automatically writes the entry to a predefined VB and VBA Program Settings subkey. Figure 2.14 shows the Windows registry entries for Chapter 2's add-in. To read the Windows registry entry for the display status of an add-in's form, you can use VB's **GetSetting** statement.

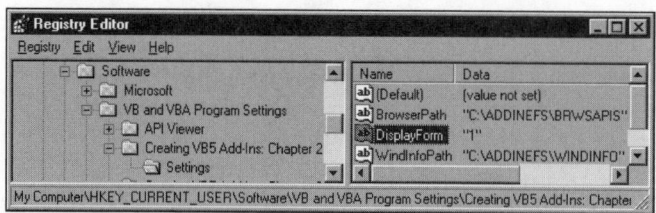

Figure 2.14
Chapter 2's add-in entries in Windows registry.

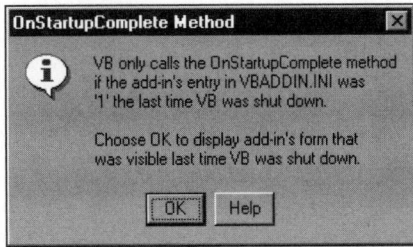

Figure 2.15
Message box explaining **OnStartupComplete** method's action.

The **OnStartupComplete** procedure in Listing 2.10 also demonstrates how you can react to a module-level cancellation flag set in the **OnConnection** method's procedure and abort an automatic connection. As with the other **IDT_ Extensibility** object methods of Chapter 2's add-in, a message box like the one in Figure 2.15 is displayed to illustrate what actions are occurring and the order in which they occur.

LISTING 2.10 ONSTARTUPCOMPLETE METHOD'S PROCEDURE.

```
Private Sub IDTExtensibility_OnStartupComplete(Custom())

    ' Constants for literals:
    Const BTNS = 64 + 65536 + &H40000
    Const C = "OnStartupComplete Method "

    ' Variables:
    Dim M               As String
    Dim Item            As String
    Dim Ch2Desc         As String
    Dim Ch2ProgID       As String
    Dim FormWasDisplayed  As Boolean

    ' If automatic connection was canceled and flag
    ' was turned on in OnConnection method:
    If mCancelConnection Then

        ' Turn flag off, uncheck add-in in Add-In
        ' Manager dialog box, and exit procedure:
        mCancelConnection = False
        Util.Connect VBE, "Chapter2.Connect", False
        Exit Sub

    End If
```

```
' If automatic connection wasn't canceled—
' * Create add-in's menu item.
' * Make sure Add-In toolbar is displayed with button on
'   it for add-in.
' * Copy button's icon to menu item.
Ch2ProgID = "Chapter2.Connect"
Ch2Desc = Util.GetDesc(VBE, Ch2ProgID)
Item = "Creating VB5 Add-Ins: Chapter &2..."
SetAIMenuItem Item, Ch2Desc
SetAIToolBar Ch2ProgID
AITBar.CopyButtonIcon VBE, Ch2Desc, mMenuItem

M = "VB only calls the OnStartupComplete method" & vbCr
M = M & "if the add-in's entry in VBADDIN.INI was" & vbCr
M = M & "'1' the last time VB was shut down."

' If demo add-in's form was visible last time VB was
' shut down and add-in's menu item was connected:
If GetSetting(App.Title, "Settings", _
            "DisplayForm", "#$%^&") = "1" Then

    M = M & vbCr & vbCr
    M = M & "Choose OK to display add-in's form that" & vbCr
    M = M & "was visible last time VB was shut down."
    FormWasDisplayed = True

End If

Util.ShowMsg M, BTNS, C, App.HelpFile, C & "Example"

If FormWasDisplayed Then DisplayForm

End Sub
```

Tweaking The OnDisconnection Method

The last of the four methods of the **IDTExtensibility** object that executes is the **OnDisconnection** method. How an add-in behaves when its **OnDisconnection** method is called is directly related to the parameter that is passed in to that method's *RemoveMode* argument. The two settings for *RemoveMode* are described in Table 2.5.

At this point, the **OnDisconnection** procedure in Listing 2.11 and what it does ought to be clear enough, as you've seen the ways the other methods of the **IDTExtensibility** object can be customized and how they interact. However,

	TABLE 2.5

SETTINGS OF ONDISCONNECTION METHOD'S *REMOVEMODE* ARGUMENT.

Setting	Description
0 - vbext_dm_HostShutdown	Add-in is disconnected when developer closes current instance of VB.
1 - vbext_dm_UserClosed	Add-in is disconnected when the developer unchecks its item in the Add-In Manager dialog box or when an add-in's code sets an add-in's Connect property to **False**.

you should note three important points. First, the code in **OnDisconnection** that reacts to VB being shut down is there strictly so that Chapter 2's add-in will behave correctly if run in debug mode. Normally if an in-process DLL add-in is connected to a VB menu item and you close the current instance of VB, it is not necessary to do anything in the method's code. When VB shuts down, it also automatically shuts down any DLL add-in that is still connected.

Second, if you connect and start an add-in by clicking on its button on the Add-In toolbar but the add-in is not also connected to a VB menu item:

- The **OnDisconnection** method is not called when you shut down VB.

- If the add-in's form is displayed when VB is shut down, it will not be redisplayed when a new instance of VB is started. This is because automatic connection does not occur unless the add-in was connected to a menu item the last time VB was shut down.

Third, it would have been nice if Microsoft's VB development team had provided a *Cancel* argument for the **OnDisconnection** method, at least when the *RemoveMode* argument's value is 1 - **vbext_dm_UserClosed**. They didn't, so the only workaround that achieves reconnection is to call the **OnConnection** method internally and pass its *ConnectMode* argument the value 2 - **vbext_cm_External**.

It does not seem possible to reconnect to a menu item; you can go through all the steps (recreate the menu item, connect it to the add-in, make it responsive to the **Click** event, and so on). However, it's an exercise in futility because, after the reconnect code in **OnConnection** is done, execution reverts back to the **OnDisconnection** method in Listing 2.11, at the line immediately below the one that programmatically called the **OnConnection** method. After execution exits the **OnDisconnection** procedure, the **Terminate** event procedure of the add-in's connection object executes. So you end up with a menu item that has no add-in connected to it.

LISTING 2.11   ONDISCONNECTION METHOD'S PROCEDURE.

```
Private Sub IDTExtensibility_OnDisconnection _
         (ByVal RemoveMode As vbext_DisconnectMode, _
         Custom())

    ' Constants for literals:
    Const C = "OnDisconnection Method "
    Const BTNS = 64 + 65536 + &H40000


    ' Variables:
    Dim M         As String
    Dim Visible   As Boolean
    Dim Mngr      As Object
    Dim Flag(0)   As Variant

    ' If developer is shutting down VB:
    If RemoveMode = vbext_dm_HostShutdown Then

        ' If running add-in in debug mode, it is necessary to
        ' explicitly unload form. Note that we do not call
        ' IsBeingDebugged method of Util object here because VB
        ' has already deinstantiated Util object at this point.
        If IsBeingDebugged Then

            If mfrmDemoSynt.Visible Then Visible = True
            Unload mfrmDemoSynt

            If Visible Then
                SaveSetting App.Title, "Settings", "DisplayForm", "1"
            End If

        End If

    ' If developer is disconnecting add-in's menu item:
    ElseIf RemoveMode = vbext_dm_UserClosed Then

        ' Remove add-in's menu item and unload its form:
        mMenuItem.Delete
        Unload mfrmDemoSynt

        ' Rest of procedure shows how to internally
        ' call method of IDTExtensibility object:
```

```
M = "Do you really want to disconnect the add-in?"
M = M & vbCr & vbCr
M = M & "Choose Yes to disconnect or No to reconnect" & vbCr
M = M & "add-in externally and redisplay its form."

If Util.ShowMsg(M, BTNS + vbYesNo, C, App.HelpFile, _
                C & "Example") = vbNo Then

    Flag(aiCancelDisconnection) = True
    IDTExtensibility_OnConnection VBE, vbext_cm_External, _
                                  mAIDemo, Flag()

Else

    If AITBar.IsDisplayed(VBE) And _
       AITBar.IsButton(VBE, "Chapter2.Connect") Then

        M = "Demo add-in's button is still on the" & vbCr
        M = M & "VB Add-In toolbar. Do you also" & vbCr
        M = M & "want to remove button from toolbar?"
        M = M & vbCr & vbCr
        M = M & "Choose Yes to remove button next" & vbCr
        M = M & "time VB is started or choose No" & vbCr
        M = M & "to leave button on Add-In toolbar."
        If Util.ShowMsg(M, BTNS + vbYesNo, C, _
                        App.HelpFile, C & "Example") _
                        = vbYes Then

            Set Mngr = CreateObject("AddInToolbar.Manager")
            Mngr.RemoveAddInFromToolbar _
                "Creating VB5 Add-Ins: Chapter 2"

        End If
    End If
    End If
End If

End Sub
```

At this point you'll have to admit that there's quite a lot to learn about customizing the **IDTExtensibility** object's interface. In fact you might be mumbling to yourself that it's precisely these kinds of issues that, as the quotation that begins this chapter says, "keep us in thrall to ourselves, concerned with our surfaces." Well, two more sections to go and you'll be free and clear of this chapter's topics and we can move on to other concerns.

Displaying An Add-In's Form Only Once

After an add-in has been connected and one of its forms has been displayed, nothing prevents you from clicking that add-in's menu item or toolbar button again. In order to avoid displaying multiple instances of the same form for the current instance of VB's IDE, you need to be able to find the add-in's form that is currently displayed and bring it to the foreground. However, if the form that is currently displayed belongs to a second instance of VB, a new instance of the form should be displayed.

I wrote the **IsFormDisplayed** method of the **Util** object of the VBAI class library to deal with this situation. **IsFormDisplayed** is a **Function** that finds the currently displayed add-in form, brings it to the foreground, and returns **True**. If the form is not displayed or is displayed by another instance of VB, **IsFormDisplayed** returns **False**. **IsFormDisplayed** takes three required arguments:

- *VBE*: An object expression that evaluates to a **VBE** object of the VBIDE class library.

- *ProgID*: A **String** expression that specifies the programmatic ID of the add-in whose forms are to be checked. If *ProgID* is set to a nonexistent programmatic ID, **IsFormDisplayed** fails. The programmatic IDs of all registered add-ins are listed in VBADDIN.INI.

- *Titles()*: A **String** array that contains one or more elements specifying the captions of the title bars of the forms to be checked.

If an add-in displays only a single form, then *Titles(0)* should be assigned the caption of that form. If the add-in displays several forms in succession, as in the case of a Wizard, then the caption of each possible form displayed by the add-in should be assigned to different element of *Titles()*. The code for the **IsFormDisplayed** method is shown in Listing 2.12.

LISTING 2.12   ISFORMDISPLAYED METHOD'S PROCEDURE.

```
Function IsFormDisplayed(VBE As VBE, _
                    ProgID As String, _
                    Titles() As String) As Integer
```

```
    ' Variables:
    Dim Title      As Variant
    Dim ClsName    As String
    Dim HWnd       As Long

    ' Check for specified failure cases:
    On Error GoTo EH
    If Not IsProgID(VBE, ProgID) Then
        IsFormDisplayed = aiFailed
        Exit Function
    End If

    ' Determine correct class name of VB form
    ' (it differs depending on run mode):
    If IsBeingDebugged(VBE, ProgID) Then
        ClsName = "ThunderForm"
    Else
        ClsName = "ThunderRT5Form"
    End If

    For Each Title In Titles

        ' Try to find add-in's form.
        HWnd = FindWindow(ClsName, Title)

        ' If form is displayed and thread ID of VB instance that
        ' created form matches thread ID of current instance of
        ' VB, bring form to foreground and return True:
        If HWnd <> False Then
            If GetWindowThreadProcessId(HWnd, 0) = _
                GetCurrentThreadId Then
                    SetForegroundWindow HWnd
                    IsFormDisplayed = True
                    Exit For
            End If
        End If

    Next Title

EH:
    If Err <> False Then IsFormDisplayed = aiFailed

End Function
```

There are three key points to note about the **IsFormDisplayed** method's code.
First, it calls the Windows API function **FindWindow** to try to find the add-in's

form; **FindWindow** takes two arguments, the class name and caption of the form that is being sought. Notice that the class name of a VB5 form differs (ThunderForm vs. ThunderRT5Form), depending on whether or not the form is being displayed while the add-in is in debug mode.

Second, **IsFormDisplayed** uses the Windows API functions **GetWindowThread-ProcessId** and **GetCurrentThreadId** to compare the identifier of the VB thread that displayed the form with the identifier of the VB thread that is running the add-in that called **IsFormDisplayed**. Third, if the thread identifiers are the same, **IsFormDisplayed** returns **True** and brings the form that is already visible to the foreground by calling the Windows API function **SetForegroundWindow**. In Chapter 2's add-in, **IsFormDisplayed** is called from the **Private DisplayForm** method of the add-in's **Connect** class; see the code in Listing 2.13 for an example of how to make the call.

LISTING 2.13   CALLING THE ISFORMDISPLAYED METHOD.

```
Private Sub DisplayForm()

    ' Variables:
    Dim ProgID        As String
    Dim Captions(0)   As String

    ' Assign variables:
    ProgID = "Chapter2.Connect"
    Captions(0) = "Demo VB5 Add-In Syntax"

    ' If add-in's form is not displayed for this instance of VB:
    If Util.IsFormDisplayed(VBE, ProgID, Captions()) = False Then

        ' Display form and save setting to Windows registry:
        mfrmDemoSynt.Show
        SaveSetting App.Title, "Settings", "DisplayForm", "1"

    End If

End Sub
```

The IsFormDisplayed method is particularly useful if the add-in is a Wizard that displays several different modeless forms in succession. Typically, a Wizard displays modal forms, which automatically prevents you from clicking the add-in's menu item or toolbar button again while one of its forms is still displayed. However, certain add-ins like the Tutor Wizard that we will discuss in Chapter 8 need to display modeless forms; this modeless display of the Tutor's forms allows the developer to interact with VB's IDE while the Wizard is running.

Displaying A Custom Message Box From An Add-In

Chapter 2's add-in illustrates all of the possible customization features of an add-in. However, as I explained earlier, its major function is to demonstrate each of the add-in language elements that VB5's Extensibility object model supports. As I began to write the routines for the language elements, I felt that I could clarify some of the demonstrations by displaying periodic message boxes that explain what is about to occur.

After experimenting for a while, I realized that VB's **MsgBox** function was not the best way to display these message boxes. The **MsgBox** function has the following shortcomings as far as add-in work is concerned:

- It can only display a modal dialog box. Because the great majority of add-ins are DLL ActiveX components, it is impossible for the developer to interact with VB's IDE while a modal message box is displayed.

- It can only display Help topics by context ID number. Sometimes, as with Chapter 2's add-in, you would like to be able to display Help topics by keyword.

- It does not enable you to display a Help topic as a popup.

- Although VB5's version of the **MsgBox** function can now display a message dialog box as the foreground window, there are situations in add-in work where the message box still gets hidden behind another application's window. This seems to occur most often when you are debugging an add-in with two instances of VB open. One way to deal with this problem would be to display the message dialog box on top of all other windows; however, the **MsgBox** function's *Buttons* argument does not support an on-top setting.

To solve these problems, I wrote the **ShowMsg** method of the **Util** object in the VBAI class library. **ShowMsg** uses the Windows API function **MessageBox-Indirect** to create and display a customized message box. In conjunction with VB5's new **AddressOf** function, **MessageBoxIndirect** supports the callback that must be made when a developer clicks the Help button. The **Util** object's **ShowMsg** method has been invaluable to me in writing the add-in code for this book. For more detailed information about its specifications, see its entry in the *Dictionary* section of the book or in ADDINEFS.HLP. The code for the **ShowMsg** method and its related procedures are shown in Listing 2.14.

 Displaying a Help topic using **MessageBoxIndirect** requires that a callback be made from the API function's procedure to the address of a procedure in the VBAI class library. VB's **AddressOf** function, which enables a callback to be made, can only point to a procedure in a standard module (named basCallBack for the **ShowMsg** method), so the **Util** object must violate encapsulation in this regard.

LISTING 2.14   SHOWMSG METHOD'S CODE.

```
Function ShowMsg(Prompt As String, _
                Optional Buttons As Long = 0, _
                Optional Title As String = "ShowMsg Method", _
                Optional HelpFile As String = "", _
                Optional Context, _
                Optional HWndOwner As Long = 0, _
                Optional Popup As Boolean = False) As Integer

    ' Variables:
    Dim Dlg        As MSGBOXPARAMS
    Dim Items(3)   As Variant

    On Error GoTo EH

    ' Set Help-related parameters for message box:
    If HelpFile <> "" And Not IsMissing(Context) Then
       If Not Buttons And vbMsgBoxHelpButton Then
          Buttons = Buttons + vbMsgBoxHelpButton
       End If
       Items(0) = HelpFile
       Items(1) = Context
       Items(2) = Popup
       Items(3) = HWndOwner
```

```
        basCallBack.HelpParams = Items
    End If

    ' Set elements of user-defined data type used
    ' by Windows API function MessageBoxIndirect:
    With Dlg

        ' Size data type and set owner (if one was passed):
        .Size = LenB(Dlg)
        .Owner = HWndOwner

        ' Set other parameters:
        .Prompt = Prompt
        .Buttons = Buttons
        .Title = Title

        ' Pass address of procedure to be called back to
        ' by Windows API function MessageBoxIndirect, if
        ' Help button on message box is clicked:
        .CallBack = ProcAddress(AddressOf basCallBack.ShowHelpTopic)

    End With

    ShowMsg = MessageBoxIndirect(Dlg)

EH:
    If Err <> False Then ShowMsg = False


End Function

' General declarations and procedures in basCallBack standard module—
' Module-level variables related to HelpParams Property procedure:
Private mHelpFile       As String    ' Path/name of .HLP file
Private mContextStr     As String    ' Keyword in .HLP file
Private mPopup          As Boolean   ' Is Help topic a popup?
Private mContextNbr     As Long      ' Context ID # of Help topic
Private mOwner          As Long      ' Dialog box that Help
                                     ' window belongs to


' DLL Functions:
Private Declare Function GetDesktopWindow& Lib "USER32" ()
Private Declare Function WinHelp& Lib "USER32" _
                    Alias "WinHelpA" _
                    (ByVal HWnd&, ByVal HelpFile$, _
                    ByVal Cmd&, ByVal Info As Any)


Property Let HelpParams(Vals As Variant)
```

```vb
    ' Set module-level variables for Help-related properties:
    mHelpFile = Vals(0)

    If VarType(Vals(1)) = vbInteger Or _
        VarType(Vals(1)) = vbLong Then
            mContextNbr = Vals(1)
            mContextStr = ""
    ElseIf VarType(Vals(1)) = vbString Then
        mContextStr = Vals(1)
    End If

    mPopup = Vals(2)
    mOwner = Vals(3)

End Property

Function ProcAddress(X As Long) As Long

    ProcAddress = X

End Function

Sub ShowHelpTopic()

    ' Constants for Windows API functions:
    Const HELP_CONTEXT = &H1
    Const HELP_KEY = &H101
    Const HELP_CONTEXTPOPUP = &H8

    ' Display Help topic by calling Windows API function—
    ' * Normal jump topic:
    If Not mPopup And mContextStr = "" Then
        WinHelp mOwner, mHelpFile, HELP_CONTEXT, mContextNbr

    ' * Topic associated with keyword:
    ElseIf mContextStr <> "" Then
        WinHelp mOwner, mHelpFile, HELP_KEY, mContextStr

    ' * Popup topic (first argument cannot
    '    be zero when displaying popup):
    ElseIf mPopup Then
        If mOwner = 0 Then mOwner = GetDesktopWindow
        WinHelp mOwner, mHelpFile, HELP_CONTEXTPOPUP, mContextNbr
    End If

End Sub
```

Well, that's all for Chapter 2 and for Part I of this book. As I promised at the beginning of the chapter, you've seen a whole bag full of customization techniques and tricks for creating complex, commercial-quality add-ins. In Part I of this book (the Introduction and Chapters 1 and 2), I:

- Provided all the generic information that a developer needs to create add-ins.

- Demonstrated with Chapter 2's add-in all of the individual language elements that comprise VB's Extensibility object model.

- Illustrated all the possible customization options that an add-in's public interface can support.

Now it's time to move on to Part II and Chapters 3 through 6. Part II breaks down VB's Extensibility object model into four general categories: manipulating VB IDE-level objects that aren't project-specific; handling project-level objects (components, designers, and controls); manipulating lower-level objects (properties, members, code modules, and code); and handling and reacting to add-in related events.

How To Use
Add-In Objects
And Members

VB IDE-LEVEL ADD-IN OBJECTS 3

But above this level, far above, separated by an abyss, is the level where the highest things are achieved. These things are essentially anonymous.

—*Simone Weil*

Part II of this book, consisting of Chapters 3 through 6, analyzes the Extensibility object model and its language elements from these four viewpoints:

- Chapter 3: Objects that are not associated with any particular project but are VB IDE-level in scope.

- Chapter 4: Objects that are associated with a project, its components, its designers, and its controls.

- Chapter 5: Objects that are at the property and code level.

- Chapter 6: Objects that respond to events raised by VB. These objects, like those discussed in Chapter 3, are VB IDE-level in scope. However, I won't be dealing with them until Chapter 6 for two reasons: They are among the most difficult elements of the add-in object model to understand and use, and using them requires detailed knowledge of all the other add-in language elements discussed in Chapters 3, 4, and 5.

The *Dictionary* section of this book deals with the add-in object model at its lowest, most discrete level of abstraction. It describes each of the 244 trees in the add-in forest. At the other end of the spectrum, this chapter discusses the add-in object model at the highest and broadest level of abstraction. It describes the characteristics of the add-in forest. More specifically, this chapter analyzes the root **VBE** object and its members, listed and described in Table 3.1.

 An accessor property returns an object or collection of the same type as signified by the property name. In this chapter, the generic **Collection** and **Parent** accessor properties are not discussed (we already mentioned and illustrated them in Chapter 1). Also, because we are not dealing with event-related objects until Chapter 6, the **VBE** object's **Events** accessor property is not covered here.

The Root VBE Object

VBE (that is, Visual Basic environment) is the root object that represents the current instance of VB's IDE and that contains all other objects and collections in the VBIDE class library. There is also a **VBE** accessor property, which is a member of 24 collections or objects in VBIDE, that is a handy way of returning the root **VBE** object.

TABLE **3.1**

VBE OBJECT'S MEMBERS BY CATEGORY.

Member Category	Description
Active Object Accessors	Four accessor properties (**ActiveCodePane, ActiveVBProject, ActiveWindow, SelectedVB Component**) that return the active or most recently selected instance of their respective VB IDE-level objects
Collection Accessors	Five accessor properties (**Addins, CodePanes, CommandBars, VBProjects, Windows**) that return their respective VB IDE-level collection objects
Other Properties	Eight other properties (**DisplayModel, FullName, LastUsedPath, MainWindow, Name, ReadOnlyMode, TemplatePath, Version**) that return or set information about VB's IDE itself
Quit Method	The **VBE** object's only method, which shuts down the development environment

---

A **VBE** object is instantiated when an add-in is connected to the current instance of VB's IDE. It is passed in to the add-in's code through the *VBInst* argument of the **OnConnection** method of the **IDTExtensibility** object. You then use the **Set** statement to assign *VBInst* to a **Public** object variable (named VBE in this book's add-ins) in a standard BAS module. An add-in's code can only access the functionality of the Extensibility object library through a **VBE** object.

The **VBE** object replaces the **Application** object used in VB4's VBEXT32.OLB Add-In type library. **Application** is a hidden member of VB5's add-in object model, and thus it (and the other 45 hidden members listed at the beginning of the book's *Dictionary* section) can't normally be accessed from a VB5 add-in. There really is no good reason to access the hidden VB4 **Application** object because all of its functionality has been replicated in a more logically consistent and easily used way in the VB5 add-in object model.

However, it is technically possible to store an object reference to **Application**; I demonstrate this in Chapter 3's add-in, using the procedures in Listing 3.1. To do this, declare and write the old VB4 connection/disconnection procedures **ConnectAddIn** and **DisconnectAddIn** in the **Connect** class. When the add-in is connected, VB passes in to the *VBInst* argument of the **ConnectAddIn** method an **Application** object, which you can then store and use in the normal manner.

LISTING 3.1 PROCEDURES TO DEMONSTRATE THE **VB4** APPLICATION OBJECT.

```
Public Sub ConnectAddIn(VBInst As VBIDE.Application)

    ' **********************************************************
    ' Demonstrates that old VB4 add-in interface (and its hidden
    ' objects) can still be used in VB5 add-in's object model.
    ' **********************************************************

    ' Assign instance of VB's IDE to public variable.
    Set basGenlPrcs.Application = VBInst

End Sub

Public Sub DisconnectAddIn(Mode As Integer)

    ' **********************************************************
    ' Demonstrates that old VB4 add-in interface (and its hidden
```

```
' objects) can still be used in VB5 add-in's object model.
' ************************************************************

' Variables:
Dim M As String

If Mode = vbext_dm_UserClosed Then
    M = "Disconnected by Add-In Manager" & vbCr
    M = M & "and executed from within VB4's" & vbCr
    M = M & "old DisconnectAddIn method."
    M = M & vbCr & vbCr
    M = M & "LastUsedPath: " & Application.LastUsedPath
    M = M & vbCr & vbCr
    M = M & "This demo's technical capacity to" & vbCr
    M = M & "use hidden VB4 add-in objects."
    MsgBox M, vbInformation + vbMsgBoxSetForeground, App.Title
End If

End Sub
```

Chapter 3's add-in, whose source code is in CHAPTER3.VBP, uses a tabbed dialog box to organize the various VB IDE-level objects and members. The tab for the **VBE** object is displayed in Figure 3.1. To demonstrate an IDE-level add-in language element, connect/run Chapter 3's add-in, check the language element's option button, and click on the Demo button. Because space is limited, in the rest of this chapter (and the rest of Part II), I will discuss in detail only language elements that are of particular significance or that exhibit odd behavior. If you need more information about a language element, check its entry in the *Dictionary* section of the book or in ADDINEFS.HLP.

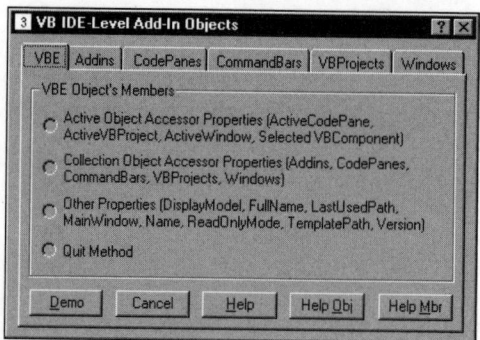

Figure 3.1
The **VBE** tab of Chapter 3's add-in dialog box.

Active Object Accessor Properties

The **CodePanes** collection crosses project boundaries, and a **CodePane** object only exists if a code module in a project is open. Reading the **ActiveCodePane** property returns either the code pane window that currently has the focus, or the one that last had the focus. Setting **ActiveCodePane** to a code pane window gives it the focus and brings it to the top of the z-order of windows in the project.

 If no code pane window is open, trying to return or set **ActiveCodePane** results in trappable error 452 (invalid ordinal).

The **ActiveVBProject** property returns the project that is selected in the Project Explorer window or the project whose component is selected. Setting the **ActiveVBProject** property to a member of the **VBProjects** collection causes that project's name to be selected in the Project Explorer window and to be displayed in the title bar of VB's menu bar window.

Chapter 3's add-in demo of **ActiveVBProject** illustrates an interesting technique. Manually double-clicking on a project item in the Project Explorer window either contracts or expands that project's component items, closing or opening all its windows in the process. The add-in object model does not provide a member to programmatically implement this contraction/expansion action; however, by setting the **ActiveVBProject** property and immediately using VB's **SendKeys** statement to pass an Enter keystroke, you can achieve the same effect.

The **Windows** collection crosses project boundaries, and the read-only **ActiveWindow** property returns the **Window** object from the **Windows** collection that currently has the focus.

 VB's Help file incorrectly states that the **ActiveWindow** property returns **Nothing** if VB's main window has the focus. Instead, it returns a **Window** object.

The **SelectedVBComponent** property returns the selected component in the Project Explorer window. If the selected item in the Project Explorer window isn't a component (that is, it's a folder or project), **SelectedVBComponent** returns **Nothing**. **SelectedVBComponent** is read-only; to select a component, you must call the **Activate** method of a **VBComponent** object.

Collection Accessor Properties

The collection accessor properties of the **VBE** object (**Addins**, **CodePanes**, **CommandBars**, **VBProjects**, **Windows**) return their respective collection objects. These collections (with the exception of **CommandBars**) all have the usual **Count**, **Item**, **Parent**, and **VBE** members, which we will not waste time on. The **CommandBars** collection object does not have a **VBE** accessor property because it does not belong to the VBIDE class library; its accessor property is part of VBIDE but the collection itself belongs to the Office (Microsoft Office 8.0 Object Library) class library.

It is possible for the **CodePanes** and **VBProjects** collections to return a count of 0. The three other collections always return counts of about 10 or more, with the **CommandBars** collection typically containing almost 30 **CommandBar** objects. We will discuss each of these collections and their respective objects later in this chapter.

Other IDE-Level Members

Five of the other properties of the **VBE** object (**FullName**, **LastUsedPath**, **Name**, **TemplatePath**, **Version**) return strings; and, of these five, only **LastUsedPath** can be set. The **DisplayModel** property returns or sets 0 - **vbext_dm_SDI** or 1 - **vbext_dm_MDI**. Setting **DisplayModel** is the same as manually selecting Tools|Options and changing the SDI Development Environment setting on the Advanced tab. When you change this setting manually, VB displays a message stating that the change will not take effect until the next instance of VB's IDE is started. When you programmatically change **DisplayModel**, no advisory message is displayed, but the change still does not affect the current instance of VB. A typical set of values for these six properties is shown in Figure 3.2.

 Setting the **LastUsedPath** property only sets the current directory for VB's IDE; it is not equivalent to using VB's **ChDir** statement.

The **MainWindow** accessor property returns a **Window** object that represents VB's main window; you can use it to add and remove docked windows or to maximize, minimize, hide, or restore the main window. This **Window** object has a **Type** property setting of 12 - **vbext_wt_MainWindow**. The main window of VB's IDE is not an item in the **Windows** collection, and the only way you can access the main window is through the **MainWindow** property.

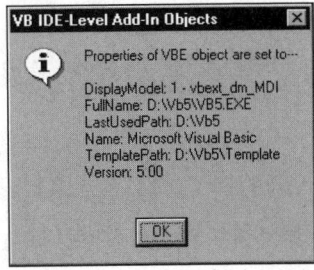

Figure 3.2
VBE object's typical property settings.

The **ReadOnlyMode** property returns an **Integer** or sets a numeric expression that determines how VB's IDE interacts with read-only files. If **ReadOnlyMode** is set to 0 - Lenient, you can modify code, designers, and the project; however, you cannot save any of these changes back to disk if they affect read-only files. If **ReadOnlyMode** is set to 1 - Strict, the Project|Remove File and Project|Add File commands are available; however, trying to select these commands causes VB to display a read-only error message. For read-only code modules, trying to edit the code causes VB to display the message "Can't edit module." For read-only designers, controls cannot be added or removed, control positions are locked, property settings can't be changed, and custom Properties dialog boxes are disabled.

 VB's Help file incorrectly states that 0 corresponds to Strict and 1 to Lenient for the **ReadOnlyMode** property's setting. Instead, it is the opposite, as already mentioned.

The **Quit** method of the **VBE** object shuts down VB. Calling the **Quit** method is equivalent to manually selecting File|Exit. However, the **Quit** method does not prompt you to save any changes to open projects. Instead it automatically saves all changes and closes VB's IDE. You can write code in the **RequestWriteFile** event procedure of a **FileControlEvents** object to intervene in this process and allow you to control which files are saved and which are not.

The Addins Collection Object

The **Addins** collection contains the **AddIn** objects listed in VBADDIN.INI and in the Add-In Manager dialog box. These **AddIn** objects cross project boundaries and exist primarily to enable you to connect and disconnect add-ins program-matically. The tab for the **Addins** collection on Chapter 3's add-in dialog box is displayed in Figure 3.3.

Members Of The AddIn Object

Of the three **String** properties of an **AddIn** object (**ProgID**, **Description**, **Guid**), the only one that works the way you would expect it to is **ProgID**. If you loop through the **Addins** collection and read **ProgID** for each **AddIn**, it returns the programmatic ID from the Windows registry. However, **Description** and **Guid** only return values for currently connected add-ins; and, if an add-in has been connected from VB's Add-In toolbar, it can't even read its own **Description** property.

The inconsistent behavior of the **Description** and **Guid** properties is confusing when you first encounter them. There is no reason why Microsoft's VB devel-opment team couldn't have programmed **Description** and **Guid** to behave like **ProgID**, because all this information is stored in the same set of entries in the Windows registry. I wrote the **GetDesc** and **GetGuid** methods of the VBAI class library to correct for these deficiencies. The code for these two methods is shown in Listing 3.2. It's a simple task to read the settings for **Description** and **Guid** from the registry.

 I already discussed the problem associated with the **Connect** prop-erty of an **AddIn** object in Chapter 2, in the section titled *The Add-In Manager Dialog Box.*

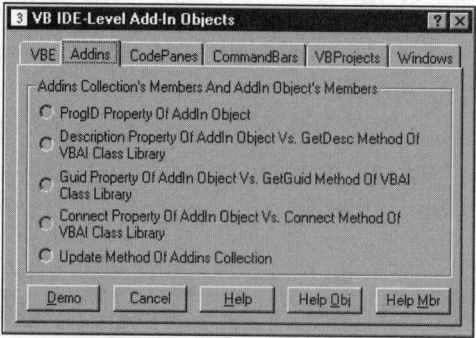

Figure 3.3
The **Addins** tab of Chapter 3's add-in dialog box.

LISTING 3.2   GETDESC AND GETGUID METHODS (VBAI).

```
Public Function GetDesc(VBE As VBE, ProgID As String) As String

    ' Check for specified failure case:
    If Not IsProgID(VBE, ProgID) Then
        GetDesc = ""
        Exit Function
    End If

    ' Get setting of add-in's Description property.
    GetDesc = Reg.GetValue(Reg.OpenSubKey(aiKTClasses, ProgID))

End Function

Public Function GetGuid(VBE As VBE, ProgID As String) As String

    ' Variables:
    Dim SubKey As String

    ' Check for specified failure case:
    If Not IsProgID(VBE, ProgID) Then
        GetGuid = ""
        Exit Function
    End If

    ' Get setting of add-in's Guid property.
    SubKey = ProgID & "\Clsid"
    GetGuid = Reg.GetValue(Reg.OpenSubKey(aiKTClasses, SubKey))

End Function
```

The Update Method Of The Addins Collection

The behavior of the **Update** method of the **Addins** collection, like that of the **Description** and **Guid** properties, is confusing and quirky. **Update** reads the entries in the Windows registry related to add-ins and, if a new add-in has been added to the registry, refreshes the **Addins** collection for the current instance of VB to reflect the addition. Unfortunately, the **Update** method fails to refresh the **Addins** collection if an add-in has been deleted from the registry. In the case of a deletion, the only way to refresh the **Addins** collection is to start another instance of VB.

Calling the **Update** method is not required to reflect a change you make to an item in the Add-In Manager dialog box's list because, in this case, VB itself automatically refreshes the **Addins** collection. However, if you programmatically change an add-in's entry in the VBADDIN.INI file by calling the Windows API function **WritePrivateProfileString**, neither the **Update** method nor VB can react to such a change. Instead you must start another instance of VB's IDE to refresh the **Addins** collection.

The demonstration of the **Update** method in Chapter 3's add-in illustrates its quirky behavior. Because the **Addins** collection does not have an **Add** or **Remove** method, it is not possible to correct for this behavior. However, the demonstration does give you a feel for how rich the add-in object model is when it programmatically:

- Loads an unregistered add-in's project
- Compiles and registers the add-in
- Calls the **Update** method to refresh the **Addins** collection
- Unregisters the add-in by deleting its entries from the Windows registry

Visual Basic Books Online, in the topic titled *Connecting Or Disconnecting Add-Ins*, makes several incorrect statements about the **Update** method of an **Addins** collection and the **Connect** property of an **AddIn** object. 1) It states that you can set **Connect** to 1; instead, **Connect** is a **Boolean** that is either **True** (-1) or **False** (0). 2) It states that after you set **Connect**, you must call **Update** to alert VB to connect the add-in; instead, VB automatically connects the add-in. 3) It states that calling **Update** forces VB to read VBADDIN.INI and react to any changes made to its entries. Instead, **Update** reads the Windows registry and has nothing to do with VBADDIN.INI.

The CodePanes Collection Object

The **CodePanes** collection contains the **CodePane** objects that represent the set of open code panes in all projects within VB's IDE. A code pane is the code window in which you enter and edit code. If no code pane is open, the **Count** property of **CodePanes** returns 0. You open a **CodePane** object by calling its **Show** method. The tab for the **CodePanes** collection on Chapter 3's add-in dialog box is displayed in Figure 3.4.

To access a particular **CodePane** object, you must drill down several layers into the add-in object model. The statement

```
VBE.ActiveVBProject.VBComponents("UserControl1").CodeModule.CodePane
```

demonstrates how to do this, using the **CodePane** accessor property of the **CodeModule** object. If you know the index number of the **CodePane** object you want to manipulate, you can access it more easily with a statement like

```
VBE.CodePanes(1)
```

but the index number approach is not reliable. Unfortunately, the **CodePanes** collection does not support **String** indexing, so the only sure way to access the right **CodePane** object is with the **CodePane** accessor property.

You use the **CodePane** object to manipulate the position of visible code or the code selection displayed in the code pane. You can't use **CodePane** to manipulate the code itself; to do this, you use the members of the **CodeModule** object, which we'll deal with in Chapter 5. I'm not going to take up space here going into all the details of the **CodePane** object demonstration in Chapter 3's add-in. If you run the demo, you can observe what it does and easily understand the behavior of the various methods and properties of **CodePane**.

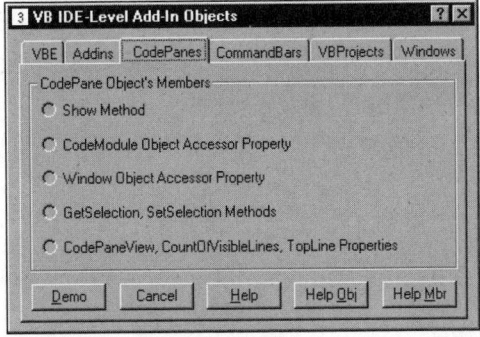

Figure 3.4
The **CodePanes** tab of Chapter 3's add-in dialog box.

The one member of the **CodePane** object that does not work the way you might expect is the **CodePaneView** property. Although you can manually set the view mode for an individual code pane by clicking the Procedure View or Full Module View button at the bottom-left corner of the pane's window (see Figure 3.5), there is no way to programmatically do so because **CodePaneView** is read-only. Microsoft ought to correct this deficiency in the next release of VB. The golden rule of the Extensibility object model should be: If you can do it manually within VB's IDE, you should be able to do it with an add-in.

The CommandBars Collection Object

The **CommandBars** collection of the Office class library is how VB5 enables you to create or modify its menus and toolbars. Every menu bar and toolbar is represented by a **CommandBar** object in this collection. In turn, every **CommandBar** object contains a **CommandBarControls** collection that contains **CommandBarControl** objects, which represent menus, menu items, popup menus, and toolbar buttons.

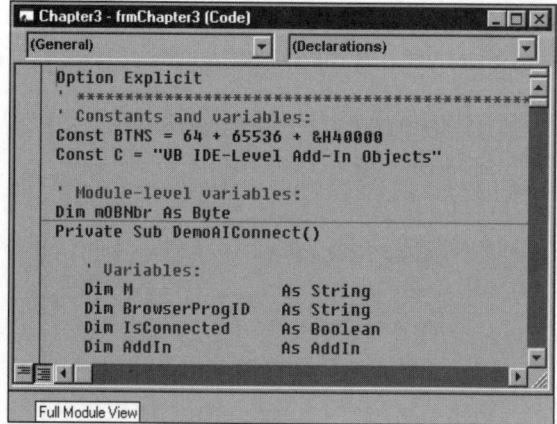

Figure 3.5
Code pane view buttons on code pane window.

The **CommandBars** collection is found in the Office class library and not in the VBIDE add-in library because Microsoft wants to position VBA as the universal corporate development language. Because any corporation that licenses VBA will be more likely to also own the license rights to Office 97 than to VB5, it was a no-brainer for Microsoft to deliver the **CommandBars** collection and its Help file with the Office library rather than the VBIDE library.

Disadvantages Of Using Office's Members

As I mentioned in Chapter 2, using the Office class library file (MSO97.DLL) can be difficult. Some of the problems you'll encounter when trying to learn how to reuse Office's members are:

- The VB documentation for the objects and members of the Office Class library is minimal. There's nothing in VB's Help file and there are only a couple of examples in Visual Basic Books Online. I challenge any VB programmer to figure out how to create an add-in popup menu with two or more menu items just by using the documentation that comes with VB.

- If you don't have a copy of Microsoft Office 97 on your PC, asking for Help for an Office member from VB's Object Browser leads you nowhere. Even if you have the Help file, it's not as well written as VB's and the example code it provides is minimal.

- The Office class library includes a lot of objects (for example, **CommandBarButton**, **CommandBarComboBox**, **CommandBarPopup**) that a VB add-in developer will not normally need to reuse. The presence of these objects (and all the syntax and language elements that go with them) obfuscates the main issues, which are how to create add-in menu items, toolbars, and toolbar buttons.

- The Office class library's syntax directly related to creating add-in menu items, toolbars, and toolbar buttons is sprawling and cumbersome. For example, to create a menu item with a graphic and separator bar, you have to call the **Add**, **SetData**, and **PasteFace** methods and set the **Caption**, **Begin-Group**, and **Style** properties. Learning how to do this is tedious at best and, without adequate documentation, almost hopeless.

Take it from me, if you need to create custom menus or toolbars for an add-in, you'll find it's a lot easier to reuse the methods of the **Cmd** object in my VBAI class library than to struggle with the Office class library syntax. The tab for the **CommandBars** collection on Chapter 3's add-in dialog box, which demonstrates the reuse of the **Cmd** object's methods, is displayed in Figure 3.6.

How To Reuse The Cmd Object's Methods

To understand how to reuse the menu and toolbar-related methods of the **Cmd** object that are described in Table 3.2, you need to be aware of the terminology I use in ADDINEFS.HLP:

- Menu: An item on the menu bar of VB's main window. In its default configuration, VB contains 11 menus (from File on the left of the bar to Help on the right).

- Popup menu: A menu item attached to one of VB's 11 menus that does nothing by itself but instead, when selected, pops up two or more menu items. For example, VB's View menu contains the Toolbars popup menu. Technically, a VB menu is also a popup menu; however, to avoid confusion, I've provided different methods for creating a menu and a popup menu.

- Menu item: An item attached to a menu or popup menu that, when selected, raises the **Click** event of an add-in's **CommandBarEvents** object. Code in this **Click** event's procedure then typically displays the add-in's form.

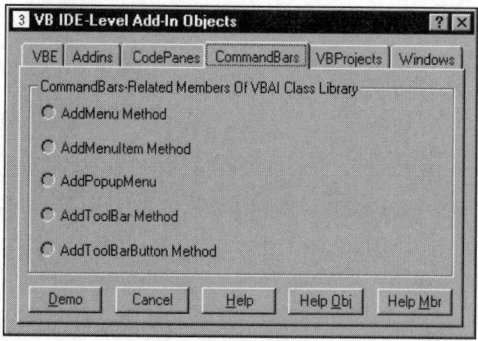

Figure 3.6
The **CommandBars** tab of Chapter 3's add-in dialog box.

TABLE 3.2

CMD OBJECT'S METHODS (VBAI).

Method Name	Description
AddMenu	Adds a menu to the VB menu bar and returns the new menu as a **CommandBarControl** object of the Office class library
AddMenuItem	Adds a menu item for an add-in to a VB menu or popup menu and returns the new menu item as a **CommandBarControl** object of the Office class library
AddPopupMenu	Adds a popup menu for an add-in to a VB menu and returns the new popup menu as a **CommandBarControl** object of the Office class library
AddToolBar	Adds a custom toolbar for add-ins to VB's IDE and returns the new toolbar as a **CommandBar** object of the Office class library
AddToolBarButton	Adds a button for an add-in to a VB toolbar and returns the new button as a **CommandBarControl** object of the Office class library
GetMenu	Returns a VB menu as a **CommandBarControl** object of the Office class library
IsMenuItem	Checks whether or not the specified menu item is attached to the specified VB menu or popup menu and returns **True** or **False** accordingly

If you run Chapter 3's add-in demonstrations of the **Cmd** object's methods, it's easy to see what they do. The most complex use of these methods occurs when you call **AddPopupMenu** and then call **AddMenuItem** to create the popup menu's items. The code for the methods themselves is shown in Listing 3.3. The code in Chapter 3's add-in that demonstrates these two methods is shown in Listing 3.4.

LISTING 3.3   ADDPOPUPMENU AND ADDMENUITEM METHODS (VBAI).

```
Public Function AddPopupMenu(VBE As VBE, _
                     Menu As Office.CommandBarControl, _
                     Caption As String, _
                     Optional Position As Byte = 0, _
                     Optional Separator As Boolean = False) _
                     As Office.CommandBarControl
```

```
    ' Variables:
    Dim Popup As Office.CommandBarControl

    On Error GoTo EH

    ' Add popup menu to VB menu:
    If Position = 0 Then Position = Menu.Controls.Count + 1
    Set Popup = Menu.Controls.Add(Type:=msoControlPopup, _
                                  Before:=Position, _
                                  Temporary:=True)

    ' Set properties of popup menu:
    Popup.Caption = Caption
    If Separator Then Popup.BeginGroup = True

EH:
    If Err = False Then Set AddPopupMenu = Popup

End Function

Public Function AddMenuItem(VBE As VBE, _
                            Menu As Office.CommandBarControl, _
                            Caption As String, _
                            Optional Position As Byte = 0, _
                            Optional Separator As Boolean = False, _
                            Optional Bitmap As String = "") _
                            As Office.CommandBarControl

    ' Variables:
    Dim Item As Office.CommandBarControl

    On Error GoTo EH
    If Bitmap <> "" Then Clipboard.SetData LoadPicture(Bitmap)

    ' Add menu item to VB menu:
    If Position = 0 Then Position = Menu.Controls.Count + 1
    Set Item = Menu.Controls.Add(Type:=msoControlButton, _
                                 Before:=Position, _
                                 Temporary:=True)

    ' Set properties of menu item:
    Item.Caption = Caption
    If Separator Then Item.BeginGroup = True
    If Bitmap <> "" Then
       Item.Style = msoButtonIconAndCaption
       Item.PasteFace
    End If
```

```
EH:
    If Err = False Then Set AddMenuItem = Item

End Function
```

LISTING 3.4   DEMONSTRATION OF ADDPOPUPMENU/ ADDMENUITEM METHODS.

```
Private Sub DemoCBAddPopupMenu()

    ' Variables:
    Dim M               As String
    Dim Item            As String
    Dim Path            As String
    Dim BMPNames(8)     As String
    Dim El              As Byte
    Dim Tools           As Office.CommandBarControl
    Dim Popup           As Office.CommandBarControl

    Item = "Creating VB5 Add-Ins"
    Set Tools = VBE.CommandBars("Menu Bar").Controls("Tools")
    M = "Choose OK to add popup menu to" & vbCr
    M = M & "bottom of VB's Tools menu."
    Util.ShowMsg M, BTNS, C

    Set Popup = Cmd.AddPopupMenu(VBE:=VBE, _
                                 Menu:=Tools, _
                                 Caption:=Item, _
                                 Separator:=True)

    M = "Click the Tools menu to see the new popup menu" & vbCr
    M = M & "and then choose OK to add nine menu items to it."
    Util.ShowMsg M, BTNS, C
    Path = App.Path
    For El = 0 To 8
        BMPNames(El) = Path & "\CHAPTER" & CStr(El + 1) & ".BMP"
        Cmd.AddMenuItem VBE:=VBE, _
                        Menu:=Popup, _
                        Caption:="Chapter &" & CStr(El + 1), _
                        Bitmap:=BMPNames(El)
    Next El

    M = "Click the Tools menu and the popup menu" & vbCr
    M = M & "to see the nine menu items added to it."
    M = M & vbCr & vbCr
    M = M & "The nine menu items are not connected to an" & vbCr
    M = M & "event handler so they are not functional."
```

```
M = M & vbCr & vbCr
M = M & "Now choose OK to delete the popup menu." & vbCr
Util.ShowMsg M, BTNS, C
Popup.Delete

End Sub
```

The VBProjects Collection Object

The **VBProjects** collection contains the **VBProject** objects open in VB's IDE. You use the members of **VBProjects** to access, add, save, or remove projects from VB. Two properties of **VBProjects**, **IconState** and **StartProject**, also allow you to assign a particular project in the collection a different status from the other projects. The tab for the **VBProjects** collection on Chapter 3's add-in dialog box is displayed in Figure 3.7.

Adding A Project To VB's IDE

The **VBProjects** collection provides three different ways of adding a project to VB's IDE:

- **Add** method: Adds a project to VB and returns it as a **VBProject** object. This is equivalent to manually choosing File|Add Project and selecting one of the first four project icons (Standard EXE, ActiveX EXE, ActiveX DLL, or ActiveX Control) in the New Project dialog box.

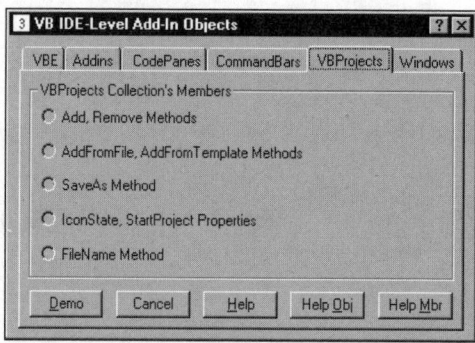

Figure 3.7
The **VBProjects** tab of Chapter 3's add-in dialog box.

- **AddFromTemplate** method: Adds a new project using an existing project on the VB path \TEMPLATE\PROJECTS as a template and returns a **VBNewProjects** collection that contains all the projects added using **AddFromTemplate**. This is equivalent to manually choosing File|Add Project and selecting a project icon other than one of the first four icons in the New Project dialog box.

- **AddFromFile** method: Adds or opens a project or group project that was previously saved and returns a **VBNewProjects** collection that contains all the projects added using **AddFromFile**.

To call the **Add** method of **VBProjects**, you typically use a statement like

```
Set ProjStd = VBE.VBProjects.Add(vbext_pt_StandardExe)
```

where **ProjStd** is an object variable of the **VBProject** type and **vbext_pt_Standard-Exe** is an intrinsic constant specifying the kind of project to be added. You can then reuse the members of the **VBProject** object to manipulate the **ProjStd** object reference. We will discuss how to manipulate an individual project in Chapter 4.

The **AddFromFile** and **AddFromTemplate** methods differ from the simpler **Add** method in the kind of object they return and the way you manipulate it. Unlike the **Add** method that directly returns a **VBProject** object, **AddFromFile** and **AddFromTemplate** return a **VBNewProjects** collection that contains one or more **VBProject** objects. You first have to store the returned collection and then store references to the **VBProject** object(s) that the collection contains. From here on, you can manipulate the **VBProject** object reference(s) in the same way as you would one returned by the **Add** method. To call **AddFromFile** or **AddFromTemplate**, use code like that in Listing 3.5. To see this code in action, run Chapter 3's add-in.

LISTING 3.5 DEMONSTRATION OF ADDFROMFILE/ ADDFROMTEMPLATE METHODS.

```
Private Sub DemoVBProjsAddFrom()

    ' Variables:
    Dim M         As String
    Dim Path      As String
    Dim FileName  As String
```

```
Dim Proj1      As VBProject
Dim Proj2      As VBProject
Dim VBProjs    As VBProjects
Dim NewProjs1  As VBNewProjects
Dim NewProjs2  As VBNewProjects

' Shorten object expression (faster and more readable).
Set VBProjs = VBE.VBProjects

M = "Choose OK to add project from file."
Util.ShowMsg M, BTNS, C
FileName = App.Path & "\FROMFILE.VBP"
Set NewProjs1 = VBProjs.AddFromFile(FileName)
Set Proj1 = NewProjs1(1)

' Find VB's path:
On Error Resume Next
Err.Raise 3
Path = Mid$(Err.HelpFile, 1, Len(Err.HelpFile) - 16)
On Error GoTo 0
FileName = Path & "TEMPLATE\PROJECTS\ACTIVEX DOCUMENT DLL.VBP"

M = "Choose OK to add ActiveX Document" & vbCr
M = M & "DLL project from VB template."
Util.ShowMsg M, BTNS, C
Set NewProjs2 = VBProjs.AddFromTemplate(FileName)
Set Proj2 = NewProjs2(1)

M = "Choose OK to remove projects that" & vbCr
M = M & "were added to VB and conclude demo."
Util.ShowMsg M, BTNS, C
VBProjs.Remove Proj1
VBProjs.Remove Proj2

End Sub
```

Saving A Group Project And Removing A Project

The add-in object model contains a **SaveAs** method that applies to three different kinds of objects: **VBProjects**, **VBProject**, and **VBComponent**. In the case of the **VBProjects** collection, **SaveAs** is called to save a VBG group project file. For more detailed information about the three different uses of the **Save-As** method, see its topic in the *Dictionary* section of the book or in ADD- INEFS.HLP.

Normally, you only use a group project file to test and debug an ActiveX control or ActiveX document.

After you are done working with a project, you can remove it from VB's IDE by calling the **Remove** method of the **VBProjects** collection. **Remove** takes one argument that is a **Variant**, which can be either the index value (number or string) of an item in the **VBProjects** collection or an object reference to an item in the collection. The procedure in Chapter 3's add-in that best demonstrates the two different uses of the **Remove** method is shown in Listing 3.6.

LISTING 3.6 DEMONSTRATION OF REMOVE METHOD.

```
Private Sub DemoVBProjsAddRemove()

    ' Variables:
    Dim M         As String
    Dim Counter   As Byte
    Dim ProjStd   As VBProject
    Dim VBProjs   As VBProjects

    ' Shorten object expression (faster and more readable).
    Set VBProjs = VBE.VBProjects

    M = "Choose OK to add ActiveX DLL, ActiveX EXE," & vbCr
    M = M & "ActiveX Control, and Standard EXE projects."
    Util.ShowMsg M, BTNS, C
    Set ProjStd = VBProjs.Add(vbext_pt_StandardExe)
    VBProjs.Add vbext_pt_ActiveXDll
    VBProjs.Add vbext_pt_ActiveXExe
    VBProjs.Add vbext_pt_ActiveXControl

    M = "Choose OK to remove the four projects that" & vbCr
    M = M & "were just added to VBProjects collection."
    M = M & vbCr & vbCr
    M = M & "We will remove the standard EXE project" & vbCr
    M = M & "by object reference and remove the other" & vbCr
    M = M & "three projects by their index values."
    Util.ShowMsg M, BTNS, C

    VBProjs.Remove ProjStd
    For Counter = 1 To 3
        VBProjs.Remove VBProjs(VBProjs.Count)
    Next Counter

End Sub
```

Other VBProjects Collection Members

The **IconState** property returns/sets the file status of a VB project or component file. **IconState** determines how an instance of VB behaves if you try to open a VB project or component file that is already open in another instance of VB. Normally, if you try to do this, VB tells you that the file name in question is already open and refuses to open the file. However, if for example you set **IconState** to 32 - **vbextSCCStatusOutOfDate** or 512 - **vbextSCCStatusShared**, you can then open the same file in another instance of VB.

The **StartProject** property returns/sets a **Variant** that represents the project that will be started when you select Run|Start or press the F5 key. The first project that is loaded into VB is automatically specified as the start project. If you add another project and want to start it, the only way to manually change the start project is by right-clicking on the project's item in the Project Explorer window and selecting the Set As Start Up item from the shortcut menu (as in Figure 3.8). Setting **StartProject** is the programmatic equivalent of doing this.

Until you have actually saved a group project file or an individual project file within a group project, the **FileName** method returns only the default name of GROUP1.VBG with no path specified. After you have saved a group project or project file, **FileName** returns a string that includes the path.

 It is easy to confuse the **FileName** method of a **VBProjects** collection with the **FileName** property of a **VBProject** object. The distinction is that the **FileName** method returns a group project

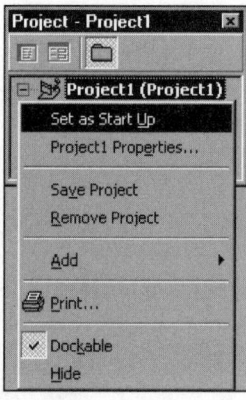

Figure 3.8
Set As Start Up shortcut menu item.

file name (VBG extension) while the **FileName** property returns a project file name (VBP extension).

The Windows Collection Object

The **Windows** collection contains two kinds of **Window** objects: permanent IDE windows and temporary windows. The fixed set of permanent IDE windows (for example, the Project and Properties windows) is always available in the **Windows** collection. Closing a permanent window hides the window but does not remove it from the collection. The set of temporary open windows is variable in number and can consist of code module or designer windows and the IDE Find and Replace windows. Opening or closing one of these temporary windows adds an item to or removes an item from the **Windows** collection. The tab for the **Windows** collection and **Window** object members on Chapter 3's add-in dialog box is displayed in Figure 3.9.

Window Object Accessor Properties

The **Window** object accessor properties, **LinkedWindowFrame** and **LinkedWindows**, exist because VB5's architecture now supports MDI (multiple document interface). The **LinkedWindowFrame** property enables you to access a **Window** object representing a window frame that has properties distinct from those of the linked window or windows it contains. If a window is not linked, its **LinkedWindowFrame** property returns **Nothing**.

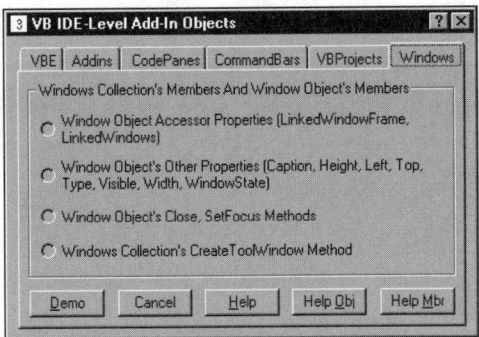

Figure 3.9
The **Windows** tab of Chapter 3's add-in dialog box.

You use the frame **Window** object returned by the **LinkedWindowFrame** property to access the **LinkedWindows** collection that the frame window contains. You can then, for example, dock and undock windows from the main window frame in VB's IDE. Linked window frames contain all windows that can be linked or docked. This includes all windows except code windows, designers, the Object Browser window, and the Find and Replace windows. You can use the **Add** method to add a window to or the **Remove** method to delete a window from a collection of currently linked windows.

If you use the **Remove** method to delete a linked window from the collection and then immediately add it back to the collection with the **Add** method, the relinked window does not necessarily appear in the same position within the frame window that it occupied before it was removed. Unfortunately, the Extensibility object model does not provide programmatic control over the positioning of a linked window.

Other Window Object Members

The **Window** object members other than its two object accessor properties generally behave the same way as the standard properties and methods you have always used when manipulating **Form** objects. **Height**, **Left**, **Top**, and **Width** need no explanation, but you need to remember that the values of these properties are always specified in pixels when you use them with a **Window** object. **Caption**, **Visible**, **WindowState**, **Close**, and **SetFocus** work the same for both **Window** and **Form** objects.

The **Type** property of a **Window** object deserves special mention. For a **Window** object, **Type** returns an intrinsic constant that is a value from 0 to 15, which specifies the kind of permanent IDE or temporary module/designer window that you are working with. With my current VB settings, Chapter 3's add-in demonstration code finds the kinds of windows displayed in Figure 3.10.

VB's Object Browser incorrectly states that **Type** returns 10 - **vbext_wt_Toolbox** for the Toolbox window. Instead, it returns 15 - **vbext_wt_ToolWindow**. Also, because VB's main window is never a member of the **Windows** collection, its **Type** setting (12 - **vbext_wt_MainWindow**) does not appear on the message box in Figure 3.10.

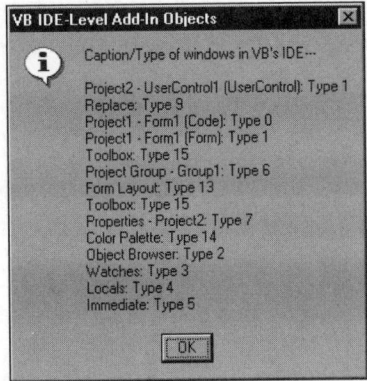

Figure 3.10
Settings of **Window** object's **Type** property.

Creating A VB Tool Window

Create ToolWindow is a method of the **Windows** collection that creates a new Tool window in VB's IDE containing an ActiveX document object. **Create-ToolWindow** allows you to extend VB's IDE by adding an ActiveX document to VB when you connect and run an add-in. The **Window** object returned by **Create ToolWindow** is, unlike the normal modal or modeless form that an add-in can display, an item in the **Windows** collection. This means that the window is dockable and has all the other properties and methods associated with a **Window** object.

You can use **Create ToolWindow** to add a text editor or any other application that can be run as an ActiveX document to VB's IDE. Although you can close the Tool window that contains the ActiveX document application, the application itself is not terminated until you disconnect the add-in with which the Tool window is associated or until you close the current instance of VB's IDE.

Chapter 3's add-in demonstration of the **Create ToolWindow** method creates a window containing a Programmer's Log ActiveX document, as in Figure 3.11. When you run this demo, the Programmer's Log is created as either a docked (MDI interface) or undocked (SDI interface) window. The **Create ToolWindow** method is a very powerful and easy-to-use feature of the add-in object model. The more difficult task is to develop the ActiveX document object that the Tool window is to contain. We don't have the space in this chapter to delve into all the details of the **Create ToolWindow** method and ActiveX document creation. See Chapter 7 for a complete discussion of this exciting new capability of VB.

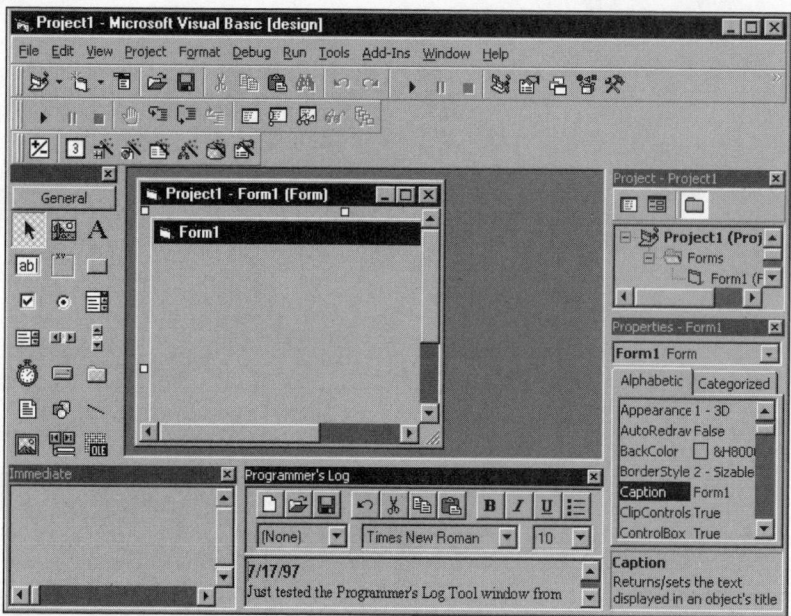

Figure 3.11
Programmer's Log Tool window docked in VB.

Now it's time to move on to Chapter 4, where we'll drill down into the add-in object model a little deeper. Instead of just dealing with high-level, IDE-related objects as in Chapter 3, we'll be working with objects on the project level. These project-level objects are the **VBProject** object, the **VBComponents** collection (a project's modules), the **References** collection (a project's ActiveX controls and class libraries), the **VBForm** object (a module's designer), and the **VBControls** collection (a designer's intrinsic and ActiveX controls). In fact, by the end of Chapter 4, you'll know everything about the add-in object model's capabilities except for handling properties, code and VB IDE-related events, which we get to in Chapters 5 and 6.

4

PROJECT-LEVEL ADD-IN OBJECTS AND MEMBERS

He had been eight years upon a project for extracting sunbeams out of cucumbers, which were to be put into vials hermetically sealed, and let out to warm the air in raw, inclement summers.

—Jonathan Swift

n Chapter 3, we adhered to the from-the-top-down philosophy of systems analysis and started at the highest level of the Extensibility object model, learning how to manipulate and use the members of the root **VBE** object. As you saw, the **VBE** object's members enable you to access various collections (**Addins, CodePanes, CommandBars, VBProjects, Windows**) and attributes (**DisplayModel, FullName, LastUsedPath, MainWindow, Name, ReadOnlyMode, TemplatePath, Version**), which are not project-specific in nature but rather relate to VB's IDE itself.

Having become familiar with VB's IDE-level objects and members in Chapter 3, you're now ready to dig deeper into the add-in object model and learn how to deal with and manipulate individual projects and their components. More specifically, this chapter analyzes the **VBProject** object and related members that are listed and described in Table 4.1.

To demonstrate any of the **VBProject** object's members described in Table 4.1, connect/run Chapter 4's add-in, select the appropriate tab on the add-in's dialog box (**VBProject, VBComponents, VBComponent, VBForm, VBControls**), check the language element's option button, and click on Demo.

A Project's References Collection

Each time you load an existing project or open a new one, it contains the set of references selected in the References dialog box (Project|References). When you manually check or uncheck an item in the References dialog box, VB adds a **Reference** object to or removes one from the **References** collection of the **VBProject** object that represents the project. You can also programmatically manipulate references with the add-in object model's **References** collection and

---

TABLE **4.1**

VB Project object's members by category.

Member Category	Description
Collection Accessors	Two accessor properties (**References, VBComponents**) that return their respective, project-level collection objects
Miscellaneous Members	Two methods and five properties (**AddToolboxProgID, Description, HelpContextID, HelpFile, IconState, ReadProperty, Type**) that return or set information about the project itself
Members To Save Project	Three properties and two methods (**FileName, IsDirty, Saved, SaveAs, WriteProperty**) that you use when saving a project
Members To Compile Project	Three properties and one method (**BuildFileName, CompatibleOleServer, MakeCompiledFile, StartMode**) that you use when compiling a project

---

(continued)

	TABLE 4.1

VBPROJECT OBJECT'S MEMBERS BY CATEGORY (*CONTINUED*).

Member Category	Description
Designers	The **VBForm** object that can represent any of the four kinds of designer that VB5 supports (forms, user controls, property pages, user document forms)
Controls	The members of the **VBControls** collection and **VBControl** object that enable you to manipulate the controls on a designer

Reference object. The option button for the **References** collection's demonstration is the first one on the tab for the **VBProject** object, as shown in Figure 4.1.

Properties Of Reference Object

You can use the properties of a **Reference** object, all of which are read-only, to verify whether a particular reference is still valid, or to return information about the reference. The **IsBroken** property returns **True** if the reference no longer points to a valid reference; this means that there is a mismatch between the GUID string of the reference stored in the ActiveX component's file and the GUID string of the component's entry in the Windows registry. This most commonly occurs on PCs used by developers who, in a client application, bind a reference to an ActiveX component early and then later change the existing public interface of the ActiveX component and recompile it.

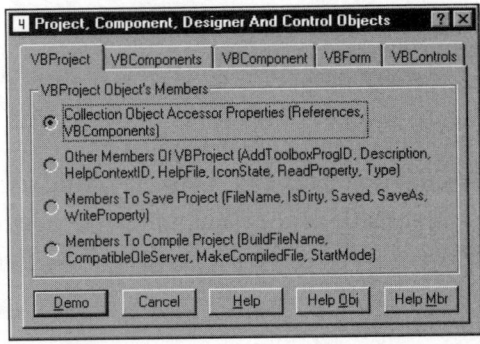

Figure 4.1
VBProject tab of Chapter 4's add-in dialog box.

A **Reference** object's **BuiltIn** property returns **True** if the reference is a default reference that can't be moved or removed. A VB project always contains the following default references, listed in the order of their priority:

- VBA: Visual Basic For Applications (VBA5.DLL)

- VBRUN: Visual Basic runtime objects and procedures (MSVBVM50.DLL)

- VB: Visual Basic objects and procedures (VB5.OLB)

If you try to manually remove a default reference from a VB project by unchecking its item in the References dialog box, VB displays a syntax error message (Can't remove control or reference; in use). If an add-in tries to remove a default reference, trappable error 57101 occurs (Can't remove default reference).

The other **Reference** object properties (**Description, FullPath, Guid, Major, Minor, Name,** and **Type**) and the values they return for this book's VBAI ActiveX server class library are shown in Figure 4.2.

Adding And Removing A Reference Object

In addition to the three default references that you can't remove from a VB project, there are other references that you can add programmatically to a project you are creating with an add-in. The **References** collection has two methods, **AddFromFile** and **AddFromGuid**, that enable you to do this. **AddFromFile** is called with code like

```
FileName = Left$(App.Path, Len(App.Path) - 8)
FileName = FileName & "VBAI\VBAI.DLL"
Set FileRef = ProjEXE.References.AddFromFile(FileName)
```

where **ProjEXE** is an object variable that represents the **VBProject** object, **FileName** is the fully qualified path and filename of the reference to be added, and **FileRef** is an object variable of the **Reference** type to which the reference is assigned. If you don't need to read the properties of the **Reference** object later on, you can dispense with storing the reference returned by **AddFromFile**.

The **AddFromGuid** method adds a reference to the **References** collection using the globally unique identifier (GUID) of the ActiveX component. **AddFromGuid** is called with code like

Figure 4.2
Reference object's property settings (VBAI).

```
Guid = "{EF404E00-EDA6-101A-8DAF-00DD010F7EBB}"
Set GuidRef = ProjEXE.References.AddFromGuid(Guid, 5, 0)
```

where **Guid** is the globally unique identifier (in this example, for the VBIDE add-in object model) and the other two arguments are numbers specifying the Major (5) and Minor (0) version numbers of the component. After you programmatically add references to a project, they are checked in the References dialog box just as if you had added them manually. To remove non-default references and uncheck them in the References dialog box, code like

```
ProjEXE.References.Remove GuidRef
ProjEXE.References.Remove FileRef
```

does the trick.

Other Project-Level Members

Besides references, a **VBProject** object has other project-level members that you can call or set before you save and compile the project. These members, two methods and five properties, are described in Table 4.2.

The only member in Table 4.2 that deserves special mention or that is not discussed in another place in this book is the **AddToolboxProgID** method. The demonstration of **AddToolboxProgID** in Chapter 4's add-in places the Microsoft Winsock ActiveX control on VB's Toolbox with the statement

```
ProjEXE.AddToolboxProgID "MSWinsock.Winsock.1", "MSWINSCK.OCX"
```

TABLE 4.2

OTHER PROJECT–LEVEL MEMBERS OF **VB**PROJECT OBJECT.

Member Name	Description
AddToolboxProgID	Method that places an ActiveX control or embedded component in VB's Toolbox, checks its item on the Controls or Insertable Object tab of the Components dialog box, and adds a reference to the component to a project
Description	Property that returns or sets a description associated with a project and is saved in its VBP text file under the key name of **Description** (for example, Description="Demo add-in project")
HelpContextID	Property that returns or sets the context ID number for a topic in a Windows Help file that is associated with a project and is saved in its VBP text file under the key name of **HelpContextID** (for example, HelpContextID="1000")
HelpFile	Property that returns or sets the fully qualified path to a Windows Help file for a project and is saved in its VBP text file under the key name of **HelpFile** (for example, HelpFile="C:\DUMMY.HLP")
IconState	Property that returns or sets the file status of a project and determines how an instance of VB behaves if you try to open a project that is already open in another instance of VB
ReadProperty	Method that returns a custom property's setting from the specified user-defined section and key in a project's VBP file
Type	Property that returns the kind of project (standard executable, ActiveX executable, ActiveX DLL, ActiveX control)

where **ProjEXE** is an object variable that represents the **VBProject** object and the two arguments of **AddToolboxProgID** specify the programmatic ID and the filename of the ActiveX component to be added. If the specified component already exists in the Toolbox, the **AddToolboxProgID** method simply does nothing.

There is no method in the Extensibility object model to delete a component from the Toolbox. However, if you manually or programmatically delete the project that is referencing the component and no other project is referencing it, VB automatically deletes the component from the Toolbox.

Saving A Project

Three properties and two methods of a **VBProject** object (**FileName, IsDirty, Saved, SaveAs, WriteProperty**) can come into play when you want to save a project. Chapter 4's add-in demonstration illustrates how these members behave in relation to each other. After adding a standard executable project to the **VBProjects** collection, the demo calls the **WriteProperty** method to save a custom property to the project's VBP file (and, in the process, turns the project's **IsDirty** flag on). After calling **WriteProperty**, the demo displays the message box shown in Figure 4.3.

The demo then calls the **SaveAs** method of the **VBProject** object with the statement

```
ProjEXE.SaveAs App.Path & "\DEMOSAVE.VBP"
```

where **ProjEXE** is an object variable that represents the **VBProject** object and the argument of **SaveAs** specifies the path and filename under which to save the project. Besides saving the project and all its files, **SaveAs** also causes VB to change the settings of the **FileName, IsDirty,** and **Saved** properties of **VBProject**, as shown in the message box in Figure 4.4.

Figure 4.3
Settings of dirty project's properties before being saved.

Figure 4.4
Settings of project's properties after being saved.

Compiling A Project

After you save a project, you will want to compile it. Three properties and one method (**BuildFileName**, **CompatibleOleServer**, **MakeCompiledFile**, **StartMode**) can come into play. Chapter 4's add-in demo illustrates how these members behave in relation to each other. After the demo adds an ActiveX executable project to the **VBProjects** collection (the only kind of project for which you can change **StartMode**), it sets the project's **BuildFileName** and **StartMode** properties and then calls the **MakeCompiledFile** method. It is only after you have called **MakeCompiledFile** that you can set the **CompatibleOleServer** property (for ActiveX component projects only) and, in the case of this demo, make the entries to the Project Properties dialog box shown in Figure 4.5.

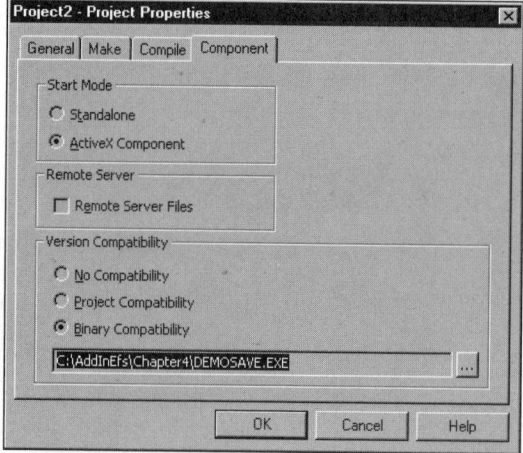

Figure 4.5
CompatibleOleServer and StartMode settings.

If you try to programmatically set **CompatibleOleServer** for a non-ActiveX component project, trappable error 50264 occurs (Method 'CompatibleOleServer' of object '_VBProject' failed). Therefore, you should always read the **Type** property of a **VBProject** object and ensure that it is not 0 - **vbext_pt_StandardExe** before setting **CompatibleOleServer**.

Adding And Removing VB Components

The typical VB development cycle is an iterative process where you add modules and controls, set properties in the Properties window, write code, run the interpreter to test/debug the changes you have made, and save the changes. In a complex project, you can repeat this cycle hundreds of times before you actually compile the project.

You organize a complex project by modules or, as they are called in VB5, VB components. Each **VBProject** object contains a **VBComponents** collection that includes all the components contained in that project. Different sorts of projects can contain various components. The kinds of components available and their corresponding **Type** property settings are:

- Forms (.FRM extension): 5 - **vbext_ct_VBForm** or 6 - **vbext_ct_VBMDIForm**

- Basic modules (.BAS extension): 1 - **vbext_ct_StdModule**

- Class modules (.CLS extension): 2 - **vbext_ct_ClassModule**

- User controls (.CTL extension): 8 - **vbext_ct_UserControl**

- Property pages (.PAG extension): 7 - **vbext_ct_PropPage**

- User document forms (.DOB extension): 9 - **vbext_ct_DocObject**

- ActiveX designers (.DSR extension): 11 - **vbext_ct_ActiveXDesigner**

- Related documents (.RES or other extension): 4 - **vbext_ct_ResFile**, 10 - **vbext_ct_RelatedDocument**, 100 - **vbext_ct_Document**

Adding VB-Created Modules

You add components to and delete them from a project manually by selecting Project|Add 'Component Type'. An add-in can programmatically add and delete certain kinds of components by calling the **Add**, **AddCustom**, **AddFile**, **AddFromTemplate**, and **Remove** methods of the **VBComponents** collection.

The **Add** method is the simplest to use and requires only one argument that specifies the component **Type** being added. **AddFile** is used to create a component from an existing file and **AddFromTemplate** creates a component from one of the template files on VB's \TEMPLATE path. The **Remove** method works in the same way for a component as it did for a project: It takes one argument (a **Variant**), which can either be the index value (number or string) of an item in the **VBComponents** collection or an object reference to an item in the collection.

Adding An ActiveX Designer Module

The **AddCustom** method is used to add an ActiveX designer component (new to VB5 and also referred to as a custom or base class) and deserves special mention. An ActiveX designer provides a custom visual interface for a development task that otherwise might require a great deal of code. You can't create an ActiveX designer with VB itself; instead, you must use a C++ compiler and the ActiveX Designer SDK, which is included with the Professional and Enterprise editions of Visual Basic. As I write this book, there are only two examples of ActiveX designer components available for use in VB:

- The UserConnection designer included in the Enterprise Edition of Visual Basic, which provides visual tools for defining complex database queries

- The Microsoft Forms designer included with Office 97, which allows forms used in Microsoft Office applications to be created with and used by VB

Manually adding an ActiveX designer component to a project is a two-step process. You first select Project|Components, click on the Designers tab of the Components dialog box, and check the designer you want to use. Then you select Project|Add ActiveX Designer and click the designer (either User-Connection or Microsoft Forms) that you want to add to the project. The **AddCustom** method is the programmatic equivalent of this manual process. If you have one of these two designers on your PC, Chapter 4's add-in demonstration shows how to call **AddCustom**.

Specifying The StartUp Module

When a project contains more than one component, you need to tell VB which module to start execution in. You do this manually by selecting Project|Properties and selecting an item from the Startup Object drop-down box. The programmatic equivalent in an add-in is to set the **StartUpObject** property of the **VBComponents** collection. **StartUpObject** returns or sets a **Variant** that specifies the startup component for the project. In addition to a **VBComponent** object reference, the other possible values of **StartUpObject** are:

- 0 - **vbext_so_SubMain**: Startup object is the **Sub** procedure named **Main**.

- 1 - **vbext_so_None**: There is no startup object (used only with ActiveX components).

> VB's Object Browser incorrectly implies that the **StartUpObject** property is read-only. Instead, it is read/write.

Manipulating VB Components

Once you have added one or more **VBComponent** objects to a project, you can do anything to them programmatically with an add-in that you can do manually. In this section of Chapter 4, we'll group the members of the **VBComponent** object into four general categories (non-designer accessor properties, designer-related members, file manipulation members, and others). The tab for the **VBComponent** object on Chapter 4's add-in dialog box is shown in Figure 4.6.

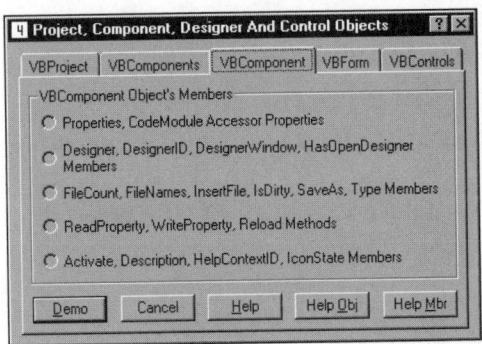

Figure 4.6
VBComponent tab of Chapter 4's add-in dialog box.

Non-Designer Accessor Properties

Although we will not explore the **CodeModule** and **Properties** accessor properties of the **VBComponent** object in depth in this chapter, we will introduce them now. You use the **CodeModule** accessor property to get a reference to the object that represents the code contained by the component. Almost all components except related documents can contain code. The **CodeModule** property returns **Nothing** if a **VBComponent** object doesn't have a code module. The members of a **CodeModule** object enable you to modify line by line (add, delete, or edit) the code associated with a component.

You use the **Properties** accessor property to get a reference to the collection that contains all the properties (that is, **Property** objects) associated with a component. Almost all components except related documents have one or more properties. The **Properties** property returns **Nothing** if a **VBComponent** object doesn't have any properties associated with it. Chapter 4's add-in demonstration reads the **Properties** accessor property for FRM and BAS modules and displays their **Count** property settings (50 and 1) with the message box shown in Figure 4.7.

Designer-Related Members

There are four kinds of **VBComponent** objects that contain a visual designer: forms, user controls, user documents, and property pages. The members of the **VBComponent** object that enable you to access a designer (**Designer**, **DesignerID**, **DesignerWindow**, **HasOpenDesigner**) are described in Table 4.3.

When you first add a module to a project, its designer window (if it has one) is open and **HasOpenDesigner** returns **True**. If you apply the **Close** method to the **Window** object that represents the module's designer window, then **HasOpenDesigner** returns **False**. **HasOpenDesigner** always returns **False** for a

Figure 4.7
Count settings of **Properties** collections.

TABLE 4.3

DESIGNER-RELATED MEMBERS OF VBCOMPONENT OBJECT.

Member Name	Description
Designer	Accessor property that returns the generic **Object** type that represents a visual designer (at this time, the reference returned by **Designer** always evaluates to a **VBForm** object)
DesignerID	Property that returns a **String** that specifies the kind of designer associated with a **VBComponent** object (for example, "VB.Form" or "VB.MDIForm")
DesignerWindow	Method that returns the **Window** object associated with a visual designer
HasOpenDesigner	Property that specifies whether a VB component has an open designer window (**True**) or not (**False**)

module that does not have a designer (for example, a standard or class module). You can determine the kind of designer a component contains by reading its **DesignerID** property. To actually work with a designer and add controls to it, you must use the **Designer** accessor property to return the **VBForm** object that represents the designer. We'll see how to do that later in this chapter.

File Manipulation Members

The members of the **VBComponent** object that enable you to manipulate its associated file (**FileCount, FileNames, InsertFile, IsDirty, SaveAs, Type**) are described in Table 4.4.

TABLE 4.4

FILE MANIPULATION MEMBERS OF VBCOMPONENT OBJECT.

Member Name	Description
FileCount	Property that returns a **Long** that specifies the number of files associated with a component (normally 1 but can be 2 if, for example, a form has an FRX file)
FileNames	Property that takes an *Index* argument and returns a **String** that specifies the name of a file associated with a component (normally 1 but can be 2 if, for example, a form has an FRX file)

(continued)

TABLE 4.4

FILE MANIPULATION MEMBERS OF VBCOMPONENT OBJECT (*CONTINUED*).

Member Name	Description
InsertFile	Method that inserts code from any file into a component's code module
IsDirty	Property that returns or sets a **Boolean** that specifies whether a component was edited since the last time it was saved
SaveAs	Method that saves a component under the same or a new file name to a specified path
Type	Property that returns the kind of component

We already listed the possible settings of the **Type** property earlier in this chapter. The best way to learn how the file manipulation members of a **VBComponent** object work together is to run the demonstration routine in Chapter 4's add-in. After adding a Standard EXE project with a BAS module, the routine calls the **InsertFile** method to add code to the BAS module's code module. You can use **InsertFile** with any kind of component except a related document, which does not have a code module.

The **InsertFile** method does not enable you to specify the insertion point but instead always inserts the contents of the file at the top of the General Declarations section of the code module. To specify the insertion point, you must first assign the contents of the file to a **String** variable with VB's **Open** statement and **Input** function and then call the **CodeModule** object's **InsertLines** method. **InsertLines** takes as one of its arguments the line number where the code is to be inserted.

The demo routine then returns the settings of **FileCount** and **FileNames** for Form1's component before and after saving FORM1.FRM, as shown in Figures 4.8 and 4.9. You should note that **FileNames** returns a zero-length string before you apply the **SaveAs** method to the component.

The demo routine then adds a **PictureBox** control to the **Controls** collection of the **VBForm** object that represents Form1's designer. It adds the control and sets its **Picture** property so Form1 will have an FRX file associated with it. The

Figure 4.8
Settings of component's properties before being saved (A).

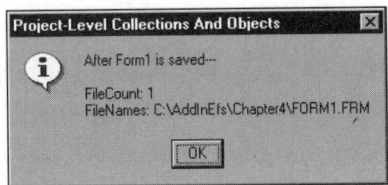

Figure 4.9
Settings of component's properties after being saved (A).

routine then resaves FORM1.FRM. The settings of **IsDirty**, **FileCount**, and **FileNames** before and after saving Form1 with the **PictureBox** control are shown in Figures 4.10 and 4.11. You should note that once the **FileCount** property returns a value of 2 as in Figure 4.11, the **FileNames** property can be read with a **For...Next** loop control structure like

```
For FileNbr = 1 To CompFRM.FileCount
   M = M & "FileNames(" & FileNbr & "): "
   M = M & CompFRM.FileNames(FileNbr) & vbCr
Next FileNbr
```

where the counter variable **FileNbr** is used as the *Index* argument of the **FileNames** property.

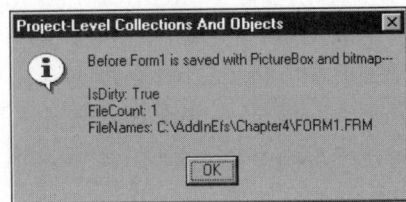

Figure 4.10
Settings of component's properties before being saved (B).

Figure 4.11
Settings of component's properties after being saved (B).

Other Members Of VBComponent Object

As far as the other members of the **VBComponent** object are concerned, we discussed five of them (**ReadProperty**, **WriteProperty**, **Description**, **HelpContextID**, **IconState**) earlier in the chapter in relation to the **VBProject** object. These five members work the same way when used with a **VBComponent** object except for these differences:

- **ReadProperty** and **WriteProperty** don't require a *Section* argument when used with the **VBComponent** object, the entry is contained in the component's file instead of the VBP file, and the entry itself takes the format of Attribute VB_Ext_KEY = "Picture" ,"C:\AddInEfs\Chapter4\-CHAPTER4.ICO".

- The entries for the **Description** and **HelpContextID** properties are contained in the component's file instead of the VBP file, and the entries themselves take the formats of Attribute VB_Description = "Splash screen form" and Attribute VB_HelpID = 2000.

The **Activate** and **Reload** methods apply only to the **VBComponent** object. **Activate** selects the specified **VBComponent** object and displays it just as if you had double-clicked on the component's item in the Project Explorer window. In the process, it also adds that component's **Window** object to the **Windows** collection. Activated VB components either display a code pane window (BAS and CLS components) or a designer window (FRM, CTL, PAG, DOB, and DSR components). The only exception is a related document component, which does not display any kind of window.

The **Reload** method reloads a VB component from its most recently saved file on disk, discarding any unsaved changes to the component in VB's IDE. This method does not affect cursor position, code window, or form visibility. **Reload** also doesn't change the **IsDirty** setting that indicates whether the component was edited since the last time it was saved.

Manipulating Designers With The VBForm Object

To manipulate a visual designer programmatically, you first use the **Designer** accessor property to return the **VBForm** object that represents the designer. Then you use the members of the **VBForm** object to work on the designer and access its three controls-related collections (**VBControls**, **SelectedVBControls**, **ContainedVBControls**). The tab for the **VBForm** object on Chapter 4's add-in dialog box is shown in Figure 4.12.

Every designer's **VBControls** collection returns a **Count** property setting of 0 when the component's designer is first loaded. The best way to see how the various members of the **VBForm** object shown in Figure 4.12 work together is to connect/run Chapter 4's add-in demo, select the **VBForm** tab, check the last option button (**CanPaste**, **Paste** Members), and click Demo. This last option button demonstrates all of the members as you might use them in a typical sequence.

First, the demo routine uses the **VBControls** accessor property to return that collection; then it calls the **Add** method of **VBControls**. Next, the demo routine

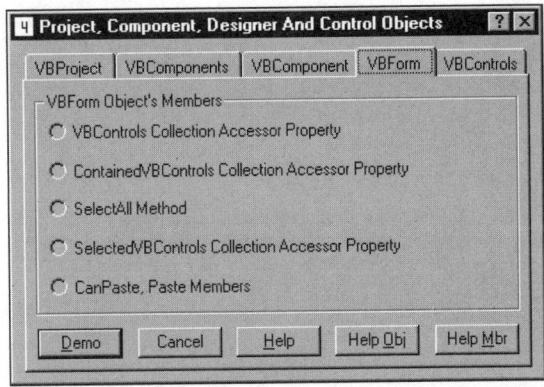

Figure 4.12
VBForm tab of Chapter 4's add-in dialog box.

adds a **CommandButton** and a **Label** control (that is, **VBControl** objects) to Form1 with the statements

```
Set CmdBtn = FormDes.VBControls.Add("VB.CommandButton")
CmdBtn.Properties("Top") = CmdBtn.Properties("Top") - 600
FormDes.VBControls.Add "VB.Label"
```

and, in the process, moves the **VBControl** object that represents the **CommandButton** up 600 twips so the **Label** control will be visible. These statements also add the two controls to the **ContainedVBControls** collection. At this point, the **Count** property of both the **VBControls** and **Contained-VBControls** collections returns 2, as shown in Figure 4.13.

Then the demo calls the **SelectAll** method of the **VBForm** object, which adds the two controls to the designer's **SelectedVBControls** collection, as shown in Figure 4.14. Next, the routine calls the **Cut** method of the **SelectedVBControls** collection to remove the controls from the designer and copy them to the Clipboard. (I could just as easily have called the **Copy** method.) Finally, the routine reads the **CanPaste** property of the **VBForm** object with the statement

```
If FormDes.CanPaste Then FormDes.Paste
```

which determines that the Clipboard currently contains **VBControl** objects (just cut there) and pastes them back on the designer, as shown in Figure 4.15. I could have just as easily pasted them onto another component's designer in the same or another project.

Handling VB Controls

The last part of the add-in object model that we'll discuss in this chapter is the **VBControls** collection and **VBControl** objects. You just saw in the previous

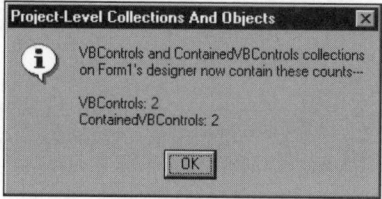

Figure 4.13
Count of VBControls and ContainedVBControls collections.

section how to add controls to and manipulate them on a visual designer. Now we'll look at the members for handling controls. The tab for the **VBControls** collection on Chapter 4's add-in dialog box is shown in Figure 4.16.

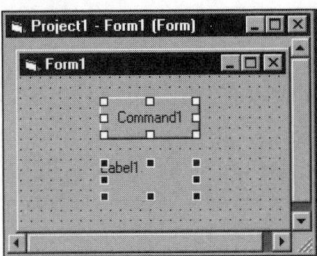

Figure 4.14
Result of calling the **SelectAll** method.

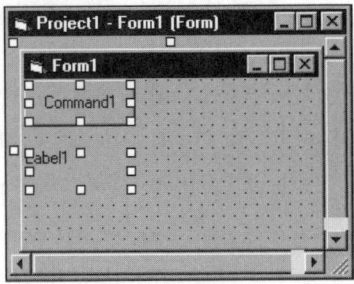

Figure 4.15
Result of calling the **Paste** method.

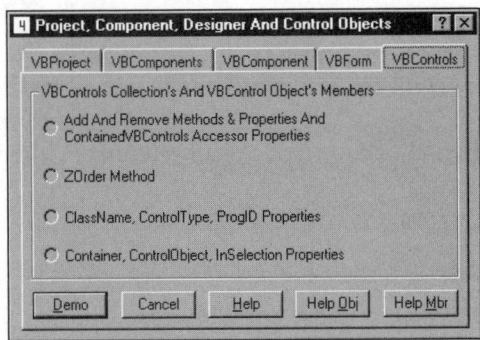

Figure 4.16
VBControls tab of Chapter 4's add-in dialog box.

Container Controls And The ZOrder Method

In the previous section, you saw how the **ContainedVBControls** collection works for a **VBForm** object that represents a visual designer. VB also supports container controls like **PictureBox** and **Frame**, which have their own individual **ContainedVBControls** collections initialized at a **Count** of 0. In Chapter 4's add-in demo, the statements

```
Set PicBox = FormDes.VBControls.Add("VB.PictureBox")
PicBox.Properties("Align") = vbAlignRight
PicBox.Properties("Align") = vbAlignBottom
Set CmdBtn = PicBox.ContainedVBControls.Add("VB.CommandButton")
```

add a **PictureBox** control (that is, a **VBControl** object) to a visual designer, use the **Properties** accessor property of the **VBControl** object to size it so that it fills the entire form by aligning it right and bottom, and use the **Contained-VBControls** accessor property of the **VBControl** object to layer a **CommandButton** control on it. At this point, the **ContainedVBControls** collection has an item in it that can be manipulated just like a control on a designer.

With VB5, you manually change the z-order of control objects by selecting Format|Order|Bring To Front or Format|Order|Send To Back. The add-in object model enables you to do this programmatically with the **ZOrder** method of the **VBControl** object. If you layer two **Label** controls on a **PictureBox** with the statements

```
Set Lbl1 = PicBox.ContainedVBControls.Add("VB.Label")
Set Lbl2 = PicBox.ContainedVBControls.Add("VB.Label")
```

where **Lbl1** and **Lbl2** are **VBControl** object references, then the statements

```
Lbl1.ZOrder vbBringToFront
Lbl1.ZOrder vbSendToBack
```

call **ZOrder** to change which **Label** control is on top.

Other VBControl Object Members

The **VBControl** object also has properties (**ClassName**, **ControlType**, **ProgID**) that enable you to differentiate between the types of controls that VB can layer

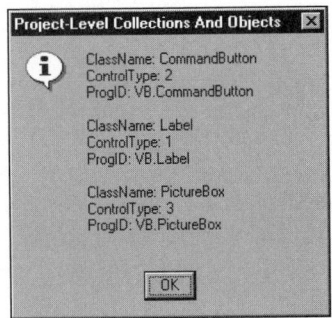

Figure 4.17
Distinguishing between types of controls.

on a designer or a container control. Chapter 4's add-in demo uses the code in Listing 4.1 to add three different kinds of controls to a designer, demonstrates these properties for the three controls, and displays their settings in the message shown in Figure 4.17.

 There is a bug in the VBIDE class library that results in the **Control Type** property always returning a value of 2 - **vbext_ct_- Standard** regardless of the kind of **VBControl** object. You should call the **GetControlType** method of a **Util** object of my VBAI class library to correct for this bug and return the correct value for all intrinsic and ActiveX controls that ship with VB5. The three values **GetControlType** returns are 1 - **vbext_ct_Light** (control has no hWnd property at runtime); 2 - **vbext_ct_Standard** (control has hWnd at runtime); and 3 - **vbext_ct_Container** (has **hWnd** at runtime and is container control).

LISTING 4.1   CLASSNAME, CONTROLTYPE, PROGID PROPERTIES.

```
Set CmdBtn = FormDes.VBControls.Add("VB.CommandButton")
CmdBtn.Properties("Top") = CmdBtn.Properties("Top") - 600
FormDes.VBControls.Add "VB.Label"
Set PicBox = FormDes.VBControls.Add("VB.PictureBox")
PicBox.Properties("Top") = PicBox.Properties("Top") + 600

M = "Choose OK to read ClassName, ControlType" & vbCr
M = M & "and ProgID properties of controls just added."
Util.ShowMsg M, BTNS, C
M = ""
```

```
' NOTE: GetControlType method of Util object is used
' because there is a bug in ControlType property.
For Each VBControl In FormDes.VBControls
   M = M & "ClassName: " & VBControl.ClassName & vbCr
   M = M & "ControlType: " & Util.GetControlType(VBControl)
   M = M & vbCr
   M = M & "ProgID: " & VBControl.ProgID & vbCr & vbCr
Next VBControl
Util.ShowMsg M, BTNS, C
```

The **VBControl** object also has a **Container** accessor property and an **InSelection** property that come in handy at times. **Container** provides an object reference to a control's container, which can be either a designer or another control like **PictureBox** or **Frame**. Once you have an object reference to the container, you can call any of the container's own members.

The code in Listing 4.2 demonstrates how to do this by calling the **SelectAll** method of a designer container. Then the code reads the **InSelection** property for each item in the designer container's **VBControls** collection and, because they are all selected, gets a return value of **True**, as shown in Figure 4.18.

LISTING 4.2 CONTAINER AND INSELECTION PROPERTIES.

```
M = "Choose OK to add PictureBox and Image to Form1."
Util.ShowMsg M, BTNS, C
Set VBCtls = ProjEXE.VBComponents("Form1").Designer.VBControls
Set PicBox = VBCtls.Add("VB.PictureBox")
PicBox.Properties("Top") = PicBox.Properties("Top") - 700
VBCtls.Add "VB.Image"

M = "Choose OK to read PictureBox's container object" & vbCr
M = M & "(that is, Form1) and call its SelectAll method."
Util.ShowMsg M, BTNS, C
PicBox.Container.SelectAll

M = "VBControl objects' InSelection property is set to---"
M = M & vbCr & vbCr
For Each VBCtl In VBCtls
   M = M & VBCtl.ClassName & ": " & VBCtl.InSelection & vbCr
Next VBCtl
Util.ShowMsg M, BTNS, C
```

Wow, Chapter 4 turned out to be quite a whirlwind tour of project-level collections, objects, and members. If your head is really spinning at this point, it's

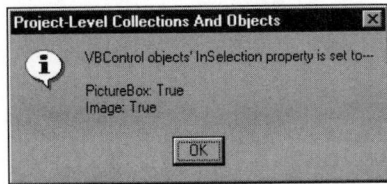

Figure 4.18
Values returned by **InSelection** property.

understandable because, as Dorothy said to Toto, "We're not in Kansas any-more." I relied heavily on screen captures in this chapter to clarify what the demo add-in code was doing because most of the work that you do with a project's components, designers, and controls is mouse-oriented and visual in nature.

Now that you've worked through Chapters 3 and 4 and run their demo add-ins, I hope you're beginning to feel that there is a method to my madness as far as how I organized this book. As I've said before, Part IV's *Dictionary* section looks at each of the 244 individual kinds of trees in the add-in forest. What I'm trying to do in Part II, in Chapters 3 through 6, is group the individual trees in the add-in forest together (if they are logically and functionally related) and show how they interact and feed off of each other.

I'll use this same approach in Chapter 5, which drills down to the code level of the add-in object model and looks at how the **CodeModule** object, **Members** collection and **Member** objects, and **Properties** collection and **Property** objects work. However, I'll end Chapter 5 by pulling all the language elements from Chapters 3, 4, and 5 together (except for the event-handling syntax, which we deal with in Chapter 6). Chapter 5 concludes with an add-in that you can use to automatically create the public interface for any other add-in. Stay tuned!

5

Properties And Code-Related Add-In Objects

We are built to make mistakes, coded for error.

—*Dr. Lewis Thomas*

Anyone who has programmed computers, even with a high-level, easy-to-use language like Visual Basic, must admit the truth of this chapter's epigraph. Although Thomas meant it in the context of Darwinian evolution, it rings true for every programmer; despite the best of intentions and mighty effort, writing error-free code is very difficult. Much of the history of programming languages (the creation of higher-level languages, the use of structured and modular programming techniques, and the relatively recent emphasis on object-oriented and component-based development) can be viewed as a continuing attempt to find better and more reliable ways of creating error-free programs.

At this point in your journey through VB5's Extensibility object model, you've reached a fork in the road where the sign says: "Automated, error-free code generation." As I write this paragraph, I'm thinking of the image of Rod Serling on an old

153

black-and-white TV many years ago. I can almost hear him saying, "Next stop, the Twilight Zone!" However, automated code generation is no longer just a fantasy. The reality is that VB5's add-in object model gives you the ability to:

- Return or set the properties of components and controls available at design-time in the Properties window.

- Write code that returns or sets the properties of components and controls that are read/write at runtime.

- Generate code to execute any kind of VB statement that you can write manually.

I want to achieve two major objectives in Chapter 5. First, I'll use this chapter's add-in demo to illustrate the property-related and code-related objects that are listed and described in Table 5.1. Second, I'll take an in-depth look at a commercial-quality add-in that automatically generates the code for and creates/compiles the public interface of a new add-in. The add-in that does this is called the Add-In Interface Builder. As you will see, it not only automates all the grunt work associated with developing an add-in's interface, but it also uses most of the elements in the add-in object model that we presented in Chapters 3, 4, and 5 (except event handlers, which we deal with in Chapter 6).

To demonstrate any of the objects and their members listed in Table 5.1, connect/run Chapter 5's add-in, check the appropriate option button on the add-in's dialog box (see Figure 5.1), and click on Demo.

TABLE 5.1

PROPERTIES AND CODE–RELATED OBJECTS.

Object Name	Description
Properties Collection	Collections of design-time properties associated with a VB component or control and displayed in the Properties window.
Property Object	Represents an item in a **Properties** collection and itself has members (**IndexedValue, Name, NumIndices, Object, Value**) that enable you to manipulate the settings of properties in the Properties window.

(continued)

	TABLE 5.1

PROPERTIES AND CODE–RELATED OBJECTS (*CONTINUED*).

Object Name	Description
CodeModule Object Methods	Seven methods (**AddFromFile, AddFromString, CreateEventProc, DeleteLines, Find, InsertLines, ReplaceLine**) that enable you to write and modify code.
CodeModule Object Properties	Nine properties (**CodePane, CountOfDeclarationLines, CountOfLines, Lines, Members, ProcBodyLine, ProcCountLines, ProcOfLine, ProcStartLine**) that enable you to write and modify code.
Member Object	Represents an item in a **Members** collection of a **CodeModule** object. A **Member** object's properties programmatically implement the manual functionality of the Procedure Attributes dialog box (Tools|Procedure Attributes).

Working With Properties

When you first start writing add-in code to work with properties, it is easy to get confused. All VB programmers are used to returning and setting the values of properties of forms or controls in a standard or ActiveX application. For example, the statements

```
Form1.Visible = False
Form2.Visible = True
```

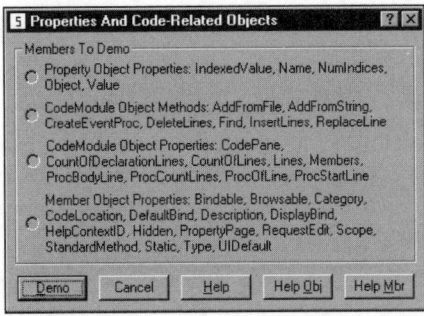

Figure 5.1
Chapter 5's demo add-in dialog box.

set the **Visible** property to hide one form and display a second form. This is not the kind of code that you write in an add-in to return and set the value of a **Property** object.

When you write add-in code, each **VBComponent** object or **VBControl** object has a **Properties** collection associated with it that includes all the object's properties that are visible in the Properties window. A **Property** object is an item in the **Properties** collection that represents one of the design-time properties of a **VBComponent** or **VBControl**. For example, assuming that you have an object reference named **CompFRM** to a **VBComponent** that represents a newly instantiated form, the statements

```
M = "Count: " & CompFRM.Properties.Count & vbCr
M = M & "Visible: " & CompFRM.Properties("Visible")
MsgBox M, vbInformation, "Form VBComponent Object"
```

generate the message box shown in Figure 5.2.

If you trouble yourself to count the number of properties displayed in the Properties window for a new form, you will see that there are exactly 50 and that **Visible** is always initially set to **True**.

The **Properties** collections for different **VBComponent** or **VBControl** objects contain various numbers and kinds of **Property** objects. For example, a BAS module component's **Properties** collection contains only 1 item (**Name**). A CLS module component's **Properties** collection can contain 1 (**Name**) or 2 items (**Name** and **Instancing**), depending on whether it is part of a standard project or an ActiveX project. A **VBControl** object that represents a **Line** control has a **Properties** collection that contains 12 items, but a **VBControl** object that represents a **ListBox** control contains 34 items.

Figure 5.2
Property-related settings of form **VBComponent**.

Properties Of Property Object

The other important concept to keep in mind when writing add-in code to work with properties is that a **Property** object, which represents a specific property of a **VBComponent** or **VBControl** object, also has properties of its own. Besides its typical **Collection** and **VBE** accessor properties, a **Property** object has the five properties listed in Table 5.2.

It's easy to work with the **Name** and **Value** properties of typical **Property** objects. For a **VBComponent** object that is a form, the statements

```
M = "Items in Properties collection-" & vbCr & vbCr
M = M & "First Item: " & CompFRM.Properties(1).Name & vbCr
M = M & "Last Item: " & CompFRM.Properties(50).Name & vbCr
M = M & "First Value: " & CompFRM.Properties(1).Value & vbCr
M = M & "Last Value: " & CompFRM.Properties(50)
MsgBox M, vbInformation, "Form VBComponent Object"
```

generate the message box shown in Figure 5.3.

	TABLE 5.2

PROPERTY OBJECT'S PROPERTIES.

Property Name	Description
IndexedValue	Returns or sets a value of a **Property** object that is an indexed list or an array.
Name	Returns the name used in code to identify a **Property** object. Read-only.
NumIndices	Returns the number of indices of a **Property** object. The value of **NumIndices** can be from 0 to 4, but for most properties **NumIndices** returns 0. It only returns a value greater than 0 for a **Property** object that is an indexed list or an array. Read-only.
Object	Returns or sets the value of a **Property** object that itself returns an object, like **Font, Icon, Picture**, and so on.
Value	Returns or sets a **Variant** that specifies the value of a **Property** object. **Value** is the default member of a **Property** object and thus need not be explicitly specified.

Figure 5.3
Settings of **Name** and **Value** properties.

You should note that the **Value** property is not explicitly specified in the statement that returns the **True** setting of the **Moveable** property and that **Value**, because it is the default member of the **Property** object, is implicitly used in all the example code in this book.

You can easily set the **Value** property of typical **Property** objects with statements like

```
CompFRM.Properties("Caption") = "Title Bar Has No Control Menu"
CompFRM.Properties("ControlBox") = False
```

which change the settings in the Properties window and display a form like the one shown in Figure 5.4 when the project is run.

Setting Properties That Return Objects

You must use the **Object** property to return or set the value of a **Property** object like **Font**, **Icon**, or **Picture** that itself returns an object. Chapter 5's

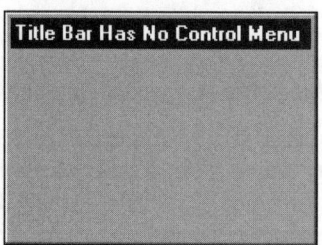

Figure 5.4
Result of **Caption** and **ControlBox** property settings.

demo add-in uses the code in Listing 5.1 to set the **Icon** property of a form **VBComponent** object.

LISTING 5.1   USING THE OBJECT PROPERTY.

```
Private Sub DemoProperty()

    ' Variables:
    Dim M        As String
    Dim Icon     As String


    .   .   .   .


    ' Get path of VB's icons and specify icon:
    On Error Resume Next
    Err.Raise 3
    Icon = Mid$(Err.HelpFile, 1, Len(Err.HelpFile) - 16)
    Icon = Icon & "GRAPHICS\ICONS\ELEMENTS\EARTH.ICO"
    On Error GoTo 0

    M = "Choose OK to set Icon property of Form1" & vbCr
    M = M & "to EARTH.ICO by using Object property."
    Util.ShowMsg M, BTNS, C
    Set CompFRM.Properties("Icon").Object = LoadPicture(Icon)


    .   .   .   .


End Sub
```

If you wanted to copy a form component's **Icon** property setting to its **Picture** property, you could use the statement

```
Set CompFRM.Properties("Picture").Object = _
    CompFRM.Properties("Icon").Object
```

where **Object** is used to both set and return the values of **Property** objects.

For some reason, setting the **Object** property while an add-in is running in debug mode results in OLE Automation error - 2147467259 (Method 'Object' of object 'Property' failed). All the demo code in this book related to the **Object** property uses the **IsBeingDebugged** method of the VBAI class library's **Util** object to check the run mode (debug or normal) of the add-in and only executes the code in normal mode.

Setting Properties That Contain Arrays

A few **Property** objects contain an indexed list or array of items as their settings. For these kinds of **Property** objects, the **IndexedValue** and **NumIndices** properties come into play. Chapter 5's demo add-in uses the code in Listing 5.2 to: add a **ListBox** control to a form component; determine which properties of a **ListBox** take an array (**List** and **ItemData**); and fill the **ListBox** at design time with numbers from 0 to 20 (as shown in Figure 5.5).

LISTING 5.2   USING INDEXEDVALUE AND NUMINDICES PROPERTIES.

```
Private Sub DemoProperty()
    .    .    .
    M = "Choose OK to add ListBox control object to Form1."
    Util.ShowMsg M, BTNS, C
    Set FormDes = CompFRM.Designer
    Set LstCtl = FormDes.VBControls.Add("VB.ListBox")
    LstCtl.Properties("Top") = 50
    LstCtl.Properties("Height") = 2000

    M = "Choose OK to see list of Property objects" & vbCr
    M = M & "of the VBControl object that is List1" & vbCr
    M = M & "whose NumIndices property is not zero."
    Util.ShowMsg M, BTNS, C

    M = "Property objects' non-zero NumIndices settings—"
    M = M & vbCr & vbCr
    For El = 1 To LstCtl.Properties.Count
        Nbr = LstCtl.Properties(El).NumIndices
        If Nbr > 0 Then
            M = M & LstCtl.Properties(El).Name & " ("
            M = M & Nbr & ")" & vbCr
        End If
    Next El
    Util.ShowMsg M, BTNS, C

    M = "Choose OK to use IndexedValue property to" & vbCr
    M = M & "set values for List property of List1."
    Util.ShowMsg M, BTNS, C

    Set ListPrp = LstCtl.Properties("List")
    For El = 0 To 20
        ListPrp.IndexedValue(El) = El
    Next El
    .    .    .    .
End Sub
```

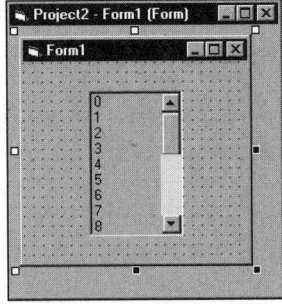

Figure 5.5
Result of setting **IndexedValue** property of **Property** object.

Working With Code

Every kind of **VBComponent** object except a Related Document has a **CodeModule** accessor property that returns the **CodeModule** object, which enables you to manipulate a component's code. You can generate, find, modify, and delete code with the **CodeModule** object's methods and properties in many ways. The best way to learn how to use its members is to study the example code in Chapter 5's demo add-in, contained in the **Sub** procedures named **DemoCodeModMets** and **DemoCodeModPrps**.

In general, you use the properties of the **CodeModule** object to determine the position of code (general declarations, procedure declarations, or statements in a procedure) that you want to manipulate. You use the methods of **CodeModule** to generate new code or manipulate existing code.

Adding And Formatting Code

You can add new code to a code module in various ways, both from sources within the add-in that is generating the code or from external sources. These sources are:

- Event procedure declarations stored in VB's type library (**CreateEventProc** method)

- External text files (**AddFromFile** method)

- Internal resource files (**AddFromString**, **InsertLines**, or **ReplaceLine** methods, after first using VB's **LoadResString** function to extract the code from the RES file)

- Internal strings contained in the add-in's procedures (**AddFromString**, **InsertLines**, or **ReplaceLine** methods)

- Developer input to controls on a dialog box of the add-in (**AddFromString**, **InsertLines**, or **ReplaceLine** methods)

When an add-in generates code from internal strings or developer input, you have to also add all the formatting codes (carriage returns, quotation marks, spaces, and so on). For example, let's assume that you want to add code to an add-in for the **OnStartupComplete** method of the **ITDExtensibility** object. The first few lines of the procedure, after it has been added to a code module, appear as in Listing 5.3.

However, the appearance of the code in Listing 5.3 is very different in the add-in that generates it and then calls the **InsertLines** method to add it to a **CodeModule** object. At that point, the code string (referred to as the **String** variable "C"), which includes formatting codes and values/variables derived from developer input to controls, appears as in Listing 5.4. You will see more examples of how this code generation process works later in this chapter, in the section titled *The Add-In Interface Builder*.

LISTING 5.3   CODE AFTER IT IS ADDED TO CODE MODULE.

```
Private Sub IDTExtensibility_OnStartupComplete _
        (Custom() As Variant)

    ' Variables:
    Dim Item       As String
    Dim AIProgID   As String
    Dim AIDesc     As String

    ' Assign local variables:
    Item = "Example Of Description..."
    AIProgID = "NewAddIn.Connect"
    AIDesc = Util.GetDesc(VBE, AIProgID)

    . . . .

End Sub
```

LISTING 5.4   CODE BEFORE IT IS ADDED TO CODE MODULE.

```
C = "Private Sub IDTExtensibility_OnStartupComplete _" & vbCr
C = C & "              (Custom() As Variant)"
C = C & vbCr & vbCr
C = C & "    ' Variables:" & vbCr
C = C & "    Dim Item        As String" & vbCr
C = C & "    Dim AIProgID    As String" & vbCr
C = C & "    Dim AIDesc      As String"
C = C & vbCr & vbCr
C = C & "    ' Assign local variables:" & vbCr
C = C & "    Item = """ & Desc & "...""" & vbCr
C = C & "    AIProgID = """ & mProgID & """ & vbCr
C = C & "    AIDesc = Util.GetDesc(VBE, AIProgID)"
C = C & vbCr & vbCr
C = C & "    .  .  .  ."
C = C & vbCr & vbCr
C = C & "End Sub"
```

Methods Of CodeModule Object

The **DemoCodeModMets** procedure in Listing 5.5, with most of the message box code deleted and replaced with comments to reduce the listing's length, shows the seven methods (**AddFromFile**, **AddFromString**, **CreateEventProc**, **DeleteLines**, **Find**, **InsertLines**, **ReplaceLine**) of the **CodeModule** object in action. Some key points about how these methods work are:

- You can generate or modify code with the **AddFromFile**, **AddFromString**, **CreateEventProc**, **InsertLines**, and **ReplaceLine** methods. **AddFromFile**, **AddFromString**, and **InsertLines** are very flexible, and you can use them all to make declarations, add single statements, or write entire procedures. **CreateEventProc** and **ReplaceLine** have more specific purposes: **CreateEventProc** declares the opening and closing statements of an event procedure; **ReplaceLine** replaces a single line of code with a specified string.

- **AddFromFile** and **AddFromString** provide little control over the insertion point of the code, always placing it on the line preceding the first procedure in the module or, if there are no procedures, at the end of the module. For control over the insertion point, use the **InsertLines** or **ReplaceLine** methods.

- Some of these methods are more prone to error than others. In some cases, the **AddFromFile** method fails if the code pane is closed, but no trappable error occurs. In other cases, **AddFromFile** works whether or not the code pane is open. **AddFromString** can incorrectly insert the invalid string "()" on the line immediately following other text that it has added. You can work around this bug by searching the module for "()" with the **Find** method and using the **DeleteLines** method to remove the invalid string. In general, the **InsertLines** and **ReplaceLine** methods are more reliable.

 None of the **CodeModule** object's methods can return a line or lines of code. To do this, you must use the **Lines** property of the **CodeModule** object. Also, none of these methods controls the selection status of code. To do this, you must use the **GetSelection** and **SetSelection** methods of the **CodePane** object.

LISTING 5.5   DEMO OF CODEMODULE OBJECT'S METHODS.

```
Private Sub DemoCodeModMets()

    ' Variables:
    Dim M          As String
    Dim Code       As String
    Dim BegLine    As Long
    Dim EndLine    As Long
    Dim BegCol     As Long
    Dim EndCol     As Long
    Dim CompFRM    As VBComponent
    Dim CompBAS    As VBComponent
    Dim FRMMod     As CodeModule
    Dim BASMod     As CodeModule
    Dim ProjEXE    As VBProject
    Dim VBProjs    As VBProjects

    ' Set up demo project, components, and object references:
    Set VBProjs = VBE.VBProjects
    Set ProjEXE = VBProjs.Add(vbext_pt_StandardExe)
    Set CompFRM = ProjEXE.VBComponents("Form1")
    Set CompBAS = ProjEXE.VBComponents.Add(vbext_ct_StdModule)

    ' Get object references to two CodeModule objects:
    Set FRMMod = CompFRM.CodeModule
    Set BASMod = CompBAS.CodeModule
```

```
' Call AddFromFile method, get code added with Lines property:
BASMod.AddFromFile App.Path & "\MAPI32.TXT"
Code = BASMod.Lines(1, BASMod.CountOfLines)

' Delete/add back code with DeleteLines/InsertLines methods:
BASMod.DeleteLines 1, BASMod.CountOfLines
BASMod.InsertLines 1, Code

' Delete/add back code with DeleteLines/AddFromString methods:
BASMod.DeleteLines 1, BASMod.CountOfLines
BASMod.AddFromString Code

' Call Find method to get position of copyright notice in code:
Code = "Copyright (C) 1994 Microsoft Corporation"
BASMod.Find Code, BegLine, BegCol, EndLine, EndCol
M = "Position of Microsoft copyright notice—"
M = M & vbCr & vbCr
M = M & "Line Nbr: " & BegLine & vbCr
M = M & "Beg Col Nbr: " & BegCol & vbCr
M = M & "End Col Nbr: " & EndCol
Util.ShowMsg M, BTNS, C

' Replace copyright notice with ReplaceLine method, declare
' event procedure, and remove demo project:
BASMod.ReplaceLine BegLine, "' Author: Gene Swartzfager"
FRMMod.CreateEventProc "Load", "Form"
VBProjs.Remove ProjEXE

End Sub
```

Properties Of CodeModule Object

The **DemoCodeModPrps** procedure in Listing 5.6, with most of the message box code deleted and replaced with comments to reduce the listing's length, shows the nine properties (**CodePane, CountOfDeclarationLines, CountOfLines, Lines, Members, ProcBodyLine, ProcCountLines, ProcOfLine, ProcStartLine**) of the **CodeModule** object in action. Some key points about how these properties work are:

- **CodePane** and **Members** are accessor properties that enable you to easily access their respective objects without having to write additional statements to drill down through the add-in object hierarchy.

- The line numbers in a code module begin at 1 in the Declarations section and include any blank lines between or in procedures. **CountOfDeclaration**

Lines includes in its returned value any blank lines that are at the bottom of the Declarations section of a code module. **CountOfLines** includes in its returned value any blank lines that are contained in the code module.

- The easiest way to work with the properties of the **CodeModule** object and to view how many lines a procedure contains (including blanks) is to check the Default To Full Module View and Procedure Separator items on the Editor tab of the Options dialog box.

- If you have just added a component to a project, and Require Variable Declaration is checked on the Editor tab of VB's Options dialog box (that is, the **Option Explicit** statement appears at the top of the module's Declarations section), both **CountOfDeclarationLines** and **CountOfLines** return 2 for the new component's **CodeModule** object, which includes one blank line at the bottom of the Declarations section. If the **Option Explicit** statement does not appear at the top of the module's Declarations section, **CountOfDeclarationLines** and **CountOfLines** both return 0.

- **Lines**, although it is listed in the Object Browser as a property, behaves like a method. In VB's Help file, **Lines** is actually listed twice, as a property and as a method. Regardless of the kind of member **Lines** actually is "under the hood," it works well enough.

LISTING 5.6   DEMO OF CODEMODULE OBJECT'S PROPERTIES.

```
Private Sub DemoCodeModPrps()

    ' Variables:
    Dim M          As String
    Dim T          As String
    Dim LineNbr    As Long
    Dim CompFRM     As VBComponent
    Dim FRMMod      As CodeModule
    Dim ProjEXE     As VBProject
    Dim VBProjs     As VBProjects

    ' Set up demo project, components, and object references:
    Set VBProjs = VBE.VBProjects
    Set ProjEXE = VBProjs.Add(vbext_pt_StandardExe)
    Set CompFRM = ProjEXE.VBComponents("Form1")
    Set FRMMod = CompFRM.CodeModule
```

```
' Declare two event procedures in FRM module:
FRMMod.CreateEventProc "Resize", "Form"
FRMMod.CreateEventProc "QueryUnload", "Form"

' Find position of procedures and add code to them:
' * Form_Resize found with ProcBodyLine property.
' * Form_QueryUnload found with ProcStartLine property.
LineNbr = FRMMod.ProcBodyLine("Form_Resize", 0) + 2
T = "    ' Constants for Windows API functions:" & vbCr
T = T & "    Const SWP_NOSIZE = &H1" & vbCr
T = T & "    Const SWP_NOMOVE = &H2"
T = T & vbCr & vbCr
T = T & "    ' Keep dialog box on top of other windows." & vbCr
T = T & "    SetWindowPos hWnd, True, 0, 0, 0, 0, _" & vbCr
T = T & "                SWP_NOSIZE + SWP_NOMOVE"
FRMMod.InsertLines LineNbr, T & vbCr

LineNbr = FRMMod.ProcStartLine("Form_QueryUnload", 0) + 3
T = "    SaveSetting App.Title, ""Settings"", _" & vbCr
T = T & "                ""DisplayForm"", ""0"""
FRMMod.InsertLines LineNbr, T & vbCr

' Add General declaration to Form1.
T = "Private mFlag As Boolean" & vbCr
FRMMod.InsertLines FRMMod.CountOfDeclarationLines + 1, T

' Read various line count properties:
M = "Line counts for Form1's code module" & vbCr
M = M & "and Form_Resize event procedure—"
M = M & vbCr & vbCr
M = M & "CountOfDeclarationLines: "
M = M & FRMMod.CountOfDeclarationLines & vbCr
M = M & "CountOfLines: " & FRMMod.CountOfLines & vbCr
M = M & "ProcCountLines: "
M = M & FRMMod.ProcCountLines("Form_Resize", vbext_pk_Proc)
M = M & vbCr
M = M & "Procedure Containing Line 15: "
M = M & FRMMod.ProcOfLine(15, vbext_pk_Proc)
Util.ShowMsg M, BTNS, C

' Demo CodePane, Members, and Lines properties:
M = "Visible Lines In CodePane: "
M = M & FRMMod.CodePane.CountOfVisibleLines & vbCr
M = M & "Members In CodeModule: "
M = M & FRMMod.Members.Count & vbCr
```

```
M = M & "Line 15: " & FRMMod.Lines(15, 1)
Util.ShowMsg M, BTNS, C

' Remove demo project.
VBProjs.Remove ProjEXE

End Sub
```

Working With Members

You can think of the code in a **CodeModule** object, at a higher level of abstraction, as consisting of members that you access through the **Members** accessor property of **CodeModule**. The **Members** collections of the various code modules in a project contain different numbers and kinds of **Member** objects. A **Member** object of a code module represents an identifier that has module-level scope. Until you select an event procedure in a code module, write a general procedure in it, or make a general declaration, a code module does not contain any **Member** objects.

Kinds Of Member Objects

When you display VB5's Object Browser, you see that it lists three kinds of members (events, properties, and methods). However, the add-in object model distinguishes 5 kinds of **Member** objects, which are identified by the values returned by the **Type** property of **Member**:

- 1 - **vbext_mt_Method**: A **Function** procedure, **Sub** procedure, or general declaration made with the **Declare** statement.

- 2 - **vbext_mt_Property**: A **Property, Get, Let**, or **Set** procedure.

- 3 - **vbext_mt_Variable**: A module-level variable (but not a user-defined data type).

- 4 - **vbext_mt_Event**: A general declaration made with the **Event** statement.

- 5 - **vbext_mt_Const**: A general declaration made with the **Const** statement (but not an intrinsic constant that is an enumerated type).

A **Member** object has 19 properties (but no methods) that enable an add-in to programmatically return and set various attributes of a member. This process is equivalent to manually selecting Tools|Procedure Attributes to display the Procedure Attributes dialog box (shown in Figure 5.6), clicking on Advanced to

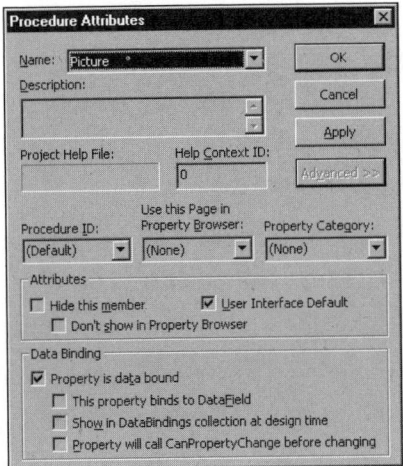

Figure 5.6
Procedure Attributes Advanced dialog box.

expand the dialog box, and setting one or more of the selected procedure's attributes.

There are three important points to keep in mind about the **Member** object and its properties. First, you should use the properties/attributes displayed on the expanded version of the Procedure Attributes dialog box only when you are creating a custom property for an ActiveX control project. Second, the documentation of these properties in VB's Help file and Visual Basic Books Online is woefully inadequate. As a result, I spent a lot of time comprehensively documenting them in the *Dictionary* section of this book and in ADDINEFS.HLP. Third, the Procedure Attributes dialog box only displays a code module's **Public** members, but the **Members** collection includes **Public**, **Private**, and **Friend** members.

The Uses Of Member Objects

Member objects are easy enough to use. You can look at the demo code in the DemoMember procedure in Chapter 5's add-in to see how to handle the mechanics of reading and setting the **Member** object's properties. It is less obvious exactly what **Member** objects are good for. Here's a brief list of some of their possible uses:

- Setting the attributes of custom properties of an ActiveX control.

- Determining whether a particular procedure already exists in a code module. For example, before you call the **CreateEventProc** method to declare an event procedure, you could read the **Name** property of all the items in the code module's **Members** collection to make sure the collection doesn't already include that procedure.

- Flagging **Public** variables. You could read the **Type** and **Scope** properties of all **Member** objects in a project and display a list of all **Public** variables in the project.

- Finding the line number where a procedure or module-level variable is declared by reading the member's **CodeLocation** property.

- Adding Help context ID numbers to all **Public** members of an ActiveX component. You could write an add-in to automate this process, which is very tedious when you do this manually by displaying the names of the members with **Label** controls and allowing the developer to input his or her **HelpContextID** property settings in **TextBox** controls.

The Add-In Interface Builder

The last section of this chapter introduces you to the first full-scale, commercial-quality add-in that we will discuss in this book: the Add-In Interface Builder. Its source code project is BUILDAI.VBP, which you can find on the path \ADDINEFS\CHAPTER5. Its purpose is to automate the creation of an add-in and its basic public interface elements, which we discussed in Chapter 2.

The Add-In Interface Builder is an ActiveX DLL that consists of four modules:

- BUILDAI.FRM: The Add-In Interface Builder form that accepts the developer's inputs.

- BUILDAI.BAS: The BAS module that contains the **Public** declarations (**VBE** object reference, enumerated type, Windows API functions, and object references to the VBAI class library) and general procedures (**AddToINI**, **IsBeingDebugged**, and **Main**).

- BUILDAI.CLS: The CLS module that serves as the add-in's connection object.

- BUILDAI.RES: The resource file that specifies the add-in's icon.

The Add-In Interface Builder was installed and registered on your PC along with all the other files from the CD-ROM enclosed with this book. Its programmatic ID in VBADDIN.INI is BuildAI.Connect and its item in the Add-In Manager dialog box is Creating VB5 Add-Ins: Add-In Interface Builder. At this point in the book, it's timely to study how this add-in is designed and works, because it demonstrates many of the add-in object library's language elements that you have seen in Chapters 3 and 4, and in this chapter.

The Interface Builder's Form

When you connect and run the Add-In Interface Builder, it displays the form shown in Figure 5.7. As you can see from Figure 5.7, the default names for the new add-in's four files are automatically entered (you can change them if you want). Inputs that you must make are:

- Kind of ActiveX file: an in-process, DLL add-in or an out-of-process, EXE add-in.

- Kind of Add-In: normal or Wizard, which determines the last part of the add-in's programmatic ID.

- Project Name: equivalent to the entry made on the General tab of the Project Properties dialog box and the first part of the add-in's programmatic ID.

- Add-In's Path: determined by the settings you select with the **DriveListBox** and **DirListBox** controls.

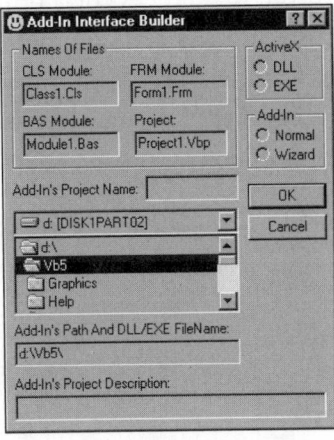

Figure 5.7
Add-In Interface Builder form.

- DLL/EXE FileName: the name of the add-in's DLL or EXE file.

- Project Description: equivalent to the entry made on the General tab of the Project Properties dialog box and listed in the Add-In Manager dialog box.

 I could have expanded upon the functionality of the Add-In Interface Builder and turned it into a multiple-dialog box Wizard that accepted inputs for and then implemented just about every possible feature of an add-in. However, the Interface Builder automates enough of the grunt work of creating an add-in to make it quite worthwhile as is. If you want to customize the interface that it creates or, more likely, add functionality to the add-in's dialog box, the Interface Builder's add-in leaves the source code's project for the new add-in open and ready for you to work on.

The Interface Builder's Code

When you choose OK, the **cmdOK_Click** event procedure performs a series of validations. The first two validations require that you have checked an option for both the kind of ActiveX file and the kind of add-in that you want to build. If these options are checked, the event procedure executes the code in Listing 5.7 and assembles the add-in project and its components. There are a couple of key points to note in Listing 5.7. First, as is the case with all add-ins in this book, it adds references to the VBIDE, Office, and VBAI class libraries so it can reuse their **Public** members. It does this by calling the **AddFromFile** and **AddFromGuid** methods of the **References** collection. Second, it uses the conventional **Name** property setting (that is, Connect or Wizard) for the CLS module used as the add-in's connection object, based on whether the Normal or Wizard option button is checked. I strongly recommend that you get in the habit of adopting these kinds of conventions.

LISTING 5.7   ASSEMBLY OF ADD-IN PROJECT AND COMPONENTS.

```
Private Sub cmdOK_Click()

    .   .   .   .


    ' Create add-in project and its components only once:
    If Not ProjAssembled Then

        ProjAssembled = True
```

```
' Shorten object expression (faster and more readable).
Set VBProjs = VBE.VBProjects

' Add new DLL or EXE project:
If optDLL Then
    Set AIProj = VBProjs.Add(vbext_pt_ActiveXDll)
Else
    Set AIProj = VBProjs.Add(vbext_pt_ActiveXExe)
End If

' Assign project reference to module-level variable:
Set mAIProj = AIProj

' Add VBIDE, Office and VBAI references to project:
GuidVBIDE = "{EF404E00-EDA6-101A-8DAF-00DD010F7EBB}"
AIProj.References.AddFromGuid GuidVBIDE, 5, 0
SubKey = "Software\Microsoft\Office\8.0\Common\Internet\Icons"
HWndSubKey = Reg.OpenSubKey(1, SubKey)
OfficeName = Reg.GetValue(HWndSubKey) & "\MSO97.DLL"
AIProj.References.AddFromFile OfficeName
VBAIName = Left$(App.Path, Len(App.Path) - 8)
VBAIName = VBAIName & "VBAI\VBAI.DLL"
AIProj.References.AddFromFile VBAIName

' Add BAS and FRM components and obtain object references:
Set CompBas = AIProj.VBComponents.Add(vbext_ct_StdModule)
Set CompFrm = AIProj.VBComponents.Add(vbext_ct_VBForm)
Set CompCls = AIProj.VBComponents("Class1")

' Assign Name property settings to components:
CompBas.Name = "basGenlPrcs"
CompFrm.Name = "frmDlgBox1"

If optNormal Then
    CompCls.Name = "Connect"
Else
    CompCls.Name = "Wizard"
End If
End If

    .   .   .   .

End Sub
```

Once the project and its components are assembled, other validations are done before the Interface Builder compiles and registers the new add-in. Most of these validations are pretty fundamental and I'll leave it up to you to check out their code; however, two of them deserve a closer look. There are two **Function** procedures in the Interface Builder's FRM module, **IsDuplicateDesc** and **IsDuplicateProgID**, that appear in Listing 5.8 and that illustrate the care you should take when you make entries to someone else's PC Windows registry.

 When you're working with add-ins, there is probably no more offensive programming error than to write over or corrupt an existing add-in's entries in the Windows registry. You might think this to be an unlikely occurrence; however, if you consistently use the conventional Connect and Wizard names for the second half of an add-in's programmatic ID, it is probable that just by chance you will someday duplicate the first half of an existing add-in's programmatic ID. The validation code in Listing 5.8 ensures that this can't happen when you use the Add-In Interface Builder.

LISTING 5.8   CHECKING FOR DUPLICATE REGISTRY ENTRIES.

```
Private Function IsDuplicateDesc() As Boolean

    ' Variables:
    Dim Desc    As String
    Dim AddIn   As AddIn

    ' Get new add-in's Project Description setting.
    Desc = txt(aiClsDesc)

    ' Check it against existing Description property
    ' settings for add-ins in Windows registry:
    For Each AddIn In VBE.Addins

        ' If setting already exists, return True and abort:
        If Desc = Util.GetDesc(VBE, AddIn.ProgID) Then
            IsDuplicateDesc = True
            Exit For
        End If

    Next AddIn

End Function

Private Function IsDuplicateProgID() As Boolean

    ' Variables:
    Dim AddIn As AddIn
```

```
' Get new add-in's programmatic ID setting:
If optNormal Then
    mProgID = txt(aiPrjName) & ".Connect"
Else
    mProgID = txt(aiPrjName) & ".Wizard"
End If

' Check it against existing ProgID property
' settings for add-ins in Windows registry:
For Each AddIn In VBE.Addins

    ' If setting already exists, return True and abort:
    If mProgID = AddIn.ProgID Then
        IsDuplicateProgID = True
        Exit For
    End If
Next AddIn

End Function
```

Once all validations have been successfully done, the Interface Builder displays the message box shown in Figure 5.8. If you realize that you need to change a setting on the dialog box, choose Cancel, change the setting, and choose OK again on the dialog box. Once you choose OK on the message box shown in Figure 5.8, the Interface Builder proceeds to compile, register, and save the new add-in and cannot be prevented from doing so.

Most of the rest of the **cmdOK_Click** event procedure involves calls to general procedures with names like **WriteFrmModCode**, **WriteBasModCode**, **WriteClsModDecls**, **WriteClsModProcs**, and so on. You can study the routines in these procedures at your leisure. They offer extensive examples of how to use an add-in to generate code for another application that you are automatically creating. After you write all the code for the add-in, which you don't actually

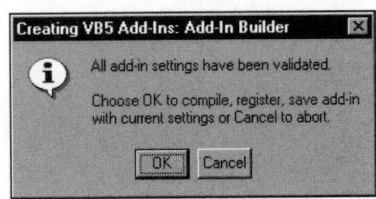

Figure 5.8
Interface Builder's last-chance message box.

see happen because redrawing of the desktop window is temporarily suspended, the Interface Builder executes the code in Listing 5.9 that compiles, registers, and saves the new add-in. At this point, if you have worked your way through Chapters 3 and 4, this code should be pretty easy to understand.

LISTING 5.9   INTERFACE BUILDER'S FINAL ACTIONS.

```
Private Sub cmdOK_Click()

    .   .   .   .


    ' Set Description properties that are equivalent to entries:
    ' * On General tab of Project Properties dialog box.
    ' * On Object Browser's Member Options dialog box.
    AIProj.Description = txt(aiClsDesc)
    CompCls.Description = txt(aiClsDesc)

    ' Write add-in's entry to VBADDIN.INI
    WritePrivateProfileString "Add-Ins32", mProgID, _
                              "0", "VBADDIN.INI"

    ' Save add-in's component files:
    CompCls.SaveAs mPath & txt(aiClsFile)
    CompBas.SaveAs mPath & txt(aiBasFile)
    CompFrm.SaveAs mPath & txt(aiFrmFile)

    ' Set StartUp Object and path:
    AIProj.VBComponents.StartUpObject = vbext_so_SubMain
    VBE.LastUsedPath = mPath

    ' Parse out DLL/EXE filename from entry:
    Name = txt(aiActXName)
    Do
        Pos = InStr(1, Name, "\")
        Name = Mid$(Name, Pos + Len("\"), Len(Name) - Pos)
    Loop Until InStr(Name, "\") = False

    ' Compile/register add-in and save its project file:
    AIProj.BuildFileName = Name
    AIProj.MakeCompiledFile
    AIProj.SaveAs mPath & txt(aiPrjFile)

    .   .   .   .


End Sub
```

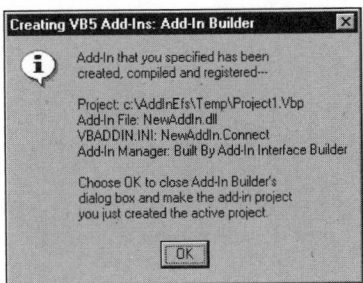

Figure 5.9
Interface Builder's final message box.

The Interface Builder finishes up by displaying the message box shown in Figure 5.9, which reminds you of the key settings of the new add-in. Then the Interface Builder makes the new add-in's project both the active and startup project, and shuts itself down. At this point, you can select Add-Ins|Add-In Manager, check the new add-in's item (in this example, Built By Add-In Interface Builder), choose OK, and start the add-in from its menu item. It displays a generic form with OK and Cancel buttons. You can customize this form and the new add-in any way you like and recompile the source code at any time.

Well, sports fans, you've just finished round 5 of a 10-round championship match (Round 10 in this book being its "Dictionary" section). Are you still on your feet? I'll bet that you are! Anybody who's gotten this far in the book has got to be a pretty tough customer. As I said early in the book, add-in development is probably the most challenging kind of VB programming that you can do. At this point, you should have gotten your second wind and be ready to work your way through the rest of the book.

Round 6 is coming up and it's going to be a doozy! Up to this point, the only add-in event that we've looked at is the **Click** event of a menu item or toolbar button, which is the most commonly used event that the add-in object model supports. Chapter 6 exposes you to the six other kinds of event-related objects that the VBIDE add-in class library provides: **FileControlEvents**, **References Events**, **SelectedVBControlsEvents**, **VBComponentsEvents**, **VBControls Events**, and **VBProjectsEvents**. Once you've completed Chapter 6 and Part II of the book, it's on to Part III and Chapters 7 through 9, which contain some intriguing case studies that demonstrate the many possible uses of add-ins.

6

EVENT-RELATED ADD-IN OBJECTS

Like a kick in the butt, the force of events wakes slumberous talents.

—Edward Hoagland

In add-in programming, the most difficult area to master in my experience is the Extensibility object model's events. Add-in events are raised by VB's IDE when a developer makes menu choices, inputs dialog box entries or checks/unchecks options, and takes actions enabled by one of VB's permanent windows (Properties, Project Explorer, Toolbox, and so on). In an event-driven add-in, the code doesn't follow a predetermined path; instead, different sequences of developer actions cause VB to raise different events that result in varying sequences of code execution in the add-in.

Each add-in event procedure can contain code that performs certain actions, depending on the event object's functionality and the purpose of the add-in. For example, you can design and code an add-in to react to the selection of some VB menu items (File|New Project, File|Open Project, and File|Add Project) by always adding references to certain ActiveX component servers (for example, Office or VBAI) to the new project. The following sequence of related steps allows you to do this:

179

- A developer loads a project with File|New Project, File|Open Project, or File|Add Project.

- VB's IDE raises the **ItemAdded** event of the **VBProjects** collection.

- VB passes an object reference to the loaded **VBProject** object as a parameter to the **VBProject** argument of this add-in's **VBProjects_ItemAdded** event procedure.

- Code in the **ItemAdded** event procedure uses the **References** property of **VBProject** to access its **References** collection and then calls the **AddFromFile** or **AddFromGuid** method to add the appropriate references.

This chapter will show you how to deal with and program the six event-related objects listed in Table 6.1. I will not deal with the **CommandBarEvents** object and its **Click** event here because we covered that material in Chapter 2 and

TABLE **6.1**

EVENT-RELATED OBJECTS.

Object Name	Description
Events	Supplies seven accessor properties that enable an add-in to connect to add-in-related events raised in VB's IDE: CommandBarEvents, FileControlEvents, ReferencesEvents, SelectedVBControlsEvents, VBComponentsEvents, VBControlsEvents, VBProjectsEvents.
FileControlEvents	Is the source of nine events raised by VB's IDE that support file control: AfterAddFile, AfterChangeFileName, AfterCloseFile, AfterRemoveFile, AfterWriteFile, BeforeLoadFile, DoGetNewFileName, RequestChangeFileName, RequestWriteFile.
ReferencesEvents	Is the source of two events raised by VB's IDE when a reference is added to or deleted from a project's References collection: ItemAdded, ItemRemoved.
SelectedVBControlsEvents	Is the source of two events raised by VB's IDE when a control is added to or deleted from a designer's SelectedVBControls collection: ItemAdded, ItemRemoved.

(continued)

TABLE **6.1**

EVENT–RELATED OBJECTS (*CONTINUED*).

Object Name	Description
VBComponentsEvents	Is the source of six events raised by VB's IDE that are related to a project's **VBComponents** collection: **ItemActivated, ItemAdded, ItemReloaded, ItemRemoved, ItemRenamed, ItemSelected.**
VBControlsEvents	Is the source of three events raised by VB's IDE that are related to a designer's **VBControls** collection: **ItemAdded, ItemRemoved, ItemRenamed.**
VBProjectsEvents	Is the source of four events raised by VB's IDE that are related to the **VBProjects** collection: **ItemActivated, ItemAdded, ItemRemoved, ItemRenamed.**

there are examples of how to use **CommandBarEvents** in every add-in in the book. In this chapter, we will study two add-ins in depth:

- Add-In Events Log: This add-in exposes all of the events supported by the add-in object model and has code that, when VB raises one of these events, displays in the Events Log window the name of the event and the values of the event procedure's arguments. When you connect/run this add-in (Creating VB5 Add-Ins: Chapter 6), you can make menu choices, take actions in dialog boxes, or do something in one of VB's permanent windows and watch the Add-In Events Log display the add-in events that are raised.

- Controls Monitor: This add-in (Creating VB5 Add-Ins: Controls Monitor) demonstrates how to take advantage of control-related events that the add-in object model exposes. More specifically, it displays a custom toolbar that enables you to perform several actions. You can automatically reset a control's default property settings (**Height, Name,** and so on) when you add it to a designer; rearrange the **TabIndex** or **Index** settings of the controls on a designer by dragging and dropping items in lists; change a control's name in code after you change its **Name** property setting in the Properties window; and cut, copy, and paste controls *and their related event procedures* from one designer to another.

It is not necessary for every add-in to expose and react to all the events listed in Table 6.1. You can create many useful add-ins, like the Add-In Interface Builder in Chapter 5, while only exposing the **Click** event of a menu item. However, if you don't expose an add-in's events, their potential power and "slumberous talents" remain dormant.

The Add-In Events Log

Before explaining how the Add-In Events Log works, let's observe it in action. First, open a Standard EXE project in VB and connect/run the Add-In Events Log add-in (Creating VB5 Add-Ins: Chapter 6). Then select File|Add Project to add a second project to VB and the Events Log displays the information for event 1 in Figure 6.1. Select File|Remove Project to delete the second project and the Events Log displays the information for events 2 and 3 in Figure 6.1. Finally, if you select Project|Add File, point and click to the path \ADDINEFS\CHAPTER6, and add the file AAF.BAS, the Events Log displays the information for events 4 through 6 in Figure 6.1.

The information in the window in Figure 6.1 was displayed in response to the three menu selections that you made and the six related add-in events that VB raised:

- File|Add Project: VB raised the **ItemAdded** event of the **VBProjects** collection in the add-in, and code in that event procedure then displayed number 1's item.

- File|Remove Project: VB raised the **ItemRemoved** event of the **VBProjects** collection in the add-in, and code in that event procedure then displayed number 2's item. Immediately after the **ItemRemoved** event, the

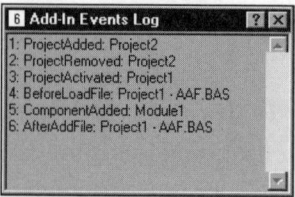

Figure 6.1
Chapter 6's Add-In Events Log dialog box.

ItemActivated event was raised as a result of a message from the operating system (that is, the first project got the focus and was activated), and code in **ItemActivated** displayed number 3's item.

- Project|Add File: Adding the standard module AAF.BAS to the project caused VB to raise three add-in events in succession. **BeforeLoadFile** (4) and **AfterAddFile** (6) belong to the **FileControl** object; **ItemAdded** (5) belongs to the **VBComponents** collection.

These three examples should give you a good feel for what the Add-In Events Log does. In order to explain in detail how the Events Log works, we first need to review the processes by which you declare an add-in event source object, declare the object's events, and make the event procedures responsive to VB-raised events. We explained these processes briefly in Chapter 1, but we'll analyze them in more detail in the next section.

Declaring Add-In Event Objects

Chapter 6's Events Log add-in contains a class module whose **Name** property is set to VBEvents. In the General declarations section of this class module, the six statements

```
Public WithEvents FileControl          As FileControlEvents
Public WithEvents References            As ReferencesEvents
Public WithEvents SelectedVBControls    As SelectedVBControlsEvents
Public WithEvents VBComponents          As VBComponentsEvents
Public WithEvents VBControls            As VBControlsEvents
Public WithEvents VBProjects            As VBProjectsEvents
```

declare the event source object variables that enable you to create the beginning and ending statements of add-in event procedures.

The **WithEvents** keyword, which must be used with the **Public** statement, specifies that you are declaring an object variable that will respond to events that an ActiveX component raises. When you use **WithEvents** in the context of an add-in, the ActiveX component that raises the events is VB's IDE. **WithEvents** is valid only in class modules. You can declare as many different object variables as you like using **WithEvents**; however, you can neither create arrays nor use the **New** keyword with **WithEvents**.

In this example, I've declared six object variables because the add-in object model supports six general categories of events (not including the **CommandBarEvents** object's **Click** event). After you type these six statements and press Enter, the names of the object variables are added to the class module's Object drop-down box, as shown in Figure 6.2.

 You can give any name you want to the add-in object variables declared with the **WithEvents** keyword, but I believe it makes the code more readable to give them the same name as the type of object being instantiated (minus the suffix *Events*).

Creating An Object's Event Procedures

Once you have declared an event source object variable and its name appears in the class module's Object drop-down box, the next step is to create the respective event procedures associated with the object. You do so by selecting the item you want in the Object drop-down box (for example, **FileControl**), which automatically creates the beginning and ending statements of its first event procedure (that is, **AfterAddFile**). You can then create the other event procedures by selecting their items in the Procedure drop-down box, as shown in Figure 6.3.

In the case of the **FileControl** object, nine event procedures are available. Other objects like the **References** and **SelectedVBControls** collections have only two event procedures. Refer back to Table 6.1 to see the event procedures associated with each event source object, or you can find them in the Object Browser. Just

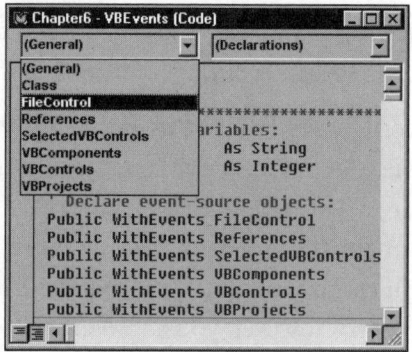

Figure 6.2
VBEvents class module's Object drop-down box.

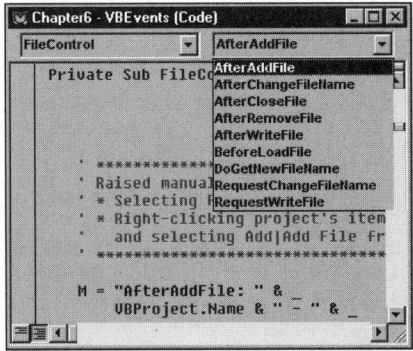

Figure 6.3
VBEvents class module's Procedure drop-down box.

as with event procedures for forms and controls, you only need to create the add-in event procedures that you want to make responsive to VB's IDE and for which you are going to write code.

After I create the beginning and ending statements of an add-in procedure, I like to add line-continuation characters to the beginning statement so that:

- I can easily view all of its arguments in the code module.

- Printed documentation of the code fits on 8.5×11-inch paper.

The lines of the opening statement for the **AfterAddFile** event procedure, with the line-continuation characters inserted and the arguments lined up, are shown in Listing 6.1.

LISTING 6.1 AFTERADDFILE EVENT PROCEDURE DECLARATION.

```
Private Sub FileControl_AfterAddFile _
                    (ByVal VBProject As VBProject, _
                    ByVal FileType As vbext_FileType, _
                    ByVal FileName As String)


End Sub
```

Making Event Procedures Responsive

Once you have created the beginning and ending statements for an object's event procedures, you must next connect that event source object to the related add-in events that VB's IDE raises and make it responsive to them. Until you accomplish these tasks, any code that you write in the event procedures will not execute. You connect an event source object (for example, **FileControl**) with a statement like

```
Set FileControl = VBE.Events.FileControlEvents(VBProject)
```

where the syntax is as follows:

- **FileControl**: Name of the event source object that you are connecting.

- **VBE**: Root object of the VBIDE class library.

- **Events**: Accessor property of **VBE** that returns the **Events** object, which in turn has accessor properties.

- **FileControlEvents**: Accessor property of **Events** object that connects the **FileControl** event source object to the add-in events raised by VB's IDE and takes a **VBProject** object reference as its argument.

- *VBProject*: Argument of **FileControlEvents** accessor property.

You connect the other five event source objects with statements like

```
Set References = VBE.Events.ReferencesEvents(VBProject)
Set VBComponents = VBE.Events.VBComponentsEvents(VBProject)
Set VBControls = VBE.Events.VBControlsEvents(VBProject, VBForm)
Set VBProjects = VBE.Events.VBProjectsEvents
Set SelectedVBControls = VBE.Events.SelectedVBControlsEvents _
                                    (VBProject, VBForm)
```

where each of the accessor properties of **Events** connects a different event source object and, except for the **VBProjectsEvents** accessor property, takes one or more arguments. The arguments always require object references to either a **VBProject** object (typically representing the active project) and a **VBForm** object (typically representing the designer of the selected component in the active project).

Listing 6.2 contains the **ConnectTo** method—declared with the **Friend** keyword to prevent it from being called from another application or component—that connects the six event source objects in the **VBEvents** class module of the Events Log add-in. The **ConnectTo** method is called from a **Timer** object that is contained by the Events Log form (frmChapter6). I explain why and how the **Timer** is used in the next section.

LISTING 6.2   CONNECTTO PROCEDURE IN VBEVENTS CLASS MODULE.

```
Friend Sub ConnectTo()

    ' Variables:
    Dim VBForm      As VBForm
    Dim VBProject   As VBProject

    ' Make VBProjects event source object responsive to its events.
    Set VBProjects = VBE.Events.VBProjectsEvents

    ' If no project is loaded, don't make other connections.
    If VBE.ActiveVBProject Is Nothing Then Exit Sub

    ' Shorten object expression (faster and more readable):
    Set VBProject = VBE.ActiveVBProject

    ' Connect event source objects that take
    ' only VBProject argument to their events:
    Set FileControl = VBE.Events.FileControlEvents(VBProject)
    Set References = VBE.Events.ReferencesEvents(VBProject)
    Set VBComponents = VBE.Events.VBComponentsEvents(VBProject)

    ' Handle error for components that don't have designer and
    ' shorten object expression (faster and more readable):
    On Error GoTo EH
    Set VBForm = VBE.SelectedVBComponent.Designer

    ' Connect event source objects that take both VBProject
    ' argument and VBForm argument to their events:
    Set VBControls = VBE.Events.VBControlsEvents(VBProject, VBForm)
    Set SelectedVBControls = VBE.Events.SelectedVBControlsEvents _
                                    (VBProject, VBForm)

EH:

End Sub
```

Refreshing Event Handlers

Using a **Timer** object to recursively call the **ConnectTo** method is an easy way to make sure all the event source connections are updated when the active project, selected component, or selected control in VB's IDE changes. This **Timer** object is started in the **Form_Load** event procedure of frmChapter6 with the statement

```
tmrWatchVBComps.Interval = 1
```

and continues to run until the form is unloaded or the Events Log add-in is disconnected. The code for the **tmrWatchVBComps_Timer** event procedure is shown in Listing 6.3 and is easy to understand. The code continuously examines the selected **VBComponent** object. Two possibilities exist:

- If the selected module hasn't changed since the last time the **Timer** routine executed, the rest of the routine is not run and the **Timer** thread continues to call itself recursively.

- If the selected module has changed, the **Timer** routine updates its **Static** object variable with the newly selected **VBComponent** object, calls the **ConnectTo** method to refresh the six event source objects, and again calls itself recursively.

That's all there is to it. The **ConnectTo** method can internally derive the active project, selected component, and selected control to get the appropriate object reference arguments it needs to connect the six event source objects. If these three object references never changed, there would be no need to call **ConnectTo** again; but they do change and, because **ConnectTo** can't call itself recursively, we use the **Timer** object's thread to call it. The **VBEvents** object variable in the statement

```
VBEvents.ConnectTo
```

is module level in scope and is declared in the General section of frmChapter6.

LISTING 6.3 TIMER ROUTINE TO REFRESH EVENT HANDLERS.

```
Private Sub tmrWatchVBComps_Timer()

   ' Variables:
   Static MostRecentVBComp As VBComponent

   ' If we have new selected component:
   If Not MostRecentVBComp Is VBE.SelectedVBComponent Then

      ' Refresh local object reference.
      Set MostRecentVBComp = VBE.SelectedVBComponent
```

```
                           ' Refresh add-in's event source objects by calling
                           ' ConnectTo method in VBEvents class module:
                           VBEvents.ConnectTo

                    End If

              End Sub
```

Writing Add-In Event Procedure Routines

For the Events Log add-in, the code in the event procedures is for demonstration purposes only. It simply records data about the add-in event that is raised (kind of event source object, kind of event, and parameters that VB passes to the event's arguments) and then calls the **ShowEventInfo Sub** to display the information on the Events Log form. If a path is part of one of the event's file name arguments, it calls the **StripPath Function** to delete it to condense the log's information. For example, the code for the **AfterAddFile** event procedure, and for the **StripPath** and **ShowEventInfo** procedures, is shown in Listing 6.4.

LISTING 6.4   EVENTS LOG EVENT PROCEDURE CODE.

```
Private Sub FileControl_AfterAddFile _
                          (ByVal VBProject As VBProject, _
                           ByVal FileType As vbext_FileType, _
                           ByVal FileName As String)

        ' ***********************************************************
        ' Raised manually by:
        ' * Selecting Project|Add File.
        ' * Right-clicking project's item in Project Explorer window
        '   and selecting Add|Add File from its shortcut menu.
        ' ***********************************************************

        M = "AfterAddFile: " & _
            VBProject.Name & " - " & _
            StripPath(FileName)

        ShowEventInfo

End Sub

Private Function StripPath(Item As String)

        ' Variables:
        Dim Pos As Byte
```

```
    Do
        Pos = InStr(1, Item, "\")
        Item = Mid$(Item, Pos + Len("\"), Len(Item) - Pos)
    Loop Until InStr(Item, "\") = False

    StripPath = UCase$(Item)

End Function

Private Sub ShowEventInfo()

    ' Constants for Windows API functions:
    Const WM_PASTE = &H302

    ' Display event's information, constructed in each event
    ' handler's procedure, on add-in's Events Log form:
    mLineNbr = mLineNbr + 1
    Clipboard.SetText CStr(mLineNbr & ": " & M & vbCrLf)
    mLog.SelStart = Len(mLog)
    SendMessage mLog.hWnd, WM_PASTE, 0, 0

End Sub
```

 In the **ShowEventInfo** procedure, I use the Clipboard and the Windows API function **SendMessage** to easily append the information about the add-in event to the end of the Events Log text.

You can experiment with the Events Log add-in by running it while you work on any of your current VB projects, because it does not actually affect a project or component in any way. It is simply intended to give you a feel for the typical sequences of add-in events that VB raises when you take certain actions in the IDE. For example, if you select a module that has already been saved under one file name, select File|Save As, and save it under another name, you will trigger a complex sequence of about six events that VB raises in response to this one action and that are displayed on the Events Log dialog box.

So, you must be wondering at this point, what kinds of procedures might you write for add-ins that perform useful work? The answer to this question is limited only by your imagination and the language elements of the Extensibility object model. I list some ideas for you to consider in the next section. Then, in the last section of this chapter, titled *The Controls Monitor Add-In,* I demonstrate a complete add-in that shows how to utilize the control-related events.

Uses For Event-Related Add-Ins

The add-in events we are dealing with in this chapter belong to one object (**FileControl**) and five collections (**References, SelectedVBControls, VBComponents, VBControls, VBProjects**). One way to brainstorm about the potential uses of these add-in events is to consider the functionality of their related members and ask yourself what kinds of automated capabilities these properties and methods might lend themselves to.

The **FileControl** object and its many events could, if you wanted to invest sufficient time and effort, support a customized project file control system. Personally, I wouldn't bother because Visual Source Safe and other similar products already exist, and they provide this kind of functionality (some in the form of a VB add-in). The following sections list some automation ideas for the **Reference, VBProject,** and **VBComponent** objects.

Reference Object Automation Ideas

A **References** collection only has three methods other than the default **Item** method (**AddFromFile, AddFromGuid, Remove**), two events (**ItemAdded, ItemRemoved**), and a **Reference** object that has just read-only properties. Still, consider these possible suggestions related to this relatively limited range of functions:

- Check the **References** collection of each project that is loaded and, if it does not include certain references, automatically add them. A Microsoft Solutions Provider or other VB shop that wants to aggressively promote reuse of objects could require that all its programmers be familiar with, and include in their projects, references to specified ActiveX servers.

- Check the settings of the **Guid, Major,** and **Minor** properties of each reference that is added to a project and roll back the attempted addition if it doesn't correspond to a certain release.

- Check the **IsPath** property of certain sharable references that are added to a project and roll back the attempted addition if the component isn't located on the shared path.

- If certain references are deleted from a project, roll back the attempted deletion.

VBProject Object Automation Ideas

A **VBProjects** collection and a **VBProject** object have lots of useful methods and properties that support a broad range of functionality. Here are some ideas:

- Assume that you (or some developer on your VB team) have created enhanced project templates for the different kinds of projects (Standard EXE, ActiveX DLL, ActiveX EXE, ActiveX Control). These enhanced templates might include module comment headers, standard code for event procedures, designer property settings other than the defaults, and so on. Then, when any attempt is made to load one of these kinds of projects from VB's New Project dialog box, roll back the addition and instead load the enhanced template project.

- Call the **AddToolboxProgID** method whenever a project is loaded to make sure certain specified ActiveX components are always referenced and included in the project.

- When a project's VBP file is renamed, display a message box that enables the developer to delete the old VBP file from the project's path or copy it to a backup path.

VBComponent Object Automation Ideas

Here are some suggestions for the **VBComponents** collection and its **VBComponent** object:

- Assume that you (or some developer on your VB team) have created enhanced component templates for the different kinds of modules (Form, MDIForm, Standard, Class, User Control, and so on). These enhanced templates might include module comment headers, standard code for event procedures, designer property settings other than the defaults, and so on. Then, when any attempt is made to load one of these kinds of modules from VB's Add 'Module Type' dialog box, roll back the addition and instead load the enhanced template module with the **AddFromTemplate** method.

- When a developer double-clicks on a component in the Project Explorer window, hide any other components' windows in the project and display only the windows (designer and/or code pane) associated with the activated component.

- When a developer clicks on a component in the Project Explorer window, bring the component's open designer window (if it has one) to the top of the z-order. If the component does not have an open designer window, bring its code pane window to the top of the z-order.

- Set properties of a newly added component to values other than the initial defaults.

- When a component's file is deleted or renamed, display a message box that enables the developer to delete the old file from the project's path or copy it to a backup path.

- When a component is deleted from a project, check if any references to that component's **Name** property setting or to **Public** members of that component still exist in the project's code. If they do, roll back the deletion and flag the references for action.

The Controls Monitor Add-In

The Controls Monitor add-in (Creating VB5 Add-Ins: Controls Monitor) demonstrates how to take advantage of control-related events that the add-in object model exposes. When you connect it, it displays the custom toolbar shown in Figure 6.4. This toolbar behaves like all other VB toolbars and can be docked or allowed to float free.

Because of its functionality, the Controls Monitor add-in is designed and runs differently than the other add-ins in this book. You can only connect it from the Add-In Manager dialog box or programmatically by calling the **Connect** method of the **Util** object in the VBAI class library; you can't connect it from the VB Add-In Toolbar.

When you connect this add-in, it does not add a menu item to the Add-Ins menu. Instead, when its **OnConnection** method's procedure creates its custom

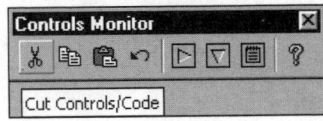

Figure 6.4
Controls Monitor add-in's custom toolbar.

toolbar and adds it to the VB IDE's **CommandBars** collection, VB automatically adds a menu item for the custom toolbar to the View|Toolbars popup menu (see Figure 6.5). You can hide and display the toolbar by unchecking and checking its menu item on the Toolbars popup menu. This is a nice feature and, because VB is hard-coded to handle custom toolbars this way, it obviously makes no sense to add a redundant menu item to the Add-Ins menu.

The Controls Monitor add-in can display two modeless forms simultaneously: SetTabIndex and SetIndex, as shown in Figure 6.6. These forms allow you to rearrange the **TabIndex** or **Index** settings of the controls on a designer by dragging and dropping items in the lists on the forms. The Controls Monitor add-in also allows you to change its parameters and demonstrates how you could set up an entire add-in suite of customized IDE settings. It does this by displaying the Set Control Monitor's Parameters form shown in Figure 6.7. If you change any parameters and choose OK, the current instance of the add-in is updated to reflect the changes, and the new parameters are saved to the Windows registry so the next instance of the add-in will reflect them.

Through the use of **Timer** threads, the Controls Monitor add-in enables two-way interaction for the **TabIndex** and **Index** properties of controls. If you change **TabIndex** or **Index** settings of controls by dragging and dropping items in the

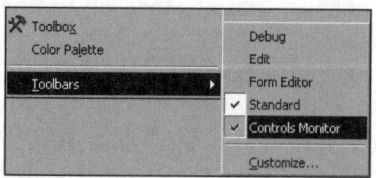

Figure 6.5
Controls Monitor toolbar's menu item.

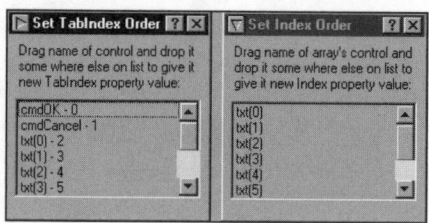

Figure 6.6
SetTabIndex and SetIndex forms.

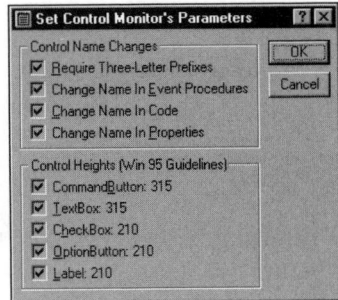

Figure 6.7
Set Control Monitor's Parameters form.

lists on the SetTabIndex and SetIndex forms, the values are changed in the Properties window. Going the other way, if you change **TabIndex** or **Index** settings of controls in the Properties window, these changes are also made in the lists on the SetTabIndex and SetIndex forms.

Now let's take a look at some of the specific techniques that I employed in this add-in to react to and take advantage of control-related events. I will not repeat the material about how you declare an event source object, create its event procedures, and make them responsive to events raised by VB's IDE (see the previous sections in this chapter). Instead, I'll focus on how the Controls Monitor add-in:

- Sets default values for the **Name** property of controls when they are added to a designer.

- Reacts to a change of a control's **Name** property setting by changing references to that control's **Name** property in the code module's event procedures, code, and properties.

- Cuts, copies, and pastes both controls and their associated event procedures.

Setting The Name Property Of Controls

After you connect the Controls Monitor add-in and its toolbar is displayed, you'll notice that when you add one of the 20 intrinsic controls on VB's Toolbox to a designer, the small Type Control Name dialog box shown in Figure 6.8 is displayed. After you type in the rest of the name and press Enter (the only way to close this dialog box), the control is instantiated with the specified **Name**

Figure 6.8
Control Name dialog box.

property setting. If the control has a **Caption** or **Text** property whose setting is normally initialized to the **Name** property setting, the routine also changes the settings of those properties. Finally, for certain controls (**CommandButton**, **TextBox**, **CheckBox**, **OptionButton**, **Label**), the routine changes their default **Height** settings to those specified by the Windows 95 GUI guidelines.

 In this example, because the control that is being added is a **CommandButton**, you are prompted with the three-letter prefix *cmd*; the appropriate prefix is provided for each of the intrinsic controls.

The code in the Controls Monitor add-in that customizes the instantiation of VB's intrinsic controls is shown in Listing 6.5, with most of the boilerplate statements that set the various prefixes omitted. The **VBControls_ItemAdded** event procedure of the **VBEvents** class module is pretty straightforward.

Once we have an object reference to the **VBControl** object that is being added—and assuming that the appropriate parameters are checked on the Monitor's Parameters dialog box—we get some information about the control: class name, **Name** property setting, and **Name** property index suffix. Then we display the Type Control Name dialog box with the three-letter prefix prompt. After the developer completes the **Name** entry and presses Enter, the control's **Name** (and in some cases **Height**) property is changed.

 You should note that to prevent the code in the **VBControls_Item Renamed** event procedure from executing, the module-level flag **mSettingPrefix** is turned on in the **VBControls_ItemAdded** event procedure until after the control has been renamed. When you write this kind of add-in, event-driven code often requires that you set flags to prevent interference effects between event procedures or redundant execution.

LISTING 6.5   VBCONTROLS_ITEMADDED EVENT PROCEDURE.

```
Private Sub VBControls_ItemAdded(ByVal VBControl As VBControl)

    ' Variables:
    Dim Prefix      As String
    Dim NameIndex   As String
    Dim OrigName    As String
    Dim NewName     As String


    On Error GoTo EH

    ' If auto-prefixing Name property feature is checked
    ' on Control Monitor's Parameters dialog box:
    If pPrefix Then

        ' Turn on flag so ItemRenamed event procedure doesn't run.
        mSettingPrefix = True

        ' Get correct three-letter prefix:
        Select Case VBControl.ClassName
            Case "PictureBox"
                Prefix = "pic"
            Case "Label"
                Prefix = "lbl"


            .   .   .   .


        End Select

        ' Derive original name and index suffix appended to name:
        OrigName = VBControl.Properties("Name")
        NameIndex = Right$(OrigName, 1)

        ' If control's not part of array:
        If Val(NameIndex) > 0 Then

            ' Display dialog box modally to input name:
            frmSetName.Prefix = Prefix
            frmSetName.Show vbModal

            ' After user inputs name and hides dialog box by
            ' pressing Enter, change Name and unload form:
            NewName = frmSetName.txtSetName
            Unload frmSetName
            VBControl.Properties("Name") = NewName
```

```
      ' Change Caption and Text properties too:
      On Error Resume Next
      VBControl.Properties("Caption") = NewName
      VBControl.Properties("Text") = NewName
      On Error GoTo 0

   End If

   ' Turn off flag.
   mSettingPrefix = False

End If

' If Win 95 heights are checked on Control Monitor's
' Parameters dialog box, change height of controls
' when they are added from Toolbox to designer:
Select Case VBControl.ClassName
   Case "CommandButton"
      If pCmd Then VBControl.Properties("Height") = 315
   Case "TextBox"
      If pTxt Then VBControl.Properties("Height") = 315
   Case "CheckBox"
      If pChk Then VBControl.Properties("Height") = 210
   Case "OptionButton"
      If pOpt Then VBControl.Properties("Height") = 210
   Case "Label"
      If pLbl Then VBControl.Properties("Height") = 210
End Select

' If TabIndex or Index forms are visible,
' refresh their lists of controls:
If pfrmTabIndex.Visible Then pfrmTabIndex.RefreshList
If pfrmIndex.Visible Then pfrmIndex.RefreshList
Exit Sub

EH:

   Util.ShowMsg "Error " & Err & vbCr & Err.Description, _
           BTNS, "VBControls_ItemAdded"

End Sub
```

Reacting To Name Property Changes

Every VB developer knows what a pain it is, after changing the **Name** property
of one or more controls, to have to manually do a find-and-replace operation

on all the references to the **Name** in the designer's code module. The Controls Monitor add-in automates this process. The code that does this is in the **VBControls_ItemRenamed** event procedure of the **VBEvents** class module and is shown in Listing 6.6. To see what this event procedure does, just put a control on a designer, create two or three simple event procedures for the control, and change its **Name** setting in the Properties window.

There are several approaches to coding the functionality in Listing 6.6. Because I want to demonstrate how to use the **Members** collection and its **Member** objects, I use that syntax to change any control-related names in event procedure declarations. Then, to change **Name** references in the body of procedures, I loop through every line of code, changing **Name** property references wherever I find them. From a practical standpoint, using these two different approaches also allows me to distinguish the two kinds of changes on the Control Monitor's Parameters dialog box.

 There is also a block of code at the end of the **VBControls_Item Renamed** event procedure that checks all items in the control's **Properties** collection and changes any, like **Caption** and **Text**, to the new **Name** property's setting.

Listing 6.6   VBControls_ItemRenamed event procedure.

```
Private Sub VBControls_ItemRenamed(ByVal VBControl As VBControl, _
                         ByVal OldName As String, _
                         ByVal OldIndex As Long)


' *********************************************************
' ItemRenamed event is raised when:
' * Name property of normal control is changed.
' * Name or Index property of item in control array
'   is changed.
' *********************************************************


' Variables:
Dim OldLine        As String
Dim OldMbrName     As String
Dim NewDecl        As String
Dim NewLine        As String
Dim NewName        As String
Dim OldSetting     As String
Dim Pos            As Byte
Dim NumLines       As Long
```

```
Dim DeclLineNbr    As Long
Dim LineNbr        As Long
Dim Member         As Member
Dim CodeModule     As CodeModule
Dim Property       As Property

On Error GoTo EH

' Except under certain circumstances, refresh lists on
' SetTabIndex and SetIndex forms (if they are visible):
If Not pChangingIndex And Not mSettingPrefix Then
    If pfrmIndex.Visible Then pfrmIndex.RefreshList
    If pfrmTabIndex.Visible Then pfrmTabIndex.RefreshList
End If

' Shorten object expression (faster and more readable).
Set CodeModule = VBControl.Container.Parent.CodeModule

' If we're changing event procedure names:
If pProc And Not mSettingPrefix Then

    ' Get Name property of renamed control:
    NewName = VBControl.Properties("Name")

    ' For...Each...Next block searches procedure declarations
    ' and replaces control's old name with new name:
    For Each Member In CodeModule.Members

        ' If it is event procedure for renamed control:
        If InStr(Member.Name, OldName & "_") Then

            ' Get line number of procedure's declaration.
            DeclLineNbr = Member.CodeLocation

            ' Parse old declaration's string, create new
            ' declaration string that uses new control
            ' name, and replace old declaration with new:
            OldMbrName = Member.Name
            Pos = InStr(OldMbrName, "_")
            NewDecl = "Private Sub " & NewName & _
                      Mid$(OldMbrName, Pos)
            CodeModule.ReplaceLine DeclLineNbr, NewDecl

        End If
    Next Member
End If
```

```
' If we're changing code reference names:
If pCode And Not mSettingPrefix Then

    ' Do...Loop block searches code and replaces
    ' control's old name with new name:
    NumLines = CodeModule.CountOfLines
    Do
        For LineNbr = 1 To NumLines

            ' If code line contains control's old name:
            If CodeModule.Find(OldName, LineNbr, _
                            NumLines, 0, 0) Then

                ' Assign code line to variable, find where:
                ' old name starts in code line, replace it
                ' with new name, and then replace code line:
                OldLine = CodeModule.Lines(LineNbr, 1)
                Pos = InStr(OldLine, OldName)
                NewLine = Left$(OldLine, Pos - 1) & NewName & _
                            Mid$(OldLine, Pos + Len(OldName))
                CodeModule.ReplaceLine LineNbr, NewLine

            Else
                Exit Do
            End If
        Next LineNbr
    Loop

End If

    .   .   .   .

End Sub
```

Cutting, Copying, And Pasting Controls/Code

VB has always supported the ability to copy and paste selected controls from one designer to another via the Clipboard. Haven't you always wished, though, that you could also copy and paste the event procedures related to those controls? The first four buttons on the Controls Monitor toolbar provide this functionality. You can cut, copy, or paste controls/code, and you can even undo previous cut or paste operations to some degree. To try out this functionality, instantiate some controls on a designer, create some simple event procedures for the controls, and have another designer available. Then select some controls and start cutting/copying/pasting/undoing and see what happens.

The **Copy** and **Paste** procedures, contained in the **Connect** class module, are shown in Listing 6.7. The **Cut** procedure is almost an exact replica of the **Copy** procedure, except that the **Cut** method of the **SelectedVBControls** collection is called instead of the collection's **Copy** method. Once you understand how the **Cut**, **Copy**, and **Paste** procedures work, figuring out the **Undo** procedure is a no-brainer.

The key technique in the **Cut** and **Copy** procedures involves looping through the event procedures for each selected control and storing their code in the module-level variable **mCode**. When the **Paste** procedure executes, the **Paste** method of the **VBForm** object handles the controls and the **AddFromString** method of the **CodeModule** object is used to insert all the event procedures stored in **mCode** into the other designer's code module.

LISTING 6.7 COPY AND PASTE PROCEDURES.

```
Private Sub TBarBtnCopy_Click(ByVal CommandBarControl As Object, _
                        Handled As Boolean, _
                        CancelDefault As Boolean)

    ' Variables:
    Dim SelVBComp    As VBComponent
    Dim CodeMod      As CodeModule
    Dim Designer     As VBForm
    Dim SelCtl       As VBControl
    Dim ContCtl      As VBControl


    On Error GoTo EH


    ' Shorten object expression (faster and more readable).
    Set SelVBComp = VBE.SelectedVBComponent

    ' Don't copy controls/code if:
    ' * No module is selected
    ' * Module's designer is not open.
    If SelVBComp Is Nothing Then Exit Sub
    If Not SelVBComp.HasOpenDesigner Then Exit Sub

    ' Shorten object expressions (faster and more readable).
    Set Designer = SelVBComp.Designer
    Set CodeMod = SelVBComp.CodeModule
```

```
' Don't copy controls/code if no control is selected.
If Designer.SelectedVBControls.Count = 0 Then Exit Sub

' Store selected module and number of selected
' controls to check next operation against:
Set mSelVBComp = SelVBComp
mNumSelCtls = Designer.SelectedVBControls.Count

' Initialize code storage variable.
mCode = ""

' Looping through each selected control:
For Each SelCtl In Designer.SelectedVBControls

    ' Check selected control's type:
    Select Case SelCtl.ClassName

        ' If it's container control:
        Case "Frame", "PictureBox"

            ' If container control actually contains controls:
            If SelCtl.ContainedVBControls.Count <> 0 Then

                ' Looping through each contained control:
                For Each ContCtl In SelCtl.ContainedVBControls

                    ' Store contained control's events procedures.
                    StoreEvtProcs ContCtl.Properties("Name"), CodeMod

                Next ContCtl
            End If
    End Select

    ' Store selected control's events procedures.
    StoreEvtProcs SelCtl.Properties("Name"), CodeMod

Next SelCtl

' Copy selected controls to Clipboard and set flag:
Designer.SelectedVBControls.Copy
mLastOper = aiCopy
Exit Sub

EH:

    Util.ShowMsg "Error " & Err & vbCr & Err.Description, _
            BTNS, "TBarBtnCopy_Click"
```

```
End Sub

Private Sub TBarBtnPaste_Click(ByVal CommandBarControl As Object, _
                              Handled As Boolean, _
                              CancelDefault As Boolean)

    ' Variables:
    Dim M          As String
    Dim SelVBComp  As VBComponent
    Dim CodeMod    As CodeModule
    Dim Designer   As VBForm

    On Error GoTo EH

    ' Shorten object expression (faster and more readable).
    Set SelVBComp = VBE.SelectedVBComponent

    ' Don't paste controls/code if:
    ' * No module is selected
    ' * Module's designer is not open.
    If SelVBComp Is Nothing Then Exit Sub
    If Not SelVBComp.HasOpenDesigner Then Exit Sub

    ' Shorten object expressions (faster and more readable).
    Set Designer = SelVBComp.Designer
    Set CodeMod = SelVBComp.CodeModule

    ' Can't paste controls/code under certain conditions:
    If Not Designer.CanPaste Then
        M = "Can't paste if no controls on Clipboard."
        Util.ShowMsg M, BTNS, App.Title
        Exit Sub
    ElseIf SelVBComp Is mSelVBComp And mLastOper = aiCopy Then
        M = "Can't paste onto same designer that was copied from."
        Util.ShowMsg M, BTNS, App.Title
        Exit Sub
    End If

    ' Paste controls from Clipboard and code from storage,
    ' set flag, and change Undo button's tooltip:
    Designer.Paste
    CodeMod.AddFromString mCode
    mLastOper = aiPaste
    TBarBtns(aiUndo).ToolTipText = "Undo Paste"
    Exit Sub

EH:
```

```
Util.ShowMsg "Error " & Err & vbCr & Err.Description, _
             BTNS, "TBarBtnPaste_Click"

End Sub
```

Changing TabIndex And Index Settings

The code contained in the **frmTabIndex** and **frmIndex** forms that supports the ability to change **TabIndex** or **Index** settings of controls by dragging and dropping items in the lists on the forms is pretty complex. I don't have room in this chapter or book to analyze it in depth. If you display and experiment with the forms, you'll see what they do. Notice their interactive nature and how, if you change a **TabIndex** or **Index** property setting in the Properties window, the change is immediately reflected in the lists; and, vice versa, if you make a drag-and-drop change in the lists, it is reflected in the Properties window.

The entire Controls Monitor add-in is yours as is; do with it as you wish. I've been using it myself while I've been writing the code for the last few chapters of this book and I find it to be a good productivity tool. Feel free to modify and enhance its code. I think it's a good illustration of the sort of event-driven add-in code that VB5's Extensibility object model supports, and I hope it will be the source of some good ideas for you.

Now it's time to move on to Part III of the book, which is devoted to an analysis of several different kinds of add-in case studies. In Part III, you'll learn how to create add-ins that:

- Generate various kinds of dialog boxes.

- Use the **CreateToolWindow** method to instantiate an ActiveX document object, a Programmer's Log that uses a VB Tool window as a container.

- Run an interactive, real-time, online tutorial that is not just a simulation but actually creates an ActiveX control and tests it right inside VB's IDE.

- Support code reuse/inheritance of different kinds.

Part

III

Case Studies
Of Add-Ins

ADD-INS AND DIALOG BOXES

7

Death is a Dialogue between,
The Spirit and the Dust.

—*Emily Dickinson*

The dialog box is one of the most familiar metaphors in Windows programming. VB developers, even in the "prehistoric" era of Visual Basic 1.0, have always been able to create and display dialog boxes with an ease that C and C++ programmers could only dream about. For example, the language has always included the **MsgBox** and **InputBox** functions to display or input simple kinds of information. The **Form** object's ability to act as a container of myriad control objects, without requiring a single line of code, is another early feature of VB that we all take for granted.

In the course of the evolution of the language, Microsoft's VB development team has continued to enhance the feature sets of the **MsgBox/Input** functions, adding new optional arguments and supporting new parameter values. And, with respect to the **Form** object, VB5 now enables you to create two new kinds of dialog box-related objects, listed on the next page.

- The **UserDocument** designer object, which you use to create a form or dialog box that can be hosted by any ActiveX component supporting the ActiveX document specification.

- The **Microsoft Forms ActiveX** designer object, which you use to create a form or dialog box that can run under both VB5 and VBA 5.0 (for example, in a Microsoft Office 97 application or some other application that hosts VBA).

In the most general sense of the word, a dialog is a conversation between two entities. In the epigraph at the beginning of this chapter, the poet, Emily Dickinson, does not say who gets the last word in the dialog between the spirit and the dust; given the mysterious and elusive nature of the human spirit, death's victory probably should not be taken for granted. In the case of a Windows dialog box, the user always gets the last word, typically by clicking OK to effect the terms of the dialog or clicking Cancel to terminate the dialog without taking action. However, in the ongoing evolution of Visual Basic, you can be certain that there will be no last word when it comes to the feature set that enables the creation of dialog boxes, because Microsoft will continue to enhance the language's dialog box-related syntax.

Chapter 7 provides two case studies of add-ins that are related to the creation of dialog boxes and that demonstrate the current state of the art. The first is the Dialog Builder add-in, which automates the writing of code required to display a message box or one of four kinds of common dialog boxes (Color, Open, Print, Save As). The second is the Tool Window or Programmer's Log add-in, which shows you how to create and encapsulate an ActiveX document within an add-in and then display the document's dialog box within a VB Tool window.

The Dialog Builder Add-In

In addition to the new features mentioned earlier in this chapter, VB5 supports one other new dialog box-related capability you should be aware of. When you select Project|Add Form, the Add Form dialog box is displayed. You can then double-click on any of its icons (for example, About Dialog) and add a predefined dialog box of the specified kind—complete with controls and code—to the active project. The FRM modules for these predefined dialog boxes are contained on the VB path \TEMPLATE\FORMS.

Besides being good templates that will increase your productivity when creating these kinds of dialog boxes, these FRM modules contain some interesting code. For example, the About Dialog's frmAbout module contains a **Function** named **GetKeyValue** that shows you how to convert a DWORD Windows registry entry to a **String**.

The Dialog Builder add-in (Creating VB5 Add-Ins: Dialog Builder) takes another approach to improving your productivity when creating certain kinds of dialog boxes. Instead of relying on predefined FRM modules, it allows you to select the kind of dialog box you want to display; in the case of a message box, it lets you specify all of the possible combinations of arguments and parameters you can use with the **MsgBox** function. Then it inserts into the active project the appropriate procedural code needed to create the dialog box and a code snippet that illustrates how to call the procedure and display the dialog box.

How The Dialog Builder Works

When you connect/run the Dialog Builder add-in, it initially displays the dialog box shown in Figure 7.1.

If you check the Message option and click OK, the add-in displays the Build Message Box dialog box shown in Figure 7.2.

If you make the selections shown in Figure 7.2 and click OK, the advisory message box shown in Figure 7.3 is displayed. Assuming that you want to continue and click on OK, the Dialog Builder then:

- Parses your selections.

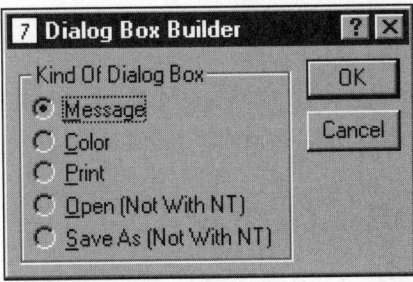

Figure 7.1
Dialog Builder add-in's initial form.

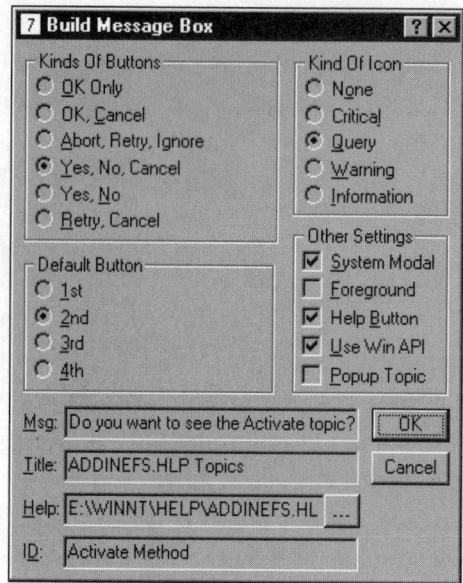

Figure 7.2
Dialog Builder's Build Message Box form.

- Inserts the code snippet required to call **MsgBox** in the selected code module and procedure, as in the example in Listing 7.1. (Please note that I manually added the line-continuation characters so the code would fit on a book-sized page.)

- Adds a BAS module to the active project that contains the code in Listing 7.2.

 The Dialog Builder only displays the advisory message shown in Figure 7.3 when you check the Use Win API option. It does so because it wants you to be aware that it must add a BAS module to your project to handle the **AddressOf** operator required by the Windows API function **MessageBoxIndirect**. If you don't check Use Win API, the Dialog Builder uses VB's **MsgBox** function and does not need to add a BAS module to the project.

MsgBox Code Created By The Dialog Builder

If you go through the steps in the previous section and execute the code in Listing 7.1, it calls the **MsgBox** function in Listing 7.2; in turn, **MsgBox** and

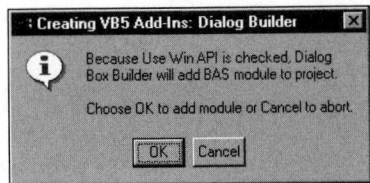

Figure 7.3
Advisory message box displayed by Dialog Builder.

its associated procedures display the message box shown in Figure 7.4. If you click the Help button on the message box, you will see that calling the Windows API function **MessageBoxIndirect** enables you to display a Help topic by keyword instead of just by context ID number (as VB's **MsgBox** function limits you).

You can learn about the rest of the capabilities of the Build Message Box dialog box by clicking the What's This? Help button on the right side of its title bar. Then click the control on the dialog box for which you want context-sensitive Help. For example, the popup Help topic for the button with three dots on it says that it "displays common dialog box that enables you to specify path and name of Help file that is used when you click Help button on message box."

LISTING 7.1   CODE TO CALL MsgBox FUNCTION.

```
Private Sub Command1_Click()

    Dim Button As Integer

    Button = MsgBox("Do you want to see the Activate topic?", _
          20771, "ADDINEFS.HLP Topics", _
          "E:\WINNT\HELP\ADDINEFS.HLP", _
          "Activate Method")

End Sub
```

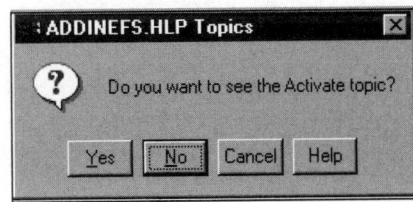

Figure 7.4
Message box displayed by code in Listings 7.1 and 7.2.

LISTING 7.2   BAS MODULE CODE FOR WIN API MSGBOX.

```
' Module-level variables:
Private mHelpFile     As String    ' Path/name of .HLP file
Private mContextStr   As String    ' Keyword in .HLP file
Private mPopup        As Boolean   ' Is Help topic a popup?
Private mContextNbr   As Long      ' Context ID # of Help topic
Private mOwner        As Long      ' Dialog box that Help
                                   ' window belongs to


' User-defined data types for DLL functions:
Private Type MSGBOXPARAMS
    Size As Long
    Owner As Long
    Inst As Long
    Prompt As String
    Title As String
    Buttons As Long
    Icon As String
    Context As Long
    CallBack As Long
    LangID As Long
End Type


' DLL Functions:
Private Declare Function MessageBoxIndirect& Lib "USER32" _
                    Alias "MessageBoxIndirectA" _
                    (Params As MSGBOXPARAMS)
Private Declare Function WinHelp& Lib "USER32" _
                    Alias "WinHelpA" _
                    (ByVal HWnd&, ByVal HelpFile$, _
                    ByVal Cmd&, ByVal Info As Any)


Function ProcAddress(X As Long) As Long

    ' ************************************************************
    ' Purpose: Function call associated with AddressOf operator
    '          used in ShowMsg procedure.
    '
    ' Called:  Internally from ShowMsg procedure.
    '
    ' Notes:   AddressOf operator causes address of procedure it
    '          precedes to be passed to API function that
    '          expects function pointer at that position in
    '          argument list. However, AddressOf can only be used
    '          from within function call. So, given how
    '          AddressOf is used in MsgBox procedure, you need
```

```
'                to call associated function like ProcAddress, which
'                exists only to return parameter that it is passed.
' ************************************************************

    ProcAddress = X

End Function

Function MsgBox(Prompt As String, _
               Optional Buttons As Long = 0, _
               Optional Title As String = "", _
               Optional HelpFile As String = "", _
               Optional Context, _
               Optional Popup As Boolean = False)


    ' Variables:
    Dim Dlg As MSGBOXPARAMS

    On Error GoTo EH

    ' Set Help-related parameters for message box:
    If HelpFile <> "" And Not IsMissing(Context) Then
        If Not Buttons And vbMsgBoxHelpButton Then
            Buttons = Buttons + vbMsgBoxHelpButton
        End If

        mHelpFile = HelpFile
        mPopup = Popup
        mOwner = Screen.ActiveForm.HWnd

        If VarType(Context) = vbInteger Or _
           VarType(Context) = vbLong Then
            mContextNbr = Context
            mContextStr = ""
        ElseIf VarType(Context) = vbString Then
            mContextStr = Context
        End If

    End If

    ' Set elements of user-defined data type used
    ' by Windows API function MessageBoxIndirect:
    With Dlg

        ' Size data type and set owner:
        .Size = LenB(Dlg)
        .Owner = Screen.ActiveForm.HWnd
```

```
        ' Set other parameters:
        .Prompt = Prompt
        .Buttons = Buttons

        If Len(Title) <> 0 Then
           .Title = Title
        Else
           .Title = App.Title
        End If

        ' Pass address of procedure to be called back to
        ' by Windows API function MessageBoxIndirect, if
        ' Help button on message box is clicked:
        .CallBack = ProcAddress(AddressOf ShowHelpTopic)

    End With

    MsgBox = MessageBoxIndirect(Dlg)

EH:
    If Err <> False Then MsgBox = False

End Function

Sub ShowHelpTopic()

    ' Constants for Windows API functions:
    Const HELP_CONTEXT = &H1
    Const HELP_KEY = &H101
    Const HELP_CONTEXTPOPUP = &H8

    ' Display Help topic by calling Windows API function—
    ' * Normal jump topic:
    If Not mPopup And mContextStr = "" Then
       WinHelp mOwner, mHelpFile, HELP_CONTEXT, mContextNbr

    ' * Topic associated with keyword:
    ElseIf mContextStr <> "" Then
       WinHelp mOwner, mHelpFile, HELP_KEY, mContextStr

    ' * Popup topic (first argument cannot
    '   be zero when displaying popup):
    ElseIf mPopup Then
       WinHelp mOwner, mHelpFile, HELP_CONTEXTPOPUP, mContextNbr
    End If

End Sub
```

MsgBox Code In The Dialog Builder

The source code in the Dialog Builder that parses the various combinations of message box arguments and parameters is where the "heavy lifting" for this add-in is done. It is found in the **cmdOK_Click** event procedure of **frmMsgBox** in BUILDDLG.VBP, as shown in Listing 7.3. The syntax of the code is pretty straightforward. However, there are three important general points to note about how the **cmdOK_Click** procedure works.

First, almost all add-in code is based on the assumption that a certain configuration of projects/components/members currently exists in VB's IDE. Bad things can happen to a good developer unless you invest the time and effort required to handle all possible errors or exceptions that can occur related to a given add-in's functionality. In the **cmdOK_Click** procedure, no fewer than seven kinds of validations are performed and advisory messages are displayed if some parameter or interdependent parameters are invalid.

Second, although I use VB-intrinsic constants in the Dialog Builder's source code when reading **MsgBox** *Button* parameters, the add-in generates code that uses a numeric value (for example, the number 20771 in Listing 7.1). It is possible, of course, to add another option to the Build Message Box form that would let the developer select intrinsic constants or not. You would then have to add more code to the **cmdOK_Click** procedure to handle this variable and substitute the individual intrinsic constants (added together) for the numeric value. I must confess that the main reason I didn't do this myself was that the deadline for finishing this book and receiving the second half of my advance was bearing down on me.

Third, in all the case study add-ins in Part III of this book, before I insert a procedure into a code module, I first run some code like the following statements

```
For Each VBComp In VBE.ActiveVBProject.VBComponents
   For Each Member In VBComp.CodeModule.Members
      If Member.Name = "MsgBox" And _
         Member.Type = vbext_mt_Method Then
            GoTo InsertCall
      End If
   Next Member
Next VBComp
```

to make sure the procedure doesn't already exist. Granted, it wouldn't hurt anything to insert a duplicate procedure. All that happens is that VB displays a Compile error (Ambiguous name detected: 'Procedure name') and the developer has to remove the redundant procedure. However, I feel that it's just common courtesy to prevent this sort of thing from happening in the first place.

LISTING 7.3   cmdOK_Click EVENT PROCEDURE OF MESSAGE BOX BUILDER.

```
Private Sub cmdOK_Click()

    ' Variables:
    Dim M          As String
    Dim C          As String
    Dim Title      As String
    Dim Msg        As String
    Dim HelpBtn    As Boolean
    Dim IDNbr      As Boolean
    Dim HelpPopup  As Boolean
    Dim JustOKBtn  As Boolean
    Dim IsMsgBox   As Boolean
    Dim B          As Long
    Dim Buttons    As Long
    Dim BegLine    As Long
    Dim CodeMod    As CodeModule
    Dim BASMod     As CodeModule
    Dim Member     As Member
    Dim BASComp    As VBComponent
    Dim VBComp     As VBComponent

    If VBE.SelectedVBComponent Is Nothing Then
        M = "Can't insert MsgBox code" & vbCr
        M = M & "unless component is selected."
        Util.ShowMsg M, BTNS, App.Title
        Exit Sub
    End If

    ' Build initial parameters for message box statement:
    Title = txtTitle
    Msg = txtMsg
    B = mBtnsConfig + mKindOfIcon + mDefBtn
    If chkSysModal = vbChecked Then B = B + vbSystemModal
    If chkForeground = vbChecked Then B = B + vbMsgBoxSetForeground
```

```
' Validate Help button parameters:
If chkHelpBtn = vbChecked Then

    ' Don't process if filename or ID parameters are missing:
    If Len(txtHelpFile) = 0 Or Len(txtHelpID) = 0 Then
       M = "If Help button is checked, you must" & vbCr
       M = M & "also specify Help file and context ID."
       Util.ShowMsg M, BTNS, App.Title
       Exit Sub
    End If

    HelpBtn = True
    B = B + vbMsgBoxHelpButton

    ' If context ID is number:
    If Val(txtHelpID) > -1 And txtHelpID <> "0" Then
       If Val(txtHelpID) > 0 Then

           ' Turn on IDNbr flag.
           IDNbr = True

           ' If Popup is checked, turn on its flag.
           If chkPopup Then HelpPopup = True

       Else
           If chkAPI = vbUnchecked Then
               M = "If Help context ID is string," & vbCr
               M = M & "Use Win API must be checked."
               Util.ShowMsg M, BTNS, App.Title
               Exit Sub
           End If
       End If
    End If
End If

' Validate Help popup parameters:
If chkPopup = vbChecked Then
    If chkHelpBtn = vbUnchecked Then
        M = "If Popup topic is checked," & vbCr
        M = M & "Help button must be checked."
        Util.ShowMsg M, BTNS, App.Title
        Exit Sub
    ElseIf chkAPI = vbUnchecked Then
        M = "If Popup topic is checked," & vbCr
        M = M & "Use Win API must be checked."
        Util.ShowMsg M, BTNS, App.Title
        Exit Sub
```

```
        ElseIf Not IDNbr Then
            M = "If Popup topic is checked," & vbCr
            M = M & "context ID must be a number."
            Util.ShowMsg M, BTNS, App.Title
            Exit Sub
        End If
End If

' If it's just OK button (that is, no need
' to read returned value), turn on flag:
If optButton(0) Then JustOKBtn = True

If JustOKBtn Then
    C = "    MsgBox """
    C = C & Msg
Else
    C = "    Dim Button As Integer" & vbCr
    C = C & "    Button = MsgBox("""
    C = C & Msg
End If

' * Prompt/Buttons/Title arguments:
C = C & """, " & B
C = C & ", """
C = C & Title & ""

' * Prompt/Buttons/Title/HelpFile/Context arguments:
If HelpBtn And IDNbr Then
    C = C & """, """
    C = C & txtHelpFile & """, " & txtHelpID
    If HelpPopup Then C = C & ", " & True

ElseIf HelpBtn And Not IDNbr Then
    C = C & """, """
    C = C & txtHelpFile & ""
    C = C & """, """
    C = C & txtHelpID & ""
End If

' Get current insertion point in module:
Set CodeMod = VBE.SelectedVBComponent.CodeModule
CodeMod.CodePane.GetSelection BegLine, 0, 0, 0

' If using Windows API MsgBox function:
If chkAPI = vbChecked Then
```

```
        ' Check if Win API MsgBox code already is in project:
        For Each VBComp In VBE.ActiveVBProject.VBComponents
            For Each Member In VBComp.CodeModule.Members
                If Member.Name = "MsgBox" And _
                    Member.Type = vbext_mt_Method Then
                        GoTo InsertCall
                End If
            Next Member
        Next VBComp

        M = "Because Use Win API is checked, Dialog" & vbCr
        M = M & "Box Builder will add BAS module to project."
        M = M & vbCr & vbCr
        M = M & "Choose OK to add module or Cancel to abort."
        Buttons = vbOKCancel + vbInformation + vbSystemModal
        If Util.ShowMsg(M, Buttons, App.Title) = vbCancel Then
            Exit Sub
        End If

        ' Add BAS module and get reference to its code module:
        Set BASComp = VBE.ActiveVBProject. _
                    VBComponents.Add(vbext_ct_StdModule)
        Set BASMod = BASComp.CodeModule

        ' Get code from DLGBUILD.TXT and add it to module:
        BASMod.InsertLines BASMod.CountOfDeclarationLines + 1, _
                    GetCode("' Module-level variables", "End Sub")

    End If

InsertCall:

    ' Append necessary characters if MsgBox called as function:
    If Not JustOKBtn Then
        If HelpBtn And IDNbr Then
            C = C & ")"
        Else
            C = C & """)"
        End If
    End If

    ' Insert message box code.
    CodeMod.InsertLines BegLine, C & vbCr

End Sub
```

Other Dialog Builder Capabilities

Sometimes you may only require a plain-vanilla version of one of the common dialog boxes and, thus, may not want to use the **CommonDialog** ActiveX control (and the extra memory it requires). It is possible to display most of the common dialog boxes by directly calling certain Windows API functions. The code in the Dialog Builder add-in that does this is shown in Listing 7.4. Except in the case of the Color dialog box, this code is skeletal in nature.

It should be clear, after seeing earlier in this chapter the degree of customization that is possible with VB's **MsgBox** function and the Windows API function **MessageBoxIndirect**, that you could customize the common dialog boxes by adding additional forms to the Dialog Builder. These forms and their controls would accept developer input to specify the various parameters associated with the display of the Open, Print, and Save As dialog boxes. In addition, you might be able to develop a simple workaround to get the code for the Open and Save As dialog boxes to work under Windows NT; however, I've never run across such a workaround in any VB book or magazine article.

 One essential difference to note about how the Dialog Builder generates message box code vs. common dialog box code is that the common dialog box code is contained in an external TXT file while the message box code is contained inside the add-in itself.

LISTING 7.4   cmdOK_Click EVENT PROCEDURE OF COMMON DIALOG BUILDER.

```
Private Sub cmdOK_Click()

    ' Variables:
    Dim M               As String
    Dim MbrName         As String
    Dim BegGen1         As String
    Dim EndGen1         As String
    Dim BegCall         As String
    Dim EndCall         As String
    Dim NumOrigLines    As Integer
    Dim NumLinesAdded   As Long
    Dim BegLine         As Long
    Dim CodeMod         As CodeModule
    Dim Member          As Member
```

```
' Build message box using another form:
If opt(aiMsg) Then
    Hide
    frmMsgBox.Show
    Exit Sub
End If


' Open and Save As Win API functions don't work with NT:
If opt(aiOpen) Or opt(aiSaveAs) Then
    If Util.IsWinNT Then
        M = "Can't insert common dialog code" & vbCr
        M = M & "for Open or Save As options when" & vbCr
        M = M & "you are running VB under Win NT."
        Util.ShowMsg M, BTNS, App.Title
        Exit Sub
    End If
End If


If VBE.SelectedVBComponent Is Nothing Then
    M = "Can't insert common dialog code" & vbCr
    M = M & "unless component is selected."
    Util.ShowMsg M, BTNS, App.Title
    Exit Sub
End If


' Get current insertion point and number
' of General declaration lines in module:
Set CodeMod = VBE.SelectedVBComponent.CodeModule
CodeMod.CodePane.GetSelection BegLine, 0, 0, 0
NumOrigLines = CodeMod.CountOfLines


' Set start and stop points in text file containing code:
If opt(aiColor) Then
    MbrName = "GetColor"
    BegGenl = "CHOOSECOLOR"
    EndGenl = "As CHOOSECOLOR"
    BegCall = "Color common dialog:"
    EndCall = "End If"
ElseIf opt(aiPrint) Then
    MbrName = "GetPrintInfo"
    BegGenl = "PRINTDLG"
    EndGenl = "As PRINTDLG"
    BegCall = "Print common dialog:"
    EndCall = "End If"
ElseIf opt(aiOpen) Then
    MbrName = "GetOpenFileName"
    BegGenl = "OPENFILENAME"
```

```
        EndGenl = "As OPENFILENAME"
        BegCall = "Open common dialog:"
        EndCall = "End If"
    ElseIf opt(aiSaveAs) Then
        MbrName = "GetSaveFileName"
        BegGenl = "SAVEFILENAME"
        EndGenl = "As SAVEFILENAME"
        BegCall = "Save As common dialog:"
        EndCall = "End If"
    End If


    ' Prevent insertion of same declaration twice:
    For Each Member In CodeMod.Members
        If Member.Name = MbrName Then GoTo JustAddCall
    Next Member


    ' Insert General declarations:
    CodeMod.InsertLines CodeMod.CountOfDeclarationLines + 1, _
                    GetCode(BegGenl, EndGenl)

JustAddCall:

    ' Insert calling code:
    NumLinesAdded = CodeMod.CountOfLines - NumOrigLines - 1
    CodeMod.InsertLines BegLine + NumLinesAdded, _
                    GetCode(BegCall, EndCall)

End Sub
```

The Programmer's Log Add-In

As I mentioned in Chapter 3, I definitely wanted to include an add-in that demonstrates VB5's capability to host an ActiveX document. When you create a typical add-in, the dialog boxes it displays are Visual Basic forms by default. While this is fine in most cases, you may occasionally want an add-in dialog box to act as other windows in VB do and dock with other IDE windows. The way to create a dialog box like this is to use an ActiveX document and the **CreateToolWindow** method of the Extensibility object library.

CreateToolWindow is a method of the **Windows** collection that creates a new Tool window in VB's IDE to contain an ActiveX document object that is encapsulated in an add-in. The **Window** object returned by **CreateToolWindow** is, unlike the normal modal or modeless form that an add-in can display, an item in the **Windows** collection. This means that the window is dockable and has all the other properties and methods associated with a **Window** object.

When you connect/run the Programmer's Log add-in (Creating VB5 Add-Ins: Tool Window), it adds to VB's IDE a text editor that you can use as a personal programming log. The Programmer's Log is created as either a docked (MDI interface) or undocked (SDI interface) window, depending on the current setting of SDI Development Environment on the Advanced tab of VB's Options dialog box. An undocked Programmer's Log dialog box is shown in Figure 7.5. For a picture of the Programmer's Log dialog box as it appears when it is docked to VB's IDE, see Figure 3.11 in Chapter 3.

Creating An ActiveX Document

Actually creating an ActiveX document with VB is no more difficult than creating a normal form. If you open the source code for TOOLWND.VBP project, you'll see that the designer for a **UserDocument** object looks exactly the same as the designer for a **Form** object, except for its control-menu icon. You can add the same kinds of controls to it as to a form except that you cannot place embedded objects or an OLE container control on it. Inside its code module, everything appears the same, except that in the Object drop-down box, its item is referred to as UserDocument instead of Form.

If you study the controls and code for the Programmer's Log ActiveX document, you'll see that they are all basically the same ones you would use on a **Form** object. After you have the ActiveX document the way you want it, you simply compile it inside the add-in and test its functionality as you would that of any form in an add-in.

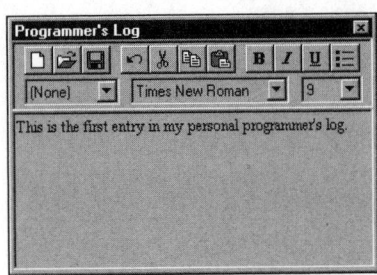

Figure 7.5
Undocked Programmer's Log dialog box.

The other major difference between the capabilities of the **UserDocument** and **Form** objects is the events that they support. The **UserDocument** object has most, but not all, of the events that are found on a **Form** object. The events present on a **Form** that are not found on a **UserDocument** include: **Activate, Deactivate, LinkClose, LinkError, LinkExecute, LinkOpen, Load, QueryUnload,** and **Unload.** Events present on a **UserDocument** but not found on a **Form** object include: **AsycReadComplete, EnterFocus, ExitFocus, Hide, InitProperties, ReadProperties, Scroll, Show,** and **WriteProperties.**

Displaying An ActiveX Document

To display an ActiveX document in an add-in, you write code in the **OnConnection** method of the **IDTExtensibility** object to call the **CreateToolWindow** method and to add a menu item to VB's View menu. As the straightforward code in Listing 7.5 suggests, it's actually quite easy to use **CreateToolWindow.** For more detailed information about how the method and its arguments work, see its topic in the *Dictionary* section of this book.

LISTING 7.5   CODE TO DISPLAY PROGRAMMER'S LOG TOOL WINDOW.

```
Private Sub IDTExtensibility_OnConnection _
          (ByVal VBInst As Object, _
           ByVal ConnectMode As vbext_ConnectMode, _
           ByVal AddInInst As AddIn, _
           Custom() As Variant)

    .   .   .   .

    ' If connected from Add-In Manager:
    ElseIf ConnectMode = vbext_cm_AfterStartup Then
       DisplayLog
    End If

End Sub

Private Sub DisplayLog()

   ' Variables:
   Dim SubKey         As String
   Dim ActXDocGuid    As String
```

```
    Dim ActXDocProgID   As String
    Dim HWndSubKey      As Long
    Dim UserDoc         As Object

    ' Read Windows registry and get GUID of ActiveX
    ' document class that new Tool window is to contain:
    ActXDocProgID = "ToolWnd.ProgLog"
    SubKey = ActXDocProgID & "\Clsid"
    HWndSubKey = Reg.OpenSubKey(aiKTClasses, SubKey)
    ActXDocGuid = Reg.GetValue(HWndSubKey)
    Reg.CloseSubKey HWndSubKey

    ' Create Tool window and instantiate ActiveX document.
    Set mProgLogWnd = VBE.Windows.CreateToolWindow _
                    (VBE.Addins("ToolWnd.Connect"), _
                    ActXDocProgID, "Programmer's Log", _
                    ActXDocGuid, UserDoc)

    ' Must explicitly display tool window.
    mProgLogWnd.Visible = True
    mProgLogWnd.SetFocus

    If VBE.DisplayModel = vbext_dm_MDI Then
        VBE.MainWindow.LinkedWindows.Add mProgLogWnd
    End If

    SetAIMenuItem "P&rogrammer's Log"

End Sub

Private Sub SetAIMenuItem(Caption As String)

    ' Variables:
    Dim Mnu As Office.CommandBarControl

    ' Create add-in's menu item with separator bar and icon:
    Set Mnu = VBE.CommandBars("Menu Bar").Controls("View")
    Set mMenuItem = Cmd.AddMenuItem _
                    (VBE:=VBE, _
                    Menu:=Mnu, _
                    Caption:=Caption, _
                    Separator:=True, _
                    Bitmap:=App.Path & "\TOOLWND.BMP")

    ' Make add-in respond to menu item's Click event.
    Set CommandBar = VBE.Events.CommandBarEvents(mMenuItem)

End Sub
```

Closing/Opening An ActiveX Document

To close an open ActiveX document's Tool window, a VB developer can click the Close icon on the right side of the title bar. To allow the developer to reopen the Tool window, a short event procedure such as

```
Private Sub CommandBar_Click _
                (ByVal CommandBarControl As Object, _
                Handled As Boolean, _
                CancelDefault As Boolean)

    If Not mProgLogWnd.Visible Then mProgLogWnd.Visible = True
    mProgLogWnd.SetFocus

End Sub
```

does the trick. This event procedure is connected to the menu item created in Listing 7.5. Finally, when the developer disconnects the add-in, statements like

```
If mProgLogWnd.Visible Then mProgLogWnd.Close
mMenuItem.Delete
```

in the **OnDisconnection** method of the **IDTExtensibility** object close the Tool window and delete its menu item. Feel free to experiment with this Programmer's Log (Tool Window) add-in and enhance it as you wish. It supports most of the conventional capabilities of a text editor except the ability to print (you can do that easily enough from Windows's WordPad).

This example of the Programmer's Log demonstrates how easy it is to create an ActiveX document in an add-in and display it within a Tool window container. Another example of this ActiveX document/Tool window technology is the VB Tab Order Window add-in that ships with VB5; you can find it on the path SAMPLES\COMPTOOL\ADDINS\TABORDER.

In the long run, Microsoft is counting on its ActiveX document technology to promote document-centric computing and to serve as another kind of reusable component. According to Visual Basic Books Online, the only applications that can currently function as ActiveX document containers are VB5 (inside a Tool window), Internet Explorer 3.0, and Office Binder 1.0. However, given the growing market share that Microsoft's ActiveX/COM/DCOM technologies enjoy, it's obvious that ActiveX documents have a bright future.

THE ACTIVEX CONTROL TUTOR ADD-IN

8

It is the supreme art of the teacher to awaken joy in creative expression and knowledge.

—Albert Einstein

As I mentioned in the *Acknowledgments* section of this book, I earn my daily bread these days by teaching VB. Whether it is classroom instruction at the University of Washington, writing books and magazine articles, or consulting for companies in the Seattle area, the common thread that knits all these activities together for me is the satisfaction that I gain from teaching others about what I love to do. For me, VB is not just a programming language; it is an infinite game whose rules and moves are always expanding. I never grow tired of playing with VB.

One day in the course of writing this book, it dawned on me that it should be possible to create a really slick online VB tutor or instructor with an add-in. Visual Basic 4.0 actually included an online tutorial on its Help menu titled *Learning Microsoft Visual Basic 4.0*. It was pretty primitive and basically was nothing more than a set of Help topics arranged in a certain order. Because online tutorials are becoming more sophisticated and commercially viable, Microsoft decided not to include one at all with VB5. Instead you must now shell out $99 to Microsoft Press to purchase the *Mastering Microsoft Visual Basic 5* CD-ROM.

The content and mode of presentation (slick, multimedia-enhanced topic pages) of the *Mastering Microsoft Visual Basic 5* CD-ROM are quite good. However, its one major defect is that although it bills itself as interactive, it is still just a simulation and doesn't actually do anything! When the student or developer is done with the tutorial, he or she hasn't actually built anything, hasn't participated in a real sequence of programming steps within VB's IDE.

This chapter shows you how to create what I refer to as a Tutor add-in (Creating VB5 Add-Ins: Tutor Demo). Adhering to the Wizard format, this Tutor add-in leads a VB developer through the process of creating a simple ActiveX control, one that adds an icon for an application to the Windows Taskbar tray. Each step that you tell the Tutor add-in to execute actually takes effect within VB; that is, a project is started, modules are loaded, controls are added, properties are set, code is written, the project is compiled, a test script/project is created, and so on. You can see all these things happening, and at any point in the process, you can go into a VB code module and review the code that the Tutor add-in just wrote, or open a VB dialog box and see the setting that was just made.

In addition to demonstrating how to create an ActiveX control, this chapter's Tutor add-in also shows you how to:

- Create an efficient, five-form Wizard that, even when compiled to native code, results in a DLL file of only about 108K.

- Create a Windows RES file that contains the string and graphic resources used by an add-in.

- Determine which one of the five forms is currently displayed modelessly and make it the foreground window without displaying another instance of the initial form.

- Write reusable procedures to add code to and remove it from code modules.

- Get the handle of any of VB's IDE windows and use it to change that window's caption by calling the Windows API function **SetWindowText**. There are times that you might want to do this in order to call attention to an IDE window (for example, the Properties window) that your add-in is working with.

I'm very excited about the potential of this Tutor add-in approach as a teaching tool. When I finish writing this book, I hope to start on a new project (maybe an online CD-ROM tutorial) that expands on the capabilities of the Tutor add-in. I found the process of writing the code for this chapter's add-in to be more fun than writing any of the other code in the book.

Designing The Tutor Add-In

The Tutor add-in, whose source code is in TUTOR.VBP, is a simple project that contains the four modules described in Table 8.1. We need to take an in-depth look at the FRM and RES modules of the Tutor add-in's project in order to understand how this add-in is designed and works.

The Tutor's FRM Module

When you connect and run the Tutor add-in's Wizard, the first form it displays is shown in Figure 8.1.

TABLE 8.1

TUTOR ADD-IN'S MODULES.

Module Filename	Description
TUTOR.FRM	The add-in's only FRM module, whose properties and controls are reconfigured and redrawn each time another of the Wizard's five forms is displayed
TUTOR.RES	The add-in's resource file, which contains all the different settings for the **Caption**, **Icon**, and **Picture** properties of the **Form** object and its control objects
TUTOR.CLS	The add-in's connection class module that implements the **IDTExtensibility** object's interface
TUTOR.BAS	A skeletal BAS module that contains nothing but the **AddToINI** procedure needed to test the add-in

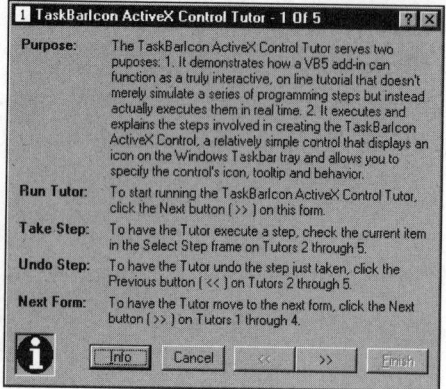

Figure 8.1
Tutor add-in's first Wizard form.

The design of the form in Figure 8.1 is straightforward. There are two sets of five **Label** controls, each set laid out from top to bottom. An **Image** control and five **CommandButton** controls are at the bottom of the form. You should note, too, that the settings of the **Icon** and **Caption** properties of the form reflect its position in the sequential order of the Wizard's forms.

As is the convention with Wizards, this initial form is meant primarily to orient the developer and provide general information about how the Tutor add-in works. Clicking the Info button displays an appropriate Help topic, clicking Cancel terminates the Tutor add-in and restores VB's IDE to its original state, and clicking the >> button displays the Wizard's next form, as shown in Figure 8.2.

Although the forms pictured in Figures 8.1 and 8.2 are actually the same **Form** object, the design of the form in Figure 8.2 is quite different from that of the form in Figure 8.1. The form in Figure 8.2 (and also forms 3 through 5) has the following controls:

- A single **Label** control at the top that describes the general purpose of the form

- A **Frame** control with the **Caption** Select Step, which contains six **CheckBox** controls

- Six **Label** controls on the right side of the form that describe what happens when you select the different **CheckBox** controls

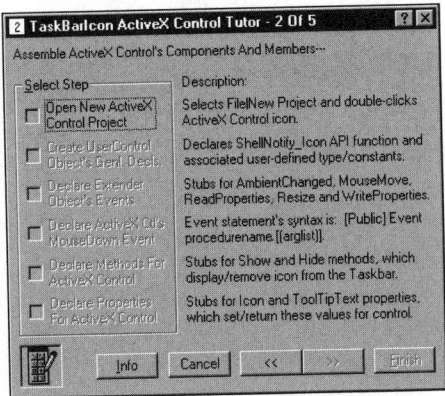

Figure 8.2
Tutor add-in's second Wizard form.

- The same **Image** control and five **CommandButton** controls that were at the bottom of the first form (although their settings and enabled states have changed)

As with all of the book's add-ins, clicking the What's This? Help button on the right of the title bar enables you to display a context-sensitive Help topic that describes what any control on the form does. The Tutor add-in allows you to do one of two things at any point on the Wizard forms 2 through 5: Either click on the enabled/current **CheckBox** control and execute the Tutor's next step or click on the << button and undo the step that you just executed. If you haven't yet executed the first step, clicking on << sends you back to the previous form. If you've executed the last step, the >> button is enabled so that you can click it and move to the next form.

Most of the essential procedural code that both handles the transition between forms and changes the visible appearance of each form is shown in Listing 8.1. The **SetIntroForm** procedure configures the **Visible** and **Enabled** property settings for the initial form. The **LoadResources** procedure reads the appropriate string and graphic resources from the add-in's RES file and sets the properties of the form's controls appropriately. The **SetTutorCaption**, **SetBegSteps**, and **SetEndSteps** procedures handle the other settings.

LISTING 8.1 PROCEDURES THAT CONFIGURE DIFFERENT TUTOR FORMS.

```
Private Sub SetIntroForm()

    ' Variables:
    Dim El     As Byte
    Dim Ctl    As Control

    ' Make all controls invisible on first form:
    For Each Ctl In Controls
        Ctl.Visible = False
    Next Ctl

    ' Make certain controls visible on first form:
    For El = aiCancel To aiInfo
        Cmd(El).Visible = True
    Next El
    imgBMP.Visible = True
    lblPurpose1.Visible = True
    lblPurpose2.Visible = True
    lblTakeStep1.Visible = True
    lblTakeStep2.Visible = True
    lblUndoStep1.Visible = True
    lblUndoStep2.Visible = True
    lblNextForm1.Visible = True
    lblNextForm2.Visible = True
    lblRunTutor1.Visible = True
    lblRunTutor2.Visible = True

    ' Enable/disable certain buttons on first form:
    Cmd(aiNext).Enabled = True
    Cmd(aiBack).Enabled = False

End Sub

Private Sub LoadResources()

    ' Variables:
    Dim Step       As Byte
    Dim Offset1    As Integer
    Dim Offset2    As Integer

    ' Set Tutor bitmap and icon:
    imgBMP = LoadResPicture(mTutorNbr, vbResBitmap)
    Icon = LoadResPicture(mTutorNbr + 1000, vbResIcon)
```

```vb
    ' Don't set captions for steps/descriptions for Tutor 1.
    If mTutorNbr = 1 Then Exit Sub

    Select Case mTutorNbr
        Case 2
            Offset1 = 20
            Offset2 = 200
        Case 3
            Offset1 = 30
            Offset2 = 300
        Case 4
            Offset1 = 40
            Offset2 = 400
        Case 5
            Offset1 = 50
            Offset2 = 500
    End Select

    ' Set appropriate captions for steps/descriptions:
    For Step = 1 To 6
        chk(Step).Caption = LoadResString(Step + Offset1)
        lbl(Step) = LoadResString(Step + Offset2)
    Next Step

    ' Set caption for heading:
    lblHeading = LoadResString(7 + Offset2)

End Sub

Private Sub SetTutorCaption()

    ' Set form's caption.
    Caption = "TaskBarIcon ActiveX Control Tutor - "
    Caption = Caption & mTutorNbr & " Of 5"

End Sub
Private Sub SetBegSteps()

    ' Variables:
    Dim Step As Byte

    ' Initialize status of check boxes:
    For Step = 1 To 6
        chk(Step) = vbUnchecked
        chk(Step).Enabled = False
    Next Step
```

```
    ' Initialize flag, enable first step, and disable Next button:
    mPrevStep = False
    chk(1).Enabled = True
    Cmd(aiNext).Enabled = False

End Sub

Private Sub SetEndSteps()

    ' Variables:
    Dim Step As Byte

    ' Reset ending status of check boxes, flag, and Next button:
    For Step = 1 To 6
        chk(Step) = vbChecked
        chk(Step).Enabled = False
    Next Step

    mPrevStep = 6
    Cmd(aiNext).Enabled = True

End Sub
```

The Tutor's RES Module

The Tutor add-in's resource module (TUTOR.RES) is the compiled binary file that contains the various string and graphic resources the **LoadResources** procedure reads. **LoadResources** uses VB's **LoadResString** and **LoadResPicture** functions to set the **Caption**, **Icon**, and **Picture** properties of the Tutor form and its controls to the values contained in TUTOR.RES. The advantages of creating a resource file and compiling it inside the add-in's DLL file (as opposed to reading string and graphics values from external files at runtime) are greater speed, fewer files to distribute, and more flexibility.

The source for TUTOR.RES is contained in the TUTOR.RC file, which is simply a text file with an .RC file extension. Snippets of the TUTOR.RC file, opened in Notepad, are shown in Figure 8.3. After I created this RC file, I ran the Microsoft Resource Compiler (RC.EXE) with the command line

```
C:\ADDINEFS\CHAPTER8\RC.EXE /r /fo TUTOR.RES TUTOR.RC
```

to create the TUTOR.RES file.

```
Tutor.rc - Notepad
File  Edit  Search  Help
STRINGTABLE DISCARDABLE

BEGIN
        //Tutor 2's Steps:
        21      "Open New ActiveX Control Project"
        22      "Create UserControl Object's Genl. Decls."
        23      "Declare Extender Object's Events"
        24      "Declare ActiveX Ctl's MouseDown Event"
        25      "Declare Methods For ActiveX Control"
        26      "Declare Properties For ActiveX Control"
END

//Icon for TUTOR.DLL:
APPICON      ICON    TUTOR.ICO

//Tutor 1 - 5's Bitmaps:
1           BITMAP PRELOAD TUTOR1.BMP
2           BITMAP PRELOAD TUTOR2.BMP
3           BITMAP PRELOAD TUTOR3.BMP
4           BITMAP PRELOAD TUTOR4.BMP
5           BITMAP PRELOAD TUTOR5.BMP

//Tutor 1 - 5's Icons:
1001        ICON DISCARDABLE TUTOR1.ICO
1002        ICON DISCARDABLE TUTOR2.ICO
1003        ICON DISCARDABLE TUTOR3.ICO
1004        ICON DISCARDABLE TUTOR4.ICO
1005        ICON DISCARDABLE TUTOR5.ICO
```

Figure 8.3
Portion of TUTOR.RC file.

You can find more information about creating these kinds of files on VB's CD-ROM in the file RESOURCE.TXT, which is located on the path TOOLS\RESOURCE. The associated files for the Microsoft Resource Compiler itself (RC.EXE, RC.HLP, and README.TXT) are also located on that path.

 There is a bug in the VB Add-In toolbar that causes it to display an error message (Error Loading Application) and fail to connect/run the Tutor add-in. This bug only appears when running the Tutor add-in in normal mode. If you run it in debug mode in a second instance of VB, the VB Add-In toolbar will connect/run the Tutor add-in correctly. I think this bug is related to the add-in's resource file and the fact that it has many other entries in it besides the single APPICON entry used in all the other resource files in this book's add-ins.

Other Design Considerations

Because the Tutor add-in is interactive in nature, all of its forms and message boxes are displayed modelessly. This is necessary so that the developer can select code modules in the Tutor's project to examine code, display VB dialog boxes to see that the Tutor add-in has changed settings, and so on. Because the forms and message boxes are modeless, there is nothing to prevent the developer from clicking the Tutor add-in's menu item and running another instance of the add-in.

This can be a problem even with a normal, one-form add-in, but the problem is magnified when you are dealing with a Wizard add-in with multiple forms. The way I handle this situation is with the **IsFormDisplayed** procedure in the CLS module of the add-in, shown in Listing 8.2. In Chapter 2, I showed how you could use a procedure similar to this to determine if a single form was displayed. However, in the case of the Tutor add-in, I'm dealing with five possible forms.

IsFormDisplayed uses the Windows API functions **GetWindowThread-ProcessId** and **GetCurrentThreadId** to compare the identifier of the VB thread that displayed any one of the five forms with the identifier of the VB thread that is running the add-in that called **IsFormDisplayed**. If the thread identifiers are the same, **IsFormDisplayed** brings the form that is already visible to the foreground by calling the Windows API function **SetForegroundWindow**. If none of the five forms is displayed, **IsFormDisplayed** returns zero and the add-in responds to the clicking of its menu item by displaying its initial form.

 In almost all of the other add-ins in this book, I have called the IsFormDisplayed method of the VBAI class library's Util object. In the Tutor add-in, I included the IsFormDisplayed procedure in the add-in itself. In fact, this is the only add-in other than the one in Chapter 1 that does not include a reference to the VBAI class library. I did not include this reference because I have been distributing standalone copies of this Tutor add-in on demonstration disks, and I wanted to minimize the number of files that I needed to include on the disks.

LISTING 8.2   ISFORMDISPLAYED PROCEDURE.

```
Private Function IsFormDisplayed() As Integer

    ' Variables:
    Dim ClsName        As String
    Dim Strs(1 To 5)   As String
```

```
Dim El          As Byte
Dim HWnd        As Long


' Assign captions to array:
For El = 1 To 5
    Strs(El) = "TaskBarIcon ActiveX Control Tutor - "
    Strs(El) = Strs(El) & El & " Of 5"
Next El


' Determine correct class name of VB form
' (it differs depending on run mode):
If IsBeingDebugged Then
    ClsName = "ThunderForm"
Else
    ClsName = "ThunderRT5Form"
End If


For El = 1 To 5

    ' Try to find add-in's form.
    HWnd = FindWindow(ClsName, Strs(El))

    ' If form is displayed and thread ID of VB instance that
    ' created form matches thread ID of current instance of
    ' VB, bring form to foreground and return True:
    If HWnd <> False Then
        If GetWindowThreadProcessId(HWnd, 0) = _
           GetCurrentThreadId Then
            SetForegroundWindow HWnd
            IsFormDisplayed = True
            Exit For
        End If
    End If

Next El

End Function
```

How The Tutor Add-In Works

One of the great things about the Tutor add-in as far as this book is concerned, is that it demonstrates so many of the language elements of the Extensibility object library. If you run this add-in in debug mode and single-step through the code for each of its steps, you can learn a lot about add-in development. As you check each of the Tutor add-in's steps on forms 2 through 5, it follows these general steps:

- Assembles the TaskBarIcon ActiveX control's project/module and declares its members (Form 2)

- Writes the procedural code for the members that are events and methods (Form 3)

- Sets the appropriate properties in the Properties window and writes custom property procedures (Form 4)

- Sets the TaskBarIcon ActiveX control's attributes, compiles/registers it, and loads a demonstration project to test it (Form 5)

The demonstration project's form, which the Tutor add-in automatically creates and runs, is shown in Figure 8.4. The icon for the ActiveX control on VB's Toolbox is shown in Figure 8.5. Click Show Icon on the demonstration form to

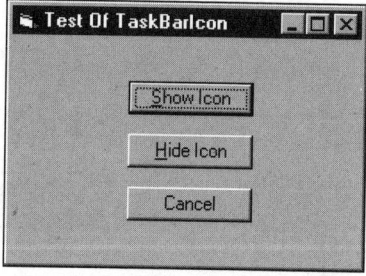

Figure 8.4
Demonstration form for TaskBarIcon ActiveX control.

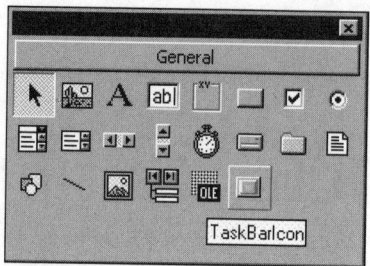

Figure 8.5
VB Toolbox with icon for TaskBarIcon ActiveX control.

add the icon to the Windows Taskbar tray; click Hide Icon to remove the icon from the Taskbar tray. If you move the mouse over the icon, the tooltip "Eureka! Demo Works" is displayed. If you click on the icon, the TaskBarIcon ActiveX control registers which mouse button was clicked on it and sends this information back to the container form.

Loading Code From TUTOR.TXT

All of the code that the Tutor add-in needs to create the TaskBarIcon ActiveX control is contained in the TUTOR.TXT file. I wrote a customized, sequential file-access procedure called **GetCode** (shown in Listing 8.3) to read TUTOR.TXT and return the specified code snippet. For example, a statement like

```
Code = GetCode("AmbientChanged", "End Sub")
```

returns the declaration of the **AmbientChanged** event procedure. **Code** is a **String** variable to which the returned code snippet is assigned. "AmbientChanged" and "End Sub" are the parameters passed to the arguments of **GetCode**. These parameters identify the opening and closing lines of the code snippet to be read and returned.

LISTING 8.3   GETCODE PROCEDURE.

```
Private Function GetCode(BegLine As String, _
                        EndLine As String) As String


   ' **********************************************************
   ' GetCode: Reads TXT file containing code and returns block
   '          that starts with specified unique line and
   '          ends with specified line.
   ' **********************************************************


   ' Variables:
   Dim M             As String
   Dim TargetStr     As String
   Dim OneLine       As String
   Dim ByteStr       As String * 1
   Dim FileNbr       As Integer
   Dim Byt           As Long
   Dim BegByte       As Long
   Dim EndByte       As Long
```

```
' Get unused file number and open file for sequential read:
On Error GoTo EH
FileNbr = FreeFile
Open mFile For Input Access Read As FileNbr

' Look for beginning string until end of file or it's found:
Do While Not EOF(FileNbr) And BegByte = False

    ' Assign one line to variable.
    Line Input #FileNbr, OneLine

    ' Beginning string is either in line or not (False).
    BegByte = InStr(OneLine, BegLine)

Loop

' Store first byte number of beginning string.
BegByte = Seek(FileNbr) - (Len(OneLine) + 3)
If BegByte = 0 Then BegByte = 1

' Look for ending string until end of file or it's found:
Do While Not EOF(FileNbr) And EndByte = False

    ' Assign one line to variable.
    Line Input #FileNbr, OneLine

    ' Ending string is either in line or not (False).
    EndByte = InStr(OneLine, EndLine)

Loop

' Store last byte number of ending string. ,
EndByte = Seek(FileNbr)

' If ending string is last line in
' file, adjust for end-of-file byte:
If EndByte > FileLen(mFile) Then
   EndByte = FileLen(mFile)

' Else adjust for normal end-of-line bytes:
Else
   EndByte = EndByte - 3
End If

' Close file and reopen for binary read:
Close FileNbr
```

```
FileNbr = FreeFile
Open mFile For Binary As FileNbr

' For each byte in file from previously recorded start-to-stop:
For Byt = BegByte To EndByte

    ' Get byte, convert it to string, and
    ' add it to string to be returned:
    Get FileNbr, Byt, ByteStr
    ByteStr = Chr$(Asc(ByteStr))
    TargetStr = TargetStr & ByteStr

Next Byt

' Clean up and return text found between
' beginning and ending strings:
Close FileNbr
GetCode = TargetStr
Exit Function

EH:

Close FileNbr
M = "Error " & Err & vbCr & Err.Description
MsgBox M, vbInformation + vbMsgBoxSetForeground, App.Title

End Function
```

Changing A VB IDE Window's Caption

Some of the Tutor add-in's steps (Steps 1, 2, and 3 on form 4) involve changing settings in the Properties window. In order to draw attention to the fact that this is happening, I temporarily change the caption of the Properties window's title bar to "**** CHANGING SETTING ****" by calling the Windows API function **SetWindowText**. Changing the caption is the easy part; what is more difficult to do is getting the handle of the Properties window, which **SetWindowText** requires as an argument.

As I explain in the *Dictionary* section of the book, the **HWnd** property of the **Window** object in the VBIDE class library does not work correctly. The only window in VB's IDE for which the **HWnd** property returns a valid value is the main window. If you want to get the handle of any of the other windows, you have to write a custom procedure that uses Windows API functions to do so.

Further complicating matters is that VB5's window structure behaves differently (parent vs. child windows) depending on whether VB's IDE is displayed in MDI or SDI mode. My solution to this problem was to write the **GetHWndProp** procedure shown in Listing 8.4. If you ever need to get the handle of one of VB's IDE windows, this procedure will reward your study.

LISTING 8.4   GETHWNDPROP PROCEDURE.

```
Private Function GetHWndProp()

   ' *****************************************************************
   ' GetHWndProp: Returns handle of VB's Properties window.
   ' *****************************************************************

   ' Constants for Windows API functions:
   Const GW_CHILD = 5
   Const GW_HWNDNEXT = 2

   ' Variables:
   Dim Caption        As String
   Dim Buff           As String * 256
   Dim ChildCaption   As String
   Dim TempCaption    As String
   Dim PropWndFound   As Boolean
   Dim HWndChild      As Long
   Dim HWndTemp       As Long
   Dim Window         As Window

   If VBE.DisplayModel = vbext_dm_MDI Then

      ' Get handle of VB's first child window.
      HWndChild = GetWindow(VBE.MainWindow.HWnd, GW_CHILD)

      ' Until all child windows are examined:
      Do Until HWndChild = False

         ' Get child's caption:
         GetWindowText HWndChild, Buff, Len(Buff)
         Caption = Trim(Left$(Buff, InStr(Buff, vbNullChar) - 1))

         ' If child is Properties window, return its handle
         ' (Properties window's parent is some frame window):
         If Left$(Caption, 10) = "Properties" Then
            GetHWndProp = HWndChild
            Exit Function
         End If
```

```
        HWndChild = GetWindow(HWndChild, GW_HWNDNEXT)

Loop

' If Properties window is floating free
' (that is, its parent is main window):
If Not PropWndFound Then

    ' Get its handle by going through Windows collection:
    For Each Window In VBE.Windows

        If Window.Type = vbext_wt_PropertyWindow Then

            Caption = Window.Caption

            ' Try to give Properties window
            ' focus and get handle returned:
            Window.SetFocus
            HWndTemp = GetForegroundWindow

            ' Check if handle returned is for Properties
            ' window (that is, it is floating window):
            GetWindowText HWndTemp, Buff, Len(Buff)
            TempCaption = Trim(Left$(Buff, InStr _
                            (Buff, vbNullChar) - 1))
            If TempCaption = Caption Then
                GetHWndProp = HWndTemp
                Exit Function
            End If

        End If

    Next Window
End If

ElseIf VBE.DisplayModel = vbext_dm_SDI Then

    For Each Window In VBE.Windows

        If Window.Type = vbext_wt_PropertyWindow Then

            ' Check if Properties window is floating free
            ' (that is, its parent is main window):
            Caption = Window.Caption

            ' Try to give Properties window
            ' focus and get handle returned:
```

```
        Window.SetFocus
        HWndTemp = GetForegroundWindow

        ' Check if handle returned is for Properties
        ' window (that is, it is floating window):
        GetWindowText HWndTemp, Buff, Len(Buff)
        TempCaption = Trim(Left$(Buff, InStr _
                        (Buff, vbNullChar) - 1))
        If TempCaption = Caption Then
          GetHWndProp = HWndTemp
          Exit Function
        End If

        ' Otherwise handle is for another frame window
        ' so get handle of frame's first child window.
        HWndChild = GetWindow(HWndTemp, GW_CHILD)

        ' Until all child windows are examined:
        Do Until HWndChild = False

          ' Get child's caption:
          GetWindowText HWndChild, Buff, Len(Buff)
          ChildCaption = Trim(Left$(Buff, InStr _
                          (Buff, vbNullChar) - 1))

          ' If child is Properties window:
          If ChildCaption = Caption Then
            GetHWndProp = HWndChild
            Exit Function
          End If

          HWndChild = GetWindow(HWndChild, GW_HWNDNEXT)

        Loop
      End If
    Next Window
  End If

End Function
```

Enhancing The Tutor Add-In

As I mentioned earlier in the chapter, I've recently been distributing standalone copies of the Tutor add-in and soliciting feedback from different people. I conceived this version of the Tutor add-in as only a prototype. Some suggestions that I've received for enhancing the interactive nature of this kind of add-in are:

- Using conditional branching to allow the developer some degree of choice as far as how a particular piece of functionality is implemented with code

- Using prompts that require the developer to actually type in some of the procedures (for example, one of the two procedures in a **Property Get** and **Property Let** pair of procedures)

- Testing code that a developer typed in to determine if a procedure or statement was validly entered

- Displaying multiple-choice or true-and-false questions that must be answered correctly before the Tutor add-in will continue

As I'm sure you realize at this point in the book, VB's add-in object model supports all of these possible enhancements. It's only a matter of my finding the time to add them, once I've finished this book. I hope that you enjoy playing with the TaskBarIcon ActiveX Control Tutor add-in and I welcome any suggestions that you might have to improve it. You can email me at 75521.3130@ compuserve.com.

THE CODE LIBRARIAN ADD-IN

9

Every library should try to be complete on something, if it were only the history of pinheads.

—Oliver Wendell Holmes

Ever since I was a child, libraries have fascinated me. At first, it was the few books that we had in our small home library. Then, when I went off to my family's parish grade school, it was the books in the modest library that the nuns maintained. One of the most exciting days in my life was when my mother first took me to the local branch of the public library, a couple blocks from our house, where I got my first library card and was amazed at the sheer number of books there. Soon enough, my mother must have realized she had "created a monster" because I can remember almost immediately starting to badger her about why I wasn't allowed in the Adults section.

I think my fascination with libraries is rooted in its basic nature. A library is a place that stores hard-won knowledge, and anyone can use it again and again without having to pay. Even though I was a very good student as a boy, I quickly realized how hard it is to learn anything from scratch. It always seemed easier to learn something new if you could find a book that had a good example or explanation. Quickly locating a book that had the

answer to the problem at hand was the trick to master. Working the card catalog was, at first, a necessary evil, but after I understood how the Dewey decimal
classification system was designed, leafing through the card catalog became,
dare I say it, almost fun.

Fast forward 40 years in my life. In one sense, little has changed, and yet everything is different. I still love libraries, but now, more often than not, it's a virtual
library, which I access through the Internet and peruse using one of the many
available search engines. When it comes to teaching Visual Basic, I adhere to
the dictum in Mr. Holmes's epigraph; my home library is complete (or almost
so) with regard to VB books.

However, when it comes to writing VB code, it often feels like I'm still a little
boy, searching for the right example, the right block of code. I know that it's out
there somewhere, in the form of a reusable procedure, class, or ActiveX component. Sometimes I realize with an awful certainty that I wrote it myself once,
but where is it? On which of the multiple 500MB partitions on my hard disk
did I save it? In which project and module? And what did I call it?

Microsoft has mapped out the future as far as reusable, component-based
development is concerned. The ActiveX protocol that has evolved, based on the
OLE/COM/DCOM cross-language and cross-platform binaries, is at this point
an obvious winner. No other horse in the race is going to come up on the
outside and overtake it. ActiveX is state-of-the-art technology that defines ease
of reuse. The developer can simply set a reference to an ActiveX component in
a VB5 project (and thus view the component's public interface in the Object
Browser), get help on any of its objects or members, and display in a code
module context-sensitive, Automatic Code Completion data related to an
object or member.

VB5 still does not explicitly support the ability to inherit a class's source code;
however, there is nothing about the ActiveX architecture that forbids it. Inheritance of a class's public interface is supported through the **Implements** statement,
which is new to VB5. Inheritance is one of those "silver bullet, magic wand"
kind of concepts that can improve programmer productivity, but only in certain conditions. If your development team is working on a very complex
application that warrants substantial, up-front investment of resources in the
design and development of a domain-specific object hierarchy, inheritance can

be useful. However, the great majority of VB developers don't work on these kinds of projects.

The last of the add-in case studies in this book is the Code Librarian. If VB developers and development teams implement this approach to reusing code with discipline and consistency, it will greatly benefit them. The focus of the Code Librarian is on the creation, archiving, and reuse of procedures. When I honestly analyze my own programming habits over the last few years, I must conclude that there is no single software technology that would have made me more productive than the one I have embodied in Chapter 9's add-in. After you have finished reading this chapter and watching the Code Librarian in action, you can make your own judgment as to its potential effectiveness.

The Case For Reusable Procedures

Regardless of which higher-level approach of reusing code you adopt (object-oriented programming, component-based development, or inheritance), what you actually spend most of your time doing while writing code is creating general, non-event procedures. Surprise? Not! Sometimes we allow ourselves to become so beguiled by the hype in our business about the NEXT GREAT THING that we forget what we really do. VB programmers write procedures for a living and, in a very real sense, that is job #1.

If I went through every VB book and magazine that I've bought and read over the last five years, the number of potentially reusable procedures that I would find would be very large. If I examined the sample code that accompanies VB5, the number of reusable procedures included would be in the hundreds.

Consider just the reusable routines I found in the BAS modules in the SETUP1.VBP project on the VB5 path \SETUPKIT\SETUP1. The names of these routines are shown in Table 9.1. There are 169 of them. Some of them are Windows API function declarations/calls, but you can think of them as reusable procedures, too. The point of this dramatic example should be clear: A very large number of VB procedures in the public domain can be reused. Why do we keep reinventing the wheel?

TABLE 9.1

ROUTINES IN SETUP1.VBP's BAS MODULES.

Name	Name
AbortAction	DetectFile
AddActionNote	DirExists
AddDirStep	DisableLogging
AddHKeyToCache	DiskSpaceFree
AddPerAppPath	DllAbortAction
AddQuotesToFN	DllAddActionNote
AddURLDirStep	DllChangeActionKey
AllocUnit	DllCommitAction
CalcDiskSpace	DllDisableLogging
CalcFinalSize	DllEnableLogging
CenterForm	DllLogError
ChangeActionKey	DllLogNote
CheckDiskSpace	DllLogWarning
CheckDrive	DllNewAction
CheckOverwritePrivateFile	DllSelfRegister
CommitAction	EnableLogging
ConcatSplitFile	EtchedLine
CopyFile	ExeSelfRegister
CopySection	ExitSetup
CountIcons	Extension
CreateIcons	fCheckFNLength
CreateOSLink	fCreateOSProgramGroup
CreateProgManGroup	fCreateShellGroup
CreateProgManItem	fDllWithinAction
CreateShellLink	FileExists
DecideIncrementRefCount	fIsDepFile

(continued)

TABLE 9.1

ROUTINES IN **SETUP1.VBP**'s **BAS** MODULES (*CONTINUED*).

Name	Name
fNTWithShell	IncrementRefCount
FSyncShell	InitDiskInfo
fValidFilename	intGetHKEYIndex
fValidNTGroupName	intGetNextFldOffset
fWithinAction	IsDisplayNameUnique
GetAppRemovalCmdLine	IsNewerVer
GetClsidFromActXFile	IsUNCName
GetDefMsgBoxButton	IsValidDestDir
GetDepFileVerStruct	IsWin32
GetDiskSpaceFree	IsWindows95
GetDrivesAllocUnit	IsWindowsNT
GetDriveType	IsWindowsNT4WithoutSP2
GetFileName	lmemcpy
GetFileSize	LogError
GetFileVersion	LogNote
GetFileVerStruct	LogSilentMsg
GetLicInfoFromVBL	LogSMSMsg
GetLongPathName	LogWarning
GetPathName	MakePath
GetRemoteSupportFileVerStruct	MakePathAux
GetShortPathName	MoveAppRemovalFiles
GetTempFileName	MsgError
GetUNCShareName	MsgFunc
GetWindowsDir	MsgWarning
GetWindowsSysDir	NewAction
GetWinPlatform	OpenConcatFile

(continued)

TABLE **9.1**

ROUTINES IN **SETUP1.VBP**'s **BAS** MODULES (*CONTINUED*).

Name	Name
OSfCreateShellGroup	RegPathWinCurrentVersion
OSfCreateShellLink	RegPathWinPrograms
OSfRemoveShellLink	RegQueryNumericValue
OSGetLongPathName	RegQueryRefCount
PackVerInfo	RegQueryStringValue
ParseDateTime	RegSetNumericValue
PerformDDE	RegSetStringValue
ProcessCommandLine	RestoreProgMan
PromptForNextDisk	SetFileDateTime
ReadIniFile	SetFormFont
ReadProtocols	SetMousePtr
ReadSetupFileLine	SetTime
ReadSetupRemoteLine	ShowLoggingError
RegCloseKey	ShowPathDialog
RegCreateKey	SrcFileMissing
RegDeleteKey	strExtractFileNameArg
RegEdit	strExtractFilenameItem
RegEnumKey	strGetCommonFilesPath
RegisterAppRemovalEXE	strGetDAOPath
RegisterDAO	strGetDriveFromPath
RegisterFiles	strGetHKEYString
RegisterLicense	strGetPredefinedHKEYString
RegisterLicenses	strGetProgramFilesPath
RegisterTLB	StripTerminator
RegisterVBLFile	strQuoteString
RegOpenKey	strRootDrive

(continued)

ROUTINES IN SETUP1.VBP'S BAS MODULES (*CONTINUED*).	
Name	**Name**
IncrementRefCount	strUnQuoteString
InitDiskInfo	TreatAsWin95
intGetHKEYIndex	UCase16
intGetNextFldOffset	UpdateStatus
IsDisplayNameUnique	WriteAccess
IsNewerVer	WriteMIF
IsUNCName	

The Obstacles To Reusing Procedures

When as a kid I got caught red-handed doing something I knew was wrong, my usual tactic was to try and spread the blame around (my brothers were also involved, I was helping a friend out, and so on). When we ask ourselves as VB developers why we don't reuse procedures more often, the temptation is also to spread the blame around:

- The current project is inadequately budgeted.

- The VB group that I work for is short-term oriented.

- There is no personal reward for investing the extra time and effort required to create truly reusable procedures.

- I had to meet the deadline for completing this book.

These kinds of conditions certainly contribute to the problem, and I don't want to discount them. However, I want to focus in this section on three technical obstacles to increasing code reuse. Because these three factors are technical in nature, their solutions are technical and thus are more subject to our own individual control.

Non-Encapsulated Procedures

With regard to a VB **Sub** or **Function**, an encapsulated general procedure is one that you can extract from one code module or file and use in a physically different code module without altering it in any way. This means that the procedure itself contains everything it requires and that, assuming valid parameters are passed to its arguments, it executes correctly and consistently in any code module in any project. When a procedure is completely encapsulated, it is said to be loosely or non-coupled.

We tend to write non-encapsulated procedures in VB for several reasons. One of the most common is that we ask too much of our procedures. If each general procedure was limited in scope and designed to do just one thing, it would be significantly easier to encapsulate its functionality.

VB's own architecture imposes constraints to some degree. If a procedure makes a call to an external Windows DLL or requires a user-defined data type, it must violate encapsulation because VB requires that you declare references to external procedures in a dynamic-link library (DLL) and user-defined data types in the General section of a code module. In a similar fashion, if you write a procedure that, in the course of its execution, uses VB's **CreateObject** function to reference and reuse a **Public** member of an ActiveX component, you have coupled that procedure to an external dependency and it is no longer encapsulated.

Non-Generic Procedures

When you write a procedure, you are tempted to do so to meet the specific need of your current application. Even if you write an encapsulated procedure, its degree of reusability also depends on how generic its functionality is, without violating the dictum that it should do only one thing. If you want others to reuse a procedure, its functionality should apply to as many different situations as possible.

Imagine that you want to write a procedure to get a certain path (for example, the Windows path). Disregarding for now the problem of declaring the associated Windows API function, it would be easy enough to write an encapsulated procedure called **GetWinDir** to do this. Later on, however, you may find yourself writing other procedures to get the Windows system path, the Windows temporary path, the VB path, and so on. It might be better to design a more generic procedure called **GetDir**, which would still perform just one basic action (that is, return a path as a string), but which, with the use of a *Kind* argument, could be written to return any of several different types of paths.

There is an obvious tradeoff involved between writing a procedure that does one specific thing and writing a procedure that is generic enough to enhance its chances for reuse. Another issue that comes into play is the documentation of procedures. It would be quicker and easier to document one generic **GetDir** procedure than five or more individual procedures, each of which returns a different kind of path.

Inadequate Librarian Tools

Let's assume that your VB development team has decided to make a concerted effort to improve your degree of procedure reuse. You've established metrics (one new procedure per developer per week), agreed on a descriptive template, set up a peer review process, and hired a part-time technical writer just to document the reusable procedures. One major stumbling block still exists. What librarian tool will you use to assist in this effort?

Your team's well-planned and adequately budgeted initiative will probably founder over the long run if the developers who are to reuse the procedures can't:

- Find them easily.

- Load them quickly into a code module without any manual copy-and-paste hassle.

- Save new procedures automatically.

- Save any associated DLL or user-defined type declarations automatically.

It's surprising, but you won't find much in the way of procedure librarian tools available for the VB developer. If you do find such a tool, it probably won't function the way you would like and will be difficult to customize. I offer the Code Librarian add-in as an answer to this problem or at least as a prototype.

How The Code Librarian Works

If you connect/run the Code Librarian add-in, it initially displays the dialog box shown in Figure 9.1. Note that at this point the caption on the first **CommandButton** control is Add Proc To Module. If you select an item in the DLLs list, the caption on the first **CommandButton** control changes to Add DLL To Module. If you select an item in the user-defined Types list, the caption changes to Add Type To Module. The caption on the button always reflects the last list from which an item was selected.

The Code Librarian enables you to automatically:

• Retrieve any general procedure, DLL declaration, or Type declaration stored in the library and add it to the selected code module.

• Store any general procedure and its associated DLL/Type declarations in the library.

• Load the code for any VB class module into the active project and, thus, inherit it to modify or enhance as you wish.

In the rest of this chapter, I'll examine the code that performs the various functions of the Code Librarian, as well as suggest some ideas for enhancing it. Although you might not have made the same design choices I did, I think you'll agree that the Code Librarian is a good working prototype. Feel free to modify its source code and customize it to suit your particular needs.

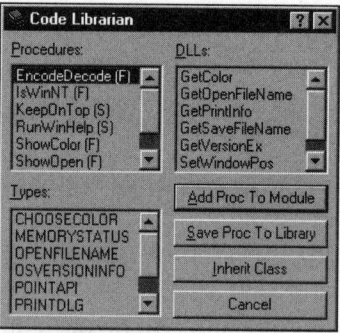

Figure 9.1
Code Librarian dialog box as initially displayed.

The File Architecture
Of The Code Librarian

I decided to store all the information the Code Librarian needs (general procedures, DLL or user-defined type declarations, and names of the items stored) in sequential text files. Although other file storage options exist, I used sequential text files because I:

- Wanted the storage/retrieval routines to execute quickly.

- Did not want to rely on the OLE Object field type supported by VB's Jet database engine.

- Had previously written reliable storage/retrieval routines for these kinds of sequential data.

The names of the TXT files that the Code Librarian uses and a description of their contents are shown in Table 9.2. The items/records in the three files containing the list of names (DLLNAMES.TXT, TYPNAMES.TXT, PRCNAMES. TXT) are delimited by carriage return/line-feed characters. The code blocks in the other files (CODEDLLS.TXT, CODETYPS.TXT, CODEPRC*.TXT) are identified by their unique names and ending strings. The files that contain code blocks also have:

- A string at the beginning of the file identifying its contents (for example, "DLL functions—" or "Procedures (A)—")

- An end-of-file marker that is the string "*** EOF ***"

TABLE 9.2

TXT FILES THAT CODE LIBRARIAN USES.

File name	Description
DLLNAMES.TXT	Contains the names of the Windows API or other DLL functions whose declarations are stored in the CODEDLLS.TXT file (**GetVersionEx, SetWindowPos**, and so on).
TYPNAMES.TXT	Contains the names of the user-defined data types whose declarations are stored in the CODETYPS.TXT file (**OSVERSIONINFO, RECT**, and so on).

(continued)

	TABLE 9.2

TXT FILES THAT CODE LIBRARIAN USES (*CONTINUED*).

Filename	Description
PRCNAMES.TXT	Contains the names of the general procedures that are stored in the various CODEPRC*.TXT files (**EncodeDecode** (F), **KeepOnTop** (S), and so on).
CODEDLLS.TXT	Contains the declarations of the Windows API or other DLL functions stored by the Code Librarian.
CODETYPS.TXT	Contains the declarations of the user-defined data types stored by the Code Librarian.
CODEPRC*.TXT	26 files (one for each letter of the alphabet) that contain the code for the general procedures stored by the Code Librarian. For example, the file CODEPRCE.TXT contains all procedures beginning with the letter "E" (like **EncodeDecode**) and the file CODEPRCK.TXT contains all procedures beginning with the letter "K" (like **KeepOnTop**).

Retrieving Code From The Library

To retrieve code from the library and add it to a code module, select the module you want to insert the code in (you do not have to open the code module) and the code item you want to insert. For example, if you select **Form1** as the module and the **IsWinNT** procedure as the code item, clicking on the Add Proc To Module button loads the procedure from its library file and inserts it, as shown in Figure 9.2.

At the same time, the Code Librarian reads that the inserted procedure requires an associated DLL (**GetVersionEx**) and user-defined type (**OSVERSIONINFO**) and automatically inserts them in the General section of the code module, as shown in Figure 9.3. The Code Librarian knows that a procedure requires a DLL or user-defined type declaration if there is a comment in the procedure's header like "DLL1:" or "Type1:" (or "DLL2:", "DLL3:", and so on). This convention for specifying a procedure's associated DLL or user-defined type is an arbitrary choice on my part, but it works well enough.

 You can also load just a DLL or user-defined type into a code module by selecting its item and clicking the Add DLL To Module or Add Type To Module buttons.

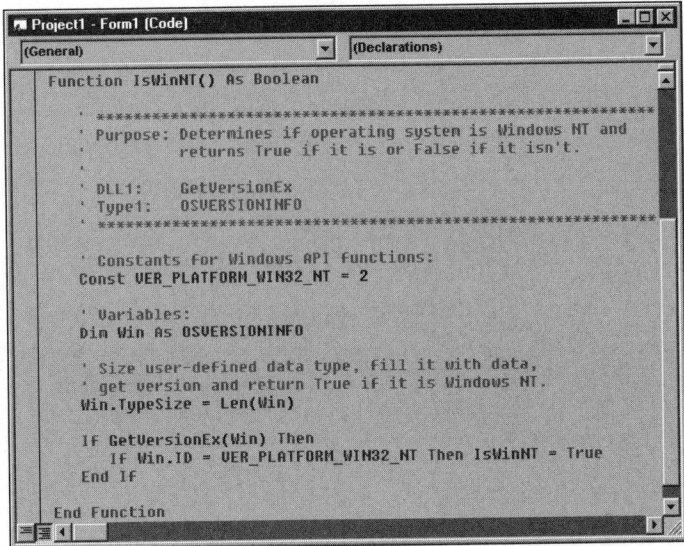

Figure 9.2
Inserted **IsWinNT** procedure.

The procedures in the Code Librarian add-in that retrieve the various kinds of code from the library are in the file CODELIBR.FRM under the names **AddProc**, **AddDLL**, and **AddType**. These three procedures in turn call the **GetCode** procedure to actually read the data from the appropriate sequential text files. You already saw a version of **GetCode** in Chapter 8 in Listing 8.3, so I won't show it again. The **AddProc** code is shown in Listing 9.1. Please note that I did not include in Listing 9.1 the last **Do** loop, which loads any required user-defined

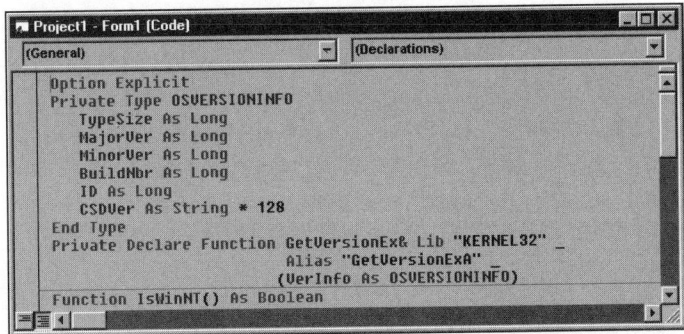

Figure 9.3
Inserted General declarations for **IsWinNT** procedure.

types, because its code is almost exactly the same as that for the loop earlier in
AddProc that loads any required DLL declarations. Once you have inserted a
particular procedure, DLL, or user-defined type in a code module, the Code
Librarian detects any attempt to insert the same code item twice and displays
an error message ('Name' already is in active code module).

LISTING 9.1   ADDPROC PROCEDURE.

```
Private Sub AddProc()

    ' ***********************************************************
    ' AddProc: Adds procedure and any DLL or Type declarations
    '           required by procedure to selected code module.
    ' ***********************************************************

    ' Variables:
    Dim FileName    As String
    Dim ProcName    As String
    Dim DLLName     As String
    Dim TypeName    As String
    Dim BegLine     As String
    Dim EndLine     As String
    Dim TmpStr      As String
    Dim CodeProc    As String
    Dim CodeDLL     As String
    Dim CodeType    As String
    Dim Counter     As Byte
    Dim Pos         As Integer
    Dim LineNbr     As Long
    Dim SelMod      As CodeModule

    ' Shorten object expression (faster and more readable).
    Set SelMod = VBE.SelectedVBComponent.CodeModule

    ' Get filename containing procedure:
    ProcName = lstProcs.List(lstProcs.ListIndex)
    FileName = App.Path & "\CODEPRC" & Left$(ProcName, 1) & ".TXT"

    ' Get name, beginning line, and ending line of procedure:
    If Right$(ProcName, 3) = "(F)" Then
        ProcName = Left$(ProcName, Len(ProcName) - 4)
        BegLine = "Function " & ProcName
        EndLine = "End Function"
    Else
        ProcName = Left$(ProcName, Len(ProcName) - 4)
```

```
        BegLine = "Sub " & ProcName
        EndLine = "End Sub"
End If

' Check if procedure already exists in code module:
If IsMbrInModule(SelMod, ProcName, True) Then Exit Sub

' Prevent redrawing of desktop.
LockWindowUpdate GetDesktopWindow

' Load procedure from file, add it to code
' module, and make sure code pane is visible:
CodeProc = GetCode(FileName, BegLine, EndLine)

With SelMod

    ' Add Function or Sub to end of module:
    LineNbr = .CountOfLines + 1
    .InsertLines LineNbr, CodeProc

    ' Remove any blank lines created when
    ' adding code and reset top line in pane:
    DelBlanksAfterAdd SelMod
    .DeleteLines LineNbr
    .CodePane.TopLine = LineNbr

End With

' Load any DLL declarations required by procedure:
Do

    ' See if DLL marker exists (for example, "DLL1:"):
    Pos = InStr(CodeProc, "DLL" & CStr(Counter + 1) & ":")

    ' If it does:
    If Pos <> False Then

        ' Work with temporary string that starts
        ' immediately after DLL marker:
        TmpStr = Mid$(CodeProc, Pos + 5)

        ' Strip spaces preceding name of DLL:
        Do
            If Mid$(TmpStr, 1, 1) = " " Then
                TmpStr = Right$(TmpStr, Len(TmpStr) - 1)
```

```
        Else
            Exit Do
        End If
    Loop

    ' Find position of carriage return at
    ' end of DLL name and pull out name:
    Pos = InStr(TmpStr, vbCrLf)
    DLLName = Mid$(TmpStr, 1, Pos - 1)
    Counter = Counter + 1

    ' If DLL doesn't already exist in code module, add it:
    If Not IsMbrInModule(SelMod, DLLName) Then
        FileName = App.Path & "\CODEDLLS.TXT"
        CodeDLL = GetCode(FileName, DLLName, ")")
        AddGenl SelMod, CodeDLL
    End If

' If DLL marker doesn't exist:
Else
    Counter = 0
    Exit Do
End If

Loop

.  .  .  .

' Redraw desktop.
LockWindowUpdate False

End Sub
```

Storing A Procedure In The Library

To store a new procedure in the library and make it available for later reuse, put the insertion point somewhere within the procedure to be saved and click the Save Proc To Library button. For example, if you write the procedure named **Sub AAA** (shown in Figure 9.4) and save it with the Code Librarian, it writes the procedure to the file CODEPRCA.TXT, which would then appear as in Figure 9.5.

I could have designed the Code Librarian to save procedures, DLLs, and user-defined types in different ways. Because DLL and Type declarations are useless unless they are used in procedures, I decided to have the Code Librarian only

Figure 9.4
Sub AAA procedure to be saved.

store code by saving a procedure and any DLLs or Types that it requires/references using the convention specified in the previous section of this chapter (a comment in the procedure's header like "DLL1:", "Type1:", and so on). If you want to be able to save a DLL or user-defined type separately, it would not be difficult to modify the Code Librarian's source code to do so.

The procedures that do most of the Code Librarian's storage work are found in CODELIBR.FRM in the **cmdSaveProc**, **SaveCode**, and **SaveIdentifier** procedures. Because of limited space, I will not provide code listings here. If you want, you can study these procedures in the source code in CODELIBR.VBP. Once you have saved a particular procedure, the Code Librarian detects any attempt to save it again and displays a query message ('Name' already is in code library. Do you want to replace it?). You can choose Yes or No and the Code Librarian proceeds accordingly.

Enhancing The Code Librarian

VB5 does not support inheritance. The Code Librarian add-in's implementation of an inheritance technique is meant primarily as food for thought. If you

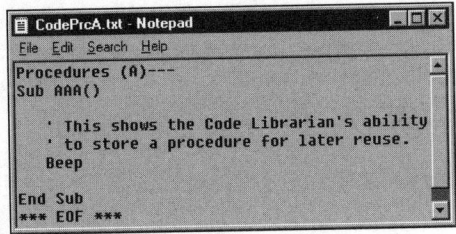

Figure 9.5
File CODEPRCA.TXT after procedure Sub AAA is saved.

click the Inherit Class button, it displays an Inherit Class common dialog box that allows you to search for a CLS module file. If you look on the path \ADDINEFS\CHAPTER9, you will see four CLS files listed (AITBAR.CLS, CODELIBR.CLS, CONNECT.CLS, and REG.CLS).

Only one of those four files, REG.CLS, is both completely encapsulated and has its **Creatable** property set to some value other than 1 or 2 (that is, it is a class that was designed to be reused). If you select AITBAR.CLS, CONNECT.CLS, or REG.CLS (don't select CODELIBR.CLS because it is part of the Code Librarian's source code), you will see the different validations that the Code Librarian performs while inheriting the CLS module's source code. These validations suggest the kinds of obstacles that a full-blown version of a Code Librarian that implemented inheritance would have to deal with.

Other possible enhancements to the Code Librarian might revolve around these kinds of issues:

- Deletion of procedures, DLLs, and user-defined types from the library: Should any developer be able to delete or should there be some type of security clearance?

- The deletion question is fundamentally related to the more general issue of administration of the code library. In a company with many VB developers, successful long-term use of an add-in like the Code Librarian would no doubt be enhanced by the existence of a Library Administrator position.

- The developer/technical writer holding the Library Administrator position could be responsible for scheduling code reviews, documenting the available procedures in Help file or HTML format, searching the VB literature for new procedures, and so on.

These are just some of the possible enhancements that you could make to the concepts and functionality embodied in the Code Librarian add-in. I personally am committed to using it in all my future work with VB and to evangelizing about it to the students that I will be teaching.

Chapter 9's case study of the Code Librarian add-in concludes Part III of this book. Part IV, of course, is the *Add-In Dictionary*, which you will use more as a reference tool than as material for study. If you have worked your way through this book and its sample add-ins, beginning with the *Introduction* and finishing with this chapter, you have seen examples of every possible kind of VB add-in language syntax. The rest is up to you and your imagination. How much artificial intelligence can you add to VB? Can you develop, market, and sell the next "killer" add-in that every VB developer will need to have? Good luck with your endeavors and may the force of AI be with you!

Part

IV

ADD-IN DICTIONARY

ADD-IN DICTIONARY

A dictionary for a programming language's object model is like a firefighter. When everything's cool and going well for you, it sits idle and goes unnoticed. However when you're getting hot under the collar because you can't figure out how to use a particular language element or syntax (for example, how to add a popup menu and its items to a VB5 menu), a well-written dictionary containing good Example code is essential in order to put out the fire.

This Dictionary for VB's Add-In Extensibility object model is especially useful for the following three reasons. First, VB5 shipped without any printed documentation. Yes, the product contains an Object Browser, a Help file, and Visual Basic Books Online and the answer to your add-in question may be in there somewhere. However, when you are dealing with a complex object model that contains well over 200 new language elements, it can be helpful to have all the pertinent information organized alphabetically in one book.

Second, the online information about add-ins and the Extensibility object model that comes with VB is inadequate, confusing, and in some cases erroneous. Here's a simple example. There is a **Description** property in the VBIDE class library, whose Help topic is shown in Figure D.1. The objects to which the **Description** property applies are listed by VB's Help file as shown in Figure D.2. Finally, the Object Browser states that for an **AddIn** object **Description** can "be set only in the **OnConnection** Event."

Here's a partial list of some major points about the **Description** property that are inadequately treated in VB's online documentation, are confusing, or are simply wrong:

- **Description** applies to five objects and not to one (as Figure D.2 suggests) or to two (as the information in Figure D.1 implies).

- Contrary to the Object Browser, it is possible to set **Description** for an **AddIn** object from other procedures besides **OnConnection**. Also, **OnConnection** is a method, not an event.

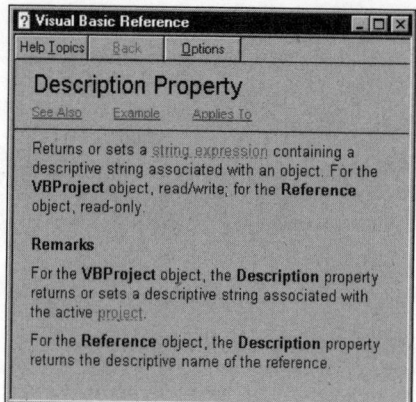

Figure D.1
VB Help topic for **Description** property.

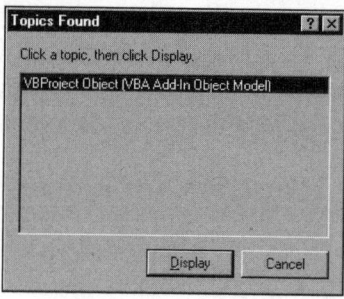

Figure D.2
Objects VB Help says **Description** property applies to.

- There is no information about how the setting of **Description** is determined by the developer of an add-in, where this information is stored in the Windows registry, or the difference between the setting of the **Description** property and the Project Description entry contained on the General tab of the Project Properties dialog box.

- There is no information at all about how the setting of the **Description** property works with a **Reference** object.

- There is no information at all about how the setting of the **Description** property is stored for a **Member, VBComponent,** or **VBProject** object.

> Detailed information about these five points regarding the **Description** property can be found in the **Description** entry in this Dictionary.

The third reason why this Add-In Dictionary is essential to any VB developer who wants to write an add-in is the Example code it contains. The Example code in VB's Help file is practically useless. It is either too skimpy, does not provide any context, or you just can't figure out how to get it to run in the first place. The Example code in this Add-In Dictionary addresses all of these deficiencies. The code is extensive and the context is always clearly explained. Most important, it is guaranteed to run because it all exists in the DEMOSYNT.VBP project on this book's CD-ROM.

How To Use This Dictionary

The Add-In Dictionary is organized alphabetically and contains an entry for each object and its members contained in the VBIDE class library (except for hidden members, as explained later in this section). It also has entries for the objects and members contained in the VBAI class library, which is a collection of methods that I wrote for add-in development. The methods in the VBAI class library can help you to:

- Enhance the capabilities of the Add-In Extensibility object model.

- Simplify some of the tasks commonly encountered in add-in development.

- Customize the behavior of the VB Add-In toolbar and of your own add-ins.

Each entry in the Add-In Dictionary defines the purpose of the language element and its syntax usage options. It then presents any information that is not explained or is inadequately explained in VB's online documentation. Finally, it tells you where you can find the entry's Example code either in ADDINEFS.HLP or the code that comes on the book's CD-ROM. If the entry is for a method in the VBAI class library that I wrote, it also tells you where you can find the method's code.

There are 46 hidden language elements (collections, objects, or members) in the VBIDE class library that you can't access through the Add-In Extensibility object model. They are not listed in VB's online documentation and, unless you right-click on the Object Browser and select Show Hidden Members from its popup menu, they are not visible in the Object Browser. As explained in the Introduction, these hidden language elements (shown in Table D.1) are included in the VBIDE class library only for internal use by Microsoft's VB development team. They are not to be used when developing VB5 add-ins and are not listed in the Add-In Dictionary.

For some reason, two of the hidden members, the **Current** and **HWnd** properties, can be accessed from the Add-In Extensibility object model and have some limited usefulness. These two hidden members do have entries in the Add-In Dictionary.

All of the information contained in the Add-In Dictionary can also be found online in the Creating Visual Basic 5 Add-Ins Help file (ADDINEFS.HLP) that comes with this book. When you are writing code for an add-in and you want to quickly scan a specific entry in the Add-In Dictionary, display ADDINEFS.HLP and find the Help topic that corresponds to the Dictionary entry.

The Example code in this Dictionary and in ADDINEFS.HLP can be used in two general ways. First, you can connect the Demo VB5 Add-In Syntax add-in to an instance of VB's IDE, start the add-in, and run the Example code from there. You can do this in either normal or debug mode. Second, you can type or copy and paste the Example code into an add-in of your own and run it from there. For more details on how to run the Example code, see the Introduction.

A-A

Table D.1   Hidden elements that do not work in VB5 add-ins.

Name of Element	Name of Element
ActiveForm Property	ControlTemplates Property
ActiveProject Property	DisconnectEvents Method
AddFormTemplate Method	DoGetAddFileName Event
AddInMenu Property	DoGetOpenProjectName Event
AddMDIFormTemplate Method	Enabled Property
AddMenu Method	Fetch Event
AddMenuTemplate Method	FileControl Object
AddReference Method	FileControl Property
AddToolboxTypelib Method	FormTemplate Object
AddToolboxVBX Method	LoadProject Method
AfterClick Event	MenuItems Collection
AfterNewProject Event	MenuItems Property
Application Object	MenuLine Object
Application Property	_NewEnum Method
Checked Property	ProjectTemplate Object
CheckIn Event	RemoveComponent Method
CheckOut Event	SelectedComponents Collection
Component Object	SelectedComponents Property
Components Collection	SelectedControlTemplates Collection
Components Property	SelectedControlTemplates Property
ConnectEvents Method	SubMenu Object
ControlTemplate Object	UncheckOut Event
ControlTemplates Collection	WizardHook Property

Activate Method

Activate is a **Sub** that selects and displays a VB component listed in the Project Explorer window.

Usage

Obj.**Activate**

The **Activate** method's syntax contains these parts:

- *Obj*: Required. An object expression that evaluates to a **VBComponent** object.

COMMENTS

In the context of the Project Explorer window, a VB component is a file that you can add to a project. The Project Explorer window can contain eight kinds of VB components:

- Forms (.FRM extension)

- Basic modules (.BAS extension)

- Class modules (.CLS extension)

- User controls (.CTL extension)

- Property pages (.PAG extension)

- User document forms (.DOB extension)

- ActiveX designers (.DSR extension)

- Related documents (.RES or other extension)

The **Activate** method selects the specified **VBComponent** object and displays it just as if you had double-clicked on the component's item in the Project Explorer window. In the process, it also adds that component's **Window** object to the **Windows** collection. Activated VB components either display a code pane window (BAS and CLS components) or a designer window (FRM, CTL, PAG, DOB, and DSR components). The only exception is a related document component, which does not display any kind of window.

A designer provides a visual design window in VB's IDE to create new classes visually. VB4 provided only a designer for forms. The Professional and Enterprise editions of VB5 also implement designers for user controls, property pages, user document forms, and active designers. Once you have displayed a designer component with the **Activate** method, you can use the **Show** method of its related **CodePane** object to display its code.

EXAMPLE CODE

See the Help topic Activate Method Example in ADDINEFS.HLP or the procedure DemoActivateMet in DEMOSYNT.VBP.

ActiveCodePane Property

ActiveCodePane returns an object instance of the **CodePane** class that is the active or last active code pane, or sets a **CodePane** object instance to be the active code pane. Read/write.

INSTANTIATION

Dim *Obj* As [VBIDE.]CodePane|Object|Variant
Set *Obj* = VBE.ActiveCodePane

USAGE

#1: *Obj* [.*Mbr*[*Args*]]
#2: *Obj*.MbrA.MbrB[= *ValB* | *ArgsB*]
#3: Set VBE.ActiveCodePane = *CodePaneObj*

The **ActiveCodePane** property's syntax supports named arguments and contains these parts:

- *Obj*: Required. A variable to be assigned an object instance. *Obj* can be named the same as the **CodePane** class being instantiated. *Obj* can also be declared as the generic **Object** or as **Variant**, but this slows performance.

- VBIDE: Optional. The VB5 Extensibility object library containing the **CodePane** class.

- *Mbr*: Optional. A member of a **CodePane** object.

- *Args*: Optional. You use *Args* when *Mbr* is a method that you are calling.

- *MbrA*: Required. A **CodePane** object's property that returns an object or collection.

- *MbrB*: Required. A member of the object or collection that is returned by *MbrA*.

- *ValB|ArgsB*: Optional. You use *ValB* if *MbrB* is a property being set or *ArgsB* if *MbrB* is a method being called.

- *CodePaneObj*: Required. An object expression that evaluates to a **CodePane** object and to which the **ActiveCodePane** property is set.

COMMENTS

Reading the **ActiveCodePane** property either returns the code pane window that currently has the focus or the one that last had the focus. Setting **ActiveCodePane** to a code pane window gives it the focus and brings it to the top of the z-order of windows in the project. If no code pane window is open, trying to return or set **ActiveCodePane** results in trappable error 452 (Invalid ordinal). This means that no **CodePane** object currently exists.

It is easy to confuse the effect of setting the **ActiveCodePane** property of a **CodePane** object with the effect of the **Activate** method of a **VBComponent** object or the effect of the **SetFocus** method of a **Window** object. If a **VBComponent** object is a BAS or CLS module, applying its **Activate** method is the same as setting **ActiveCodePane** to that component's code pane window. If a **Window** object is a code pane window, applying its **SetFocus** method is the same as setting **ActiveCodePane** to that code pane window.

EXAMPLE CODE

See the Help topic ActiveCodePane Property Example in ADDINEFS.HLP or the procedure DemoActiveCodePanePrp in DEMOSYNT.VBP.

ActiveVBProject Property

ActiveVBProject returns an object instance of the **VBProject** class that is the selected/active project in the Project Explorer window, or sets a **VBProject** object instance to be the active project. Read/write.

INSTANTIATION

Dim *Obj* **As** [VBIDE.]**VBProject|Object|Variant**
Set *Obj* = VBE.**ActiveVBProject**

A-A

USAGE
#1: *Obj*[.*Mbr*[*Args*]]
#2: *Obj.MbrA.MbrB*[= *ValB*\ *ArgsB*]
#3: **Set VBE.ActiveVBProject** = *VBProjectObj*

The **ActiveVBProject** property's syntax supports named arguments and contains these parts:

- *Obj*: Required. A variable to be assigned an object instance. *Obj* can be named the same as the **VBProject** class being instantiated. *Obj* can also be declared as the generic **Object** or as **Variant**, but this slows performance.

- VBIDE: Optional. The VB5 Extensibility object library containing the **VBProject** class.

- *Mbr*: Optional. A member of a **VBProject** object.

- *Args*: Optional. You use *Args* when *Mbr* is a method that you are calling.

- *MbrA*: Required. A **VBProject** object's property that returns an object or collection.

- *MbrB*: Required. A member of the object or collection that is returned by *MbrA*.

- *ValB**ArgsB*: Optional. You use *ValB* if *MbrB* is a property being set or *ArgsB* if *MbrB* is a method being called.

- *VBProjectObj*: Required. An object expression that evaluates to a **VBProject** object and to which the **ActiveVBProject** property is set.

COMMENTS
The **ActiveVBProject** property returns the project that is selected in the Project Explorer window or the project whose component is selected. Setting the **ActiveVBProject** property to a member of the **VBProjects** collection causes that project's name to be selected in the Project Explorer window and to be displayed in the title bar of VB's menu bar window.

> Both VB's Help file and the Object Browser incorrectly state that the **ActiveVBProject** property is read-only. Instead, it is read/write.

EXAMPLE CODE
See the Help topic ActiveVBProject Property Example in ADDINEFS.HLP or the procedure DemoActiveVBProjectPrp in DEMOSYNT.VBP.

ActiveWindow Property
ActiveWindow returns an object instance of the **Window** class that is the active window in VB's IDE. Read-only.

INSTANTIATION
Dim *Obj* **As** [VBIDE.]**Window****Object****Variant**
Set *Obj* = **VBE.ActiveWindow**

USAGE

#1: *Obj*[.*Mbr*[= *Val*]]

#2: *Obj.MbrA.MbrB*[= *ValB* | *ArgsB*]

The **ActiveWindow** property's syntax supports named arguments and contains these parts:

- *Obj*: Required. A variable to be assigned an object instance. *Obj* can be named the same as the **Window** class being instantiated. *Obj* can also be declared as the generic **Object** or as **Variant**, but this slows performance.

- VBIDE: Optional. The VB5 Extensibility object library containing the **Window** class.

- *Mbr*: Optional. A member of a **Window** object.

- *Val*: Optional. You use *Val* when *Mbr* is a property that you are setting.

- *MbrA*: Required. A **Window** object's property that returns an object or collection.

- *MbrB*: Required. A member of the object or collection that is returned by *MbrA*.

- *ValB* | *ArgsB*: Optional. You use *ValB* if *MbrB* is a property being set or *ArgsB* if *MbrB* is a method being called.

COMMENTS

When more than one window is open in the development environment, the **ActiveWindow** property setting is the window with the focus. Do not confuse the **ActiveWindow** property of a **VBE** object with the **ActiveForm** property of a **Form** object or the **Screen** object. **ActiveWindow** belongs to the VBIDE class library while **ActiveForm** belongs to the VB class library.

> VB's Help file incorrectly states that the **ActiveWindow** property returns **Nothing** if the main window has the focus. Instead, it returns a **Window** object. See the Example code (Usage #1) for a demonstration of this.

EXAMPLE CODE

See the Help topic ActiveWindow Property Example in ADDINEFS.HLP or the procedure DemoActiveWindowPrp in DEMOSYNT.VBP.

Add Method

Add is a **Function** that adds an item to an add-in collection and, except in the case of a **LinkedWindows** collection, returns a reference to the object instance that is added.

USAGE

#1: [**Set** *ObjAdded* =] *Obj*.**Add**(*ProjectType*, [*Exclusive* = **False**])

#2: [**Set** *ObjAdded* =] *Obj*.**Add**(*ComponentType*)

#3: [**Set** *ObjAdded* =] *Obj*.**Add**(*ProgID*, [*RelativeVBControl*], [*Before* = **False**])

#4: *Obj*.**Add**(*Window*)

The **Add** method's syntax supports named arguments and contains these parts:

- *Obj*: Required. An object expression that evaluates to a **ContainedVBControls, LinkedWindows, VBComponents, VBControls** or **VBProjects** collection.

- *ObjAdded*: Optional. A variable that is assigned the object instance returned by **Add**. *ObjAdded* is usually declared as and can be named the same as the type of object being added. *ObjAdded* can also be declared as the generic **Object** or as **Variant**, but this slows performance.

- *ProjectType*: Required. A constant or value that specifies the kind of VB project being added, as listed in Settings.

- *Exclusive*: Optional. A **Boolean** expression that specifies whether the new project is added as the only project (**True**) or is added to an existing set of projects (**False**). If *Exclusive* is not passed, it defaults to **False**.

- *ComponentType*: Required. A constant or value that specifies the kind of VB component being added, as listed in Settings.

- *ProgID*: Required. A **String** expression that specifies the programmatic ID of the VB control to be added. Examples of programmatic ID strings for VB controls are "VB.CommandButton" and "VB.TextBox".

- *RelativeVBControl*: Optional. An object expression that evaluates to an existing **VBControl** object and that specifies the point where the new control is to be inserted.

- *Before*: Optional. A **Boolean** expression that specifies whether the new **VBControl** object is placed before (**True**) or after (**False**) *RelativeVBControl*. If *Before* is not passed, it defaults to **False**.

- *Window*: Required. An object expression that evaluates to a **Window** object. It represents a permanent VB IDE window to be added to a **LinkedWindows** collection.

SETTINGS

The *ProjectType* argument's possible values are:

- 0 - **vbext_pt_StandardExe:** Standard executable

- 1 - **vbext_pt_ActiveXExe:** ActiveX executable

- 2 - **vbext_pt_ActiveXDll:** ActiveX DLL

- 3 - **vbext_pt_ActiveXControl:** ActiveX control

The *ComponentType* argument's possible values are:

- 1 - **vbext_ct_StdModule:** Standard module

- 2 - **vbext_ct_ClassModule: ClassModule** object

- 3 - **vbext_ct_MSForm:** Microsoft form

- 4 - **vbext_ct_ResFile:** Resource file

A-A

- 5 - vbext_ct_VBForm: **Form** object

- 6 - vbext_ct_VBMDIForm: **MDIForm** object

- 7 - vbext_ct_PropPage: **PropertyPage** object

- 8 - vbext_ct_UserControl: **UserControl** object

- 9 - vbext_ct_DocObject: **UserDocument** object

- 10 - vbext_ct_RelatedDocument: **RelatedDocument** object

- 100 - vbext_ct_Document: **Document** object

COMMENTS

In usage #1, **Add** adds a new project to a **VBProjects** collection. If *Exclusive* is specified as **True**, then any existing group or standalone project is closed and the new project becomes the only project in the collection. In usage #2, **Add** adds a new VB component to the **VBComponents** collection of a **VBProject** object. In usage #3, **Add** adds a new VB control (intrinsic or ActiveX) to the **VBControls** collection of a **VBForm** object or the **ContainedVBControls** collection of a **VBForm** or **VBControl** object. In usage #4, **Add** adds one of VB's permanent IDE windows (for example, the Toolbox window) to a **LinkedWindows** collection. When you call the **Add** method, VB raises the **ItemAdded** event.

 VB's Help file incorrectly states that *ProjectType* must evaluate to a **VBProject** object. Instead, it must be a constant or value, as specified in the Settings section.

EXAMPLE CODE

See the Help topic Add Method Example in ADDINEFS.HLP or the procedure DemoAddMet in DEMOSYNT.VBP.

AddButton Method (VBAI)

AddButton is a **Function** that adds the entries for an add-in button to VB's Add-In toolbar Windows registry subkey, immediately adds the button to the toolbar, and returns **True**.

USAGE

Obj.**AddButton**(*VBE, ProgID*) **As Boolean**

The **AddButton** method's syntax supports named arguments and contains these parts:

- *Obj*: Required. An object expression that evaluates to an **AITBar** object of the VBAI class library.

- *VBE*: Required. An object expression that evaluates to a **VBE** object of the VBIDE class library.

- *ProgID*: Required. A **String** expression that specifies the programmatic ID of the add-in to be added to the toolbar. The programmatic IDs of all registered add-ins are listed in VBADDIN.INI. If *ProgID* is set to "AddInToolbar.Connect" (that is, the VB Add-In Toolbar add-in itself) or to a nonexistent programmatic ID, **AddButton** fails.

ERROR HANDLING

AddButton returns **False** upon failure.

COMMENTS

AddButton improves upon the **AddToAddInToolbar** method of a **Manager** object of the VB Add-In Toolbar add-in. When you call the **AddToAddInToolbar** method, the new button is not displayed on the Add-In toolbar until the next instance of VB's IDE is started; also, its *ForceAddInToolBar* argument must be set to **True** to ensure that the toolbar itself is displayed when the next instance of VB's IDE is started. **AddButton** corrects these deficiencies of the **AddToAddInToolbar** method by immediately displaying the toolbar (if it is not already displayed) and immediately adding the button.

AddButton fails if the add-in button that *ProgID* specifies is already displayed on the toolbar. An add-in can check if a button exists for a particular add-in by calling the **IsButton** method of an **AITBar** object.

METHOD'S CODE

See the Help topic AddButton Method in ADDINEFS.HLP or the **AddButton** method's procedure in VBAI.VBP.

EXAMPLE CODE

See the Help topic AddButton Method Example in ADDINEFS.HLP or the procedure DemoAITBarObj in DEMOSYNT.VBP.

AddCustom Method

AddCustom is a **Function** that adds a custom component (that is, an ActiveX designer) to a project and returns it as an object instance of the **VBComponent** class.

USAGE

Obj.**AddCustom**(*ProgID*) **As VBComponent**

The **AddCustom** method's syntax supports named arguments and contains these parts:

- *Obj*: Required. An object expression that evaluates to a **VBComponents** collection.

- *ProgID*: Required. A **String** expression that specifies the programmatic ID of the ActiveX designer whose object instance is to be added to the project.

COMMENTS

An ActiveX designer is a VB component that provides a custom visual interface for a task that otherwise might require a great deal of code. ActiveX designers are similar in concept to VB's built-in form designer and are very flexible. Some, like the UserConnection designer included with VB's Enterprise Edition, create classes whose run-time instances are programmable, but not visible. Others, like the Microsoft Forms designer used by Microsoft Office, produce visible objects similar to Visual Basic forms. ActiveX designers are available only in the development environment.

When you run an ActiveX designer's setup program, it registers itself in the Windows registry under the appropriate component category. It is then available from the Designers tab of the

Components dialog box. Microsoft distributes two ActiveX designers with its products: Microsoft UserConnection with the Enterprise Edition of VB and Microsoft Forms 2.0 Form with Office 97.

Calling the **AddCustom** method is the same as manually adding an ActiveX designer to a VB project. To manually add an ActiveX designer, follow these steps:

- Select Project|Components and click on the Designers tab of the Components dialog box.

- Check the ActiveX designer you want to appear as an item on the Project menu and click on OK.

- Select Project|Add ActiveX Designer and click on the designer item on the popup menu that you want to add to your VB project.

 You cannot create an ActiveX designer with VB. VB's Professional and Enterprise editions include the ActiveX Designer SDK, which can be used to create new ActiveX designers; however, this SDK requires a C++ compiler, such as Visual C++.

EXAMPLE CODE

See the Help topic AddCustom Method Example in ADDINEFS.HLP or the procedure DemoAddCustomMet in DEMOSYNT.VBP.

AddFile Method

AddFile is a **Function** that creates a new VB component from a file, adds it to a project, and returns it as an object instance of the **VBComponent** class.

USAGE

Obj.**AddFile**(*PathName*, [*RelatedDocument* = **False**]) **As VBComponent**

The **AddFile** method's syntax supports named arguments and contains these parts:

- *Obj*: Required. An object expression that evaluates to a **VBComponents** collection.

- *PathName*: Required. A **String** expression that specifies the path and filename of the component's file to add to the project.

- *RelatedDocument*: Optional. A **Boolean** expression that specifies whether the file is to be treated as a standard module (the default of **False**) or as a text file (**True**).

COMMENTS

Files that are normally VB components, such as FRM files, cause an error if *RelatedDocument* is set to **True**. *RelatedDocument* should be passed only when adding text files that can be treated as either standard modules or documents.

EXAMPLE CODE

See the Help topic AddFile Method Example in ADDINEFS.HLP or the procedure DemoAddFileMet in DEMOSYNT.VBP.

AddFromFile Method

AddFromFile is a **Sub** that adds the contents of a file to a code module or adds a reference to a project from a file.

USAGE

Obj.**AddFromFile** *FileName*

The **AddFromFile** method's syntax supports named arguments and contains these parts:

- *Obj*: Required. An object expression that evaluates to a **CodeModule**, **References**, or **VBProjects** object.

- *FileName*: Required. A **String** expression that specifies the path and name of a file you want to add to the code module or project. If *FileName* does not contain a path name, **AddFromFile** searches for the file in the same directories as does the Windows API function **OpenFile**.

COMMENTS

For a **CodeModule** object, the **AddFromFile** method inserts the contents of the file starting on the line preceding the first procedure in the code module. If the module does not contain procedures, **AddFromFile** places the contents of the file at the end of the module. In some cases, the **AddFromFile** method fails if the code pane is closed, but no trappable error occurs. In other cases, **AddFromFile** works whether or not the code pane is open.

Adding the contents of a file to a code module can change the **Name** property of a **VBComponent** object that contains the code module (see the Example code). You can deal with this behavior by reading the original setting of the **Name** property and then, after applying the **AddFromFile** method, resetting the name of the component. This works because the **Name** property of a **VBComponent** object is read/write.

EXAMPLE CODE

See the Help topic AddFromFile Method Example in ADDINEFS.HLP or the procedure DemoAddFromFileMet in DEMOSYNT.VBP.

AddFromGuid Method

AddFromGuid is a **Function** that adds a reference to a project using the globally unique identifier (GUID) of the reference and returns it as an object instance of the **Reference** class.

USAGE

Obj.**AddFromGuid**(*Guid, Major, Minor*) **As Reference**

The **AddFromGuid** method's syntax supports named arguments and contains these parts:

- *Obj*: Required. An object expression that evaluates to a **References** collection.

- *Guid*: Required. A **String** expression that specifies the GUID of the reference to be added.

- *Major*: Required. A numeric expression that specifies the major version number of the reference.

- *Minor*: Required. A numeric expression that specifies the minor version number of the reference.

COMMENTS

The **AddFromGuid** method searches the Windows registry to find the reference you want to add. The GUID can be a type library, control, class identifier, and so on. Programmatically calling **AddFromGuid** has the same effect as manually selecting Project|References and checking the item in the References dialog box list.

A GUID (globally unique identifier) is a 128-bit value that is automatically assigned when a class is registered with Windows. The GUID is generated using a combination of the date, time, and a unique network card number (if the system has a network card installed). Because each bit of a binary number can have only two values, and because the GUID is 128 bits in length, the number of possible GUIDs is 2 raised to the 128th power. An example of a GUID is {FFAE6620-850D-11D0-BD69-8D0496BC6751}, which happens to be the value that Windows assigned on my PC to the WinAPIBrowser.Connect add-in (free demo version).

 If you know where the file that contains the reference's type library, control, or class identifier is located, it is easier to add a reference to a project by calling the **AddFromFile** method of the **References** collection. See the Example code for a demonstration of how to do this.

EXAMPLE CODE

See the Help topic AddFromGuid Method Example in ADDINEFS.HLP or the procedure DemoAddFromGuidMet in DEMOSYNT.VBP.

AddFromString Method

AddFromString is a **Sub** that adds text to a code module.

USAGE

Obj.**AddFromString** *Text*

The **AddFromString** method's syntax supports named arguments and contains these parts:

- *Obj*: Required. An object expression that evaluates to a **CodeModule** object.

- *Text*: Required. A **String** expression that specifies the text you want to add to the code module.

COMMENTS

The **AddFromString** method adds the text starting on the line preceding the first procedure in the code module. If the module does not contain procedures, **AddFromString** places the text at the end of the module. To add text that contains a word in quotation marks, use double quotation marks around that word. To add text that includes line breaks, use the intrinsic constant **vbCr**.

You can add an entire procedure or procedures. When you want to add more than one procedure, you should apply the **AddFromString** method individually to the text of each procedure (see the Example code). If you add the text of a procedure to a code module and that same procedure's name already exists in the module, VB will not warn you until you try to run the project, at which time it displays a syntax error message (Ambiguous name detected: 'Procedure name').

 **AddFromString** can incorrectly insert the invalid string "()" on the line immediately following other text that it has added. You can work around this bug by searching the module for "()" with the **Find** method and using the **DeleteLines** method to remove the invalid string. See the Example code for how to do this. To avoid this problem entirely, use the **InsertLines** method instead of **AddFromString**.

EXAMPLE CODE
See the Help topic AddFromString Method Example in ADDINEFS.HLP or the procedure DemoAddFromStringMet in DEMOSYNT.VBP.

AddFromTemplate Method

AddFromTemplate is a **Function** that creates a new VB project or component from a template file and returns it as an object instance of the **VBNewProjects** or **VBComponents** class.

USAGE
#1: *Obj*.**AddFromTemplate**(*FileName*, [*Exclusive* = **False**]) **As VBNewProjects**
#2: *Obj*.**AddFromTemplate**(*FileName*) **As VBComponents**

The **AddFromTemplate** method's syntax supports named arguments and contains these parts:

- *Obj*: Required. An object expression that evaluates to a **VBComponents** or **VBProjects** collection.

- *FileName*: Required. A **String** expression that specifies the path and file name of the file to create from the template.

- *Exclusive*: Optional. Used only when adding a project template, *Exclusive* is a **Boolean** expression. If **True**, the existing group project is closed and the new project is created from the template as the only open project. If **False** (the default), the new project is created from the template as an additional project and a group project is created in the Project Explorer window.

COMMENTS
The **AddFromTemplate** method is intended to be used with files installed on VB5's \TEMPLATE path. There are eight subdirectories on the \TEMPLATE path (for example, \CLASSES, \FORMS and \PROJECTS) that contain the template files that correspond to the template icons displayed on VB's Add <Item> dialog boxes.

If all you need to do is add a generic project or component type, you should call the **Add** method of a **VBProjects** or **VBComponents** collection. You only need to call the **AddFromTemplate** method when you want to add a more complex template that is not supported by the **Add** method.

VB's Help file incorrectly states that the *FileName* argument of the **AddFromTemplate** method of a **VBProjects** collection takes a **String** expression that specifies the path to the file to use as the template. Instead, *FileName* must specify both the path and the name of the project file (VBP or VBG).

EXAMPLE CODE

See the Help topic AddFromTemplate Method Example in ADDINEFS.HLP or the procedure DemoAddFromTemplateMet in DEMOSYNT.VBP.

AddIn Object

AddIn is an item in an **Addins** collection and it provides information about an add-in to other add-ins.

INSTANTIATION

Dim *Obj* **As** [VBIDE.]**AddIn**|**Object**|**Variant**
Set *Obj* = **VBE.Addins**[.**Item**](*Index*)

USAGE

#1: *Obj*[.*Mbr*[= *Val*]]
#2: *Obj.MbrA.MbrB*[= *ValB* | *ArgsB*]

An **AddIn** object's syntax supports named arguments and contains these parts:

- *Obj*: Required. A variable to be assigned an object instance. *Obj* can be named the same as the **AddIn** class being instantiated. *Obj* can also be declared as the generic **Object** or as **Variant,** but this slows performance.

- VBIDE: Optional. The VB5 Extensibility object library containing the **AddIn** class.

- *Index*: Required. Used with the default **Item** method, *Index* is a numeric or **String** expression that specifies the position of an **AddIn** object in an **Addins** collection. If *Index* is a **String** expression, it must evaluate to the **ProgID** property of an **AddIn** object.

- *Mbr*: Optional. A member of an **AddIn** object.

- *Val*: Optional. You use *Val* when setting a property of *Mbr*.

- *MbrA*: Required. An **AddIn** object's property that returns an object or collection.

- *MbrB*: Required. A member of the object or collection that is returned by *MbrA*.

- *ValB* | *ArgsB*: Optional. You use *ValB* if *MbrB* is a property being set or *ArgsB* if *MbrB* is a method being called.

MEMBERS

- Events: None at this time

- Methods: None at this time

- Properties: **Collection, Connect, Description, Guid, Object, ProgID, VBE**

COMMENTS

Whenever you start a new instance of VB, an **AddIn** object is created for each add-in that is listed in the VBADDIN.INI file, which only stores information about VB5 add-ins. Information about VB4 add-ins is stored in VB.INI. You can run a VB4 add-in under VB5; to do so, however, you must write an entry for it to VBADDIN.INI and remake and reregister it using VB5.

To see a list of **AddIn** objects while working within VB's IDE, select Add-Ins|Add-In Manager to display the Add-In Manager dialog box. If an add-in in the list is checked, its entry in VBADDIN.INI is 1; if unchecked, its entry is 0. You can access an **AddIn** object by:

- Calling the **Item** method of an **Addins** collection.

- Using a **For...Each...Next** statement to loop through the items of an **Addins** collection until you find the **AddIn** object you want.

EXAMPLE CODE

See the Help topic AddIn Object Example in ADDINEFS.HLP or the procedure DemoAddInObj in DEMOSYNT.VBP.

Addins Collection/Property

An **Addins** collection contains the VB5 **AddIn** objects listed in VBADDIN.INI and in the Add-In Manager dialog box. The read-only **Addins** property of a **VBE** object returns an object instance of the **Addins** class.

INSTANTIATION

Dim *Obj* **As** [**VBIDE.**]**Addins|Object|Variant**
Set *Obj* = VBE.Addins

USAGE

#1: *Obj.Mbr*
#2: *Obj*[.**Item**](*Index*)[.*MbrA*[= *ValA*]
#3: *Obj.MbrB.MbrC*[= *ValC*| *ArgsC*]

The **Addins** syntax supports named arguments and contains these parts:

- *Obj*: Required. A variable to be assigned an object instance. *Obj* can be named the same as the **Addins** class being instantiated. *Obj* can also be declared as the generic **Object** or as **Variant,** but this slows performance.

- VBIDE: Optional. The VB5 Extensibility object library containing the **Addins** class.

- *Mbr*: Required. A member of an **Addins** collection other than the **Item** method.

- *Index*: Required. Used with the default **Item** method, *Index* is a numeric or **String** expression that specifies the ordinal position of an **AddIn** object in an **Addins** collection. If *Index* is a **String** expression, it must evaluate to the **ProgID** property of an **AddIn** object.

- *MbrA*: Optional. A property of an **AddIn** object.

- *ValA*: Optional. You use *ValA* when *MbrA* is a property that you are setting.

- *MbrB*: Required. An **Addins** collection's property (**Parent** or **VBE**) that returns a **VBE** object.

- *MbrC*: Required. A member of the **VBE** object that is returned by *MbrB*.

- *ValC* | *ArgsC*: Optional. You use *ValC* if *MbrC* is a property being set or *ArgsC* if *MbrC* is a method being called.

MEMBERS

- Events: None at this time

- Methods: **Item, Update**

- Properties: **Count, Parent, VBE**

COMMENTS

Whenever you start a new instance of VB, an **AddIn** object is created for each add-in that is listed in the VBADDIN.INI file, which only stores information about VB5 add-ins. These **AddIn** objects comprise the items in the **Addins** collection. To see a list of the items in the **Addins** collection while working within VB's IDE, select Add-Ins|Add-In Manager to display the Add-In Manager dialog box.

You can access an **AddIn** object by first using the **Addins** property to return an **Addins** collection. Then you can apply that collection's **Item** method or use a **For...Each...Next** statement to loop through the items in that collection to find the add-in you want. The **Addins** collection replaces the **ExternalObjects** collection used in VB4's VBEXT32.OLB Add-In class library.

EXAMPLE CODE

See the Help topic Addins Collection/Property Example in ADDINEFS.HLP or the procedure DemoAddinsObj in DEMOSYNT.VBP.

AddMenu Method (VBAI)

AddMenu is a **Function** that adds a menu to the VB menu bar and returns the new menu as a **CommandBarControl** object of the Office class library.

USAGE

Set *mVar* = *Obj*.**AddMenu**(*VBE, Caption,* [*Position*]) **As** Office.**CommandBarControl**

The **AddMenu** method's syntax supports named arguments and contains these parts:

- *Obj*: Required. An object expression that evaluates to a **Cmd** object of the VBAI class library.

- *mVar*: Required. A module-level object variable declared in the add-in's **ClassModule** connection object as a **CommandBarControl** object of the Office class library. It is assigned the object instance returned by **AddMenu**.

- *VBE*: Required. An object expression that evaluates to a **VBE** object of the VBIDE class library.

- *Caption*: Required. A **String** expression that specifies the new menu's caption.

- *Position*: Optional. A numeric expression that specifies where on the VB menu bar to place the new menu. For example, passing a parameter of 11 to *Position* would place the menu just to the left of the Help menu. If *Position* is not passed, the menu is placed to the far right of the menu bar.

ERROR HANDLING

AddMenu returns an object instance that evaluates to **Nothing** upon failure.

COMMENTS

Before you declare *mVar* as a **CommandBarControl** object and call the **AddMenu** method, you must set a reference to the Microsoft Office 8.0 Object Library. After calling **AddMenu**, you must do two more things:

- Add menu items to the **CommandBarControl** object returned by **AddMenu**. You can do this by calling the **AddMenuItem** method of a **Cmd** object.

- Make the menu items responsive to a mouse click with the **CommandBarEvents** property of an **Events** object. See the Dictionary entries for the **CommandBarEvents** property and **CommandBarEvents** object for details about how to do this.

To delete a VB menu that was previously added with **AddMenu**, apply the **Delete** method of a **CommandBarControl** object to the module-level object variable that was assigned the menu. When you delete a menu, any menu items or popup menus attached to it are also deleted.

 Instead of calling **AddMenu**, you should consider calling the **AddToolBar** method of a **Cmd** object. Conventional VB add-in programming practice dictates that you not add a custom menu to VB's menu bar. You should only create a custom VB menu with **AddMenu** as a last resort.

METHOD'S CODE

See the Help topic AddMenu Method (Cmd) in ADDINEFS.HLP or the **AddMenu** method's procedure in VBAI.VBP.

EXAMPLE CODE

See the Help topic AddMenu Method (Cmd) Example in ADDINEFS.HLP or the procedure DemoAddMenuMet in DEMOSYNT.VBP.

AddMenuItem Method (VBAI)

AddMenuItem is a **Function** that adds a menu item for an add-in to a VB menu or popup menu and returns the new menu item as a **CommandBarControl** object of the Office class library.

USAGE

Set *mVar* = *Obj*.**AddMenuItem**(*VBE, Menu, Caption*, [*Position*], [*Separator*], [*Bitmap*]) **As** Office.**CommandBarControl**

A-A

The **AddMenuItem** method's syntax supports named arguments and contains these parts:

- *Obj*: Required. An object expression that evaluates to a **Cmd** object of the VBAI class library.

- *mVar*: Required. A module-level object variable declared in the add-in's **ClassModule** connection object as a **CommandBarControl** object of the Office class library. It is assigned the object instance returned by **AddMenuItem**.

- *VBE*: Required. An object expression that evaluates to a **VBE** object of the VBIDE class library.

- *Menu*: Required. An object expression that evaluates to a **CommandBarControl** object of the Office class library and that represents the VB menu or popup menu to which the menu item is to be added. To provide *Menu*, you can either call the **GetMenu** or **AddPopupMenu** method of a **Cmd** object or specify it yourself as demonstrated in the Example code.

- *Caption*: Required. A **String** expression that specifies the new menu item's caption.

- *Position*: Optional. A numeric expression that specifies where on the VB menu to place the menu item. For example, passing a parameter of 1 to *Position* places the menu item at the top of the menu. If *Position* is not passed, the menu item is placed at the bottom of the menu.

- *Separator*: Optional. A **Boolean** expression that specifies that the menu item being added is to have a separator bar above it on the menu (**True**) or is just an ordinary menu item (the default of **False**).

- *Bitmap*: Optional. A **String** expression that specifies the path and file name of a bitmap that is to be placed to the left of the menu item. For the best appearance, this BMP file should be 16 x 16 pixels, like the files on the VB5 path \GRAPHICS\BITMAPS\TLBR_W95. **AddMenuItem** will compress and use a larger bitmap but its appearance will be distorted. Passing a non-BMP graphic file causes **AddMenuItem** to fail.

ERROR HANDLING
AddMenuItem returns an object instance that evaluates to **Nothing** upon failure.

COMMENTS
Before you declare *mVar* as a **CommandBarControl** object and call the **AddMenuItem** method, you must set a reference to the Microsoft Office 8.0 Object Library. After calling **AddMenuItem**, you must make the menu item responsive to a mouse click with the **CommandBarEvents** property of an **Events** object. See the Dictionary entries for the **CommandBarEvents** property and **CommandBarEvents** object for details about how to do this.

To delete a menu item that was previously added with **AddMenuItem**, apply the **Delete** method of a **CommandBarControl** object to the module-level object variable that was assigned the menu item.

A-A

METHOD'S CODE

See the Help topic AddMenuItem Method in ADDINEFS.HLP or the **AddMenuItem** method's procedure in VBAI.VBP.

EXAMPLE CODE

See the Help topic AddMenuItem Method Example in ADDINEFS.HLP or the procedure DemoAddMenuItemMet in DEMOSYNT.VBP.

AddPopupMenu Method (VBAI)

AddPopupMenu is a **Function** that adds a popup menu for an add-in to a VB menu and returns the new popup menu as a **CommandBarControl** object of the Office class library.

USAGE

Set *mVar* = *Obj*.**AddPopupMenu**(*VBE*, *Menu*, *Caption*, [*Position*], [*Separator*]) **As** Office.**CommandBarControl**

The **AddPopupMenu** method's syntax supports named arguments and contains these parts:

- *Obj*: Required. An object expression that evaluates to a **Cmd** object of the VBAI class library.

- *mVar*: Required. A module-level object variable declared in the add-in's **ClassModule** connection object as a **CommandBarControl** object of the Office class library. It is assigned the object instance returned by **AddPopupMenu**.

- *VBE*: Required. An object expression that evaluates to a **VBE** object of the VBIDE class library.

- *Menu*: Required. An object expression that evaluates to a **CommandBarControl** object of the Office class library and that represents the VB menu to which the popup menu is to be added. To provide *Menu*, you can either call the **GetMenu** method of a **Cmd** object or specify it yourself as demonstrated in the Example code.

- *Caption*: Required. A **String** expression that specifies the new popup menu's caption.

- *Position*: Optional. A numeric expression that specifies where on the VB menu to place the popup menu. For example, passing a parameter of 1 to *Position* places the popup menu at the top of the VB menu. If *Position* is not passed, the popup menu is placed at the bottom of the menu.

- *Separator*: Optional. A **Boolean** expression that specifies that the popup menu being added is to have a separator bar above it on the menu (**True**) or is just an ordinary popup menu (the default of **False**).

ERROR HANDLING

AddPopupMenu returns an object instance that evaluates to **Nothing** upon failure.

A-A

COMMENTS

Before you declare *mVar* as a **CommandBarControl** object of the Office class library and call the **AddPopupMenu** method, you must set a reference to the Microsoft Office 8.0 Object Library. After calling **AddPopupMenu**, you must do two more things:

- Add menu items to the **CommandBarControl** object returned by **AddPopupMenu**. You can do this by calling the **AddMenuItem** method of a **Cmd** object.

- Make the menu items responsive to a mouse click with the **CommandBarEvents** property of an **Events** object. See the topics for the **CommandBarEvents** property and **CommandBarEvents** object for details about how to do this.

To delete a VB popup menu that was previously added with **AddPopupMenu**, apply the **Delete** method of a **CommandBarControl** object to the module-level object variable that was assigned the popup menu. When you delete a popup menu, any menu items attached to it are also deleted.

 It is possible to call the **AddPopupMenu** method to add a popup menu to an existing popup menu (and so on, up to a maximum of four nested levels). However, nesting popup menus is not good programming practice and is not recommended. You should follow VB's own design principles in this regard and only attach a popup menu to a VB menu.

METHOD'S CODE

See the Help topic AddPopupMenu Method in ADDINEFS.HLP or the **AddPopupMenu** method's procedure in VBAI.VBP.

EXAMPLE CODE

See the Help topic AddPopupMenu Method Example in ADDINEFS.HLP or the procedure DemoAddPopupMenuMet in DEMOSYNT.VBP.

AddToAddInToolbar Method

AddToAddInToolbar is a **Sub** that adds a button that references an add-in to the Add-In toolbar that will be displayed the next time an instance of VB's IDE is started.

USAGE

Obj.**AddToAddInToolbar** *sFileName, sProgID, sAddInName, ShowOnToolbar, ForceAdd-InToolBar*

The **AddToAddInToolbar** method's syntax supports named arguments and contains these parts:

- *Obj*: Required. An object expression that evaluates to a **Manager** object of the VB Add-In Toolbar ActiveX component (AITOOL.DLL).

- *sFileName*: Required. A **String** expression that specifies the path and name of the add-in's DLL or EXE file.

- *sProgID*: Required. A **String** expression that specifies the programmatic ID of the add-in. The value for *sProgID* is listed in VBADDIN.INI.

- *sAddInName*: Required. A **String** expression that specifies the name of the add-in whose button is to be added. The value for *sAddInName* is listed in the Add-In Manager dialog box.

- *ShowOnToolbar*: Required. A **Boolean** expression that specifies whether the add-in will appear on the Add-In toolbar (**True**) or not (**False**) the next time an instance of VB is started.

- *ForceAddInToolBar*: Required. A **Boolean** expression that specifies that the Add-In toolbar is automatically displayed the next time an instance of VB is started (**True**). If *ForceAddInToolBar* is **False**, no change to the Add-In toolbar's current display status is made the next time an instance of VB is started.

COMMENTS

You can call **AddToAddInToolbar** from any VB application, not just an add-in. To call it, you must first instantiate the Manager class of the VB Add-In Toolbar ActiveX component. You can create a **Manager** object either by setting a reference to the ActiveX component and declaring an object variable **As New** AddInToolbar.Manager (early binding), or by declaring an object variable as **Object** and assigning it a reference to a **Manager** object with the **CreateObject** function (late binding). To delete a button from the Add-In toolbar, call the **RemoveAddInFromToolbar** method of a **Manager** object.

When you make changes to the Add-In toolbar with the Add/Remove Toolbar Items dialog box, the toolbar is refreshed as soon as you close the dialog box. However, when you call the **AddToAddInToolbar** method, the Add-In toolbar is not refreshed until the next instance of VB's IDE is started. The **AddButton** method of an **AITBar** object compensates for this deficiency by adding a button and immediately refreshing the toolbar for the current instance of VB.

What the **AddToAddInToolbar** method actually does is write entries to the Windows registry and VBADDIN.INI. For example, to add a button for the API Text Viewer add-in, it writes either a "0" (*ShowOnToolbar* is **False**) or a "1" (*ShowOnToolbar* is **True**) to the ShowOnToolbar entry of the appropriate registry subkey. If the subkey does not exist, **AddToAddInToolbar** creates it. HKEY_CURRENT_USER\Software\Microsoft\Visual Basic\5.0\AddInToolbar\VB API Viewer would be the subkey for the API Text Viewer add-in. If *ForceAddInToolBar* is set to **True**, **AddToAddInToolbar** also writes "1" to VBADDIN.INI for the API Text Viewer add-in's entry.

1) VB's Help file misleadingly implies that the *ForceAddInToolBar* argument of **AddToAddInToolbar** determines the display status of the Add-In toolbar the next time VB is started (**True** = Yes, **False** = No). This suggests that if you set *ForceAddInToolBar* to **False**, the Add-In toolbar will not be displayed. Instead, setting *ForceAddInToolBar* to **False** does not write an entry to VBADDIN.INI and so has no effect at all on the display status of the Add-In toolbar the next time an instance of VB is started. 2) The sample code in VB's Help file for **AddToAddInToolbar** will not run (there is a comma missing immediately following the string "MyAddIn Title").

A-A

See the Help topic AddToAddInToolbar Method Example in ADDINEFS.HLP or the procedure DemoManagerObj in DEMOSYNT.VBP.

AddToolBar Method (VBAI)

AddToolBar is a **Function** that adds a custom toolbar for add-ins to VB's IDE and returns the new toolbar as a **CommandBar** object of the Office class library.

USAGE

Set *mVar* = *Obj*.**AddToolBar**(*VBE, Caption,* [*Floating*]) **As** Office.**CommandBar**

The **AddToolBar** method's syntax supports named arguments and contains these parts:

- *Obj*: Required. An object expression that evaluates to a **Cmd** object of the VBAI class library.

- *mVar*: Required. A module-level object variable declared in the add-in's **ClassModule** connection object as a **CommandBar** object of the Office class library. It is assigned the object instance returned by **AddToolBar**.

- *VBE*: Required. An object expression that evaluates to a **VBE** object of the VBIDE class library.

- *Caption*: Required. A **String** expression that specifies the caption that appears on the new toolbar's title bar (if it is floating).

- *Floating*: Optional. A **Boolean** expression that specifies that the toolbar being added is to be docked at the bottom of VB's main window (the default of **False**) or is not to be docked (**True**). If the toolbar is not docked, it is initially displayed in the center of the screen. Once the toolbar has been added, it behaves like other VB toolbars and can be floated/docked by double-clicking on it and toggling between the two states.

ERROR HANDLING

AddToolBar returns an object instance that evaluates to **Nothing** upon failure.

COMMENTS

Before you declare *mVar* as a **CommandBar** object of the Office class library and call the **AddToolBar** method, you must set a reference to the Microsoft Office 8.0 Object Library. After calling **AddToolBar**, you must do two more things:

- Add buttons to the **CommandBar** object returned by **AddToolBar**. You can do this by calling the **AddToolBarItem** method of a **Cmd** object.

- Make the buttons responsive to a mouse click with the **CommandBarEvents** property of an **Events** object. See the Dictionary entries for the **CommandBarEvents** property and **CommandBarEvents** object for details about how to do this.

After you add a custom toolbar with **AddToolBar**, it appears on the list of VB toolbars (View|Toolbars command). To delete a custom toolbar, apply the **Delete** method of the **CommandBar** object to the module-level object variable that was assigned the toolbar.

Method's Code

See the Help topic AddToolBar Method in ADDINEFS.HLP or the **AddToolBar** method's procedure in VBAI.VBP.

Example Code

See the Help topic AddToolBar Method Example in ADDINEFS.HLP or the procedure DemoAddToolBarMet in DEMOSYNT.VBP.

AddToolBarButton Method (VBAI)

AddToolBarButton is a **Function** that adds a button for an add-in to a VB toolbar and returns the new button as a **CommandBarControl** object of the Office class library.

Usage

Set *mVar* = *Obj*.**AddToolBarButton**(*VBE, ToolBar, Caption, Bitmap,* [*Position*], [*Separator*]) **As** Office.**CommandBarControl**

The **AddToolBarButton** method's syntax supports named arguments and contains these parts:

- *Obj*: Required. An object expression that evaluates to a **Cmd** object of the VBAI class library.

- *mVar*: Required. A module-level object variable declared in the add-in's **ClassModule** connection object as a **CommandBar** object of the Office class library. It is assigned the object instance returned by **AddToolBarButton**.

- *VBE*: Required. An object expression that evaluates to a **VBE** object of the VBIDE class library.

- *ToolBar*: Required. An object expression that evaluates to a **CommandBar** object of the Office class library and that represents the VB toolbar to which the button is to be added. To provide *ToolBar*, you should first call the **AddToolBar** method of a **Cmd** object.

- *Caption*: Required. A **String** expression that specifies the button's tooltip.

- *Bitmap*: Required. A **String** expression that specifies the path and file name of a bitmap that is to be placed on the button. For the best appearance, this BMP file should be 16 x 16 pixels, like the files on the VB5 path \GRAPHICS\BITMAPS\TLBR_W95. **AddToolBarButton** will compress and use a larger bitmap but its appearance will be distorted. Passing a non-BMP graphic file or a zero-length string (that is, "" or **vbNullString**) causes **AddToolBarButton** to fail.

- *Position*: Optional. A numeric expression that specifies where on the VB toolbar to place the button. For example, passing a parameter of 1 to *Position* places the button at the left of the toolbar. If *Position* is not passed, the button is placed at the right of the toolbar.

- *Separator*: Optional. A **Boolean** expression that specifies that the button being added is to have a separator bar before it on the toolbar (**True**) or is just an ordinary button (the default of **False**).

A-A

ERROR HANDLING

AddToolBarButton returns an object instance that evaluates to **Nothing** upon failure.

COMMENTS

Before you declare *mVar* as a **CommandBarControl** object of the Office class library and call the **AddToolBarButton** method, you must set a reference to the Microsoft Office 8.0 Object Library. After calling **AddToolBarButton**, you must make the button responsive to a mouse click with the **CommandBarEvents** property of an **Events** object. See the Dictionary entries for the **CommandBarEvents** property and **CommandBarEvents** object for details about how to do this.

To delete a button that was previously added with **AddToolBarButton**, apply the **Delete** method of the **CommandBarControl** object to the module-level object variable that was assigned the button.

 It is possible to add a button for an add-in to one of the four built-in VB toolbars (Debug, Edit, Form Editor, and Standard); however, conventional VB add-in programming practice dictates that you not do so. Instead, if you only have one or two buttons to add, you should add them to the VB Add-In toolbar with the **AddButton** method of an **AITBar** object. If you have a larger set of related add-ins, then create a custom toolbar and populate it with buttons by calling the **AddToolBar** and **AddToolBarButton** methods of a **Cmd** object.

METHOD'S CODE

See the Help topic AddToolBarButton Method in ADDINEFS.HLP or the **AddToolBarButton** method's procedure in VBAI.VBP.

EXAMPLE CODE

See the Help topic AddToolBarButton Method Example in ADDINEFS.HLP or the procedure DemoAddToolBarButtonMet in DEMOSYNT.VBP.

AddToolboxProgID Method

AddToolboxProgID is a **Sub** that places an ActiveX control or embedded component in the toolbox, checks its item on the Controls or Insertable Object tab of the Components dialog box, and adds a reference to the component to a project.

USAGE

Obj.**AddToolboxProgID** *ProgID*, [*FileName*]

The **AddToolboxProgID** method's syntax supports named arguments and contains these parts:

- *Obj*: Required. An object expression that evaluates to a **VBProject** object.

- *ProgID*: Required. A **String** expression that specifies the programmatic identifier of the ActiveX control or embedded component to add to VB's toolbox and whose item is to be checked on the Controls or Insertable Object tab of the Components dialog box. Either a version-independent or version-dependent programmatic ID can be used. If a version-independent programmatic ID is specified, the most recent version is used. If the component has an associated type library, this type library is referenced as well.

- *FileName*: Optional. A **String** expression that specifies the file name of the desired type library to be added as a reference to the project. A fully qualified path can be used, but if the file isn't found, the directories searched by the Windows API function **OpenFile** are searched, even if a complete path name is specified.

COMMENTS

If the component specified by *ProgID* already exists in the toolbox, the **AddToolboxProgID** method simply does nothing. There is no method in the Extensibility object model to delete a component from the toolbox. However, if you manually or programmatically delete the project that is referencing the component and no other project is referencing it, VB automatically deletes the component from the toolbox.

EXAMPLE CODE

See the Help topic AddToolboxProgID Method Example in ADDINEFS.HLP or the procedure DemoAddToolboxProgIDMet in DEMOSYNT.VBP.

AfterAddFile Event

AfterAddFile is raised by VB's IDE after you add a VB component's module or other file to a project with the Project|Add File command or add it programmatically with an add-in.

USAGE

*Obj*_AfterAddFile(**ByVal** *VBProject*, **ByVal** *FileType*, **ByVal** *FileName*)

The **AfterAddFile** event's syntax contains these parts:

- *Obj*: An object expression that evaluates to a **FileControlEvents** object.

- *VBProject*: A **VBProject** object that specifies the name of the project to which the file was added.

- *FileType*: An intrinsic constant of the enumerated type **vbext_FileType**, which specifies the type of file that was added. See the Details section in the **FileControlEvents** object's entry in the Dictionary for a list of these constants.

- *FileName*: A **String** expression that specifies the path and name of the file that was added.

COMMENTS

VB raises the **AfterAddFile** event only for files you add from the Project menu by selecting its Add File command. **AfterAddFile** does not occur if you select Project|Add 'VB Component'. It also does not occur when an FRX file associated with an FRM file is created. In VB4, **AfterAddFile** did occur for FRX files.

VB raises the **AfterAddFile** event if you add a VB component's file either by manually selecting Project|Add File or by adding it programmatically through an add-in. You can write code in the **AfterAddFile** event procedure to perform such tasks as logging information about the event and updating information about the file.

A-A

To make an add-in responsive to an **AfterAddFile** event raised by VB, you first need to declare an object variable as a **FileControlEvents** object and assign it the object returned by the **FileControlEvents** property of an **Events** object. For detailed information about how to do this, see the **FileControlEvents** object's entry in the Dictionary.

VB's Help file incorrectly states that **AfterAddFile** is a member of the **FileControl** object. Instead, it is a member of the **FileControlEvents** object (in VB4 it was the **FileControl** object).

EXAMPLE CODE

See the Help topic AfterAddFile Event Example in ADDINEFS.HLP or the procedure DemoAfterAddFileEvt in DEMOSYNT.VBP.

AfterChangeFileName Event

AfterChangeFileName is raised by VB's IDE after you save a VB file with the File|Save 'Name' or File|Save Project command for a new file, with the File|Save 'Name' As or File|Save Project As command for an existing file, with the File|Make 'Name' command, or save it programmatically with an add-in.

USAGE

*Obj*_**AfterChangeFileName**(ByVal *VBProject*, **ByVal** *FileType*, **ByVal** *NewName*, **ByVal** *OldName*)

The **AfterChangeFileName** event's syntax contains these parts:

- *Obj*: An object expression that evaluates to a **FileControlEvents** object.

- *VBProject*: A **VBProject** object that specifies the name of the project for which the file's name was changed.

- *FileType*: An intrinsic constant of the enumerated type **vbext_FileType**, which specifies the type of file that was added. See the Details section in the **FileControlEvents** object's entry in the Dictionary for a list of these constants.

- *NewName*: A **String** expression that specifies the new path and name of the file.

- *OldName*: A **String** expression that specifies the old path and name of the file.

COMMENTS

AfterChangeFileName does not occur for an FRX file associated with an FRM file whose name is changed. In VB4, **AfterChangeFileName** did occur for FRX files. An add-in cannot prevent a file from being saved or renamed/saved because the operation is complete; however, it can log information about the event, prompt the user to delete the original file, and so on.

To make an add-in responsive to an **AfterChangeFileName** event raised by VB, you first need to declare an object variable as a **FileControlEvents** object and assign it the object returned by the **FileControlEvents** property of an **Events** object. For detailed information about how to do this, see the **FileControlEvents** object's entry in the Dictionary.

A-A

Example Code

See the Help topic AfterChangeFileName Event Example in ADDINEFS.HLP or the procedure DemoAfterChangeFileNameEvt in DEMOSYNT.VBP.

AfterCloseFile Event

AfterCloseFile is raised by VB's IDE after you close a project with the File|New Project, File|Open Project, or File|Remove Project command; after you shut down VB with the File|Exit command or the Close command of the Control menu; or after you perform these actions programmatically with an add-in.

Usage

*Obj*_**AfterCloseFile**(**ByVal** *VBProject*, **ByVal** *FileType*, **ByVal** *FileName*, **ByVal** *WasDirty*)

The **AfterCloseFile** event's syntax contains these parts:

- *Obj*: An object expression that evaluates to a **FileControlEvents** object.

- *VBProject*: A **VBProject** object that specifies the name of the project that was closed.

- *FileType*: An intrinsic constant of the enumerated type **vbext_FileType**, which specifies the type of file that was closed. See the Details section in the **FileControlEvents** object's entry in the Dictionary for a list of these constants.

- *FileName*: A **String** expression that specifies the path and name of the file that was closed.

- *WasDirty*: A **Boolean** expression that specifies whether changes were saved to a file prior to it being closed, as listed in Settings.

Settings

The *WasDirty* argument's possible values are:

- *True*: The file was dirty when it was closed; that is, the user elected to not save changes made to the file prior to closing it.

- *False*: The file was not dirty when it was closed; that is, the user elected to save changes made to the file prior to closing it.

Comments

The **AfterCloseFile** event can occur once for each add-in connected to a **FileControlEvents** object in each project; once for each form, module, class, and control file; and once for the project file. **AfterCloseFile** does not occur if the form is dirty and the user selects No on the Save Changes to the Following Files dialog box. It also does not occur for FRX files when a project is closed. In VB4, **AfterCloseFile** did occur for FRX files.

An add-in cannot prevent a file from being written to disk or the project from being closed because the operation is complete when **AfterCloseFile** is raised; however, it can perform other tasks such as logging information about the event, backing up the file, or comparing versions of an EXE or DLL file.

To make an add-in responsive to an **AfterCloseFile** event raised by VB, you first need to declare an object variable as a **FileControlEvents** object and assign it the object returned by the **FileControlEvents** property of an **Events** object. For detailed information about how to do this, see the **FileControlEvents** object's entry in the Dictionary.

 VB's Help file incorrectly states that **AfterCloseFile** is a member of the **FileControl** object. Instead, it is a member of the **FileControlEvents** object (in VB4 it was the **FileControl** object).

EXAMPLE CODE

See the Help topic AfterCloseFile Event Example in ADDINEFS.HLP or the procedure DemoAfterCloseFileEvt in DEMOSYNT.VBP.

AfterRemoveFile Event

AfterRemoveFile is raised by VB's IDE after you remove a VB component's module or other file from a project with the Project|Remove 'File Name' command or remove it programmatically with an add-in.

USAGE

*Obj*_**AfterRemoveFile**(**ByVal** *VBProject*, **ByVal** *FileType*, **ByVal** *FileName*)

The **AfterRemoveFile** event's syntax contains these parts:

- *Obj*: An object expression that evaluates to a **FileControlEvents** object.

- *VBProject*: A **VBProject** object that specifies the name of the project from which the file was removed.

- *FileType*: An intrinsic constant of the enumerated type **vbext_FileType**, which specifies the type of file that was removed. See the Details section in the **FileControlEvents** object's entry in the Dictionary for a list of these constants.

- *FileName*: A **String** expression that specifies the path and name of the file that was removed.

COMMENTS

The **AfterRemoveFile** event occurs in all add-ins that are connected to a **FileControlEvents** object. The **AfterRemoveFile** does not occur for files that are removed before they have been saved at least once. It also does not occur for an FRX file associated with an FRM file. In VB4, **AfterRemoveFile** did occur for FRX files.

An add-in cannot prevent the removed file from being written to disk because the operation is complete; however, it can perform other tasks such as logging information about the event, updating information about the project, or prompting the user to delete the removed file from the hard disk.

To make an add-in responsive to an **AfterRemoveFile** event raised by VB, you first need to declare an object variable as a **FileControlEvents** object and assign it the object returned by the **FileControlEvents** property of an **Events** object. For detailed information about how to do this, see the **FileControlEvents** object's entry in the Dictionary.

 VB's Help file incorrectly states that **AfterRemoveFile** is a member of the **FileControl** object. Instead, it is a member of the **FileControlEvents** object (in VB4 it was the **FileControl** object).

EXAMPLE CODE

See the Help topic AfterRemoveFile Event Example in ADDINEFS.HLP or the procedure DemoAfterRemoveFileEvt in DEMOSYNT.VBP.

AfterWriteFile Event

AfterWriteFile is raised by VB's IDE after you save a file to disk with the File|Save 'Name', File|Save 'Name' As, File|Save Project or File|Save Project As command; or after you programmatically save it with an add-in.

USAGE

*Obj*_**AfterWriteFile**(**ByVal** *VBProject*, **ByVal** *FileType*, **ByVal** *FileName*, **ByVal** *Result*)

The **AfterWriteFile** event's syntax contains these parts:

- *Obj*: An object expression that evaluates to a **FileControlEvents** object.

- *VBProject*: A **VBProject** object that specifies the name of the project to which the file was saved.

- *FileType*: An intrinsic constant of the enumerated type **vbext_FileType**, which specifies the type of file that was saved. See the Details section in the **FileControlEvents** object's entry in the Dictionary for a list of these constants.

- *FileName*: A **String** expression that specifies the path and name of the file that was saved.

- *Result*: An **Integer** expression that specifies the result of the save operation, as listed in Settings.

Settings

The possible values for *Result* are:

- 0: Save operation succeeded.

- 1: Save operation was canceled.

- 2: Save operation failed.

COMMENTS

The **AfterWriteFile** event occurs in all add-ins that are connected to a **FileControlEvents** object. An add-in cannot prevent the file from being written to disk because the operation is complete; however, it can use this event to perform other tasks such as logging information about the event, updating information about the file, backing up the file, or comparing versions of an EXE or DLL file.

To make an add-in responsive to an **AfterWriteFile** event raised by VB, you first need to declare an object variable as a **FileControlEvents** object and assign it the object returned by the **FileControlEvents** property of an **Events** object. For detailed information about how to do this, see the **FileControlEvents** object's entry in the Dictionary.

> VB's Help file incorrectly states that **AfterWriteFile** is a member of the **FileControl** object. Instead, it is a member of the **FileControlEvents** object (in VB4 it was the **FileControl** object).

EXAMPLE CODE

See the Help topic AfterWriteFile Event Example in ADDINEFS.HLP or the procedure DemoAfterWriteFileEvt in DEMOSYNT.VBP.

AITBar Object (VBAI)

AITBar provides methods for an add-in to call to manipulate the VB Add-In toolbar.

USAGE

Obj.Mbr Args

An **AITBar** object's syntax supports named arguments and contains these parts:

- *Obj*: Required. An object expression that evaluates to an **AITBar** object of the VBAI class library.

- *Mbr*: Required. A member of an **AITBar** object.

- *Args*: Required. An argument or arguments of *Mbr*. All members of an **AITBar** object have at least one required argument.

MEMBERS

- Events: None at this time

- Methods: **AddButton, CopyButtonIcon, DelButton, Hide, IsButton, IsDisplayed, Show (AITBar)**

- Properties: None at this time

COMMENTS

To find out if the VB Add-In toolbar is displayed, call the **IsDisplayed** method. To display or hide the toolbar, call the **Show** or **Hide** method. To find out if there is a button for an add-in on the toolbar, call the **IsButton** method. To add a button to or remove a button from the toolbar, call the **AddButton** or **DelButton** method.

> Do not confuse the methods of an **AITBar** object with the **AddToolBar** and **AddToolBarButton** methods of a **Cmd** object. An **AITBar** object's methods work only with the VB Add-In toolbar, while a **Cmd** object's toolbar-related methods are designed to create and manipulate a custom toolbar.

EXAMPLE CODE

See the Help topic AITBar Object Example in ADDINEFS.HLP or the procedure
DemoAITBarObj in DEMOSYNT.VBP.

BeforeLoadFile Event

BeforeLoadFile is raised by VB's IDE before you add a VB component's module or other file
to a project with the Project|Add File command or add it programmatically with an add-in.

USAGE

*Obj*_BeforeLoadFile(**ByVal** *VBProject*, **ByVal** *FileNames()*)

The **BeforeLoadFile** event's syntax contains these parts:

- *Obj*: An object expression that evaluates to a **FileControlEvents** object.

- *VBProject*: A **VBProject** object that specifies the name of the project to which the file is to
  be added.

- *FileNames()*: A **String** expression that specifies the path and name of the file(s) to be added.

COMMENTS

VB raises the **BeforeLoadFile** event only for files you add from the Project menu by selecting
its Add File command. **BeforeLoadFile** does not occur if you select Project|Add 'VB Compo-
nent'. It also does not occur when an FRX file associated with an FRM file is created. In VB4,
BeforeLoadFile did occur for FRX files.

VB raises the **BeforeLoadFile** event if you add a VB component's file either by manually
selecting Project|Add File or by adding it programmatically through an add-in. You can write
code in the **BeforeLoadFile** event procedure to perform such tasks as logging information
about the event, preparing the files to be loaded, and checking out the files.

To make an add-in responsive to a **BeforeLoadFile** event raised by VB, you first need to
declare an object variable as a **FileControlEvents** object and assign it the object returned by
the **FileControlEvents** property of an **Events** object. For detailed information about how to
do this, see the **FileControlEvents** object's entry in the Dictionary.

 1) VB's Help file incorrectly states that **BeforeLoadFile** is a mem-
ber of the **FileControl** object. Instead, it is a member of the **FileControlEvents**
object (in VB4 it was the **FileControl** object). 2) VB's Help file incorrectly
implies that **BeforeLoadFile** will occur when you select File|Project Add (once
for the VBP file and once for each VB component file in the project). In-
stead, **BeforeLoadFile** occurs only when you select Project|Add File or execute
the programmatic equivalent in an add-in.

EXAMPLE CODE

See the Help topic BeforeLoadFile Event Example in ADDINEFS.HLP or the procedure
DemoBeforeLoadFileEvt in DEMOSYNT.VBP.

B-B

Bindable Property

Bindable is a **Boolean** that returns or sets the Bindable attribute associated with a **Member** object. Read/write.

Usage

Obj.**Bindable**[= *Val*]

The **Bindable** property's syntax contains these parts:

- *Obj*: Required. An object expression that evaluates to a **Member** object.

- *Val*: Optional. Only used when you set **Bindable**, *Val* is a **Boolean** expression that specifies whether Data Binding - Property Is Data Bound on the Procedure Attributes Advanced dialog box is checked for a member (**True**) or not (the default of **False**).

Comments

You only set the Bindable attribute of a public **Property** procedure to **True** when you are creating an ActiveX control and are working with the code module of a User Control VB component. You must first do this to enable other data binding options available to an ActiveX control (for example, **DefaultBind** and **DisplayBind**).

You can use the Procedure Attributes Advanced dialog box, accessed from the Tools menu, to manually make a public **Property** procedure bindable (check the Property Is Data Bound checkbox). You can also programmatically make a public **Property** procedure bindable by setting its corresponding **Member** object's **Bindable** property to **True**. When you save the User Control component that contains the **Property** procedure, VB writes a line to the component's text file (for example, Attribute *Name*.VB_MemberFlags = "4", where *Name* is the **Property** procedure's name).

VB does not permit you to manually set **Bindable** for a member that is not a public **Property** procedure. Unfortunately, VB does permit an add-in to programmatically set **Bindable** to **True** for a non-property **Member** object without causing a trappable error. This results in contradictory settings on the Procedure Attributes Advanced dialog box; that is, the Property Is Data Bound checkbox is checked but disabled and the other three checkboxes related to Data Binding are enabled. It can also, under certain circumstances, crash the current instance of VB's IDE.

Example Code

See the Help topic Bindable Property Example in ADDINEFS.HLP or the procedure DemoBindablePrp in DEMOSYNT.VBP.

Browsable Property

Browsable is a **Boolean** that returns or sets the Browsable attribute associated with a **Member** object. Read/write.

USAGE

Obj.**Browsable**[= *Val*]

The **Browsable** property's syntax contains these parts:

- *Obj*: Required. An object expression that evaluates to a **Member** object.

- *Val*: Optional. Only used when you set **Browsable**, *Val* is a **Boolean** expression that specifies whether Don't Show In Property Browser on the Procedure Attributes Advanced dialog
box is checked for a member (**False**) or not (the default of **True**).

COMMENTS

You only set the Browsable attribute of a public **Property** procedure to **False** when you are
creating an ActiveX control and are working with the code module of a User Control VB
component. You would do this to mark a property of the ActiveX control to not be displayed
in VB's Properties window.

You can use the Procedure Attributes Advanced dialog box, accessed from the Tools menu, to
manually make a public **Property** procedure not browsable (check the Don't Show In Property
Browser checkbox). You can also programmatically make a public **Property** procedure not
browsable by setting its corresponding **Member** object's **Browsable** property to **False**. When
you save the User Control component that contains the **Property** procedure, VB writes a line
to the component's text file (for example, Attribute *Name*.VB_MemberFlags = "400", where
Name is the **Property** procedure's name).

VB does not permit you to manually set **Browsable** for a member that is not
a public **Property** procedure. Unfortunately, VB does permit an add-in to
programmatically set **Browsable** to **True** for a non-property **Member** object
without causing a trappable error. This results in contradictory settings on
the Procedure Attributes Advanced dialog box; that is, the Don't Show In
Property Browser checkbox is checked but disabled. It can also, under certain circumstances, crash the current instance of VB's IDE.

EXAMPLE CODE

See the Help topic Browsable Property Example in ADDINEFS.HLP or the procedure
DemoBrowsablePrp in DEMOSYNT.VBP.

BuildFileName Property

BuildFileName returns or sets a **String** that specifies the EXE, DLL, or OCX file name that is
used when the project is compiled. Read/write.

USAGE

Obj.**BuildFileName**[= *Val*]

The **BuildFileName** property's syntax contains these parts:

- *Obj*: Required. An object expression that evaluates to a **VBProject** object.

- *Val*: Optional. Only used when you set **BuildFileName**, *Val* is a **String** expression that specifies the file name and extension to be used for the compiled file. The path is not included in *Val*.

COMMENTS

After you set the **BuildFileName** property, ensure that the **StartUpObject** and **LastUsedPath** properties are set to the values you want. Then you can call the **MakeCompiledFile** method of a **VBProject** object to compile the active project as an EXE, DLL, or OCX file.

EXAMPLE CODE

See the Help topic BuildFileName Property Example in ADDINEFS.HLP or the procedure DemoBuildFileNamePrp in DEMOSYNT.VBP.

BuiltIn Property

BuiltIn returns a **Boolean** that specifies whether a reference is a default reference and cannot be removed (**True**) or is not a default reference and can be removed (**False**). Read-only.

USAGE

Obj.**BuiltIn**

The **BuiltIn** property's syntax contains these parts:

- *Obj*: Required. An object expression that evaluates to a **Reference** object.

COMMENTS

A VB project always contains these three default references, listed in the order of their priority:

- VBA: Visual Basic For Applications (VBA5.DLL)

- VBRUN: Visual Basic runtime objects and procedures (MSVBVM50.DLL)

- VB: Visual Basic objects and procedures (VB5.OLB)

If you try to manually remove a default reference from a VB project by unchecking its item in the References dialog box, VB displays a syntax error message (Can't remove control or reference; in use). If an add-in tries to remove a default reference, trappable error 57101 occurs (Can't remove default reference). See the Example code for a demonstration of this run-time error. If an add-in removes a non-default reference (that is, its **BuiltIn** property is **False**), VB unchecks that reference's item in the References dialog box.

EXAMPLE CODE

See the Help topic BuiltIn Property Example in ADDINEFS.HLP or the procedure DemoBuiltInPrp in DEMOSYNT.VBP.

CanPaste Property

CanPaste returns a **Boolean** that is **True** if the contents of the Clipboard can be pasted to a **VBForm** object or **False** if the contents cannot be pasted. Read-only.

C-C

USAGE

Obj.**CanPaste**

The **CanPaste** property's syntax contains these parts:

- *Obj*: Required. An object expression that evaluates to a **VBForm** object.

COMMENTS

You read **CanPaste** to determine if the Clipboard contains appropriate information (that is, VB control objects) for pasting to a **VBForm** object.

EXAMPLE CODE

See the Help topic CanPaste Property Example in ADDINEFS.HLP or the procedure DemoCanPastePrp in DEMOSYNT.VBP.

Caption Property

Caption returns a **String** that is the text in the title bar of a VB IDE window, or returns or sets the text of a menu item. Read/write.

USAGE

Obj.**Caption**[= *Val*]

The **Caption** property's syntax contains these parts:

- *Obj*: Required. An object expression that evaluates to a **MenuLine** (Hidden), **SubMenu** (Hidden), or **Window** object.

- *Val*: Optional. Only used when you set **Caption**, *Val* is a **String** expression that specifies a menu item. **Caption** is read-only for a **Window** object.

COMMENTS

The title bars of two permanent IDE windows (Toolbox and Color Palette) do not contain text. For these windows the **Caption** property returns a zero-length string (that is, "" or **vbNullString**). Although the **Caption** property of a **Window** object is read-only, you can use the Windows API function **SetWindowText** to change the title of a window. This change remains in effect as long as the window remains open. The new title can be read by the Windows API function **GetWindowText** but not by the **Caption** property. To see how to change the title of an IDE window in VB, run the Example code (normal run mode only).

 The Extensibility object model includes hidden **MenuLine** and **SubMenu** objects to maintain upward compatibility with VB4 add-ins. Microsoft advises that you not use hidden objects or members when developing VB5 add-ins because they may not be available in a future release of VB.

EXAMPLE CODE

See the Help topic Caption Property Example in ADDINEFS.HLP or the procedure DemoCaptionPrp in DEMOSYNT.VBP.

Category Property

Category is a **String** that returns or sets the Category attribute associated with a **Member** object. Read/write.

Usage

Obj.**Category**[= *Val*]

The **Category** property's syntax contains these parts:

- *Obj*: Required. An object expression that evaluates to a **Member** object.

- *Val*: Optional. Only used when you set **Category**, *Val* is a **String** expression that specifies the Category attribute of a **Member** object. The default setting is a zero-length string (that is, "" or **vbNullString**).

Comments

You only set the Category attribute of a public **Property** procedure when you are creating an ActiveX control and are working with the code module of a User Control VB component. You would do this to mark a property of the ActiveX control to be displayed under a particular category in the Properties window. Assigning a category for the public properties of an ActiveX control is highly recommended because VB places all unassigned properties in the Misc category.

You can use the Procedure Attributes Advanced dialog box, accessed from the Tools menu, to manually assign a category to a public **Property** procedure (select an item from the Property Category drop-down box or type an entry). You can also programmatically assign a category to a public **Property** procedure by setting its corresponding **Member** object's **Category** property. The possible settings for the *Val* argument of **Category** are Appearance, Behavior, Data, DDE, Font, List, Misc, Position, Scale, and Text. You can also specify a new, custom category. When you save the User Control component that contains the **Property** procedure, VB writes a line to the component's text file (for example, Attribute *Name*.VB_ProcData.VB_Invoke_Property = ";*Val*", where *Name* is the **Property** procedure's name and *Val* is the category's name).

VB does not permit you to manually set **Category** for a member that is not a public **Property** procedure. Unfortunately, VB does permit an add-in to programmatically set **Category** for a non-property **Member** object without causing a trappable error. This can, under certain circumstances, crash the current instance of VB's IDE.

Example Code

See the Help topic Category Property Example in ADDINEFS.HLP or the procedure DemoCategoryPrp in DEMOSYNT.VBP.

ClassName Property

ClassName returns a **String** that specifies the class name of a **VBControl** object. Read-only.

USAGE

*Obj.*ClassName

The **ClassName** property's syntax contains these parts:

- *Obj*: Required. An object expression that evaluates to a **VBControl** object.

COMMENTS

The class name of a **VBControl** object is listed at the top of the Properties window for each control on a **VBForm** object and is the generic name to the right of the **Name** property setting of the control. Some class names of commonly used controls are **CommandButton, ListBox, TextBox,** and **Label.**

You read **ClassName** to determine the specific kind of **VBControl** object that is selected or is to be manipulated. You can read the **ControlType** property of the **VBControl** object to determine the type of runtime window that a control creates.

EXAMPLE CODE

See the Help topic ClassName Property Example in ADDINEFS.HLP or the procedure DemoClassNamePrp in DEMOSYNT.VBP.

Clear Method

Clear is a **Sub** that deselects all the selected controls on a **VBForm** object.

USAGE

*Obj.*Clear

The **Clear** method's syntax contains these parts:

- *Obj*: Required. An object expression that evaluates to a **SelectedVBControls** collection.

COMMENTS

You can call the **SelectAll** method or set the **InSelection** property of a **VBForm** object to select the **VBControl** objects you want to work with. Prior to doing so, you can call the **Clear** method to initialize the **SelectedVBControls** collection.

EXAMPLE CODE

See the Help topic Clear Method Example in ADDINEFS.HLP or the procedure DemoClear-Met in DEMOSYNT.VBP.

Click Event

Click is raised by VB's IDE after you click on a menu item that is connected to an add-in and to a **CommandBarEvents** object.

Usage

*Obj*_**Click**(**ByVal** *CommandBarControl, Handled, CancelDefault*)

The **Click** event's syntax contains these parts:

- *Obj*: An object expression that evaluates to a **CommandBarEvents** object.

- *CommandBarControl*: A generic **Object** type that evaluates to a **CommandBarControl** object of the Office class library (Microsoft Office 8.0 Object Library) and that represents the menu item that is clicked.

- *Handled*: A **Boolean** expression that specifies that if **True**, another add-in should handle the event; or if **False** (the default), the action of the menu item should not be handled.

- *CancelDefault*: A **Boolean** expression that specifies that if **True**, default behavior is performed unless canceled by a downstream add-in; or if **False** (the default), default behavior is not performed unless restored by a downstream add-in.

Comments

The **Click** event occurs in all add-ins that are connected to a menu item and to a **CommandBarEvents** object. To make an add-in responsive to a **Click** event raised by VB, you first need to declare an object variable as a **CommandBarEvents** object and assign it the object returned by the **CommandBarEvents** property of an **Events** object. For detailed information about how to do this, see the **CommandBarEvents** object's topic.

 The **Click** event does not occur for an add-in that is connected and started from the VB Add-In toolbar.

Example Code

See the Help topic Click Event Example in ADDINEFS.HLP or the procedure DemoClickEvt in DEMOSYNT.VBP.

Close Method

Close is a **Sub** that closes and destroys or closes and hides a window within VB's IDE.

Usage

Obj.**Close**

The **Close** method's syntax contains these parts:

- *Obj*: Required. An object expression that evaluates to a **Window** object.

Comments

The **Close** method behaves differently depending on the kind of window that it is applied to:

- For a window that is a code pane, **Close** destroys the code pane.

- For a window that is a designer, **Close** destroys the contained designer. There are five kinds of designer windows: 1. Forms; 2. User controls; 3. Property pages; 4. User document forms; 5. ActiveX designers.

- For permanent IDE windows that are always available on the View menu (for example, the Properties window), **Close** merely hides the window.

If you want to close a specific kind of window (designer, code pane, or IDE window), you can use the **Type** property of a **Window** object to read which kind of window you are dealing with. **Type** returns 0 - vbext_wt_CodeWindow, 1 - vbext_wt_Designer, or a value greater than 1 for a specific IDE window. There are many different kinds of IDE windows, ranging from 2 - vbext_wt_Browser to 15 - vbext_wt_ToolWindow. See the **Type** Property entry in the Dictionary for a list of them.

There is no **Open** or **Show** method that you can use after applying the **Close** method to a window. To open an IDE window, you can set its **Visible** property to **True**, because setting the **Visible** property of an IDE window to **False** has the same effect as applying the **Close** method to it. To open a designer or code pane window, which is destroyed by the **Close** method, you must first return its related **VBComponent** object and then apply the **Activate** method to it.

EXAMPLE CODE
See the Help topic Close Method Example in ADDINEFS.HLP or the procedure DemoCloseMet in DEMOSYNT.VBP.

CloseSubKey Method (VBAI)

CloseSubKey is a **Function** that releases the handle to a subkey in the Windows registry and returns **True**.

USAGE
Obj.**CloseSubKey**(*HWndSubKey*) **As Boolean**

The **CloseSubKey** method's syntax supports named arguments and contains these parts:

- *Obj*: Required. An object expression that evaluates to a **Reg** object of the VBAI class library.

- *HWndSubKey*: Required. A **Long** expression that is the handle to an open subkey. An add-in can provide *HWndSubKey* by calling the **OpenSubKey** method of a **Reg** object.

ERROR HANDLING
CloseSubKey returns **False** upon failure.

COMMENTS
The handle to a subkey should not be used after it has been closed, because it will no longer be valid. Subkey handles should not be left open any longer than necessary. **CloseSubKey** is a proxy or wrapper method for the Windows API function **RegCloseKey**.

CloseSubKey does not necessarily write information to the registry before returning **True**; it can take as long as several seconds for the contents of the cache to be written to the hard disk. If you must explicitly write registry information to the hard disk, call the Windows API function **RegFlushKey** directly. However, you should only call **RegFlushKey** if you require absolute certainty that registry changes are on disk. In general, **RegFlushKey** rarely, if ever, needs to be used.

Method's Code

See the Help topic CloseSubKey Method in ADDINEFS.HLP or the **CloseSubKey** method's procedure in VBAI.VBP.

Example Code

See the Help topic CloseSubKey Method Example in ADDINEFS.HLP or the procedure DemoRegObj in DEMOSYNT.VBP.

Cmd Object (VBAI)

Cmd provides methods for an add-in to call to manipulate VB menus and custom toolbars.

Usage

Obj.Mbr Args

A **Cmd** object's syntax supports named arguments and contains these parts:

- *Obj*: Required. An object expression that evaluates to a **Cmd** object of the VBAI class library.

- *Mbr*: Required. A member of a **Cmd** object.

- *Args*: Required. An argument or arguments of *Mbr*. All members of a **Cmd** object have at least one required argument.

Members

- Events: None at this time

- Methods: **AddMenu (Cmd)**, **AddMenuItem**, **AddPopupMenu**, **AddToolBar**, **AddToolBarButton**, **GetMenu**, **IsMenuItem**

- Properties: None at this time

Comments

To get an object reference to an existing menu in VB's IDE, call the **GetMenu** method. To add a new menu or a custom toolbar to VB's IDE, call the **AddMenu** or **AddToolBar** method. To add a menu item or popup menu to a menu in VB's IDE, call the **AddMenuItem** or **AddPopupMenu** method. To add a button to a custom toolbar in VB's IDE, call the **AddToolBarButton** method.

Do not confuse the **AddToolBar** and **AddToolBarButton** methods of a **Cmd** object with the methods of an **AITBar** object. A **Cmd** object's toolbar-related methods are designed to create and manipulate a custom toolbar while an **AITBar** object's methods work only with the VB Add-In toolbar.

Example Code

See the Example code for the individual methods of a **Cmd** object.

CodeLocation Property

CodeLocation returns a **Long** that is the line number in the code module where a member is declared. Read-only.

Usage

Obj.**CodeLocation**

The **CodeLocation** property's syntax contains these parts:

- *Obj*: Required. An object expression that evaluates to a **Member** object.

Comments

Under certain circumstances, the **CodeLocation** property of a **Member** object can return the same value as the **ProcBodyLine** property of a **CodeModule** object.

 1) VB's Help file incorrectly states that **CodeLocation** takes an optional *PropKind* argument that specifies the kind of **Property** procedure (**Get, Let,** or **Set**). Instead, **CodeLocation** never takes an argument. 2) VB's Help file incorrectly states that the enumerated type **vbext_PropertyKind** exists in the VBIDE class library. It does not exist.

Example Code

See the Help topic CodeLocation Property Example in ADDINEFS.HLP or the procedure DemoCodeLocationPrp in DEMOSYNT.VBP.

CodeModule Object/Property

A **CodeModule** object represents the code contained by a **VBComponent** object, such as a form, class, or document. The read-only **CodeModule** property of a **VBComponent** or **CodePane** object returns an object instance of the **CodeModule** class.

Instantiation

Dim *Obj* **As** [VBIDE.]**CodeModule|Object|Variant**
Set *Obj* = **VBE.ActiveVBProject.VBComponents**[.**Item**](*Index*).**CodeModule**
Set *Obj* = **VBE.CodePanes**[.**Item**](*Index*).**CodeModule**

Usage

#1: *Obj*[.*Mbr*[*Args*]]
#2: *Obj*.*MbrA*.*MbrB*[= *ValB* | *ArgsB*]

The **CodeModule** syntax supports named arguments and contains these parts:

- *Obj*: Required. A variable to be assigned an object instance. *Obj* can be named the same as the **CodeModule** class being instantiated. *Obj* can also be declared as the generic **Object** or as **Variant**, but this slows performance.

- VBIDE: Optional. The VB5 Extensibility object library containing the **CodeModule** class.

- *Index*: Required. Used with the default **Item** method, *Index* is a numeric or **String** expression that specifies the ordinal position of a **VBComponent** object in a **VBComponents** collection or of a **CodePane** object in a **CodePanes** collection. If *Index* is a **String** expression, it must evaluate to the **Name** property of a **VBComponent** object. *Index* cannot accept a **String** expression for a **CodePanes** collection.

- *Mbr*: Required. A member of a **CodeModule** object.

- *Args*: Optional. You use *Args* when *Mbr* is a method that you are calling.

- *MbrA*: Required. A **CodeModule** object's property that returns an object.

- *MbrB*: Required. A member of the object that is returned by *MbrA*.

- *ValB | ArgsB*: Optional. You use *ValB* if *MbrB* is a property being set or *ArgsB* if *MbrB* is a method being called.

MEMBERS

- Events: None at this time

- Methods: **AddFromFile**, **AddFromString**, **CreateEventProc**, **DeleteLines**, **Find**, **InsertLines**, **ReplaceLine**

- Properties: **CodePane**, **CountOfDeclarationLines**, **CountOfLines**, **Lines**, **Members**, **Parent**, **ProcBodyLine**, **ProcCountLines**, **ProcOfLine**, **ProcStartLine**, **VBE**

COMMENTS

You can access a **CodeModule** object by:

- Returning the **CodeModule** property of a **VBComponent** object.

- Returning the **CodeModule** property of a **CodePane** object.

The **CodeModule** property returns **Nothing** if a **VBComponent** object doesn't have a code module associated with it. The members of a **CodeModule** object enable you to modify (add, delete, or edit) the code associated with a component on a line-by-line basis. For example, the **InsertLines** method adds statements and procedures to a code module and the **ProcBodyLine** property returns the starting line number of a code module's procedure.

It is easy to get confused by the **CodeModule** and **CodePane** objects/properties. They are different entities with different methods and properties. You can easily toggle back and forth between a **CodeModule** and **CodePane** object by reading their respective **CodePane** and **CodeModule** properties.

VB's Help file incorrectly states that a single **CodeModule** object can have multiple **CodePane** objects associated with it. Instead, the **CodePane** property of a **CodeModule** object always returns the same single **CodePane** object.

EXAMPLE CODE

See the Help topic CodeModule Object/Property Example in ADDINEFS.HLP or the procedure DemoCodeModuleObj in DEMOSYNT.VBP.

CodePane Object/Property

A **CodePane** object is an item in a **CodePanes** collection and it represents the code pane that is used for entering and editing code. The read-only **CodePane** property of a **CodeModule** object returns an object instance of the **CodePane** class.

INSTANTIATION

Dim *Obj* As [VBIDE.]**CodePane|Object|Variant**
Set *Obj* = **VBE.ActiveVBProject.VBComponents**[.**Item**](*Index*).**CodeModule.CodePane**
Set *Obj* = **VBE.CodePanes**[.**Item**](*Index*)

USAGE

#1: *Obj*[.*Mbr*[*Args*]]
#2: *Obj.MbrA.MbrB*[= *ValB* |*ArgsB*]

The **CodePane** syntax supports named arguments and contains these parts:

- *Obj*: Required. A variable to be assigned an object instance. *Obj* can be named the same as the **CodePane** class being instantiated. *Obj* can also be declared as the generic **Object** or as **Variant,** but this slows performance.

- VBIDE: Optional. The VB5 Extensibility object library containing the **CodePane** class.

- *Index*: Required. Used with the default **Item** method, *Index* is a numeric or **String** expression that specifies the ordinal position of a **VBComponent** object in a **VBComponents** collection or of a **CodePane** object in a **CodePanes** collection. If *Index* is a **String** expression, it must evaluate to the **Name** property of a **VBComponent** object. *Index* cannot accept a **String** expression for a **CodePanes** collection.

- *Mbr*: Required. A member of a **CodePane** object.

- *Args*: Optional. You use *Args* when *Mbr* is a method that you are calling.

- *MbrA*: Required. A **CodePane** object's property that returns an object.

- *MbrB*: Required. A member of the object that is returned by *MbrA*.

- *ValB* |*ArgsB*: Optional. You use *ValB* if *MbrB* is a property being set or *ArgsB* if *MbrB* is a method being called.

MEMBERS

- Events: None at this time

- Methods: **GetSelection, SetSelection, Show**

- Properties: **CodeModule, CodePaneView, Collection, CountOfVisibleLines, TopLine, VBE, Window**

COMMENTS

Each **CodePane** object is associated with and contained by one **CodeModule** object. It is easy to get confused by the **CodePane** and **CodeModule** objects/properties. They are different entities with different methods and properties. You can easily toggle back and forth between a

CodePane and a **CodeModule** object by reading their respective **CodeModule** and **CodePane** properties.

 VB's Help file incorrectly states that multiple **CodePane** objects can be associated with one **CodeModule** object. Instead, the **CodePane** property of a **CodeModule** object always returns the same, single **CodePane** object.

EXAMPLE CODE
See the Help topic CodePane Object/Property Example in ADDINEFS.HLP or the procedure DemoCodePaneObj in DEMOSYNT.VBP.

CodePanes Collection/Property
A **CodePanes** collection contains the active **CodePane** objects in VB's IDE. The read-only **CodePanes** property of a **VBE** object returns an object instance of the **CodePanes** class.

INSTANTIATION
Dim *Obj* **As** [**VBIDE.**]**CodePanes|Object|Variant**
Set *Obj* = **VBE.CodePanes**

USAGE
#1: *Obj.Mbr*
#2: *Obj*[.**Item**](*Index*)[.*MbrA*[= *ValA*| *ArgsA*]]
#3: *Obj.MbrB.MbrC*[= *ValC*| *ArgsC*]

The **CodePanes** syntax supports named arguments and contains these parts:

- *Obj*: Required. A variable to be assigned an object instance. *Obj* can be named the same as the **CodePanes** class being instantiated. *Obj* can also be declared as the generic **Object** or as **Variant**, but this slows performance.

- VBIDE: Optional. The VB5 Extensibility object library containing the **CodePanes** class.

- *Mbr*: Required. A member of a **CodePanes** collection other than the **Item** method.

- *Index:* Required. Used with the default **Item** method, *Index* is a numeric expression that specifies the ordinal position of a **CodePane** object in a **CodePanes** collection. For a **CodePanes** collection, *Index* cannot be a **String** expression.

- *MbrA*: Optional. A member of a **CodePane** object.

- *ValA*|*ArgsA*: Optional. You use *ValA* if *MbrA* is a property being set or *ArgsA* if *MbrA* is a method being called.

- *MbrB*: Required. A **CodePanes** collection's property that returns a **VBE** object.

- *MbrC*: Required. A member of the **VBE** object that is returned by *MbrB*.

- *ValC*|*ArgsC*: Optional. You use *ValC* if *MbrC* is a property being set or *ArgsC* if *MbrC* is a method being called.

C-C

MEMBERS

- Events: None at this time

- Methods: **Item**

- Properties: **Count, Parent, VBE**

COMMENTS

A **CodePanes** collection that contains **CodePane** objects represents the set of open code panes in all VB projects within VB's IDE. A code pane is the code window in which you enter and edit code. You can access a **CodePane** object by calling the **Item** method of a **CodePanes** collection or by using a **For...Each...Next** statement to loop through the items of a **CodePanes** collection until you find the **CodePane** object you want. You can use the **Count** property to return the number of **CodePane** objects in the collection.

 VB's Help file incorrectly states that multiple **CodePane** objects can be associated with one **CodeModule** object. Instead, the **CodePane** property of a **CodeModule** object always returns the same, single **CodePane** object.

EXAMPLE CODE

See the Help topic CodePanes Collection/Property Example in ADDINEFS.HLP or the procedure DemoCodePanesObj in DEMOSYNT.VBP.

CodePaneView Property

CodePaneView returns a **Long** indicating whether a code pane window is in Procedure view or Full Module view. Read-only.

USAGE

Obj.**CodePaneView**

The **CodePaneView** property's syntax contains these parts:

- *Obj*: Required. An object expression that evaluates to a **CodePane** object.

COMMENTS

CodePaneView returns either 0 - **vbext_cv_ProcedureView** or 1 - **vbext_cv_FullModuleView**. You establish the default setting for **CodePaneView** on the Editor tab of the Options dialog box when you check or uncheck Default To Full Module View. However, once an individual code pane window is displayed with the default setting, you can manually toggle between the two views by clicking on the Procedure View or Full Module View button on the left side of the code pane's horizontal scroll bar. Manually changing the view mode setting of one code pane window does not affect the settings of other code panes.

 Although you can manually set the view mode for an individual **CodePane** object, there is no way to do so programmatically.

C-C

EXAMPLE CODE

See the Help topic CodePaneView Property Example in ADDINEFS.HLP or the procedure DemoCodePaneViewPrp in DEMOSYNT.VBP.

Collection Property

Collection returns an object instance of the collection class that contains the object you are working with. Read-only.

INSTANTIATION

Dim *Col* **As** [**VBIDE.**] *Cls* | **Object** | **Variant**
Set *Col* = **VBE.** *Obj.***Collection**

The **Collection** property's syntax supports named arguments and contains these parts:

- *Col*: Required. A variable to be assigned an object instance. *Col* can be named the same as the collection class (**Addins, CodePanes, Members, Properties, References, VBComponents, VBControls, VBProjects** or **Windows**) being instantiated. *Col* can also be declared as the generic **Object** or as **Variant**, but this slows performance.

- VBIDE: Optional. The VB5 Extensibility object library containing the collection class.

- *Cls*: Required. The name of the collection class being instantiated.

- *Obj*: Required. An object that has the **Collection** property as a member.

For information on how to use *Col*, see the Dictionary entries for the individual collection entries (that is, **Addins, CodePanes, Members,** and so on).

COMMENTS

Most objects in the Extensibility object model have either a **Parent** property or a **Collection** property that points to the object's container object. You use the **Collection** property to access the properties and methods of the collection to which an object belongs.

The **Collection** property is the default member of a **Member** object and does not have to be explicitly specified. In the Object Browser, a default member is marked with a small cyan circle at the top-left of the member's icon.

EXAMPLE CODE

See the Help topic Collection Property Example in ADDINEFS.HLP or the procedure DemoCollectionPrp in DEMOSYNT.VBP.

CommandBarEvents Object/Property

A **CommandBarEvents** object represents the **Click** event raised by VB's IDE when a developer clicks on a menu item connected to an add-in. The read-only **CommandBarEvents** property of an **Events** object returns a **CommandBarEvents** object.

USAGE

#1: **Public WithEvents** *CommandBar* **As CommandBarEvents**
#2: **Set** *CommandBar* = **VBE.Events.CommandBarEvents**(*Item*)

The **CommandBarEvents** syntax contains these parts:

C-C

- *CommandBar*: Required. A module-level object variable, in an add-in's **ClassModule** object, that is assigned the **CommandBarEvents** object returned by the **CommandBarEvents** property. *CommandBar* must be declared with the **Public** statement and the **WithEvents** keyword and may not be declared as the generic **Object** or as **Variant**.

- *Item*: Required. An object expression that evaluates to a **CommandBarControl** object representing the menu item whose **Click** event you want to monitor.

 In Usage #1, **CommandBarEvents** is the object. In Usage #2, **CommandBarEvents** is a property of an **Events** object. This property returns a **CommandBarEvents** object.

MEMBERS

- Events: **Click**

- Methods: None at this time

- Properties: None at this time

COMMENTS

A **CommandBarEvents** object allows an add-in to receive and react to a specified menu item's **Click** event raised by VB's IDE. To use a **CommandBarEvents** object, follow these steps in a **ClassModule** object in the add-in's project:

- Use the **Public** statement and the **WithEvents** keyword to declare an object variable that will respond to a menu item's **Click** event raised by VB. You do this in the Declarations section. The declaration statement adds a **CommandBarEvents** object, under the name of the object variable, to the class module's Object drop-down box. You can give this object variable any name you want, but *CommandBar* makes the most sense.

- Select CommandBar from the Object drop-down box of the class module and VB automatically creates the beginning and ending statements of the **Click** event procedure.

- Write code in the **Click** event procedure that will execute when VB raises the **Click** event.

- Make the add-in responsive to the menu item's **Click** event. You do this by using the **CommandBarEvents** property of an **Events** object to return a **CommandBarEvents** object that is assigned to *CommandBar*. You can write this assignment statement in the **OnConnection** method of an add-in's **IDTExtensibility** object or you can call another procedure from **OnConnection** and make the assignment there. See the **SetAIMenuItem** procedure in DEMOSYNT.VBP for a demonstration of how to do this.

EXAMPLE CODE

See the Help topic CommandBarEvents Object/Property Example in ADDINEFS.HLP or the procedures DemoCommandBarEventsObj and SetAIMenuItem in DEMOSYNT.VBP.

C-C

CommandBars Collection/Property

CommandBars returns an object instance of the **CommandBars** collection class that contains the command bars in VB's IDE, including command bars that support shortcut menus. Read-only.

INSTANTIATION

Dim *Obj* **As** [Office.]**CommandBars**|**Object**|**Variant**
Set *Obj* = VBE.CommandBars

USAGE

#1: *Obj.Mbr*
#2: *Obj*[**.Item**](*Index*)[*.MbrA*[= *ValA* | *ArgsA*]]
#3: *Obj.MbrB.MbrC*[= *ValC* | *ArgsC*]

The **CommandBars** syntax supports named arguments and contains these parts:

- *Obj*: Required. A variable to be assigned an object instance. *Obj* can be named the same as the **CommandBars** class being instantiated. *Obj* can also be declared as the generic **Object** or as **Variant**, but this slows performance.

- Office: Optional. The Microsoft Office 8.0 object library containing the **CommandBars** class.

- *Mbr*: Required. A member of a **CommandBars** collection other than the **Item** method.

- *Index*: Required. Used with the default **Item** method, *Index* is a numeric or **String** expression that specifies the ordinal position of a **CommandBar** object in a **CommandBars** collection. If *Index* is a **String** expression, it must evaluate to the **Name** property of a **CommandBar** object.

- *MbrA*: Optional. A member of a **CommandBar** object.

- *ValA* | *ArgsA*: Optional. You use *ValA* if *MbrA* is a property being set or *ArgsA* if *MbrA* is a method being called.

- *MbrB*: Required. A **CommandBars** collection's property that returns an object.

- *MbrC*: Required. A member of the object that is returned by *MbrB*.

- *ValC* | *ArgsC*: Optional. You use *ValC* if *MbrC* is a property being set or *ArgsC* if *MbrC* is a method being called.

COMMENTS

A **CommandBars** collection contains all the **CommandBar** objects in VB's IDE. A **CommandBar** object is the new programmable object from the Office class library that you use in VB to control a menu or toolbar. All the following items are represented by **CommandBar** objects:

- Menu bars, toolbars, and shortcut menus

- Menus on menu bars and toolbars

- Submenus on menus, submenus, and shortcut menus

You can access a **CommandBar** object by calling the **Item** method of a **CommandBars** collection or by using a **For...Each...Next** statement to loop through the items of a **CommandBars** collection until you find the **CommandBar** object you want. You can use either the name or index number for the *Index* argument of the **Item** method to specify a menu bar or toolbar. However, you must use the name to specify a menu, shortcut menu, or submenu. You can use the **Count** property to return the number of **CommandBar** objects in the collection and you can call the **Add** method to add an item to the **CommandBars** collection.

The **CommandBars** property is part of the VBIDE class library. However, the **CommandBars** collection that it returns and the methods and properties of a **CommandBars** collection belong to the Office class library.

 The documentation in VB's Help file and Books Online regarding a **CommandBars** collection, **CommandBar** object, other associated objects, and their members is inadequate. Also, the Microsoft Office 8.0 object library's Help file (VBAOFF8.HLP) is not included with VB; you must purchase Microsoft Office 97 to get that Help file. If you are struggling with Office's command bar syntax, try calling the methods of a **Cmd** object of the VBAI class library. They are both easy to use and well-documented in ADDINEFS.HLP.

EXAMPLE CODE

See the Help topic CommandBars Collection/Property Example in ADDINEFS.HLP or the procedure DemoCommandBarsPrp in DEMOSYNT.VBP.

CompatibleOleServer Property

CompatibleOleServer returns or sets a **String** that specifies the compatible OLE Automation server for an ActiveX component's project. Read/write.

USAGE

Obj.**CompatibleOleServer**[= *Val*]

The **CompatibleOleServer** property's syntax contains these parts:

- *Obj*: Required. An object expression that evaluates to a **VBProject** object.

- *Val*: Optional. Only used when you set **CompatibleOleServer**, *Val* is a **String** expression that specifies the path and file name of the EXE, DLL, or OCX file that is to be compatible with the ActiveX component's project.

COMMENTS

You manually set **CompatibleOleServer** on the Component tab of the Project Properties dialog box. This setting is only enabled if the project is an ActiveX component (EXE or DLL ActiveX server, OCX ActiveX control, EXE or DLL ActiveX Add-In, and so on). If you try to programmatically set **CompatibleOleServer** for a non-ActiveX component project, trappable error 50264 occurs (Method 'CompatibleOleServer' of object '_VBProject' failed). Therefore, you should always read the **Type** property of a **VBProject** object and ensure that it is not 0 - **vbext_pt_StandardExe** before setting **CompatibleOleServer**.

In addition to only being able to set **CompatibleOleServer** for an ActiveX component project, you must also have first made the ActiveX component project into a DLL, EXE, or OCX file. See the Example code for how to do this programmatically. When you set **CompatibleOleServer** programmatically, the Binary Compatibility setting on the Component tab is always the option that is checked.

EXAMPLE CODE

See the Help topic CompatibleOleServer Property Example in ADDINEFS.HLP or the procedure DemoCompatibleOleServerPrp in DEMOSYNT.VBP.

Connect Method (VBAI)

Connect is a **Function** that connects or disconnects an add-in, checks or unchecks the add-in's item in the Add-In Manager's dialog box, and returns **True**.

USAGE

Obj.**Connect**(*VBE, ProgID, Flag*) **As Boolean**

The **Connect** method's syntax supports named arguments and contains these parts:

- *Obj*: Required. An object expression that evaluates to a **Util** object of the VBAI class library.

- *VBE*: Required. An object expression that evaluates to a **VBE** object of the VBIDE class library.

- *ProgID*: Required. A **String** expression that specifies the **ProgID** property's setting of the **AddIn** object that is being connected or disconnected. The programmatic IDs of all registered add-ins are listed in VBADDIN.INI. If *ProgID* is set to a nonexistent programmatic ID or to "AddInToolbar.Connect", **Connect** fails.

- *Flag*: Required. A **Boolean** expression that specifies whether the add-in is being connected (**True**) or disconnected (**False**).

ERROR HANDLING

Connect returns **False** upon failure.

COMMENTS

If an add-in sets another **AddIn** object's **Connect** property to **True** or **False**, VB connects or disconnects the add-in represented by that **AddIn** object; however, VB does not check or uncheck the related item in the Add-In Manager dialog box's list and the Extensibility object model does not provide a way to programmatically do so. A **Util** object's **Connect** method both sets an **AddIn** object's **Connect** property to **True** or **False** and checks or unchecks the related item in the Add-In Manager dialog box's list.

Encapsulation Violation **Connect** runs a separate thread in a **Timer** object (tmrAIMgrDlgBox) on a hidden **Form** object (frmTimer) in the VBAI class library that, after **Connect** opens the Add-In Manager dialog box, finds the dialog box's window, checks or unchecks the add-in's item, and closes the dialog box. This **Timer** thread executes while drawing of the desktop window is suspended and, as a result, these actions are not visible to the developer. Although this technique violates the encapsulation of a **Util** object, it is necessary because the Add-In Manager dialog box is displayed modally and cannot be closed programmatically except by a separate thread.

METHOD'S CODE

See the Help topic Connect Method in ADDINEFS.HLP or the **Connect** method's procedure in VBAI.VBP.

EXAMPLE CODE

See the Help topic Connect Method Example in ADDINEFS.HLP or the procedure DemoAITBarObj in DEMOSYNT.VBP.

Connect Property

Connect returns or sets a **Boolean** that specifies the connected state of an add-in. Read/write.

USAGE

Obj.**Connect**[= *Val*]

The **Connect** property's syntax contains these parts:

- *Obj*: Required. An object expression that evaluates to an **AddIn** object.

- *Val*: Optional. Only used when you set **Connect**, *Val* is a **Boolean** expression that specifies whether to connect an add-in to a VB menu (**True**) or disconnect an add-in from a VB menu (**False**).

COMMENTS

When you set an add-in's **Connect** property to **True**, VB calls the **OnConnection** method of an **IDTExtensibility** object implemented in the **ClassModule** object that serves as the add-in. If you set the **Connect** property of an add-in that is already connected to **False**, VB calls an **IDTExtensibility** object's **OnDisconnection** method. A currently running add-in can programmatically disconnect itself by setting its own **Connect** property to **False**. When you run an add-in from the Add-In Toolbar, the add-in is active but is not connected to a VB menu and so **Connect** returns **False**.

 If you set an add-in's **Connect** property to **True** or **False**, VB either adds the add-in to or removes it from a menu; however, if you then manually display the Add-In Manager dialog box, the add-in's item in the Available Add-Ins list will not reflect the change in its **Connect** property's value. The Extensibility object model does not provide a way to programmatically check or uncheck an item in the Add-In Manager dialog box's list nor does it provide a way to run a connected item. You can work around these limitations by using the **Connect** method of a **Util** object and another technique, as shown in the Example code.

EXAMPLE CODE

See the Help topic Connect Property Example in ADDINEFS.HLP or the procedure DemoConnectPrp in DEMOSYNT.VBP.

ContainedVBControls Collection/Property

A **ContainedVBControls** collection contains the **VBControl** objects that are on a **VBForm** object or that are contained by another **VBControl** object. The read-only **ContainedVBControls** property of a **VBForm** or **VBControl** object returns an object instance of the **Contained-VBControls** class.

INSTANTIATION

Dim *Obj* **As** [**VBIDE.**]**ContainedVBControls|Object|Variant**
Set *Obj*=**VBE.ActiveVBProject.VBComponents**[**.Item**](*IndexA*)**.Designer. ContainedVBControls**
Set *Obj*=**VBE.ActiveVBProject.VBComponents**[**.Item**](*IndexA*)**.Designer.VBControls** [**.Item**](*IndexB*)**.ContainedVBControls**

In order to read the **ContainedVBControls** property, first use the **Designer** property of a **VBComponent** object to return a **VBForm** object. Then you can access the **ContainedVBControls** property, as illustrated by the **Set** statements, to return a **ContainedVBControls** collection.

USAGE

#1: *Obj.Mbr*
#2: *Obj* [**.Item**](*IndexC*)[*.MbrA*[*ArgsA*]]
#3: *Obj.MbrB.MbrC*[= *ValC* | *ArgsC*]

The **ContainedVBControls** syntax supports named arguments and contains these parts:

- *Obj*: Required. A variable to be assigned an object instance. *Obj* can be named the same as the **ContainedVBControls** class being instantiated. *Obj* can also be declared as the generic **Object** or as **Variant**, but this slows performance.

- VBIDE: Optional. The VB5 Extensibility object library containing the **Contained VBControls** class.

- *IndexA*: Required. Used with the default **Item** method, *IndexA* is a numeric or **String** expression that specifies the ordinal position of a **VBComponent** object in a **VBComponents** collection. If *IndexA* is a **String** expression, it must evaluate to the **Name** property of a **VBComponent** object.

- *IndexB*: Required. Used with the default **Item** method, *IndexB* is a numeric or **String** expression that specifies the ordinal position of a **VBControl** object in a **VBControls** collection. If *IndexB* is a **String** expression, it must evaluate to the **Name** property of the control represented by a **VBControl** object.

- *Mbr*: Required. A member of a **ContainedVBControls** collection other than the **Item** method.

- *IndexC*: Required. Used with the default **Item** method, *IndexC* is a numeric or **String** expression that specifies the ordinal position of a **VBControl** object in a **ContainedVBControls** collection. If *IndexC* is a **String** expression, it must evaluate to the **Name** property of the control represented by a **VBControl** object.

- *MbrA*: Optional. A member of a **VBControl** object.

- *ArgsA*: Optional. You use *ArgsA* if *MbrA* is a method being called.

- *MbrB*: Required. A **ContainedVBControls** collection's property that returns an object.

- *MbrC*: Required. A member of the object that is returned by *MbrB*.

- *ValC* | *ArgsC*: Optional. You use *ValC* if *MbrC* is a property being set or *ArgsC* if *MbrC* is a method being called.

MEMBERS

- Events: None at this time

- Methods: **Add, Item, Remove**

- Properties: **Count, Parent, VBE**

COMMENTS

A **ContainedVBControls** collection that contains **VBControl** objects represents the intrinsic and ActiveX controls contained on a form or by a container control. For controls contained on a form, that form's **VBControls** and **ContainedVBControls** collections are equivalent and you normally use the **VBControls** collection/property syntax because it is simpler.

The major use for a **ContainedVBControls** collection is to enable you to manipulate controls that are contained by another **VBControl** object. Only a **ContainedVBControls** collection can give you access to controls layered on a **PictureBox** or **Frame** control.

You use a **ContainedVBControls** collection to add controls to or delete them from a container control. You can access a **VBControl** object by calling the **Item** method of a **ContainedVBControls** collection or by using a **For...Each...Next** statement to loop through the items of a **ContainedVBControls** collection until you find the **VBControl** object you want. You can use the **Count** property to return the number of **VBControl** objects in the collection.

EXAMPLE CODE

See the Help topic ContainedVBControls Collection/Property Example in ADDINEFS.HLP or the procedure DemoContainedVBControlsObj in DEMOSYNT.VBP.

Container Property

Container returns an **Object** type that represents a containing **VBControl** or **VBForm** object. Read-only.

USAGE

Obj.**Container**

The **Container** property's syntax contains these parts:

- *Obj*: Required. An object expression that evaluates to a **VBControl** object.

COMMENTS

Container returns an object reference that evaluates to either the **VBControl** or the **VBForm** object that contains a **VBControl** object. Once you have the object reference returned by **Container**, you can return or set any of its properties and call any of its methods.

EXAMPLE CODE

See the Help topic Container Property Example in ADDINEFS.HLP or the procedure DemoContainerPrp in DEMOSYNT.VBP.

ControlObject Property

ControlObject returns an **Object** type that represents an instance of the design-time IDispatch pointer provided by a **VBControl** object. Read-only.

USAGE

Obj.**ControlObject**

The **ControlObject** property's syntax contains these parts:

- *Obj*: Required. An object expression that evaluates to a **VBControl** object.

COMMENTS

For example, a **Toolbar** control object provides an object through a **PropertyPage** object's **ControlObject** property to set the number of buttons. If there is no design-time IDispatch pointer provided by a **VBControl** object, **ControlObject** returns **Nothing**.

EXAMPLE CODE

See the Help topic ControlObject Property Example in ADDINEFS.HLP or the procedure DemoControlObjectPrp in DEMOSYNT.VBP.

ControlType Property

ControlType returns a **Long** that specifies the kind of runtime window that a **VBControl** object creates. Read-only.

USAGE

Obj.**ControlType**

The **ControlType** property's syntax contains these parts:

- *Obj*: Required. An object expression that evaluates to a **VBControl** object.

COMMENTS

The **ControlType** property is supposed to return one of three possible values:

- 1 - **vbext_ct_Light**: A lightweight control that has no **hWnd** property at runtime (for example, a **Label** object).

- 2 - **vbext_ct_Standard**: A control that has an **hWnd** property at runtime (for example, a **CommandButton** object).

- 3 - **vbext_ct_Container**: A control that has an **hWnd** property at runtime and that can contain other controls (for example, a **PictureBox** object).

 There is a bug in the VBIDE class library that results in the **ControlType** property always returning a value of 2 - **vbext_ct_Standard**, regardless of the kind of **VBControl** object. See the Example code for a demonstration of this bug. You can call the **GetControlType** method of a **Util** object to correct for this bug and return the correct value for all intrinsic and ActiveX controls that ship with VB5.

EXAMPLE CODE

See the Help topic ControlType Property Example in ADDINEFS.HLP or the procedure DemoControlTypePrp in DEMOSYNT.VBP.

Copy Method

Copy is a **Sub** that copies the selected controls on a **VBForm** object to the Clipboard.

USAGE

Obj.**Copy**

The **Copy** method's syntax contains these parts:

- *Obj*: Required. An object expression that evaluates to a **SelectedVBControls** collection.

COMMENTS

Before you call **Copy**, you can call the **SelectAll** method of a **VBForm** object or set the **InSelection** property of a **VBControl** object to select the controls you want to copy. After you call **Copy**, you can read the **CanPaste** property of a **VBForm** object and, if it returns **True**, call the **Paste** method to paste the controls from the **Clipboard** object to a **VBForm** object.

EXAMPLE CODE

See the Help topic Copy Method Example in ADDINEFS.HLP or the procedure DemoCopyMet in DEMOSYNT.VBP.

CopyButtonIcon Method (VBAI)

CopyButtonIcon is a **Function** that copies the icon from an add-in's toolbar button to an add-in's menu item and returns **True**.

USAGE

Obj.**CopyButtonIcon**(*VBE, Desc, Menu*) **As Boolean**

The **CopyButtonIcon** method's syntax supports named arguments and contains these parts:

- *Obj*: Required. An object expression that evaluates to an **AITBar** object of the VBAI class library.

- *VBE*: Required. An object expression that evaluates to a **VBE** object of the VBIDE class library.

- *Desc*: Required. A **String** expression that specifies the setting of the Project Description entry of the add-in whose toolbar button's icon is to be copied. This entry is made on the General tab of the Project Properties dialog box for the add-in's project. If Show Tool has been checked on the General tab of VB's Options dialog box, **Desc** is displayed when you move the mouse over the button. If *Desc* is set to a value for which no button is displayed, **CopyButtonIcon** fails.

- *Menu*: Required. An object expression that evaluates to a **CommandBarControl** object of the Office class library and that represents the menu item for a connected add-in. You can get *Menu* by first calling the **AddMenuItem** method of a **Cmd** object of the VBAI class library.

ERROR HANDLING

CopyButtonIcon returns **False** upon failure.

COMMENTS

When you connect an add-in to a VB menu item, you want to give that menu item the same icon that appears on the add-in's VB Add-In toolbar button. You can call **CopyButtonIcon** to do this immediately after calling the **AddMenuItem** method from the **OnConnection** method of an **IDTExtensibility** object. If the VB Add-in toolbar or the add-in's button is not displayed, **CopyButtonIcon** does nothing and returns **False**.

 Before you call **CopyButtonIcon**, make sure the VB Add-In toolbar and the add-in's button are displayed first by calling some combination of the **IsDisplayed**, **Show**, **IsButton**, and **AddButton** methods of an **AITBar** object.

METHOD'S CODE

See the Help topic CopyButtonIcon Method in ADDINEFS.HLP or the **CopyButtonIcon** method's procedure in VBAI.VBP.

EXAMPLE CODE

See the Help topic CopyButtonIcon Method Example in ADDINEFS.HLP or the procedure DemoCopyButtonIconMet in DEMOSYNT.VBP.

Count Property

Count returns a **Long** that specifies the number of items in an add-in collection. Read-only.

USAGE

Obj.**Count**

The **Count** property's syntax contains these parts:

- *Obj*: Required. An object expression that evaluates to a collection object.

COMMENTS

You can use the **Count** property with a **For...Next** statement to carry out an operation on the items in a collection. Instead of using **Count** with a **For...Next** statement, you can use a **For...Each...Next** statement to loop through the items in a collection until you find the one you want. Add-in collections are one-based, so when looping through a collection's items, you do not need to offset the value of **Count** by -1 (as you must, for example, for the zero-based **ListCount** property of a **ListBox** object).

EXAMPLE CODE

See the Help topic Count Property Example in ADDINEFS.HLP or the procedure DemoCountPrp in DEMOSYNT.VBP.

CountOfDeclarationLines Property

CountOfDeclarationLines returns a **Long** that contains the number of lines of code in the Declarations section of a code module. Read-only.

USAGE

Obj.**CountOfDeclarationLines**

The **CountOfDeclarationLines** property's syntax contains these parts:

- *Obj*: Required. An object expression that evaluates to a **CodeModule** object.

COMMENTS

The line numbers in a code module begin at 1 in the Declarations section. **CountOfDeclarationLines** includes in its returned value any blank lines that are at the bottom of the Declarations section of a code module.

If you have just added a code module to the project and Require Variable Declaration is checked on the Editor tab of VB's Options dialog box (that is, the **Option Explicit** statement appears at the top of the module's Declarations section), **CountOfDeclarationLines** returns 2, which includes one blank line at the bottom of the Declarations section. If the **Option Explicit** statement does not appear at the top of the module's Declarations section, **CountOfDeclarationLines** initially returns 0.

If you use the **InsertLines** method to add an entire procedure to a code module, you can always safely use the value returned by **CountOfDeclarationLines** + 1 for the *Line* argument of **InsertLines**.

Example Code

See the Help topic CountOfDeclarationLines Property Example in ADDINEFS.HLP or the procedure DemoCountOfDeclarationLinesPrp in DEMOSYNT.VBP.

CountOfLines Property

CountOfLines returns a **Long** that contains the number of lines of code in a code module. Read-only.

Usage

Obj.CountOfLines

The **CountOfLines** property's syntax contains these parts:

- *Obj*: Required. An object expression that evaluates to a **CodeModule** object.

Comments

The line numbers in a code module begin at 1 in the Declarations section. **CountOfLines** includes in its returned value any blank lines that are contained in the code module.

For a form module, **CountOfLines** does not include the beginning and ending code stubs for any of a form's event procedures in its line count until you either manually select an event procedure in the code pane or use the **CreateEventProc** method of a code module to define an event procedure.

If you have just added a code module to the project and Require Variable Declaration is checked on the Editor tab of VB's Options dialog box (that is, the **Option Explicit** statement appears at the top of the module's Declarations section), **CountOfLines** returns 2, which includes one blank line at the bottom of the Declarations section. If the **Option Explicit** statement does not appear at the top of the module's Declarations section, **CountOfLines** initially returns 0.

Example Code

See the Help topic CountOfLines Property Example in ADDINEFS.HLP or the procedure DemoCountOfLinesPrp in DEMOSYNT.VBP.

CountOfVisibleLines Property

CountOfVisibleLines returns a **Long** that contains the number of lines visible in a code pane. Read-only.

USAGE

Obj.CountOfVisibleLines

The **CountOfVisibleLines** property's syntax contains these parts:

- *Obj*: Required. An object expression that evaluates to a **CodePane** object.

COMMENTS

The line numbers in a code module begin at 1 in the Declarations section. **CountOfVisibleLines** includes in its returned value any blank lines that are visible in the code pane. If you change the height of the code pane by resizing it with the mouse, you either increase or decrease the number of visible lines in the code pane.

The number of visible lines in a code pane can also be affected by the screen resolution, with VB's IDE displaying more visible lines at higher resolutions. The default number of visible lines for the most common screen resolutions are:

- 640×480 pixels: 10 lines (Windows) or 12 lines (NT)

- 800×600 pixels: 18 lines (Windows) or 20 lines (NT)

- 1024×768 pixels: 29 lines (Windows) or 31 lines (NT)

- 1280×1024 pixels: 47 lines (Windows) or 48 lines (NT)

 These figures for the number of visible lines in a code pane apply only when VB's display mode is SDI (single document interface) and the code pane is first opened.

EXAMPLE CODE

See the Help topic CountOfVisibleLines Property Example in ADDINEFS.HLP or the procedure DemoCountOfVisibleLinesPrp in DEMOSYNT.VBP.

CreateEventProc Method

CreateEventProc is a **Function** that writes the beginning and ending statements of an event procedure in a code module.

USAGE

Obj.CreateEventProc *EventName, ObjName*

The **CreateEventProc** method's syntax supports named arguments and contains these parts:

- *Obj*: Required. An object expression that evaluates to a **CodeModule** object.

- *EventName*: Required. A **String** expression that specifies the name of the event procedure to add to the module (for example, QueryUnload).

- *ObjName*: Required. A **String** expression that specifies the name of the object that is the source of the event (for example, Form).

RETURNS

CreateEventProc returns a **Long** that specifies the line number on which the **Sub** statement of the event procedure starts. This is the same value that the **ProcBodyLine** property returns.

COMMENTS

No event procedure exists until you manually select an event procedure in the code pane of a module or until you use the **CreateEventProc** method to write one. Using **CreateEventProc** also has the effect of opening the code pane window, just as if you had applied the **Show** method to a **CodePane** object.

If its *ObjName* argument refers to a nonexistent object, **CreateEventProc** causes trappable error 57102 (Event handler is invalid). If its *EventName* argument refers to a nonexistent event, **CreateEventProc** causes trappable error 440 (Event handler is invalid).

EXAMPLE CODE

See the Help topic CreateEventProc Method Example in ADDINEFS.HLP or the procedure DemoCreateEventProcMet in DEMOSYNT.VBP.

CreateToolWindow Method

CreateToolWindow is a **Function** that creates a new Tool window in VB's IDE containing an ActiveX document object and returns an object instance of the **Window** class.

USAGE

Obj.**CreateToolWindow**(*AddInInst, ProgID, Caption, GuidPosition, DocObj*)

The **CreateToolWindow** method's syntax supports named arguments and contains these parts:

- *Obj*: Required. An object expression that evaluates to a **Windows** collection.

- *AddInInst*: Required. An object expression that evaluates to the **AddIn** object with which the Tool window is to be associated.

- *ProgID*: Required. A **String** expression that specifies the programmatic ID of the ActiveX document object. The ActiveX document object is a component in the add-in project referenced by *AddInInst*.

- *Caption*: Required. A **String** expression that specifies the caption to be displayed on the Tool window's title bar.

- *GuidPosition*: Required. A **String** expression that specifies a unique identifier for the Tool window. You must assign *GuidPosition*. See the Example code for a demonstration of how to do this.

- *DocObj*: Required. An object expression that evaluates to the generic **Object** type and that is to represent the ActiveX document object. This object will be set by reference in the call to the **CreateToolWindow** method. You can then use *DocObj* to programmatically control the ActiveX document application.

COMMENTS

CreateToolWindow allows you to extend VB's IDE by adding an ActiveX document to it when you connect and run an add-in. A **Window** object returned by **CreateToolWindow** is, unlike the normal modal or modeless form that an add-in can display, an item in a **Windows** collection. This means that the window is dockable and has all the other properties and methods associated with a **Window** object.

You can use **CreateToolWindow** to add to VB's IDE a text editor or any other application that can be run as an ActiveX document. Although you can close the Tool window that contains the ActiveX document application, the application itself is not terminated until you disconnect the add-in, referenced by *AddInInst*, with which the Tool window is associated or until you close the current instance of VB's IDE.

 VB's Help file incorrectly states that **CreateToolWindow** applies to a **Window** object. Instead, it applies to a **Windows** collection and returns a **Window** object.

EXAMPLE CODE

See the Help topic CreateToolWindow Method Example in ADDINEFS.HLP or the procedure DemoCreateToolWindowMet in DEMOSYNT.VBP.

Current Property (Hidden)

Current is a hidden property of a **CodePanes** collection that returns the active **CodePane** object. Read-only.

USAGE

Obj.**Current**

The **Current** property's syntax contains these parts:

*   *Obj*: Required. An object expression that evaluates to a **CodePanes** collection.

COMMENTS

Although **Current** is hidden, it is accessible and seems to return the same **CodePane** object as the **ActiveCodePane** property does. See the Example code for a demonstration of its behavior.

EXAMPLE CODE

See the Help topic Current Property (Hidden) Example in ADDINEFS.HLP or the procedure DemoCurrentPrp in DEMOSYNT.VBP.

Cut Method

Cut is a **Sub** that deletes the selected controls from a **VBForm** object and copies them to the Clipboard.

USAGE

Obj.**Cut**

C-D

The **Cut** method's syntax contains these parts:

- *Obj*: Required. An object expression that evaluates to a **SelectedVBControls** collection.

COMMENTS

Before you call **Cut**, you can call the **SelectAll** method of a **VBForm** object or set the **InSelection** property of a **VBControl** object to select the controls you want to cut. After you call **Cut**, you can read the **CanPaste** property of a **VBForm** object and, if it returns **True**, call the **Paste** method to paste the controls on the Clipboard onto a **VBForm** object.

EXAMPLE CODE

See the Help topic Cut Method Example in ADDINEFS.HLP or the procedure DemoCutMet in DEMOSYNT.VBP.

DefaultBind Property

DefaultBind is a **Boolean** that returns or sets the DefaultBind attribute associated with a **Member** object. Read/write.

USAGE

Obj.**DefaultBind**[= *Val*]

The **DefaultBind** property's syntax contains these parts:

- *Obj*: Required. An object expression that evaluates to a **Member** object.

- *Val*: Optional. Only used when you set **DefaultBind**, *Val* is a **Boolean** expression that specifies whether Data Binding—This Property Binds To DataField on the Procedure Attributes Advanced dialog box is checked for a member (**True**) or not (the default of **False**).

COMMENTS

You only set the DefaultBind attribute of a public **Property** procedure to **True** when you are creating an ActiveX control and are working with the code module of a User Control VB component. DefaultBind specifies a property of the ActiveX control as the one property that binds to the field specified by the **DataField** property of the ActiveX control. Before you can set DefaultBind, however, you must first set the Bindable attribute of the public **Property** procedure to **True**.

You can use the Procedure Attributes Advanced dialog box, accessed from the Tools menu, to manually make a public **Property** procedure default bound (check the This Property Binds To DataField checkbox). You can also programmatically make a public **Property** procedure default bound by setting its corresponding **Member** object's **DefaultBind** property to **True**. When you save the User Control component that contains the **Property** procedure, VB writes a line to the component's text file (for example, Attribute *Name*.VB_MemberFlags = "24", where *Name* is the **Property** procedure's name).

VB does not permit you to manually set **DefaultBind** for a member that is not a public **Property** procedure. Unfortunately, VB does permit an add-in to programmatically set **DefaultBind** to **True** for a non-property **Member** object without causing a trappable error. This results in contradictory settings on the Procedure Attributes Advanced dialog box; that is, the Property Is Data Bound checkbox is unchecked but the This Property Binds To DataField checkbox is checked. It can also, under certain circumstances, crash the current instance of VB's IDE.

EXAMPLE CODE
See the Help topic DefaultBind Property Example in ADDINEFS.HLP or the procedure DemoDefaultBindPrp in DEMOSYNT.VBP.

DelButton Method (VBAI)

DelButton is a **Function** that turns off the entry for an add-in button in VB's Add-In toolbar Windows registry subkey, immediately removes the button from the toolbar, and returns **True**.

USAGE
Obj.**DelButton**(*VBE, ProgID*) **As Boolean**

The **DelButton** method's syntax supports named arguments and contains these parts:

- *Obj*: Required. An object expression that evaluates to an **AITBar** object of the VBAI class library.

- *VBE*: Required. An object expression that evaluates to a **VBE** object of the VBIDE class library.

- *ProgID*: Required. A **String** expression that specifies the programmatic ID of the add-in to be removed from the toolbar. The programmatic IDs of all registered add-ins are listed in VBADDIN.INI. If *ProgID* is set to "AddInToolbar.Connect" (that is, the VB Add-In Toolbar add-in itself) or to a nonexistent programmatic ID, **DelButton** fails.

ERROR HANDLING
DelButton returns **False** upon failure.

COMMENTS
DelButton improves upon the **RemoveAddInFromToolbar** method of a **Manager** object of the VB Add-In Toolbar add-in. When you call the **RemoveAddInFromToolbar** method, the new button is not removed from the Add-In toolbar until the next instance of VB's IDE is started. **DelButton** corrects this deficiency of the **RemoveAddInFromToolbar** method by immediately removing the button if the toolbar is displayed. If the toolbar is not displayed, **DelButton** only turns off the button's entry in VB's Add-In toolbar Windows registry subkey; the next time the toolbar is displayed, the button will not appear.

DelButton fails if the VB Add-In toolbar is not displayed or if the add-in button specified by *ProgID* is not displayed on the toolbar. You can check if the toolbar is displayed by calling the **IsDisplayed** method of an **AITBar** object or check if a button exists for a particular add-in by calling the **IsButton** method of an **AITBar** object.

METHOD'S CODE

See the Help topic DelButton Method in ADDINEFS.HLP or the **DelButton** method's procedure in VBAI.VBP.

EXAMPLE CODE

See the Help topic DelButton Method Example in ADDINEFS.HLP or the procedure DemoAITBarObj in DEMOSYNT.VBP.

DeleteLines Method

DeleteLines is a **Sub** that removes a line or lines of code from a code module.

USAGE

Obj.**DeleteLines** *StartLine,*[*Count* = 1]

The **DeleteLines** method's syntax supports named arguments and contains these parts:

- *Obj*: Required. An object expression that evaluates to a **CodeModule** object.

- *StartLine*: Required. A **Long** expression or integer that specifies the first line that you want to remove from the code module. *StartLine* must be greater than zero.

- *Count*: Optional. A **Long** expression or integer that specifies the number of lines that you want to remove from the code module.

COMMENTS

If you omit the *Count* argument, it defaults to 1 and **DeleteLines** removes one line. The way VB's Object Browser shows that a default value is assigned to *Count*, if it is omitted, is to display the optional argument as [*Count* = 1]. If *Count* is 0, **DeleteLines** executes but no lines are removed and no trappable error occurs.

VB's Help file incorrectly states that when trappable error 5 occurs (for example, when *StartLine* is set to 0), the **Description** property of the **Err** object is set to "Invalid procedure call". Instead, **Description** is set to "Invalid procedure call or argument".

EXAMPLE CODE

See the Help topic DeleteLines Method Example in ADDINEFS.HLP or the procedure DemoDeleteLinesMet in DEMOSYNT.VBP.

DelSubKey Method (VBAI)

DelSubKey is a **Function** that removes a subkey and its value(s) from the Windows registry and returns **True**.

USAGE

Obj.**DelSubKey**(*HWnd*, [*SubKey* = ""]) **As Boolean**

The **DelSubKey** method's syntax supports named arguments and contains these parts:

- *Obj*: Required. An object expression that evaluates to a **Reg** object of the VBAI class library.

- *HWnd*: Required. A **Long** expression that is the handle to a predefined key (Windows 95) or open subkey (Windows 95 or Windows NT4). *HWnd* can be one of the intrinsic constants of the enumerated type **aiKeyType** listed under Settings below or a handle retuned by the **OpenSubKey** method of a **Reg** object.

- *SubKey*: Optional. For Windows 95, a **String** expression that specifies the name of a subkey that is a descendant of *HWnd*. If *SubKey* is not passed, it defaults to a zero-length string (that is, "" or **vbNullString**). For Windows NT4, an add-in should not pass *SubKey*.

SETTINGS
The predefined key values for *HWnd* (**aiKeyType**) are:

- 0 - **aiKTClasses**: HKEY_CLASSES_ROOT key

- 1 - **aiKTCurUser**: HKEY_CURRENT_USER key

- 2 - **aiKTMachine**: HKEY_LOCAL_MACHINE key

- 3 - **aiKTUsers**: HKEY_USERS key

- 5 - **aiKTCurConfig**: HKEY_CURRENT_CONFIG key

- 6 - **aiKTDynData**: HKEY_DYN_DATA key

ERROR HANDLING
DelSubKey returns **False** upon failure.

COMMENTS
Under Windows 95, **DelSubKey** can remove a subkey and all its descendent subkeys. For example, the statement

```
Reg.DelSubKey aiKTCurUser, "Software"
```

would remove the subkey Software of the predefined key HKEY_CURRENT_USER and all the descendent subkeys under Software. (DO NOT DO THIS!) Needless to say, **DelSubKey** should be used with extreme care under Windows 95.

Under Windows NT4, **DelSubKey** cannot remove a subkey that contains descendent subkeys; instead, *HWnd* must be the handle to a fully qualified subkey (that is, containing no descendants) and *SubKey* should not be passed. In the Example code for **DelSubKey**, the statement

```
Reg.DelSubKey HWndSubKey2C
```

removes the descendent subkey Developing VB 5.0 Add-Ins\ Windows API Browser Add-In, leaving the subkey Developing VB 5.0 Add-Ins and any of its other descendent subkeys in place.

DelSubKey does not release the handle to a subkey after it removes it. You should do this and free system resources by calling the **CloseSubKey** method of a **Reg** object. **DelSubKey** is a proxy or wrapper method for the Windows API function **RegDeleteKey**.

METHOD'S CODE

See the Help topic DelSubKey Method in ADDINEFS.HLP or the **DelSubKey** method's procedure in VBAI.VBP.

EXAMPLE CODE

See the Help topic DelSubKey Method Example in ADDINEFS.HLP or the procedure DemoRegObj in DEMOSYNT.VBP.

DelValue Method (VBAI)

DelValue is a **Function** that removes a named value from a Windows registry subkey and returns **True**.

USAGE

Obj.**DelValue**(*HWndSubKey, ValName*) **As Boolean**

The **DelValue** method's syntax supports named arguments and contains these parts:

- *Obj*: Required. An object expression that evaluates to a **Reg** object of the VBAIclass library.

- *HWndSubKey*: Required. A **Long** expression that is the handle to an open subkey. You can provide *HWndSubKey* by calling the **OpenSubKey** method of a **Reg** object.

- *ValName*: Required. A **String** expression that specifies the name of a value of the subkey. You can provide *ValName* either by knowing it or calling the **GetValueName** method of a **Reg** object (Windows 95 only).

ERROR HANDLING

DelValue returns **False** upon failure.

COMMENTS

DelValue can remove all the values of a subkey except the default value. To remove the default value, you must remove the subkey itself by calling the **DelSubKey** method of a **Reg** object. **DelValue** does not release the handle to the subkey after it removes its value. You should do this and free system resources by calling the **CloseSubKey** method of a **Reg** object. **DelValue** is a proxy or wrapper method for the Windows API function **RegDeleteValue**.

METHOD'S CODE

See the Help topic DelValue Method in ADDINEFS.HLP or the **DelValue** method's procedure in VBAI.VBP.

EXAMPLE CODE

See the Help topic DelValue Method Example in ADDINEFS.HLP or the procedure DemoRegObj in DEMOSYNT.VBP.

Description Property

Description returns or sets a **String** that specifies a description associated with an object. Read/write.

USAGE

Obj.**Description**[= *Val*]

The **Description** property's syntax contains these parts:

- *Obj*: Required. An object expression that evaluates to an **AddIn**, **Member**, **Reference**, **VBComponent**, or **VBProject** object.

- *Val*: Optional. Only used when you set **Description**, *Val* is a **String** expression that describes the purpose or nature of an object. **Description** is read-only for a **Reference** object.

COMMENTS (ADD-IN OBJECT)

The setting of the **Description** property is determined by the Description entry for the add-in's **ClassModule** object in which an **IDTExtensibility** object is implemented. You make this entry in the Object Browser's Member Options dialog box. If no Description entry is made, VB substitutes the add-in's programmatic ID. **Description** is the default member of an **AddIn** object and does not have to be explicitly specified. In the Object Browser, a default member is marked with a small cyan circle at the top-left of the member's icon.

The **Description** property's setting is stored in the Windows registry as the default value of the add-in's programmatic ID string, under the key HKEY_CLASSES_ROOT. For example, the Windows API Browser demo add-in that is included with this book is found under the subkey HKEY_CLASSES_ROOT\WinAPIBrowser.Connect. The **Description** property's setting appears in the Add-In Manager dialog box's list.

If an **AddIn** object is checked/connected in the Add-In Manager dialog box's list, you can read its design-time **Description** property from any add-in. However, you can only programmatically change the **Description** property of such an **AddIn** object from within the **OnConnection** method of that add-in's **IDTExtensibility** object. If an **AddIn** object is only connected through the Add-In toolbar, trying to read its design-time **Description** property returns a zero-length string (that is, "" or **vbNullString**). However, you can change the **Description** property of such an add-in from outside the **OnConnection** method (although it reverts back to its design-time setting when it is disconnected).

The Project Description entry of an add-in's project, made on the General tab of the Project Properties dialog, is not the same setting as that returned by the add-in's **Description** property. Instead, the Project Description's setting is stored as the Description attribute in the add-in project's VBP file.

COMMENTS (REFERENCE OBJECT)

The **Description** property of a **Reference** object in a VB project appears as a checked item in the References dialog box's list. Each project contains, in its **References** collection, three default references that cannot be removed (Visual Basic for Applications, Visual Basic runtime objects and procedures, Visual Basic objects and procedures).

If a VB project has references other than its three default ones, these non-default references are stored in the project's VBP text file under the key name of Reference. For example, the OLE Automation reference is stored in a project's VBP file as this string:

```
Reference=*\G{00020430-0000-0000-C000-000000000046}
#2.0#0#..\WINNT\System32\STDOLE2.TLB#OLE Automation
```

The **Description** property returns only the portion of the string that follows the last pound (#) sign. The rest of the reference string stored in the VBP file consists of, from left to right, this other information about the ActiveX component:

- Its global unique identifier (GUID), including the curly brackets.

- Its major version number.

- The path and name of its type library (TLB), executable (DLL or EXE), or ActiveX control (OCX) file.

COMMENTS (MEMBER, VBCOMPONENT, VBPROJECT OBJECTS)

The **Description** property of a **Member**, **VBComponent**, or **VBProject** object is initially a zero-length string. You can set the **Description** property of one of these objects to some string and save it with its component or project file:

- The **Description** property of a **Member** object is saved in its component's text file under the key name of Attribute 'Member Name'.VB_Description (for example, Attribute GetPrivateProfileString.VB_Description = "WIN API function that reads INI file").

- The **Description** property of a **VBComponent** object is saved in its component's text file under the key name of Attribute VB_Description (for example, Attribute VB_Description = "Splash screen form").

- The **Description** property of a **VBProject** object is saved in its VBP text file under the key name of Description (for example, Description = "Demo add-in project").

1) VB's Help file fails to state that the **Description** property applies to **AddIn**, **Member**, and **VBComponent** objects. 2) Although the **Description** property setting of a **VBComponent** object is saved to its text file, if you programmatically add the component to another project with the **AddFile** method, its **Description** property returns a zero-length string. However, if you manually add the component to a project, its **Description** property returns the saved setting. 3) If you try to programmatically set an add-in's **Description** property from outside of the **OnConnection** method and it was checked/connected in the Add-In Manager, OLE Automation error -2147467259 occurs (Method '~' of object '~' failed). Note that the error message itself is incorrect when it refers to **Description** as a method.

EXAMPLE CODE

See the Help topic Description Property Example in ADDINEFS.HLP or the procedure DemoDescriptionPrp in DEMOSYNT.VBP.

Designer Property

Designer returns the generic **Object** type that represents an object that enables you to access the design characteristics of a VB component. Read-only.

USAGE

Obj.**Designer**

The **Designer** property's syntax contains these parts:

* *Obj*: Required. An object expression that evaluates to a **VBComponent** object.

COMMENTS

If the component has an open designer window, the **Designer** property returns it; otherwise a new designer window is created. A designer window is a feature of certain **VBComponent** objects. A component can have only one designer window, and it's always the same designer.

Although **Designer** returns the generic **Object** type, at this time it always evaluates to a **VBForm** object; see the Example code for a demonstration of this. Some components, such as standard modules and class modules, do not support a designer window. **Designer** returns **Nothing** if a **VBComponent** object doesn't have a designer.

EXAMPLE CODE

See the Help topic Designer Property Example in ADDINEFS.HLP or the procedure DemoDesignerPrp in DEMOSYNT.VBP.

DesignerID Property

DesignerID returns a **String** that specifies the kind of designer associated with a **VBComponent** object. Read-only.

USAGE

Obj.**DesignerID**

The **DesignerID** property's syntax contains these parts:

* *Obj*: Required. An object expression that evaluates to a **VBComponent** object.

COMMENTS

DesignerID returns "VB.Form" for a component that is a **Form** object and "VB.MDIForm" for a component that is a **MDIForm** object. If a component does not support a designer window or does not have a designer identification string associated with it, **DesignerID** returns a zero-length string (that is, "" or **vbNullString**). See the Example code for a demonstration of this.

EXAMPLE CODE

See the Help topic DesignerID Property Example in ADDINEFS.HLP or the procedure DemoDesignerIDPrp in DEMOSYNT.VBP.

D-D

DesignerWindow Method

DesignerWindow is a **Function** that returns a **Window** object that represents a VB component's designer window.

USAGE

Obj.**DesignerWindow**

The **DesignerWindow** method's syntax contains these parts:

- *Obj*: Required. An object expression that evaluates to a **VBComponent** object.

COMMENTS

If a component supports a designer window but doesn't have an open designer, calling the **DesignerWindow** method creates the designer, but it isn't visible. To make the window visible, set the designer's **Window** object's **Visible** property to **True**.

VB's Help file incorrectly states that **DesignerWindow** is a property. Instead, the Object Browser lists it as a method.

EXAMPLE CODE

See the Help topic DesignerWindow Method Example in ADDINEFS.HLP or the procedure DemoDesignerWindowMet in DEMOSYNT.VBP.

DisplayBind Property

DisplayBind is a **Boolean** that returns or sets the DefaultBind attribute associated with a **Member** object. Read/write.

USAGE

Obj.**DisplayBind**[= *Val*]

The **DisplayBind** property's syntax contains these parts:

- *Obj*: Required. An object expression that evaluates to a **Member** object.

- *Val*: Optional. Only used when you set **DisplayBind**, *Val* is a **Boolean** expression that specifies whether Data Binding - Show In DataBindings Collection At Design Time on the Procedure Attributes Advanced dialog box is checked for a member (**True**) or not (the default of **False**).

COMMENTS

You only set the DisplayBind attribute of a public **Property** procedure to **True** when you are creating an ActiveX control and are working with the code module of a User Control VB component. Setting DisplayBind specifies that a bindable property of the ActiveX control be visible in the Data Bindings dialog box at design time. Before you can set DisplayBind, however, you must first set the Bindable attribute of the public **Property** procedure to **True**.

You can use the Procedure Attributes Advanced dialog box, accessed from the Tools menu, to manually make a public **Property** procedure displayable at design time (check the Show In DataBindings Collection At Design Time checkbox). You can also programmatically make a public **Property** procedure displayable by setting its corresponding **Member** object's **DisplayBind** property to **True**. When you save the User Control component that contains the **Property** procedure, VB writes a line to the component's text file (for example, Attribute *Name*.VB_MemberFlags = "14", where *Name* is the **Property** procedure's name).

> VB does not permit you to manually set **DisplayBind** for a member that is not a public **Property** procedure. Unfortunately, VB does permit an add-in to programmatically set **DisplayBind** to **True** for a non-property **Member** object without causing a trappable error. This results in contradictory settings in the Procedure Attributes Advanced dialog box; that is, the Property Is Data Bound checkbox is unchecked, but the Show In DataBindings Collection At Design Time checkbox is checked. It can also, under certain circumstances, crash the current instance of VB's IDE.

EXAMPLE CODE

See the Help topic DisplayBind Property Example in ADDINEFS.HLP or the procedure DemoDisplayBindPrp in DEMOSYNT.VBP.

DisplayModel Property

DisplayModel returns a **Long** or sets a constant or value that specifies the display model being used by the current instance of VB's IDE.

USAGE

Obj.**DisplayModel**[= *Val*]

The **DisplayModel** property's syntax contains these parts:

- *Obj*: Required. An object expression that evaluates to a **VBE** object.

- *Val*: Optional. Only used when you set **DisplayModel**, *Val* is a constant or value that is either 0 - **vbext_dm_SDI** (Single Document Interface) or 1 - **vbext_dm_MDI** (Multiple Document Interface).

COMMENTS

If you programmatically set **DisplayModel**, it is the same as manually selecting Tools|Options and changing the SDI Development Environment setting on the Advanced tab. When you change this setting manually, VB displays a message stating that the change will not take effect until the next instance of VB's IDE is started. When you programmatically change **DisplayModel**, no advisory message is displayed.

EXAMPLE CODE

See the Help topic DisplayModel Property Example in ADDINEFS.HLP or the procedure DemoDisplayModelPrp in DEMOSYNT.VBP.

DoGetNewFileName Event

DoGetNewFileName is raised by VB's IDE before you save a VB file with the File|Save 'Name' or File|Save Project command for a new file, with the File|Save 'Name' As or File|Save Project As command for an existing file, or with the File|Make 'Name' command; or before you remove a project programmatically with an add-in.

Usage

*Obj*_**DoGetNewFileName**(**ByVal** *VBProject*, **ByVal** *FileType*, *NewName*, **ByVal** *OldName*, *CancelDefault*)

The **DoGetNewFileName** event's syntax contains these parts:

- *Obj*: An object expression that evaluates to a **FileControlEvents** object.

- *VBProject*: A **VBProject** object that specifies the name of the project in which the file's name was changed.

- *FileType*: An intrinsic constant of the enumerated type **vbext_FileType**, which specifies the type of file whose name was changed. See the Details section in the **FileControlEvents** object's entry in the Dictionary for a list of these constants.

- *NewName*: A **String** expression that specifies the new path and name of the file. If no path is specified, the current directory is used.

- *OldName*: A **String** expression that specifies the old path and name of the file. If no path is specified, the current directory is used.

- *CancelDefault*: A **Boolean** expression that specifies the default VB action, as described in Settings.

Settings

The values for *CancelDefault* are:

- **True**: Stops raising this event for any subsequent add-ins connected to a **FileControlEvents** object. If *NewName* is a zero-length string (that is, "" or **vbNullString**) when *CancelDefault* is set to **True**, the event is canceled; otherwise, the name entered in *NewName* is used as the new file name.

- **False**: Continues raising this event for subsequent add-ins connected to a **FileControlEvents** object. If no add-in sets *CancelDefault* to **True**, the Save File As or Make Project dialog box is displayed with the string you entered in *NewName*.

Comments

If the *CancelDefault* argument is set to **True**, the Save File As dialog box is not displayed. If *CancelDefault* is set to **False**, the Save File As dialog box is displayed. If more than one add-in is connected, and *CancelDefault* is set to **True** at any time during a Save As operation, the Save File As dialog box will not display for any of the add-ins until the next Save As operation is performed.

The *NewName* argument is initially set to the same value as *OldName*, but any add-in that receives this event can change it. One way to do this is through a custom user interface where you obtain the new name of the file and set *NewName* to the user's selection. However, if *CancelDefault* is **True** (that is, a previous add-in has set it to **True**), you should not set *NewName* again.

The **DoGetNewFileName** event does not occur for an FRX file associated with an FRM file that is saved under a new name. In VB4, **DoGetNewFileName** did occur for FRX files. An add-in cannot prevent a file from being saved or renamed/saved because the operation is complete; however, it can log information about the event, update information about the file, back up the file, and so on.

You cannot raise **DoGetNewFileName** with an add-in with the programmatic equivalents of the File|Save 'Name' or File|Save Project command for a new file, with the File|Save 'Name' As or File|Save Project As command for an existing file, or with the File|Make 'Name' command. The only way you can raise **DoGetNewFileName** with an add-in is to call the **Remove** method of a **VBProjects** collection.

To make an add-in responsive to a **DoGetNewFileName** event raised by VB, you first need to declare an object variable as a **FileControlEvents** object and assign it the object returned by the **FileControlEvents** property of an **Events** object. For detailed information about how to do this, see the **FileControlEvents** object's entry in the Dictionary.

 VB's Help file incorrectly states that **DoGetNewFileName** is a member of the **FileControl** object. Instead, it is a member of the **FileControlEvents** object (in VB4 it was the **FileControl** object).

EXAMPLE CODE

See the Help topic DoGetNewFileName Event Example in ADDINEFS.HLP or the procedure DemoDoGetNewFileNameEvt in DEMOSYNT.VBP.

Events Object/Property

An **Events** object supplies properties that enable an add-in to connect to all add-in related events raised in VB's IDE. The read-only **Events** property of a **VBE** object returns an object instance of the **Events** class.

INSTANTIATION

Dim *Obj* **As** [VBIDE.]**Events|Object|Variant**
Set *Obj* = **VBE.Events**

USAGE

Set *mObj* = *Obj*.*Mbr*[(*Args*)]

The **Events** syntax supports named arguments and contains these parts:

- *Obj*: Required. A variable to be assigned an object instance. *Obj* can be named the same as the **Events** class being instantiated. *Obj* can also be declared as the generic **Object** or as **Variant**, but this slows performance.

- VBIDE: Optional. The VB5 Extensibility object library containing the **Events** class.

- *mObj*: Required. A module-level variable to be assigned an object instance. It is declared in an add-in's **ClassModule** object with the **Public** statement and the **WithEvents** keyword and may not be declared as the generic **Object** or as **Variant**. The naming convention for *mObj* is to name it the same as the event source object that is being assigned to it, minus the suffix "Events". For example, if you are assigning a **FileControlEvents** object to it, you would give *mObj* the name *FileControl*. It can also be declared as the generic **Object** or as **Variant**, but this slows performance.

- *Mbr*: Required. A member of an **Events** object.

- *Args*: Optional. You use *Args* if *Mbr* is any property other than the **VBProjectsEvents** property.

MEMBERS

- Events: None at this time

- Methods: None at this time

- Properties: **CommandBarEvents**, **FileControlEvents**, **ReferencesEvents**, **SelectedVBControlsEvents**, **VBComponentsEvents**, **VBControlsEvents**, **VBProjectsEvents**

COMMENTS

An **Events** object provides properties that return event source objects. You use the properties to return event source objects that notify you of changes in VB's IDE. The properties of an **Events** object return objects of the same type as the property name. For example, the **CommandBarEvents** property returns a **CommandBarEvents** object.

When you are returning the **CommandBarEvents** object, you can write the assignment statement in the **OnConnection** method of an add-in's **IDTExtensibility** object or you can call another private method from **OnConnection** and make the assignment there. See the SetAIMenuItem method in DEMOSYNT.VBP for a demonstration of how to do this.

When you are reading any of the other properties of an **Events** object to return an event source object, you may want to do so in a separate **ClassModule** object that exists solely to respond to add-in related events raised in VB's IDE. See the **ClassModule** object named VBEvents and the **ConnectTo** method declared as **Friend** in DEMOSYNT.VBP for a demonstration of how to do this.

EXAMPLE CODE

See the Help topic Events Object/Property Example in ADDINEFS.HLP or the **SetAIMenuItem** and **ConnectTo** methods in DEMOSYNT.VBP.

FileControlEvents Object/Property

A **FileControlEvents** object represents all events raised by VB's IDE that support file control. The read-only **FileControlEvents** property of an **Events** object returns an object instance of the **FileControlEvents** class.

USAGE

#1: **Public WithEvents** *FileControl* **As FileControlEvents**

#2: **Set** *FileControl* = **VBE.Events.FileControlEvents**(*VBProjectObj*)

The **FileControlEvents** syntax contains these parts:

- *FileControl*: Required. A module-level object variable, in an add-in's **ClassModule** object, that is assigned the **FileControlEvents** object returned by the **FileControlEvents** property. *FileControl* must be declared with the **Public** statement and the **WithEvents** keyword, and it may not be declared as the generic **Object** or as **Variant**.

- *VBProjectObj*: Required. An object expression that evaluates to a **VBProject** object whose file control events you want to monitor.

 In Usage #1, **FileControlEvents** is the object. In Usage #2, **File-ControlEvents** is a property of an **Events** object. This property returns a **FileControlEvents** object.

MEMBERS

- Events: See Table D.2 under Details

- Methods: None at this time

- Properties: None at this time

COMMENTS

A **FileControlEvents** object allows an add-in to receive and react to file control-related events raised by VB's IDE. When more than one running add-in is receiving file control-related events, VB notifies the add-ins in the order in which they were connected.

To use a **FileControlEvents** object, follow these steps in a **ClassModule** object in the add-in's project:

- Use the **Public** statement and the **WithEvents** keyword to declare an object variable that will respond to the file control-related events raised by VB. You do this in the Declarations section. The declaration statement adds a **FileControlEvents** object, under the name of the object variable, to the class module's Object drop-down box. You can give this object variable any name you want but it is most readable to name it *FileControl*.

- Select FileControl from the Object drop-down box of the class module and VB automatically creates the beginning and ending statements of the **AfterAddFile** event procedure. Then, from the Procedure drop-down box, select the other file control-related events for which you want to create procedures.

- Write code in the various event procedures that will execute when VB raises their events.

- Make the add-in responsive to VB's file control-related events. You do this by using the **FileControlEvents** property of an **Events** object to return a **FileControlEvents** object that is assigned to *FileControl*. You can write this assignment statement in the **OnConnection** method of an add-in's **IDTExtensibility** object; or, if you want more flexibility, you can write it in a separate **ClassModule** object that exists solely to respond to add-in related events raised in VB's IDE. See the **ClassModule** object named VBEvents and the **ConnectTo** method declared as **Friend** in DEMOSYNT.VBP for a demonstration of how to do this.

A single action by a developer can raise several different events of a **FileControlEvents** object. For example, adding a file to a project raises the **DoGetAddFileName** and **AfterAddFile** events. A more complex example is changing a file name, which raises this sequence of events: **DoGetNewFileName**, **RequestChangeFileName**, **RequestWriteFile**, **AfterWriteFile**, and **AfterChangeFileName**. The kinds of files that a **FileControlEvents** object gives you control over are listed in Table D.3 under Details.

 A FileControlEvents object replaces a FileControl object in VB4. It works the same as before except that its events have been changed to support the new file types and the multiple-project capability of VB5.

DETAILS

Table D.2   Events of a FileControlEvents object.

Event	Description
AfterAddFile	Occurs after a VB component's module or other file has been added to a current project with the Project|Add File command.
AfterChangeFileName	Occurs after a file in the current project has been renamed and saved or when an EXE or DLL file is created.
AfterCloseFile	Occurs after a project has been closed, either directly by the user or by VB when the user shuts down the IDE.
AfterRemoveFile	Occurs after a file is removed from the active project.
AfterWriteFile	Occurs after a file is written to disk.
BeforeLoadFile	Occurs before a VB component's module or other file is loaded into the active project.
DoGetNewFileName	Occurs when a user selects the Save Project or Save Form command from the File menu for a new file, selects the Save Project As or Save Form As command from the File menu for an existing file, or selects the Make File Name command from the File menu.
RequestChangeFileName	Occurs after specifying a new file name for a VB component's module or other file.
RequestWriteFile	Occurs prior to saving any VB component's module with unsaved changes.

Table D.3   Kinds of files a FileControlEvents object controls.

Value/Constant	Description
0 - vbext_ft_Form	Form (FRM) module
1 - vbext_ft_Module	Basic (BAS) module
2 - vbext_ft_Class	Class (CLS) module
3 - vbext_ft_Project	Project (VBP) file
4 - vbext_ft_Exe	Executable (EXE) file
5 - vbext_ft_Frx	Binary Form (FRX) file
6 - vbext_ft_Res	Resource (RES) file
7 - vbext_ft_UserControl	User control (CTL) module
8 - vbext_ft_PropertyPage	Property page (PAG) module
9 - vbext_ft_DocObject	User document (DOB) module
10 - vbext_ft_Binary	Binary file
11 - vbext_ft_GroupProject	Group project (VBG) file
12 - vbext_ft_Designers	Designer (DSR) file

F-F

EXAMPLE CODE
See the Example code for the individual events of a **FileControlEvents** object.

FileCount Property
FileCount returns a **Long** that specifies the number of files associated with a VB component. Read-only.

USAGE
Obj.**FileCount**

The **FileCount** property's syntax contains these parts:

- *Obj*: Required. An object expression that evaluates to a **VBComponent** object.

COMMENTS
The primary use for **FileCount** is to enable you to determine whether a component has an associated file (for example, an FRX file for a component that is a **Form** or **MDIForm** object).

EXAMPLE CODE
See the Help topic FileCount Property Example in ADDINEFS.HLP or the procedure DemoFileCountPrp in DEMOSYNT.VBP.

FileName Method

FileName is a **Function** that returns a **String** that specifies the file name or the fully qualified path and file name of a group project file.

USAGE

Obj.FileName

The **FileName** method's syntax contains these parts:

- *Obj*: Required. An object expression that evaluates to a **VBProjects** collection.

COMMENTS

Until you have actually saved a group project file or an individual project file within the group project, the **FileName** method returns only the default name of GROUP1.VBG with no path specified. After you have saved a group project or project file, **FileName** returns a string that includes the path. The path name returned will always be provided as an absolute path (for example, C:\PROJECTS\MYGROUP.VBG), even if it is shown as a relative path in a VB IDE common dialog box (such as ..\PROJECTS).

It is easy to confuse the **FileName** method of a **VBProjects** collection with the **FileName** property of a **VBProject** object. Actually the **FileName** method of **VBProjects** works exactly like a property but it is listed as a method in the Object Browser. Regardless, the important point to note is that the **FileName** method returns a group project file name (VBG extension) while the **FileName** property returns a project file name (VBP extension).

EXAMPLE CODE

See the Help topic FileName Method Example in ADDINEFS.HLP or the procedure DemoFileNameMet in DEMOSYNT.VBP.

FileName Property

FileName returns a **String** that specifies the file name or the fully qualified path and file name of a project file. Read-only.

USAGE

Obj.FileName

The **FileName** property's syntax contains these parts:

- *Obj*: Required. An object expression that evaluates to a **VBProject** object.

COMMENTS

Until you have actually saved a project file, **FileName** returns only the default name of PROJECT1.VBP with no path specified or it returns a zero-length string (that is, "" or **vbNullString**). After you have saved a project file, **FileName** includes the path. The path name returned will always be provided as an absolute path (for example, C:\PROJECTS \MYPROJ.VBP), even if it is shown as a relative path in a VB IDE common dialog box (such as ..\PROJECTS).

It is easy to confuse the **FileName** property of a **VBProject** object with the **FileName** method of a **VBProjects** collection. Actually the **FileName** method of **VBProjects** works exactly like a property but it is listed as a method in the Object Browser. Regardless, the important point to note is that the **FileName** property returns a project file name (VBP extension) while the **FileName** method returns a group project file name (VBG extension).

> VB's Object Browser incorrectly states that **FileName** is read/write. Instead, **FileName** is read-only.

F-F

EXAMPLE CODE
See the Help topic FileName Property Example in ADDINEFS.HLP or the procedure DemoFileNamePrp in DEMOSYNT.VBP.

FileNames Property

FileNames returns a **String** that specifies the name of a file associated with a VB component. Read-only.

USAGE
Obj.**FileNames**(*Index*)

The **FileNames** property's syntax contains these parts:

- *Obj*: Required. An object expression that evaluates to a **VBComponent** object.

- *Index*: Required. A numeric expression that specifies the element in an array of file names whose value is to be returned. The array is one-based.

COMMENTS
You can find the number of elements in the array that contains the file name(s) by reading the **FileCount** property of a **VBComponent** object. The array for classes and modules contains only one file name, while the array for forms can contain elements for both the FRM and FRX file name of the form. The settings of the file names are updated when you call the **SaveAs** method of a **VBComponent** object.

If you have not yet saved the component, **FileCount** returns 1 and **FileNames**(1) returns a zero-length string (that is, "" or **vbNullString**). The path name portion of the string returned by **FileNames** is always provided as an absolute path (for example, C:\VB5\FORM1), even if it is shown as a relative path in a VB common dialog box (such as ..\VB5).

> VB's Help file incorrectly states that **FileNames** returns the current path name(s) in which the VB component will be stored. Instead, it returns both the path and file name(s) associated with a saved component.

EXAMPLE CODE

See the Help topic FileNames Property Example in ADDINEFS.HLP or the procedure DemoFileNamesPrp in DEMOSYNT.VBP.

Find Method

Find is a **Function** that searches a code module for the next occurrence of text or pattern-matching text and, if found, returns line and column numbers by reference and **True**.

USAGE

Obj.**Find**(*Target, StartLine, StartCol, EndLine, EndCol,* [*WholeWord*], [*MatchCase*], [*PatternSearch*]) **As Boolean**

The **Find** method's syntax supports named arguments and contains these parts:

- *Obj*: Required. An object expression that evaluates to a **CodeModule** object.

- *Target*: Required. A **String** expression that specifies the text or pattern you want to find.

- *StartLine*: Required. A **Long** expression that specifies the line number at which you want to start the search; will be set to the line number of the match if one is found. If you do not pass a variable, **Find** does the search but cannot set *StartLine* to the line number of a match.

- *StartCol*: Required. A **Long** expression that specifies the column number at which you want to start the search; will be set to the column number containing the first character of the match if one is found. If you do not pass a variable, **Find** does the search but cannot set *StartCol* to the beginning column number of a match.

- *EndLine*: Required. A **Long** expression that **Find** sets to the last line number of the match if one is found. If you do not pass a variable, **Find** ignores any **Long** value that you pass.

- *EndCol*: Required. A **Long** expression that **Find** sets to the last column number following the match if one is found. If you do not pass a variable, **Find** ignores any **Long** value that you pass.

- *WholeWord*: Optional. A **Boolean** expression that specifies whether to only match whole words. If **True**, **Find** only matches whole words. **False** is the default.

- *MatchCase*: Optional. A **Boolean** expression that specifies whether to match case. If **True**, **Find** is case sensitive. **False** is the default.

- *PatternSearch*: Optional. A **Boolean** expression that specifies whether or not *Target* is a valid expression pattern. If **True**, **Find** assumes *Target* to be a pattern-matching expression. **False** is the default.

RETURNS

Find returns a **Boolean** that is **True** if a match is found and **False** (the default) if a match is not found. You can also determine whether a match is found by reading the value set by **Find** in *StartLine*. If a match is not found, *StartLine* is always set to 1; however, if a match is found, *StartLine* is set to the line number of the match, which 99 percent of the time will not be 1.

COMMENTS

The *Target* argument can include or be one of the following pattern-matching expressions:

- ? - Matches any single character.

- * - Matches zero or more characters.

- # - Matches any single digit.

- [*CharList*] - Matches any single character in *CharList*.

- [!*CharList*] - Matches any single character not in *CharList*.

The *MatchCase* and *PatternSearch* arguments are mutually exclusive. If both arguments are passed as **True** and *Target* is passed a pattern-matching expression, **Find** fails and returns **False** even if text matching the pattern exists. Always set *MatchCase* to **False** when searching for pattern-matching text. The settings of VB's Find dialog box are not affected by the use of the **Find** method.

1) VB's Help file incorrectly states that the *EndCol* argument specifies the last line of the match if one is found. Instead, *EndCol* specifies the last column of the match if one is found. 2) In the Remarks section, it incorrectly refers to the *PatternSearch* argument as *PatternMatch*.

EXAMPLE CODE

See the Help topic Find Method Example in ADDINEFS.HLP or the procedure DemoFindMet in DEMOSYNT.VBP.

FullName Property

FullName returns a **String** that specifies the fully qualified path and file name of the Visual Basic application. Read-only.

USAGE

Obj.**FullName**

The **FullName** property's syntax contains these parts:

- *Obj*: Required. An object expression that evaluates to a **VBE** object.

COMMENTS

The path returned by **FullName** is where VB5.EXE was run. The path name returned is always provided as an absolute path (for example, C:\PROJECTS\MYPROJ.VBP), even if it is shown as a relative path in Visual Basic (such as ..\PROJECTS).

EXAMPLE CODE

See the Help topic FullName Property Example in ADDINEFS.HLP or the procedure DemoFullNamePrp in DEMOSYNT.VBP.

FullPath Property

FullPath returns a **String** containing the path and file name of the referenced class library. Read-only.

Usage

Obj.**FullPath**

The **FullPath** property's syntax contains these parts:

- *Obj*: Required. An object expression that evaluates to a **Reference** object.

Comments

The **FullPath** property of a **Reference** object returns the path and file name of the reference listed at the bottom of the References dialog box, under the Location heading.

Example Code

See the Help topic FullPath Property Example in ADDINEFS.HLP or the procedure DemoFullPathPrp in DEMOSYNT.VBP.

GetControlType Method (VBAI)

GetControlType is a **Function** that returns a **Byte** that is the setting of the **ControlType** property of a **VBControl** object.

Usage

Obj.**GetControlType**(*Ctl*) **As Byte**

The **GetControlType** method's syntax supports named arguments and contains these parts:

- *Obj*: Required. An object expression that evaluates to a **Util** object of the VBAIclass library.

- *Ctl*: Required. An object expression that evaluates to a **VBControl** object of the VBIDE class library.

Error Handling

GetControlType returns 0 (that is, **False**) upon failure.

Comments

The **GetControlType** method returns one of three possible values:

- 1 - vbext_ct_Light: A lightweight control that has no **hWnd** property at runtime (for example, a **Label** object).

- 2 - vbext_ct_Standard: A control that has an **hWnd** property at runtime (for example, a **CommandButton** object).

- 3 - vbext_ct_Container: A control that has an **hWnd** property at runtime and that can contain other controls (for example, a **PictureBox** object).

There is a bug in the VBIDE class library that results in the **ControlType** property always returning a value of 2 - **vbext_ct_Standard**, regardless of the kind of **VBControl** object. See the Example code for a demonstration of this bug. You can call the **GetControlType** method of a **Util** object to correct for this bug and return the correct value for all intrinsic and ActiveX controls that ship with VB5.

Method's Code
See the Help topic GetControlType Method in ADDINEFS.HLP or the **GetControlType** method's procedure in VBAI.VBP.

Example Code
See the Help topic GetControlType Method Example in ADDINEFS.HLP or the procedure DemoGetControlTypeMet in DEMOSYNT.VBP.

GetDesc (VBAI)
GetDesc is a **Function** that returns a **String** that is the setting of the **Description** property of an **AddIn** object from the Windows registry.

Usage
Obj.**GetDesc**(*VBE, ProgID*) **As String**

The **GetDesc** method's syntax supports named arguments and contains these parts:

- *Obj*: Required. An object expression that evaluates to a **Util** object of the VBAI class library.

- *VBE*: Required. An object expression that evaluates to a **VBE** object of the VBIDE class library.

- *ProgID*: Required. A **String** expression that specifies the **ProgID** property's setting of the **AddIn** object whose Description value is being returned. The programmatic IDs of all registered add-ins are listed in VBADDIN.INI. If *ProgID* is set to a nonexistent programmatic ID, **GetDesc** fails.

Error Handling
GetDesc returns a zero-length string (that is, "" or **vbNullString**) upon failure.

Comments
The Description value of an add-in is stored in the Windows registry as the default value of the add-in's programmatic ID string, under the predefined key HKEY_CLASSES_ROOT. For example, the Windows API Browser add-in (free demo version) that is included with this book is found under the subkey HKEY_CLASSES_ROOT\WinAPIBrowser.Connect and the subkey's default or Description value is creating VB5 Add-Ins: Windows API Browser. For the book's demonstration add-in, the subkey is HKEY_CLASSES_ROOT\Chapter 2.Connect and the Description value is Creating VB5 Add-Ins: Chapter 2.

The Description value of an add-in that is stored in the Windows registry is the same as the **Description** property setting of the corresponding **AddIn** object. However, if an **AddIn** object is only connected through the Add-In toolbar, trying to read its **Description** property returns a zero-length string. The **GetDesc** method compensates for this deficiency and returns the **Description** property setting of an **AddIn** object regardless of how it was connected.

METHOD'S CODE

See the Help topic GetDesc Method in ADDINEFS.HLP or the **GetDesc** method's procedure in VBAI.VBP.

EXAMPLE CODE

See the Help topic GetDesc Method Example in ADDINEFS.HLP or the procedure DemoGetDescMet in DEMOSYNT.VBP.

GetMenu Method (VBAI)

GetMenu is a **Function** that returns a VB menu as a **CommandBarControl** object of the Office class library.

USAGE

Set *mVar* = *Obj*.**GetMenu**(*VBE, Caption*) **As** Office.**CommandBarControl**

The **GetMenu** method's syntax supports named arguments and contains these parts:

- *Obj*: Required. An object expression that evaluates to a **Cmd** object of the VBAI class library.

- *mVar*: Required. A module-level object variable declared in the add-in's **ClassModule** connection object as a **CommandBarControl** object of the Office class library. It is assigned the object instance returned by **GetMenu**.

- *VBE*: Required. An object expression that evaluates to a **VBE** object of the VBIDE class library.

- *Caption*: Required. A **String** expression that specifies the caption of the VB menu to be returned. If *Caption* refers to a nonexistent menu, **GetMenu** fails.

ERROR HANDLING

GetMenu returns an object instance that evaluates to **Nothing** upon failure.

COMMENTS

Before you declare *mVar* as a **CommandBarControl** object of the Office class library and call the **GetMenu** method, you must set a reference to the Microsoft Office 8.0 Object Library. After calling **GetMenu**, you can use the **AddMenuItem** method of a **Cmd** object to add an item to the menu or the **AddPopupMenu** method of a **Cmd** object to add a popup menu to the menu.

If you mistakenly try to delete a built-in VB menu returned by **GetMenu**, VB will permit you to do so without crashing the IDE; however, that menu and its items will not be available for use while the current instance of VB is running.

METHOD'S CODE
See the Help topic GetMenu Method in ADDINEFS.HLP or the **GetMenu** method's procedure in VBAI.VBP.

EXAMPLE CODE
See the Help topic GetMenu Method Example in ADDINEFS.HLP or the procedure DemoGetMenuMet in DEMOSYNT.VBP.

GetSelection Method

GetSelection is a **Sub** that returns, by reference in its arguments, the position of the selected text in a code pane.

USAGE
Obj.**GetSelection** *StartLine, StartCol, EndLine, EndCol*

The **GetSelection** method's syntax supports named arguments and contains these parts:

- *Obj*: Required. An object expression that evaluates to a **CodePane** object.

- *StartLine*: Required. A **Long** variable that returns a value specifying the first line of the selection.

- *StartCol*: Required. A **Long** variable that returns a value specifying the first column of the selection.

- *EndLine*: Required. A **Long** variable that returns a value specifying the last line of the selection.

- *EndCol*: Required. A **Long** variable that returns a value specifying the last column of the selection.

COMMENTS
When you call the **GetSelection** method, information is returned by reference in the method's arguments. As a result, you must pass in variables as parameters because the variables will be modified to contain the information that is returned. To select text in a code pane, call the **SetSelection** method of a **CodePane** object.

EXAMPLE CODE
See the Help topic GetSelection Method Example in ADDINEFS.HLP or the procedure DemoGetSelectionMet in DEMOSYNT.VBP.

GetSubKeyName Method (VBAI)

GetSubKeyName is a **Function** that returns a **String** that is the name of a subkey descended from a predefined key or another subkey.

USAGE
Obj.**GetSubKeyName**(*HWnd, Index*) **As String**

The **GetSubKeyName** method's syntax supports named arguments and contains these parts:

- *Obj:* Required. An object expression that evaluates to a **Reg** object of the VBAI class library.

- *HWnd*: Required. A **Long** expression that is the handle to a predefined key or open subkey. *HWnd* can be one of the intrinsic constants of the enumerated type **aiKeyType** (see Settings) or a handle returned by the **OpenSubKey** method of a **Reg** object.

- *Index:* Required. A **Long** expression that specifies the index value of the descendent subkey whose name is to be returned.

SETTINGS

The predefined key values for *HWnd* (**aiKeyType**) are:

- 0 - **aiKTClasses**: HKEY_CLASSES_ROOT key

- 1 - **aiKTCurUser**: HKEY_CURRENT_USER key

- 2 - **aiKTMachine**: HKEY_LOCAL_MACHINE key

- 3 - **aiKTUsers**: HKEY_USERS key

- 5 - **aiKTCurConfig**: HKEY_CURRENT_CONFIG key

- 6 - **aiKTDynData**: HKEY_DYN_DATA key

ERROR HANDLING

GetSubKeyName returns a zero-length string (that is, "" or **vbNullString**) upon failure.

COMMENTS

Before calling **GetSubKeyName**, you can call the **GetSubKeysCount** method of a **Reg** object to determine how many descendent subkeys a predefined key or another subkey has. To enumerate the names of subkeys, call **GetSubKeyName** within a loop as many times as the value returned by **GetSubKeysCount**, with *Index* being incremented from the value of 1 on up.

The Windows registry stores the names of the subkeys descended from a predefined key or another subkey in a zero-based array. However, **GetSubKeyName** takes as its *Index* argument the nominal number of the element (for example, the first subkey in the array is specified by an *Index* parameter of 1). Likewise, the **GetSubKeysCount** method of a **Reg** object returns the nominal number of elements in the array (for example, it returns 3 for an array containing three subkeys).

You can use **GetSubKeyName**, in combination with **GetSubKeysCount**, to find a specific subkey. For example, you could search all the subkey names descended from the predefined key HKEY_CLASSES_ROOT to determine if a particular class (for example, Access.Application.8) is registered on a PC. **GetSubKeyName** does not release the handle passed to *HWnd* after it returns its result. You should do this and free system resources by calling the **CloseSubKey** method of a **Reg** object. **GetSubKeyName** is a proxy or wrapper method for the Windows API function **RegEnumKey**.

METHOD'S CODE

See the Help topic GetSubKeyName Method in ADDINEFS.HLP or the **GetSubKeyName** method's procedure in VBAI.VBP.

EXAMPLE CODE

See the Help topic GetSubKeyName Method Example in ADDINEFS.HLP or the procedure DemoRegObj in DEMOSYNT.VBP.

GetSubKeysCount Method (VBAI)

GetSubKeysCount is a **Function** that returns a **Long** that is the number of subkeys (zero or some larger value) descended from a predefined key or another subkey.

USAGE

Obj.**GetSubKeysCount**(*HWnd*) **As Long**

The **GetSubKeysCount** method's syntax supports named arguments and contains these parts:

- *Obj* : Required. An object expression that evaluates to a **Reg** object of the VBAI class library.

- *HWnd* : Required. A **Long** expression that is the handle to a predefined key or open subkey. *HWnd* can be one of the intrinsic constants of the enumerated type **aiKeyType** (see Settings below) or a handle returned by the **OpenSubKey** method of a **Reg** object.

SETTINGS

The predefined key values for *HWnd* (**aiKeyType**) are:

- 0 - **aiKTClasses**: HKEY_CLASSES_ROOT key

- 1 - **aiKTCurUser**: HKEY_CURRENT_USER key

- 2 - **aiKTMachine**: HKEY_LOCAL_MACHINE key

- 3 - **aiKTUsers**: HKEY_USERS key

- 5 - **aiKTCurConfig**: HKEY_CURRENT_CONFIG key

- 6 - **aiKTDynData**: HKEY_DYN_DATA key

ERROR HANDLING

GetSubKeysCount returns -2 (the intrinsic constant **aiFailed**) upon failure.

COMMENTS

After calling **GetSubKeysCount**, you can call the **GetSubKeyName** method of a **Reg** object within a loop to enumerate the names of the subkeys. **GetSubKeyName** is called as many times as the count returned by **GetSubKeysCount**.

The Windows registry stores the names of the subkeys descended from a predefined key or another subkey in a zero-based array. However, **GetSubKeysCount** returns the nominal number of elements in the array (for example, it returns 3 for an array containing three subkeys).

Likewise, the **GetSubKeyName** method of a **Reg** object takes as its *Index* argument the nominal number of the element (for example, the first subkey in the array is specified by an *Index* parameter of 1).

You can use **GetSubKeysCount**, in combination with **GetSubKeyName**, to find a specific subkey. For example, you could search all the subkey names descended from the predefined key HKEY_CLASSES_ROOT to determine if a particular class (for example, Access.Application.8) is registered on a PC. **GetSubKeysCount** does not release the handle passed to *HWnd* after it returns its result. You should do this and free system resources by calling the **CloseSubKey** method of a **Reg** object. **GetSubKeysCount** is a proxy or wrapper method for the Windows API functions **RegEnumKey** and **RegQueryInfoKey**.

METHOD'S CODE

See the Help topic GetSubKeysCount Method in ADDINEFS.HLP or the **GetSubKeysCount** method's procedure in VBAI.VBP.

EXAMPLE CODE

See the Help topic GetSubKeysCount Method Example in ADDINEFS.HLP or the procedure DemoRegObj in DEMOSYNT.VBP.

GetValue Method (VBAI)

GetValue is a **Function** that returns a **String** that is the entry for a value of a subkey in the Windows registry. If the value is not set or it is not a string, **GetValue** returns a zero-length string.

USAGE

Obj.GetValue(*HWndSubKey*, [*ValName* = ""]) **As String**

The **GetValue** method's syntax supports named arguments and contains these parts:

- *Obj*: Required. An object expression that evaluates to a **Reg** object of the VBAI class library.

- *HWndSubKey*: Required. A **Long** expression that is the handle to an open subkey. You can get *HWndSubKey* by calling the **OpenSubKey** method of a **Reg** object.

- *ValName*: Optional. A **String** expression that specifies the name of a value of the subkey. If *ValName* is not passed, it defaults to a zero-length string (that is, "" or **vbNullString**) and the entry for the default value of the subkey is returned.

ERROR HANDLING

GetValue returns the string "Failed" upon failure.

COMMENTS

GetValue is a proxy or wrapper method for a simplified version of the Windows API function **RegQueryValueEx**. **GetValue** is only intended to return a subkey's value that contains a string as its entry. To return a subkey's value that contains data other than a string, you must declare and call **RegQueryValueEx** directly. **GetValue** does not release the handle of the subkey after it returns its result. You should do this and free system resources by calling the **CloseSubKey** method of a **Reg** object.

Method's Code

See the Help topic GetValue Method in ADDINEFS.HLP or the **GetValue** method's procedure in VBAI.VBP.

Example Code

See the Help topic GetValue Method Example in ADDINEFS.HLP or the procedure DemoRegObj in DEMOSYNT.VBP.

GetValueName Method (VBAI)

GetValueName is a **Function** that returns a **String** that is the name of a value of a subkey in the Windows registry (Windows 95 only).

Usage

Obj.**GetValueName**(*HWndSubKey, Index*) **As String**

The **GetValueName** method's syntax supports named arguments and contains these parts:

- *Obj*: Required. An object expression that evaluates to a **Cmd** object of the VBAI class library.

- *HWndSubKey*: Required. A **Long** expression that is the handle to an open subkey. You can get *HWndSubKey* by calling the **OpenSubKey** method of a **Reg** object.

- *Index*: Required. A **Long** expression that specifies the index value of the name of the subkey value to return. If *Index* is less than 1, **GetValueName** fails.

Error Handling

GetValueName returns "Failed" upon failure.

Comments

The Windows registry stores the names of the values of a subkey in a zero-based array. However, **GetValueName** takes as its *Index* argument the nominal number of the element; for example, the first value name in the array is specified by an *Index* parameter of 1. You can use **GetValueName**, in combination with the **GetValuesCount** method of a **Reg** object, to loop through all the names of the values of a subkey that contain an entry. For example, searching through all the value names under the subkey HKEY_CURRENT_CONFIG\Display\Fonts returns the display fonts currently available on a PC. **GetValueName** does not release the handle of the subkey after it returns its result. You should do this and free system resources by calling the **CloseSubKey** method of a **Reg** object.

It is conventional Windows programming practice that the six predefined keys in the Windows registry are only supposed to have descendent subkeys and not values. If an add-in passes *HWndSubKey* the handle of a predefined key, **GetValueName** fails. To get the name of a subkey that a predefined registry key contains, call the **GetSubKeyName** method of a **Reg** object.

GetValueName is a proxy or wrapper method for a simplified version of the Windows API function **RegEnumValue**. **RegEnumValue** does not work under Windows NT4 and always returns an error value; so, if you call **GetValueName** under Windows NT4, the method fails.

G-G

METHOD'S CODE

See the Help topic GetValueName Method in ADDINEFS.HLP or the **GetValueName** method's procedure in VBAI.VBP.

EXAMPLE CODE

See the Help topic GetValueName Method Example in ADDINEFS.HLP or the procedure DemoRegObj in DEMOSYNT.VBP.

GetValuesCount Method (VBAI)

GetValuesCount is a **Function** that returns a **Long** that is the number of values with entries contained by a subkey (Windows 95 only).

USAGE

Obj.GetValuesCount(*HWndSubKey*) **As Long**

The **GetValuesCount** method's syntax supports named arguments and contains these parts:

- *Obj*: Required. An object expression that evaluates to a **Cmd** object of the VBAI class library.

- *HWndSubKey*: Required. A **Long** expression that is the handle to an open subkey. You can get *HWndSubKey* by calling the **OpenSubKey** method of a **Reg** object.

ERROR HANDLING

GetValuesCount returns -2 (the intrinsic constant **aiFailed**) upon failure.

COMMENTS

You can call **GetValuesCount**, in combination with the **GetValueName** method of a **Reg** object, to loop through all the names of the values of a subkey that contain an entry. For example, if you search through all of the value names under the subkey HKEY_CURRENT_CONFIG\Display\Fonts returns the display fonts currently available on a PC. **GetValuesCount** does not include the default value in its count if its entry is not set. **GetValuesCount** does not release the handle of the subkey after it returns its result. You should do this and free system resources by calling the **CloseSubKey** method of a **Reg** object.

It is conventional Windows programming practice that the six predefined keys in the Windows registry are only supposed to have descendent subkeys and not values. If an add-in passes *HWndSubKey* the handle of a predefined key, **GetValuesCount** fails. To get the number of subkeys that a predefined registry key contains, call the **GetSubKeysCount** method of a **Reg** object.

GetValuesCount is a proxy or wrapper method for a simplified version of the Windows API function **RegQueryInfoKey**. **RegQueryInfoKey** does not work under Windows NT4 and always returns an error value; so, if you call **GetValuesCount** under Windows NT4, the method fails.

METHOD'S CODE

See the Help topic GetValuesCount Method in ADDINEFS.HLP or the **GetValuesCount** method's procedure in VBAI.VBP.

EXAMPLE CODE

See the Help topic GetValuesCount Method Example in ADDINEFS.HLP or the procedure DemoRegObj in DEMOSYNT.VBP.

Guid Property

Guid returns a **String** that is an object's unique class identifier and that is stored in the Windows registry. Read-only.

USAGE

Obj.**Guid**

The **Guid** property's syntax contains these parts:

- *Obj*: Required. An object expression that evaluates to an **AddIn** or **Reference** object.

G-H

COMMENTS

A GUID (globally unique identifier) is a 128-bit value that is automatically assigned when a class is registered with Windows. The GUID is generated using a combination of the date, time, and a unique network card number (if the system has a network card installed). Because each bit of a binary number can have only two values and because the GUID is 128 bits in length, the number of possible GUIDs is 2 raised to the 128th power. The GUID of an add-in's class is stored in the Windows registry as the Clsid subkey's default entry (for example, HKEY_CLASSES_ROOT\WinAPIBrowser.Connect\Clsid).

An example of a GUID is {FFAE6620-850D-11D0-BD69-8D0496BC6751}, which happens to be the value that Windows assigned on my PC to the WinAPIBrowser.Connect add-in (free demo version).

An add-in can only read the **Guid** property of an add-in that is checked/connected in the Add-In Manager dialog box's list. If an add-in is only connected through the Add-In toolbar, **Guid** returns a zero-length string (that is, "" or **vbNullString**). A **Reference** object's GUID is stored both in the Windows registry and in the VB project's VBP file.

EXAMPLE CODE

See the Help topic Guid Property Example in ADDINEFS.HLP or the procedure DemoGuidPrp in DEMOSYNT.VBP.

HasOpenDesigner Property

HasOpenDesigner is a **Boolean** that specifies whether a VB component has an open designer window (**True**) or not (**False**). Read-only.

USAGE

Obj.**HasOpenDesigner**

The **HasOpenDesigner** property's syntax contains these parts:

- *Obj*: Required. An object expression that evaluates to a **VBComponent** object.

COMMENTS

When you first add a VB component to a project, its designer window (if it has one) is open and **HasOpenDesigner** returns **True**. If you apply the **Close** method to a **Window** object that represents the component's designer window, then **HasOpenDesigner** returns **False**. **HasOpenDesigner** always returns **False** for a component that does not have a designer window (for example, a standard or class module).

EXAMPLE CODE

See the Help topic HasOpenDesigner Property Example in ADDINEFS.HLP or the procedure DemoHasOpenDesignerPrp in DEMOSYNT.VBP.

H-H

Height Property

Height returns a **Long** or sets a numeric expression that specifies the height of a window in VB's IDE. Read/write.

USAGE

Obj.**Height**[= *Val*]

The **Height** property's syntax contains these parts:

- *Obj*: Required. An object expression that evaluates to a **Window** object.

- *Val*: Optional. Only used when you set **Height**, *Val* is a numeric expression that specifies in pixels the height of a VB IDE window.

COMMENTS

There is a difference between the **Height** property of a VB IDE designer **Window** object (specified in pixels) and the **Height** property of a VB **Form** object (specified in twips). The value returned by the **Height** property of a **Window** object depends on whether or not the window is linked or docked. If the window is linked, the value of **Height** is actually for the frame window to which it is linked. If the window is not linked, the value of **Height** is for the window itself.

If you set the height of a VB IDE window to a value greater than the height of the **Screen** object, VB adjusts the window's height to that of a maximized **Form** object plus four pixels. Setting the **Height** property of VB's main window or of a linked window has no effect.

 1) VB's Help file and the Object Browser incorrectly state that the **Height** property of a **Window** object is specified in twips. Instead, it is specified in pixels. 2) VB's Help file incorrectly states that **Height** returns a **Single**. Instead, it returns a **Long**.

EXAMPLE CODE

See the Help topic Height Property Example in ADDINEFS.HLP or the procedure DemoHeightPrp in DEMOSYNT.VBP.

HelpContextID Property

HelpContextID returns a **Long** or sets a numeric expression that specifies the context ID number for a topic in a Microsoft Windows Help file. Read/write.

USAGE

Obj.**HelpContextID**[= *Val*]

The **HelpContextID** property's syntax contains these parts:

- *Obj*: Required. An object expression that evaluates to a **Member**, **VB component**, or VB Project Object.

- *Val*: Optional. Only used when you set Help Context ID, *Val* is a Numeric expression that specifies the context ID number of a Help topic.

COMMENTS

In VB's Object Browser, there are three kinds of items listed: Projects/Libraries, Classes, and Members. If a Windows Help file exists for a VB project, each of these can have a Help topic associated with it. You specify which topic is associated with which item by setting the **HelpContextID** property of a **VBProject**, **VBComponent**, or **Member** object. After you programmatically assign context ID numbers with an add-in, you can view them with the Object Browser by right-clicking on the item and choosing Properties from the shortcut menu. When you save the project, VB writes these kinds of lines to the project's and component's text files:

- Project: HelpContextID = 1000

- Component: Attribute VB_HelpID = 2000

- Member: Attribute *Name*.VB_HelpID = 3000 (where *Name* is the member's name)

Both VB's Help file and the Object Browser incorrectly state that HelpContextID returns or sets a **String**. Instead, it returns or sets a **Long**.

EXAMPLE CODE

See the Help topic HelpContextID Property Example in ADDINEFS.HLP or the procedure DemoHelpContextIDPrp in DEMOSYNT.VBP.

HelpFile Property

HelpFile returns or sets a **String** that specifies the fully qualified path to a Microsoft Windows Help file for a VB project. Read/write.

USAGE

Obj.**HelpFile**[= *Val*]

The **HelpFile** property's syntax contains these parts:

- *Obj*: Required. An object expression that evaluates to a **VBProject** object.

H-H

- *Val*: Optional. Only used when you set **HelpFile**, *Val* is a **String** expression that specifies the path and name of the HLP file to be associated with *Obj*.

COMMENTS

If a Windows Help file exists for a VB project, you can programmatically associate it with a project by setting the **HelpFile** property of a **VBProject** object. This has the same effect as manually selecting Project|Properties and specifying an entry for Help File Name on the General tab. When you save the project, VB writes a line to the project's text file (for example, HelpFile="C:\DUMMY.HLP"). The string assigned to **HelpFile** becomes the value returned at runtime by the **HelpFile** property of the **App** object.

EXAMPLE CODE

See the Help topic HelpFile Property Example in ADDINEFS.HLP or the procedure DemoHelpFilePrp in DEMOSYNT.VBP.

Hidden Property

Hidden is a **Boolean** that returns or sets the Hidden attribute associated with a **Member** object. Read/write.

USAGE

Obj.**Hidden**[= *Val*]

The **Hidden** property's syntax contains these parts:

- *Obj*: Required. An object expression that evaluates to a **Member** object.

- *Val*: Optional. Only used when you set **Hidden**, *Val* is a **Boolean** expression that specifies whether Hide This Member on the Procedure Attributes Advanced dialog box is checked for a member (**True**) or not (the default of **False**).

COMMENTS

Setting the **Hidden** property of a **Member** object to **True** can be useful when you are creating any kind of ActiveX component. You can use the Procedure Attributes Advanced dialog box, accessed from the Tools menu, to manually set **Hidden** (check the Hide This Member checkbox). You can also do this programmatically by setting the **Member** object's **Hidden** property to **True**. When you save the User Control component that contains the hidden member, VB writes the setting of **Hidden** to the ActiveX control's type library.

When a Member object's **Hidden** property is set to **True**, the Object Browser does not display it in the list of available members and, if the member is a property, it does not appear in the Properties window. However, if you check the Show Hidden Members item on the Object Browser's shortcut menu, the Members list will then display items marked as hidden in the type library. Hidden members are shown in light gray type.

 You set **Hidden** to **True** for a member to warn developers who reuse the ActiveX component that the member is secret and not supported for reuse. This may indicate that the member is designed to only be used internally within the class library (for example, to support upward compatibility with a previous release of the ActiveX component). Normally, only developers who have documentation for hidden members can write programs that reuse them.

EXAMPLE CODE

See the Help topic Hidden Property Example in ADDINEFS.HLP or the procedure DemoHiddenPrp in DEMOSYNT.VBP.

Hide Method (VBAI)

Hide is a **Function** that removes the VB Add-In toolbar from the main window of the current instance of VB's IDE and returns **True**.

USAGE

Obj.**Hide**(*VBE*, *ProgID*) **As Boolean**

The **Hide** method's syntax supports named arguments and contains these parts:

- *Obj*: Required. An object expression that evaluates to an **AITBar** object of the VBAI class library.

- *VBE*: Required. An object expression that evaluates to a **VBE** object of the VBIDE class library.

- *ProgID*: Required. A **String** expression that specifies the programmatic ID of the add-in that is calling the **Hide** method. The programmatic IDs of all registered add-ins are listed in VBADDIN.INI. If *ProgID* is set to "*AddInToolbar.Connect*" (that is, the VB Add-In Toolbar add-in itself) or to a nonexistent programmatic ID, **Hide** fails.

ERROR HANDLING

Hide returns **False** upon failure.

COMMENTS

It is possible to remove the Add-In toolbar from VB's main window by simply setting the **Connect** property of the toolbar's **AddIn** object to **False**. Unfortunately, this does not cause VB to uncheck the toolbar's item in the Add-In Manager dialog box's list. As a result, the next time an instance of VB runs, the toolbar reverts back to its previous setting and is displayed. **Hide** prevents this from happening and keeps the setting in the Add-In Manager dialog box's list synchronized with its **Connect** property setting. If the Add-In toolbar is not displayed, the **Hide** method fails.

Encapsulation Violation Hide runs a separate thread in a **Timer** object (tmrAIMgrDlgBox) on a hidden **Form** object (frmTimer) in the VBAI class library that, after **Hide** opens the Add-In Manager dialog box, finds the dialog box's window, unchecks the VB Add-In Toolbar item, and closes the dialog box. This **Timer** thread executes while drawing of the desktop window is suspended and, as a result, these actions are not visible to the developer. Although this technique violates the encapsulation of an **AITBar** object, it is necessary because the Add-In Manager dialog box is displayed modally and cannot be closed programmatically except by a separate thread.

METHOD'S CODE

See the Help topic Hide Method in ADDINEFS.HLP or the **Hide** method's procedure in VBAI.VBP.

EXAMPLE CODE

See the Help topic Hide Method Example in ADDINEFS.HLP or the procedure DemoAITBarObj in DEMOSYNT.VBP.

HWnd Property (Hidden)

HWnd returns a **Long** that is the handle to a window in VB's IDE. Read-only.

USAGE

Obj.HWnd

The **HWnd** property's syntax contains these parts:

* *Obj*: Required. An object expression that evaluates to a **Window** object.

COMMENTS

Do not confuse the **HWnd** property of a window in VB's IDE with the **hWnd** property of various VB objects at runtime (note that the second property has a lowercase "h"). Although they both return the handle of a window, they are different properties that apply to different objects.

The Microsoft Windows operating system identifies each window in VB's IDE by assigning it a handle. The handle of a window is used with Windows API function calls, many of which require a handle as an argument. To the Windows operating system, a window is any object on the screen that has a handle, including all VB control objects with the **hWnd** property.

Although **HWnd** worked correctly in VB4's Add-In language, it doesn't in VB5's Extensibility object model. **HWnd** returns a value of 0 for all members of a **Windows** collection. Only VB's main window, which is not a member of a **Windows** collection, returns a valid handle from **HWnd**. The Example code demonstrates this deficiency and a technique to work around it using Windows API functions. If you use Windows API functions to return the handle of a VB IDE window that is linked, the handle is for the frame window that contains the linked window.

> The Extensibility object model includes the hidden **HWnd** property to maintain upward compatibility with VB4 add-ins. Microsoft advises not using hidden objects or members when creating VB5 add-ins because they may not be available in a future release of VB.

EXAMPLE CODE

See the Help topic HWnd Property Example in ADDINEFS.HLP or the procedure DemoHWndPrp in DEMOSYNT.VBP.

IconState Property

IconState is a **Long** that returns the file status of a VB project or component file, or it is a numeric expression that sets the file status. Read/write.

USAGE

Obj.**IconState**[= *Val*]

The **IconState** property's syntax contains these parts:

- *Obj*: Required. An object expression that evaluates to a **VBComponent**, **VBProject**, or **VBProjects** object.

- *Val*: Optional. Only used when you set **IconState**, *Val* is a constant or value that specifies the file's status, as described in Settings.

SETTINGS

- 0 - **vbextSCCStatusNotControlled**: File is not under source code control.

- 1 - **vbextSCCStatusControlled**: File is under source code control.

- 2 - **vbextSCCStatusCheckedOut**: File is checked out to current user.

- 4 - **vbextSCCStatusOutOther**: File is checked out to another user.

- 32 - **vbextSCCStatusOutOfDate**: File is not the most recent.

- 512 - **vbextSCCStatusShared**: File is shared between projects.

COMMENTS

The **IconState** property determines how an instance of VB behaves if you try to open a VB project or component file that is already open in another instance of VB. Normally if you try to do this, VB tells you that the file name in question is already open and refuses to open the file. However, if for example you set **IconState** to 32 - **vbextSCCStatusOutOfDate** or 512 - **vbextSCCStatusShared**, you can then open the same file in another instance of VB.

All VB files have **IconState** set to 0 - **vbextSCCStatusNotControlled** when they are opened in an initial instance of VB. Changing the setting of **IconState** only affects a file's status while it is open within an instance of VB; when you save the file, the setting of **IconState** is not saved. Calling the **Reload** method of a **VBComponent** object causes the **IconState** setting of the component's file to revert to 0 - **vbextSCCStatusNotControlled**. The **IconState** property can be logically **OR**'ed together to form combined states.

If you do not have the Enterprise Edition of VB, which is the only edition that includes the Visual SourceSafe version control application, the **IconState** property, **Reload** method, and the various event procedures returned by the properties of the **Events** object would enable you to write your own add-in to handle version control.

 VB's Help file incorrectly states that **IconState** sets the source code control icon (or "glyph") for a file in the Project Explorer's window, indicating its status. Instead, setting **IconState** has no effect on the appearance of the file's source code control icon in the Project Explorer's window.

EXAMPLE CODE

See the Help topic IconState Property Example in ADDINEFS.HLP or the procedure DemoIconStatePrp in DEMOSYNT.VBP.

IDTExtensibility Object

IDTExtensibility provides methods that the current instance of VB's IDE calls when an add-in is connected to it through the Add-In Manager dialog box, the Add-In toolbar, or programmatically.

USAGE

Private Sub IDTExtensibility_*Mbr* (*Args*)

An **IDTExtensibility** object's syntax supports named arguments and contains these parts:

* *Mbr*: Required. A method of an **IDTExtensibility** object.

* *Args*: Required. An argument or arguments of *Mbr*.

MEMBERS

* Events: None at this time

* Methods: **OnAddInsUpdate, OnConnection, OnDisconnection, OnStartupComplete**

* Properties: None at this time

COMMENTS

Object interfaces like **IDTExtensibility** are new to VB5. They enable you to select a pre-configured method template from a **ClassModule** object's Procedure drop-down box, eliminating argument entry errors and allowing you to develop your applications more easily.

To use an **IDTExtensibility** object interface, you must first do two things:

* Select the Project|References command and, from the list of available references, select the Microsoft Visual Basic 5.0 Extensibility item.

* Have a **ClassModule** object in a project that is to be compiled into a VB add-in. An **IDTExtensibility** object interface is only for use in a **ClassModule** object that is to serve as a connection add-in.

An **IDTExtensibility** object's methods are exposed when you use the **Implements** statement, which is also new to VB5. After you enter the statement *Implements IDTExtensibility* in the Declarations section of a **ClassModule** object, VB makes an **IDTExtensibility** object available in the module's Object drop-down box. It also makes the object's methods available in the module's Procedure drop-down box. To add an **IDTExtensibility** object or one of its methods to the module, select it from the appropriate drop-down box.

An **IDTExtensibility** object interface currently contains four methods: **OnAddInsUpdate, OnConnection, OnDisconnection,** and **OnStartupComplete.** While these are technically methods, to you as a VB developer they act and behave like events. For example, when an add-in is connected to VB's IDE, the **OnConnection** method is called automatically by VB, just as if an event had been raised.

I-I

EXAMPLE CODE

Because the methods of an **IDTExtensibility** object are called by VB itself, it is not possible to demonstrate the normal kind of Example code for it. See the code in DEMOSYNT.VBP, which illustrates the kind of code you would write for the **IDTExtensibility** object.

Implements Statement

Implements specifies an interface or class that will be implemented in a **ClassModule** object in which **Implements** is declared.

USAGE

Implements *InterfaceName\Class*

The **Implements** statement's syntax contains these parts:

- *InterfaceName\Class*: Required. Specifies either the name of an object interface or a class in a class library, whose methods will be implemented by corresponding methods in a VB **ClassModule** object.

COMMENTS

An interface is a collection of prototypes representing the members (methods and properties) the interface encapsulates; that is, it contains only the opening and closing statements of the member procedures. A class provides an implementation of all of the methods and properties of one or more interfaces. Classes provide the code used when each member is called by a controller of the class. All classes implement at least one interface, which is considered the default interface of the class. In VB, any member that is not explicitly a member of an implemented interface is implicitly a member of the default interface.

The **Implements** statement can only appear in the Declarations section of a **ClassModule** object. After you type the statement and the name of an object interface or class, press Enter to add the implemented object to the code module's Object drop-down box. When you use **Implements** to specify an interface in a VB **ClassModule** object, the VB class provides its own versions of all the public members specified in the type library of the interface. However, VB's versions of the interface's public members may be declared as **Private**, as is the case with the members of an **IDTExtensibility** object interface.

When you implement an interface or class, you must include all the public members. Each member must contain at least one remark or statement. A missing member in an implementation causes a VB compilation error (Object module needs to implement 'member' for interface\class 'name'). If you choose not to write code in one of the implemented members, you can raise the appropriate error (*Const E_NOTIMPL = &H80004001*) to warn the user of the implementation that the member does nothing.

For more information about interfaces that can be used with the **Implements** statement, find the index entry titled *Implements statement* in VB's Help file, double-click on it, and display the topic titled *Description of interfaces that can be used with Implements (Read Me)*.

VB's Help file incorrectly places brackets around the *Interface-Name\Class* argument, signifying that it is optional. Instead, the *InterfaceName\Class* argument is required.

EXAMPLE CODE

See the Help topic Implements Statement Example in ADDINEFS.HLP or the procedure DemoImplementsStm in DEMOSYNT.VBP.

IndexedValue Property

IndexedValue returns or sets a value in an indexed list or an array of a property of a VB component or control. Read/write.

USAGE

Obj.**IndexedValue**(*Index1*, [*Index2*], [*Index3*], [*Index4*])[= *Val*]

The **IndexedValue** property's syntax contains these parts:

- *Obj*: Required. An object expression that evaluates to a **Property** object.

- *IndexNbr*: Required. A numeric expression that specifies the index position. **IndexedValue** accepts up to four indices. The number of indices accepted by **IndexedValue** is the value returned by the **NumIndices** property of the same **Property** object.

- *Val*: Optional. Only used when you set **IndexedValue**, *Val* is an expression that evaluates to a data type acceptable to the component or control.

COMMENTS

If the **Property** object is a list (as indicated by its **NumIndices** setting), then **IndexedValue** returns the element of the list specified by the *IndexNbr* parameters. **IndexedValue** is used only if the value of the **NumIndices** property is greater than zero. Values in indexed lists, as in the **List** property of a **ListBox** control, are set or returned with a single index. See the Example code for a demonstration of how to do this.

EXAMPLE CODE

See the Help topic IndexedValue Property Example in ADDINEFS.HLP or the procedure DemoIndexedValuePrp in DEMOSYNT.VBP.

InSelection Property

InSelection is a **Boolean** that returns or sets the selection status of a **VBControl** object in VB's IDE. Read/write.

USAGE

Obj.**InSelection**[= *Val*]

The **InSelection** property's syntax contains these parts:

- *Obj*: Required. An object expression that evaluates to a **VBControl** object.

- *Val*: Optional. Only used when you set **InSelection**, *Val* is a **Boolean** expression that specifies whether a control on a **VBForm** object is selected (**True**) or not (**False**).

COMMENTS

The **SelectedVBControls** collection does not have an **Add** or **Remove** method. Instead, setting the **InSelection** property to **True** is the equivalent of **Add** and setting it to **False** is the equivalent of **Remove**. Setting **InSelection** to **True** raises the **ItemAdded** event and setting it to **False** raises the **ItemRemoved** event. If the **InSelection** property of a control contained within another control is set to **True**, then any controls not within that control (or any controls within other controls) will be unselected.

The Object Browser does not indicate that **InSelection** can be set. However, VB's Help file does state that **InSelection** is read/write.

EXAMPLE CODE

See the Help topic InSelection Property Example in ADDINEFS.HLP or the procedure DemoInSelectionPrp in DEMOSYNT.VBP.

InsertLines Method

InsertLines is a **Sub** that inserts a line or lines of code at a specified location in a code module.

USAGE

Obj.**InsertLines** *Line, Code*

The **InsertLines** method's syntax supports named arguments and contains these parts:

- *Obj*: Required. An object expression that evaluates to a **CodeModule** object.

- *Line*: Required. A **Long** expression that specifies the line number directly above which you want to insert the code.

- *Code*: Required. A **String** expression containing the code you want to insert.

COMMENTS

To insert a general declaration, general procedure, or procedures, set the *Line* argument to the value returned by the **CountOfDeclarations** property + 1. You should always add one to the setting of the **CountOfDeclarations** property to prevent the *Line* argument from being set to zero (as when a newly inserted module lacks an **Option Explicit** statement).

To insert code that contains a word in quotation marks, use double quotation marks around that word. To insert code that includes line breaks, use the intrinsic constant **vbCr**. You can insert one long text string containing multiple general declarations and procedures with just one call to the **InsertLines** method. To do this, however, you must make sure the general declarations are placed at the beginning of the text string.

Unlike the **AddFromString** method, **InsertLines** never inserts the invalid string "()" on the line immediately following the inserted text. Because of this, and because it provides a greater degree of control over the insertion point, **InsertLines** is the preferred method for adding code to a module.

If you use **InsertLines** to add the text of a general procedure to a code module and that same procedure's name already exists in the module, VB will not warn you until you try to run the project, when it displays a syntax error message (Ambiguous name detected: 'Procedure name').

EXAMPLE CODE

See the Help topic InsertLines Method Example in ADDINEFS.HLP or the procedure DemoInsertLinesMet in DEMOSYNT.VBP.

IsBeingDebugged Method (VBAI)

IsBeingDebugged is a **Function** that checks whether an add-in is being run/debugged in one instance of VB while being connected to another instance of VB and returns **True** or **False** accordingly.

USAGE

Obj.**IsBeingDebugged**(*VBE*, *ProgID*) **As Integer**

The **IsBeingDebugged** method's syntax supports named arguments and contains these parts:

- *Obj*: Required. An object expression that evaluates to a **Util** object of the VBAI class library.

- *VBE*: Required. An object expression that evaluates to a **VBE** object of the VBIDE class library.

- *ProgID*: Required. A **String** expression that specifies the **ProgID** property's setting of the **AddIn** object that is being checked. The programmatic IDs of all registered add-ins are listed in VBADDIN.INI. If *ProgID* is set to a nonexistent programmatic ID, **IsBeingDebugged** fails.

ERROR HANDLING

IsBeingDebugged returns -2 (the intrinsic constant **aiFailed**) upon failure.

COMMENTS

Some kinds of routines in an add-in can behave differently depending on whether they are being run in debug mode or in normal mode. For example, the code in the book's demonstration add-in that displays VB's Add-In toolbar does not run correctly in debug mode. You can call **IsBeingDebugged** to set a flag to prevent the execution of such code.

IsBeingDebugged uses the Windows API function **FindWindow** to search for a VB main window whose caption contains the add-in's Project Name entry, which is set on the General tab of the Project Properties dialog box. If such a window exists and if its caption includes the string "[run]" or "[break]", then **IsBeingDebugged** assumes that the add-in is being debugged.

METHOD'S CODE

See the Help topic IsBeingDebugged Method in ADDINEFS.HLP or the **IsBeingDebugged** method's procedure in VBAI.VBP.

EXAMPLE CODE

See the Help topic IsBeingDebugged Method Example in ADDINEFS.HLP or the procedure DemoIsBeingDebuggedMet in DEMOSYNT.VBP.

IsBroken Property

IsBroken returns a **Boolean** that specifies whether a **Reference** object points to a valid reference in the registry (**True**) or no longer points to a valid reference (**False**). Read-only.

USAGE

Obj.**IsBroken**

The **IsBroken** property's syntax contains these parts:

- *Obj*: Required. An object expression that evaluates to a **Reference** object.

COMMENTS

When you load a project into VB, if a **Reference** object no longer points to a valid reference (that is, **IsBroken** is **True**), its item in the References dialog box is still checked but it has *MISSING:* prefixed to its description. This means that there is a mismatch between the GUID string of the reference stored in the project's VBP file and the GUID string of the entry in the Windows registry. This most commonly occurs on PCs used by developers who, in a client application, early bind a reference to an ActiveX component and then later change the existing public interface of the ActiveX component and recompile it.

When you load a project into VB, if a **Reference** object points to a file that no longer exists, VB immediately displays a syntax error message (Could not create reference: 'Path and file name'). After you clear the error message box, VB finishes loading the project but does not add the reference.

EXAMPLE CODE

See the Help topic IsBroken Property Example in ADDINEFS.HLP or the procedure DemoIsBrokenPrp in DEMOSYNT.VBP.

IsButton Method (VBAI)

IsButton is a **Function** that checks whether the entry for an add-in button in VB's Add-In toolbar Windows registry subkey is turned on, and returns an **Integer** that is **True/False** accordingly.

USAGE

Obj.**IsButton**(*VBE*, *ProgID*) **As Integer**

The **IsButton** method's syntax supports named arguments and contains these parts:

- *Obj*: Required. An object expression that evaluates to an **AITBar** object of the VBAI class library.

- *VBE*: Required. An object expression that evaluates to a **VBE** object of the VBIDE class library.

- *ProgID*: Required. A **String** expression that specifies the programmatic ID of the add-in whose button entry is to be checked. The programmatic IDs of all registered add-ins are listed in VBADDIN.INI. If *ProgID* is set to "*AddInToolbar.Connect*" (that is, the VB Add-In Toolbar add-in itself) or to a nonexistent programmatic ID, **IsButton** fails.

ERROR HANDLING

IsButton returns -2 (the intrinsic constant **aiFailed**) upon failure.

COMMENTS

Although it is possible to read the appropriate information directly from the Windows registry, the easiest way to check if the entry for an add-in button is turned on or not is to call **IsButton**. To check if VB's Add-In toolbar is displayed or not, call the **IsDisplayed** method of an **AITBar** object.

METHOD'S CODE

See the Help topic IsButton Method in ADDINEFS.HLP or the **IsButton** method's procedure in VBAI.VBP.

EXAMPLE CODE

See the Help topic IsButton Method Example in ADDINEFS.HLP or the procedure DemoAITBarObj in DEMOSYNT.VBP.

I-I

IsDirty Property

IsDirty returns or sets a **Boolean** that specifies whether a VB component or project was edited since the last time it was saved. Read/write.

USAGE

Obj.**IsDirty**[= *Val*]

The **IsDirty** property's syntax contains these parts:

- *Obj*: Required. An object expression that evaluates to a **VBComponent** or **VBProject** object.

- *Val*: Optional. Only used when you set **IsDirty**, *Val* is a **Boolean** expression that specifies that *Obj* needs to be saved (**True**) or does not need to be saved (**False**).

COMMENTS

Setting the **IsDirty** property of a **VBProject** to **False** also causes the **Saved** property of the **VBProject** object to return **True**, while setting **IsDirty** to **True** causes the **Saved** property to return **False**. See the Example code for a demonstration of this.

 Both VB's Help file and the Object Browser incorrectly state that IsDirty is read-only. Instead, IsDirty is read/write.

EXAMPLE CODE

See the Help topic IsDirty Property Example in ADDINEFS.HLP or the procedure DemoIsDirtyPrp in DEMOSYNT.VBP.

IsDisplayed Method (VBAI)

IsDisplayed is a **Function** that checks if VB's Add-In toolbar is displayed on the main window of the current instance of VB's IDE and returns a **Boolean** that is **True/False** accordingly.

USAGE

Obj.**IsDisplayed**(*VBE*) **As Boolean**

The **IsDisplayed** method's syntax supports named arguments and contains these parts:

- *Obj*: Required. An object expression that evaluates to an **AITBar** object of the VBAI class library.

- *VBE*: Required. An object expression that evaluates to a **VBE** object of the VBIDE class library.

COMMENTS

VB's Add-In toolbar behaves differently than the other VB toolbars in that a developer can display any other VB toolbar by selecting View|Toolbars and checking the desired toolbar's menu subitem. The Add-In toolbar, however, is itself an add-in. Therefore, you must initially display it by checking the VB Add-In Toolbar item in the Add-In Manager dialog box's list or by calling the **Show** method of an **AITBar** object. Once the Add-In toolbar has been displayed in this manner, you can select View|Toolbars and toggle the Add-In toolbar's menu item off to hide it or on to display it. Toggling the menu item off or on, however, does not uncheck or check the toolbar's item in the Add-In Manager dialog box's list.

The setting that determines if VB's Add-In toolbar is displayed or not when a new instance of VB's IDE is started is contained in VBADDIN.INI, under the key name of AddIn-Toolbar.Connect. If this key is set to "1" (that is, its item is checked in the Add-In Manager), the toolbar is displayed. If this key is set to "0" (that is, its item is not checked in the Add-In Manager), the toolbar is not displayed.

METHOD'S CODE

See the Help topic IsDisplayed Method in ADDINEFS.HLP or the **IsDisplayed** method's procedure in VBAI.VBP.

EXAMPLE CODE

See the Help topic IsDisplayed Method Example in ADDINEFS.HLP or the procedure DemoAITBarObj in DEMOSYNT.VBP.

IsFormDisplayed Method (VBAI)

IsFormDisplayed is a **Function** that finds an add-in's form that is currently displayed, brings the form to the foreground, and returns **True**. If the form is not displayed or is displayed by another instance of VB, **IsFormDisplayed** returns **False**.

USAGE

Obj.**IsFormDisplayed** (*VBE*, *ProgID*, *Titles()*) **As Integer**

The **IsFormDisplayed** method's syntax supports named arguments and contains these parts:

- *Obj*: Required. An object expression that evaluates to a **Util** object of the VBAI class library.

- *VBE*: Required. An object expression that evaluates to a **VBE** object of the VBIDE class library.

- *ProgID*: Required. A **String** expression that specifies the programmatic ID of the add-in whose forms are to be checked. If *ProgID* is set to a nonexistent programmatic ID, **IsFormDisplayed** fails. The programmatic IDs of all registered add-ins are listed in VBADDIN.INI.

- *Titles()*: Required. A **String** array that contains elements specifying the captions of the title bars of the forms to be checked.

ERROR HANDLING
IsFormDisplayed returns -2 (the intrinsic constant **aiFailed**) upon failure.

COMMENTS
IsFormDisplayed is meant to prevent another instance of an add-in's form from being displayed. Instead it brings the form that is already visible to the foreground. The *Titles()* argument's array may contain just one element, or it may contain several elements. If the add-in displays only a single form, then *Titles*(0) should be assigned the caption of that form. If the add-in displays several forms in succession, as in the case of a Wizard, then the caption of each possible form displayed by the add-in should be assigned to a different element of *Titles()*. **IsFormDisplayed** can detect if different instances of the same add-in are being run by different instances of VB and, in such a case, it returns **False**, which signals to the second add-in that it should display the form in question.

IsFormDisplayed uses the Windows API functions **GetWindowThreadProcessId** and **GetCurrentThreadId** to compare the identifier of the thread that displayed the form with the identifier of the thread that is running the add-in. If the thread identifiers are the same, **IsFormDisplayed** returns **True** and brings the form that is already visible to the foreground; if the identifiers are different, it returns **False**.

METHOD'S CODE
See the Help topic IsFormDisplayed Method in ADDINEFS.HLP or the **IsFormDisplayed** method's procedure in VBAI.VBP.

EXAMPLE CODE
See the Help topic IsFormDisplayed Method Example in ADDINEFS.HLP or the procedure DemoIsFormDisplayedMet in DEMOSYNT.VBP.

IsMenuItem (VBAI)

IsMenuItem is a **Function** that checks whether the specified menu item is attached to the specified VB menu or popup menu and returns **True** or **False** accordingly.

USAGE

Obj.**IsMenuItem**(*VBE, Menu, MenuItem,* [*PopupMenu* = ""]) **As Integer**

The **IsMenuItem** method's syntax supports named arguments and contains these parts:

- *Obj*: Required. An object expression that evaluates to a **Cmd** object of the VBAI class library.

- *VBE*: Required. An object expression that evaluates to a **VBE** object of the VBIDE class library.

- *Menu*: Required. A **String** expression that specifies the caption of the VB menu to be searched (for example, "Tools", "Add-Ins", and so on). The ampersand that specifies the underscored character in the caption does not need to be included.

- *MenuItem*: Required. A **String** expression that specifies the caption of the add-in menu item to be searched for.

- *PopupMenu*: Optional. A **String** expression that specifies the caption of the VB popup menu to be searched (for example, "Toolbars" under the View menu or "Bookmarks" under the Edit menu). The ampersand that specifies the underscored character in the caption does not need to be included. If *PopupMenu* is not passed, it defaults to a zero-length string (that is, "" or **vbNullString**).

ERROR HANDLING

IsMenuItem returns -2 (the intrinsic constant **aiFailed**) upon failure.

COMMENTS

The major use for the **IsMenuItem** method is to determine if an add-in has been connected to a VB menu (that is, the *ConnectMode* argument of the **IDTExtensibility** object's **OnConnection** method was either 0 - **vbext_cm_AfterStartup** or 1 - **vbext_cm_Startup**). Some elements of the Extensibility object model behave differently (for example, the **Description** property of an **AddIn** object), depending on whether an add-in has been connected to a menu item or not. You can also use **IsMenuItem** to determine if a custom VB toolbar menu item exists or not.

IsMenuItem is only designed to verify the existence of a menu item that is attached to either a VB menu or to a popup menu, which itself is attached to a VB menu. **IsMenuItem** fails if used on nested popup menus. Although VB supports nesting menus to a maximum of four levels, it is not good programming practice and is not recommended. You should follow VB's own design principles in this regard and only attach a popup menu to a VB menu.

METHOD'S CODE

See the Help topic IsMenuItem Method in ADDINEFS.HLP or the **IsMenuItem** method's procedure in VBAI.VBP.

EXAMPLE CODE

See the Help topic IsMenuItem Method Example in ADDINEFS.HLP or the procedure DemoIsMenuItemMet in DEMOSYNT.VBP.

IsSubKey Method (VBAI)

IsSubKey is a **Function** that returns a **Long** handle to the specified subkey if it exists in the Windows registry. If the subkey does not exist, **IsSubKey** returns **False**.

USAGE

Obj.IsSubKey(*Key*, *SubKey*) **As Long**

The **IsSubKey** method's syntax supports named arguments and contains these parts:

- *Obj*: Required. An object expression that evaluates to a **Reg** object of the VBAI class library.

- *Key*: Required. A constant or value that is one of the intrinsic constants of the enumerated type **aiKeyType** (see Settings) and that represents the handle to one of the Windows registry's six predefined keys.

- *SubKey*: Required. A **String** expression that specifies the subkey to be opened. If you pass *SubKey* a zero-length string (that is, "" or **vbNullString**), **IsSubKey** fails and returns **aiFailed**.

SETTINGS

The predefined values for *Key* (**aiKeyType**) are:

- 0 - **aiKTClasses**: HKEY_CLASSES_ROOT key

- 1 - **aiKTCurUser**: HKEY_CURRENT_USER key

- 2 - **aiKTMachine**: HKEY_LOCAL_MACHINE key

- 3 - **aiKTUsers**: HKEY_USERS key

- 5 - **aiKTCurConfig**: HKEY_CURRENT_CONFIG key

- 6 - **aiKTDynData**: HKEY_DYN_DATA key

ERROR HANDLING

IsSubKey returns -2 (the intrinsic constant **aiFailed**) upon failure.

COMMENTS

The difference between the **OpenSubKey** method of a **Reg** object and the **IsSubKey** method is that **OpenSubKey** creates the specified subkey if it does not already exist while **IsSubKey** does not create it and returns **False**. **IsSubKey** is useful for determining if a particular class is registered on a PC. For example, you could call **IsSubKey** and pass it "Outlook.Application" as *SubKey* to determine if Microsoft Office 97's Outlook is installed on a given PC. See the Example code for a demonstration of how to do this.

After calling **IsSubKey** to get a handle to a subkey, depending on the context, you could use that handle to call the **DelSubKey**, **DelValue**, **GetSubKeyName**, **GetSubKeysCount**, **GetValue**, **GetValueName**, **GetValuesCount**, or **SetValue** method of a **Reg** object. After you are done using the handle to a subkey, you should call the **CloseSubKey** method of a **Reg** object to release the handle and free system resources.

METHOD'S CODE
See the Help topic IsSubKey Method in ADDINEFS.HLP or the **IsSubKey** method's procedure in VBAI.VBP.

EXAMPLE CODE
See the Help topic IsSubKey Method Example in ADDINEFS.HLP or the procedure DemoRegObj in DEMOSYNT.VBP.

IsWinNT Method (VBAI)

IsWinNT is a **Function** that checks whether an add-in is being run under Windows NT and returns a **Boolean** that is **True** or **False** accordingly.

USAGE
Obj.**IsWinNT**() **As Boolean**

The **IsWinNT** method's syntax contains these parts:

- *Obj*: Required. An object expression that evaluates to a **Util** object of the VBAI class library.

COMMENTS
Some add-in routines that make calls to Windows API functions can behave differently depending on whether they are being run under Windows NT4 or Windows. You can call **IsWinNT** to set a flag that specifies the kind of Windows operating system being run.

METHOD'S CODE
See the Help topic IsWinNT Method in ADDINEFS.HLP or the **IsWinNT** method's procedure in VBAI.VBP.

EXAMPLE CODE
See the Help topic IsWinNT Method Example in ADDINEFS.HLP or the procedure DemoIsWinNTMet in DEMOSYNT.VBP.

Item Method

Item is a **Function** that returns the indexed object in an add-in collection.

USAGE
#1: *Obj*[.**Item**](*Index*)[.*Mbr*[(*Args*)]]
#2: **Set** *Var* = *Obj*[.**Item**](*Index*)

The **Item** method's syntax supports named arguments and contains these parts:

- *Obj*: Required. An object expression that evaluates to an add-in collection that has **Item** as a method. See Table D.4 for a list of the collections.

- *Item:* Optional. Because **Item** is the default member of a collection, it is itself optional.

- *Index*: Required. An expression that specifies the position of a member of a collection. If it is a numeric expression, *Index* must be a number from 1 to the value of a collection's **Count** property. If it is a **String** expression, *Index* must correspond to the *Key* argument specified when the item was added to a collection. See Table 4 for a list of the *Key* argument's values for the various add-in collections.

- *Mbr*: Optional. A member of the object returned by **Item**.

- *Args*: Optional. Argument(s) of a member of the object returned by **Item**.

- *Var*: Required. A variable declared as the specific object data type returned by **Item**, as the generic **Object** data type, or as a **Variant**. Usage #2 shortens an object expression by assigning the expression to *Var*. This results in faster-running and more readable code.

Table D.4 *Key argument's possible values.*

Kind Of Collection	Key Argument
Addins	**ProgID** property setting of **AddIn** object
CodePanes	No unique string for item in this collection
Components (Hidden)	Cannot be accessed from Extensibility object model
ContainedVBControls	**Name** property setting of control
ControlTemplates (Hidden)	Cannot be accessed from Extensibility object model
LinkedWindows	**Caption** property setting of **Window** object
Members	Declared name of public member
MenuItems (Hidden)	Cannot be accessed from Extensibility object model
Properties	**Name** property setting of **Property** object
References	**Name** property setting of **Reference** object
SelectedComponents (Hidden)	Cannot be accessed from Extensibility object model
SelectedControlTemplates (Hidden)	Cannot be accessed from Extensibility object model
SelectedVBControls	No unique string for item in this collection
VBComponents	**Name** property setting of **VBComponent** object
VBControls	**Name** property setting of control
VBNewProjects	**Name** property setting of **VBProject** object
VBProjects	**Name** property setting of **VBProject** object
Windows	**Caption** property setting of **Window** object

I-I

COMMENTS

The **Item** method is the default member of all collections to which it applies, so it does not have to be explicitly specified. In the Object Browser, a default member is marked with a small cyan circle at the top-left of the member's icon. Except for the Example code that demonstrates the **Item** method itself, the code on the book's CD-ROM does not explicitly specify the **Item** method when it calls it.

Another way to return an item in a collection is to use a **For...Each...Next** statement. According to Microsoft, **For...Each...Next** executes faster and is more readable than a **For...Next** counter loop.

1) VB's Help file fails to list all of the add-in collections that have **Item** as a method. 2) Microsoft advises that you not use the hidden collections **MenuItems**, **SelectedComponents**, and **SelectedControl-Templates** when creating VB5 add-ins because they may not be available in a future release of VB.

EXAMPLE CODE

See the Help topic Item Method Example in ADDINEFS.HLP or the procedure DemoItemMet in DEMOSYNT.VBP.

ItemActivated Event

ItemActivated is raised by VB's IDE after you manually or programmatically activate a VB component or project in the Project Explorer window.

USAGE

*Obj*_ItemActivated(**ByVal** *Item*)

The **ItemActivated** event's syntax contains these parts:

- *Obj*: An object expression that evaluates to a **VBComponentsEvents** or **VBProjectsEvents** object.

- *Item*: An object reference that is the **VBComponent** or **VBProject** object that has been activated.

COMMENTS

VB raises the **ItemActivated** event when you double-click on a component in the Project Explorer window or when you click on a project in the Project Explorer window (if there are multiple projects loaded in VB's IDE). The **ItemActivated** event does not occur when a project is double-clicked in the Project Explorer window because this action is hard-coded to toggle the project's hierarchical list of components between expanded/displayed and compressed/hidden.

I-1

You can raise the **ItemActivated** event programmatically by:

- Calling the **Activate** method of a **VBComponent** object.

- Setting the **ActiveVBProject** property of a **VBE** object to a different project.

The Example code demonstrates how you could write code in an **ItemActivated** event procedure to respond to the activation of a component. Each time you double-click on a component in the demo project in the Project Explorer window, the Example code hides any other components' windows in the demo project and displays only the windows (that is, designer and/or code pane) associated with the activated component.

 VB's Help file incorrectly states that the **ItemActivated** event does not occur when a *component* is double-clicked in the Project Explorer window. Instead, it does not occur when a *project* is double-clicked in the Project Explorer window.

I-I

EXAMPLE CODE

See the Help topic ItemActivated Event Example in ADDINEFS.HLP or the procedure DemoItemActivatedEvt in DEMOSYNT.VBP.

ItemAdded Event

ItemAdded is raised by VB's IDE after you call the **Add** method, after you manually add a reference, control, or component to a project, or after you manually add a project to VB's IDE.

USAGE

*Obj*_**ItemAdded**(ByVal *Item*)

The **ItemAdded** event's syntax contains these parts:

- *Obj*: An object expression that evaluates to a **ReferencesEvents**, **SelectedVBControlsEvents**, **VBComponentsEvents**, **VBControlsEvents**, or **VBProjectsEvents** object.

- *Item*: An object reference that is the **Reference**, **VBControl**, **VBComponent**, or **VBProject** object that a developer or an add-in has added to a collection.

COMMENTS

You can write code in the different **ItemAdded** event procedures to perform many kinds of tasks. Some examples are:

- Check whether a reference to an ActiveX component is for a particular version.

- Size specific controls to accord with the Windows 95 interface guidelines instead of the defaults that VB sets. For example, VB's default height for a **CommandButton** or **TextBox** object is 510 twips. The Windows 95 guidelines call for them to be 315 twips in height. See the Example code for how to do this.

- Set properties of a VB component to values other than the initial defaults. For example, you may want all forms that are to be used as dialog boxes to display a certain icon, have

AutoRedraw set to **True** and **ClipControls** set to **False**, and provide the What's This style of context-sensitive Help. See the Example code for how to do this.

- Add initialization comments to the different kinds of code modules that can comprise a new **VBProject** object.

To make an add-in responsive to an **ItemAdded** event raised by VB, you first need to declare an object variable as a **ReferencesEvents**, **SelectedVBControlsEvents**, **VBComponentsEvents**, **VBControlsEvents**, or **VBProjectsEvents** object and assign it the object returned by the **ReferencesEvents**, **SelectedVBControlsEvents**, **VBComponentsEvents**, **VBControlsEvents**, or **VBProjectsEvents** property of an **Events** object. For detailed information about how to do this, see the object's topic.

VB's Help file incorrectly states that *Item* specifies the name of the object that has been added. Instead, *Item* is passed the object reference itself.

EXAMPLE CODE

See the Help topic ItemAdded Event Example in ADDINEFS.HLP or the procedure DemoItemAddedEvt in DEMOSYNT.VBP.

ItemReloaded Event

ItemReloaded is raised by VB's IDE after you programmatically reload a VB component.

USAGE

*Obj*_**ItemReloaded**(**ByVal** *VBComponent*)

The **ItemReloaded** event's syntax contains these parts:

- *Obj*: An object expression that evaluates to a **VBComponentsEvents** object.

- *VBComponent*: An object reference that is the **VBComponent** object that has been selected.

COMMENTS

VB raises the **ItemReloaded** event when you programmatically reload a VB component into a project by calling the **Reload** method of a **VBComponent** object. The **ItemReloaded** event does not provide any way to cancel the reloading of a component, nor does it offer you a chance to save any changes to the component to a backup file. Instead, the **Reload** method immediately and irrevocably removes the component from the project.

There does not appear to be any single-step, manual equivalent to the Reload method in VB's IDE. If you have made changes to a component and then decide to discard the changes and revert to the last-saved version of the component, you must first remove the component from the project (Project|Remove) and then add the component's file back to the project (Project|Add File). This series of steps does not cause VB's IDE to raise the ItemReloaded event.

EXAMPLE CODE

See the Help topic ItemReloaded Event Example in ADDINEFS.HLP or the procedure
DemoItemReloadedEvt in DEMOSYNT.VBP.

ItemRemoved Event

ItemRemoved is raised by VB's IDE after you call the **Remove** method, after you manually
delete a reference, control or component from a project, or after you manually delete a project
from VB's IDE.

USAGE

*Obj*_ItemRemoved(ByVal *Item*)

The **ItemRemoved** event's syntax contains these parts:

- *Obj*: An object expression that evaluates to a **ReferencesEvents**, **SelectedVBControlsEvents**,
  VBComponentsEvents, **VBControlsEvents**, or **VBProjectsEvents** object.

- *Item*: An object reference that is the **Reference**, **VBControl**, **VBComponent**, or **VBProject**
  object that a developer or an add-in has deleted from a collection.

COMMENTS

You can write code in the different **ItemRemoved** event procedures to perform many different
kinds of tasks. Some examples are:

- Check whether any event procedures for a removed control exist in the project's code
  modules and delete them. See the Example code for how to do this.

- Check whether any references to the **Name** property of the removed control exist in the
  project's code and flag and interactively display such lines of code to the developer for
  action. See the Example code for how to do this.

- Allow the developer to delete a removed component's or project's file from the project's
  path or save the file to another, backup path.

To make an add-in responsive to an **ItemRemoved** event raised by VB, you first need
to declare an object variable as a **ReferencesEvents**, **SelectedVBControlsEvents**,
VBComponentsEvents, **VBControlsEvents**, or **VBProjectsEvents** object and assign it the object
returned by the **ReferencesEvents**, **SelectedVBControlsEvents**, **VBComponentsEvents**,
VBControlsEvents, or **VBProjectsEvents** property of an **Events** object. For detailed information about how to do this, see the object's topic.

VB's Help file incorrectly states that *Item* specifies the name of the object that has been added. Instead, *Item* is passed the object reference
itself.

EXAMPLE CODE

See the Help topic ItemRemoved Event Example in ADDINEFS.HLP or the procedure
DemoItemRemovedEvt in DEMOSYNT.VBP.

ItemRenamed Event

ItemRenamed is raised by VB's IDE after you manually or programmatically rename a control, component, or project.

USAGE

*Obj*_**ItemRenamed**(**ByVal** *Item*)

The **ItemRenamed** event's syntax contains these parts:

- *Obj*: An object expression that evaluates to a **VBComponentsEvents**, **VBControlsEvents**, or **VBProjectsEvents** object.

- *Item*: An object reference that is the **VBControl**, **VBComponent**, or **VBProject** object that a developer or an add-in has renamed.

COMMENTS

You can write code in the different **ItemRenamed** event procedures to perform many different kinds of tasks. Some examples are:

- Check whether any event procedures for a renamed control exist in the project's code modules and rename them. See the Example code for how to do this.

- Check whether any references to the old **Name** property of the renamed control exist in the project's code and rename them. See the Example code for how to do this.

- Check whether any references to the old **Name** property of the renamed control exist in the control's property settings and rename them. See the Example code for how to do this.

- Allow the developer to delete a renamed component's or project's old file from the project's path or save the old file to another, backup path.

To make an add-in responsive to an **ItemRenamed** event raised by VB, you first need to declare an object variable as a **ReferencesEvents**, **SelectedVBControlsEvents**, **VBComponentsEvents**, **VBControlsEvents**, or **VBProjectsEvents** object and assign it the object returned by the **ReferencesEvents**, **SelectedVBControlsEvents**, **VBComponentsEvents**, **VBControlsEvents**, or **VBProjectsEvents** property of an **Events** object. For detailed information about how to do this, see the object's topic.

VB's Help file incorrectly states that *Item* specifies the name of the object that has been added. Instead, *Item* is passed the object reference itself.

EXAMPLE CODE

See the Help topic ItemRenamed Event Example in ADDINEFS.HLP or the procedure DemoItemRenamedEvt in DEMOSYNT.VBP.

ItemSelected Event

ItemSelected is raised by VB's IDE after you manually select a VB component in the Project Explorer window or after you manually or programmatically give the focus to a designer window of a component.

Usage

*Obj*_ItemSelected(**ByVal** *VBComponent*)

The **ItemSelected** event's syntax contains these parts:

- *Obj*: An object expression that evaluates to a **VBComponentsEvents** object.

- *VBComponent*: An object reference that is the **VBComponent** object that has been selected.

Comments

VB raises the **ItemSelected** event when you click on a component in the Project Explorer window, whether it is a left- or right-click. In addition, any statement in an add-in that gives the focus to a designer window of a component also causes VB to raise the **ItemSelected** event.

The Example code demonstrates how to write code in an **ItemSelected** event procedure to respond to the selection of a component in the Project Explorer window. Each time you select a component in the demo project, the Example code brings the component's open designer window (if it has one) to the top of the z-order. If the component does not have an open designer window, its code pane window is brought to the top of the z-order. Normally, of course, clicking on a component in the Project Explorer window has no effect on the z-order of the component's window.

Example Code

See the Help topic ItemSelected Event Example in ADDINEFS.HLP or the procedure DemoItemSelectedEvt in DEMOSYNT.VBP.

LastUsedPath Property

LastUsedPath returns a **String** that specifies the last path used in a file dialog box in VB's IDE or sets a **String** that specifies the new path to be used. Read/write.

Usage

Obj.**LastUsedPath**[= *Val*]

The **LastUsedPath** property's syntax contains these parts:

- *Obj*: Required. An object expression that evaluates to a **VBE** object.

- *Val*: Optional. Only used when you set **LastUsedPath**, *Val* is a **String** expression that specifies the subdirectory that you want to be the current path.

Comments

You will want to read the **LastUsedPath** and possibly change it before you call the **SaveAs** method of a **VBComponent** object or the **MakeCompiledFile** method of a **VBProject** object.

Example Code

See the Help topic LastUsedPath Property Example in ADDINEFS.HLP or the procedure DemoLastUsedPathPrp in DEMOSYNT.VBP.

Left Property

Left returns a **Long** or sets a numeric expression that specifies the position of the left side of a window in a **Windows** collection. Read/write.

USAGE

Obj.**Left** [= *Val*]

The **Left** property's syntax contains these parts:

- *Obj*: Required. An object expression that evaluates to a **Window** object.

- *Val*: Optional. Only used when you set **Left**, *Val* is a numeric expression that specifies in pixels the distance between the external left side of a window and the internal left side of its container.

COMMENTS

There is a difference between the **Left** property of a VB IDE designer **Window** object (specified in pixels) and the **Left** property of a VB **Form** object (specified in twips). The value returned by the **Left** property of a **Window** object depends on whether or not the window is linked or docked. If the window is linked, the value of **Left** is actually for the frame window to which it is linked. If the window is not linked, the value of **Left** is for the window itself.

Setting the **Left** property of a linked window has no effect. You can set the **Left** property of any VB IDE window to a value so small or so large that the window is positioned entirely off the screen. See the Example code for a demonstration of this effect on VB's main window.

 1) VB's Help file and the Object Browser incorrectly state that the **Left** property of a **Window** object is specified in twips. Instead, it is specified in pixels. 2) VB's Help file incorrectly states that **Left** returns a **Single**. Instead, it returns a **Long**.

EXAMPLE CODE

See the Help topic Left Property Example in ADDINEFS.HLP or the procedure DemoLeftPrp in DEMOSYNT.VBP.

Lines Property

Lines returns a **String** containing a line or lines of code. Read-only.

USAGE

Obj.**Lines**(*StartLine, Count*)

The **Lines** property's syntax contains these parts:

- *Obj*: Required. An object expression that evaluates to a **CodeModule** object.

- *StartLine*: Required. A **Long** expression that specifies the first line number of the code you want to return from a code module. *StartLine* must be greater than zero.

- *Count*: Required. A **Long** expression that specifies the number of lines of code you want to return. *Count* must be greater than zero.

COMMENTS

The line numbers in a code module begin at 1 in the Declarations section. If *Count* is zero or a negative number, trying to return the setting of **Lines** results in OLE Automation trappable error -2147024809 (Invalid procedure call or argument).

 VB's Help file incorrectly states that **Lines** is a method. Instead, the Object Browser correctly identifies it as a property.

EXAMPLE CODE

See the Help topic Lines Property Example in ADDINEFS.HLP or the procedure DemoLinesPrp in DEMOSYNT.VBP.

LinkedWindowFrame Property

LinkedWindowFrame returns an object instance of the **Window** class that is the frame that contains the specified window. Read-only.

INSTANTIATION

Dim *Obj* **As** [**VBIDE.**]**Window|Object|Variant**
Set *Obj* = **VBE.Windows**[**.Item**] (*Index*).**LinkedWindowFrame**

USAGE

#1: *Obj* [.*Mbr* [= *Val*]]
#2: *Obj.MbrA.MbrB* [= *ValB* | *ArgsB*]

The **LinkedWindowFrame** property's syntax supports named arguments, and it also contains these parts:

- *Obj*: Required. A variable to be assigned an object instance. *Obj* can be named the same as the **Window** class being instantiated. *Obj* can also be declared as the generic **Object** or as **Variant**, but this slows performance.

- VBIDE: Optional. The VB5 Extensibility object library containing the **Window** class.

- *Index*: Required. Used with the default **Item** method, *Index* is a numeric or **String** expression that specifies the ordinal position of a **Window** object in a **Windows** collection. If *Index* is a **String** expression, it must evaluate to the **Caption** property of a **Window** object.

- *Mbr*: Optional. A member of a **Window** object.

- *Val*: Optional. You use *Val* if *Mbr* is a property being set.

- *MbrA*: Required. A **Window** object's property that returns an object or collection.

- *MbrB*: Required. A member of the object or collection that is returned by *MbrA*.

- *ValB* | *ArgsB*: Optional. You use *ValB* if *MbrB* is a property being set or *ArgsB* if *MbrB* is a method being called.

COMMENTS

The **LinkedWindowFrame** property enables you to access an object representing a window frame that has properties distinct from the linked window or windows it contains. If the window is not linked, the **LinkedWindowFrame** property returns **Nothing**. You can use the object returned by the **LinkedWindowFrame** property to access the **LinkedWindows** collection that the object contains.

EXAMPLE CODE

See the Help topic LinkedWindowFrame Property Example in ADDINEFS.HLP or the procedure DemoLinkedWindowFramePrp in DEMOSYNT.VBP.

LinkedWindows Collection/Property

A **LinkedWindows** collection contains VB's IDE **Window** objects that are enclosed in a particular linked window frame. The read-only **LinkedWindows** property of the **Window** object returns an object instance of the **LinkedWindows** class.

INSTANTIATION

Dim *Obj* **As** [VBIDE.]**LinkedWindows|Object|Variant**
Set *Obj* = VBE.**ActiveWindow.LinkedWindowFrame.LinkedWindows**

USAGE

#1: *Obj.Mbr*
#2: *Obj*[.**Item**](*Index*) [.*MbrA* [= *ValA*]]
#3: *Obj.MbrB.MbrC* [= *ValC* | *ArgsC*]

The **LinkedWindows** syntax supports named arguments and contains these parts:

- *Obj*: Required. A variable to be assigned an object instance. *Obj* can be named the same as the **LinkedWindows** class being instantiated. *Obj* can also be declared as the generic **Object** or as **Variant**, but this slows performance.

- VBIDE: Optional. The VB5 Extensibility object library containing the **LinkedWindows** class.

- *Mbr*: Required. A member of a **LinkedWindows** collection other than the **Item** method.

- *Index*: Required. Used with the default **Item** method, *Index* is a numeric or **String** expression that specifies the ordinal position of a **Window** object in a **LinkedWindows** collection. If *Index* is a **String** expression, it must evaluate to the **Caption** property of a **Window** object.

- *MbrA*: Optional. A member of a **Window** object.

- *ValA*: Optional. You use *ValA* if *MbrA* is a property being set.

- *MbrB*: Required. A **LinkedWindows** collection's property that returns a **VBE** object.

- *MbrC*: Required. A member of the **VBE** object that is returned by *MbrB*.

- *ValC* | *ArgsC*: Optional. You use *ValC* if *MbrC* is a property being set or *ArgsC* if *MbrC* is a method being called.

L-L

MEMBERS

- Events: None at this time

- Methods: **Add**, **Item**, **Remove**

- Properties: **Count**, **Parent** (Hidden), **VBE**

COMMENTS

You must first use the **LinkedWindowFrame** property of a **Window** object to return a **Window** object that contains a valid **LinkedWindows** collection. Then you can use that **LinkedWindows** collection to dock and undock windows from the main window frame in the development environment. Linked window frames contain all windows that can be linked or docked. This includes all windows except code windows, designers, the Object Browser window, and the Search and Replace window.

You can use the **Add** method to add a window to a collection of currently linked windows. A window that is a pane in one linked window frame can be added to another linked window frame. Use the **Remove** method to delete a window from a collection of currently linked windows; this results in the window being unlinked or undocked. If all the panes from one linked window frame are moved to another window, the linked window frame with no panes is destroyed. However, if all the panes are removed from the main window, it isn't destroyed.

 If you use the **Remove** method to delete a linked window from the collection and then immediately add it back to the collection with the **Add** method, the relinked window does not necessarily appear in the same position within the frame window that it occupied before it was removed. Unfortunately, the Extensibility object model does not provide programmatic control over the positioning of a linked window.

EXAMPLE CODE

See the Help topic LinkedWindows Collection/Property Example in ADDINEFS.HLP or the procedure DemoLinkedWindowsObj in DEMOSYNT.VBP.

MainWindow Property

MainWindow returns a **Window** object that represents the main window of Visual Basic's IDE. Read-only.

USAGE

Obj.**MainWindow**

The **MainWindow** property's syntax contains these parts:

- *Obj*: Required. An object expression that evaluates to a **VBE** object.

COMMENTS

You can use the **Window** object returned by the **MainWindow** property to add and remove docked windows or to maximize, minimize, hide, or restore the main window of VB's IDE.

The **Window** object returned by **MainWindow** has a **Type** property setting of 12 - vbext_wt_MainWindow. The **Window** object returned by **MainWindow** is the only one whose **HWnd** property returns a non-zero value.

 The main window of VB's IDE is not an item in a **Windows** collection. The only way you can access the main window is through the **MainWindow** property.

EXAMPLE CODE
See the Help topic MainWindow Property Example in ADDINEFS.HLP or the procedure DemoMainWindowPrp in DEMOSYNT.VBP.

Major Property
Major returns a **Long** containing the major version number of the referenced class library. Read-only.

USAGE
Obj.**Major**

The **Major** property's syntax contains these parts:

- *Obj*: Required. An object expression that evaluates to a **Reference** object.

COMMENTS
The value of the **Major** property of a **Reference** object corresponds to the major version or release number. This can be set for a VB project on the Make tab of the Project Properties dialog box.

EXAMPLE CODE
See the Help topic Major Property Example in ADDINEFS.HLP or the procedure DemoMajorPrp in DEMOSYNT.VBP.

MakeCompiledFile Method
MakeCompiledFile is a **Sub** that, depending on the project type, writes out the active project as an EXE, DLL, or OCX file.

USAGE
Obj.**MakeCompiledFile**

The **MakeCompiledFile** method's syntax contains these parts:

- *Obj*: Required. An object expression that evaluates to a **VBProject** object.

COMMENTS
After you set the **BuildFileName** property, ensure that the **StartUpObject** and **LastUsedPath** properties are set to the values you want. Then you can call the **MakeCompiledFile** method to compile the active project as an EXE, DLL, or OCX file.

M-M

EXAMPLE CODE

See the Help topic MakeCompiledFile Method Example in ADDINEFS.HLP or the procedure DemoMakeCompiledFileMet in DEMOSYNT.VBP.

Manager Object

Manager provides methods to manipulate the VB Add-In toolbar.

USAGE

Obj.Mbr Args

A **Manager** object's syntax supports named arguments and contains these parts:

- *Obj*: Required. An object expression that evaluates to a **Manager** object of the in-process, VB Add-In Toolbar add-in (AITOOL.DLL). As with all ActiveX components, you can instantiate the **Manager** class in one of two ways. The first way is to set a reference to the ActiveX component and then declare an object variable **As New** AddInToolbar.Manager. The second way is to declare an object variable as **Object** and then instantiate the **Manager** class by using the **CreateObject** function.

- *Mbr*: Required. A method of a **Manager** object.

- *Args*: Required. Arguments of a method of a **Manager** object.

MEMBERS

- Events: None at this time

- Methods: **AddToAddInToolbar**, **RemoveAddInFromToolbar**

- Properties: None at this time

COMMENTS

You can display the Add-In toolbar in the current instance of VB's IDE by checking the VB Add-In Toolbar item in the Add-In Manager dialog box. Unlike the other VB toolbars, when the Add-In toolbar is first displayed, it is docked to the main window. You can then toggle back and forth between its docked and floating state by double-clicking on a non-button area of the toolbar.

The first time you display the Add-In toolbar, it has seven buttons on it, six of which connect and start add-ins that are installed with VB. To add a button to or remove a button from the Add-In toolbar, click on the first button on the Add-In toolbar to display and use the Add/Remove Toolbar Items dialog box. A **Manager** object of the VB Add-In Toolbar add-in provides methods to programmatically add a button to (**AddToAddInToolbar**) or remove a button from (**RemoveAddInFromToolbar**) the Add-In toolbar.

 The two methods of a **Manager** object provide programmatic control over the buttons that are displayed on the Add-In toolbar, but not in the same way as provided by the Add/Remove Toolbar Items dialog box. When you make changes with the Add/Remove Toolbar Items dialog box, the Add-In toolbar is refreshed as soon as you close the dialog box. When you make changes with the **AddToAddInToolbar** and **RemoveAddInFromToolbar** methods, the Add-In toolbar is not refreshed until the next instance of VB's IDE is started. You can correct for these deficiencies by calling the **AddButton** and **DelButton** methods of an **AITBar** object.

EXAMPLE CODE
See the Help topic Manager Object Example in ADDINEFS.HLP or the procedure DemoManagerObj in DEMOSYNT.VBP.

Member Object
Member is an item in a **Members** collection. It represents a mixture of code-based and class library-based attributes of members of a code module.

INSTANTIATION
Dim *Obj* **As** [VBIDE.]**Member|Object|Variant**
Set *Obj* = **VBE.VBComponents**[.**Item**](*IndexA*).**CodeModule.Members**[.**Item**](*IndexB*)

USAGE
#1: *Obj*[.*Mbr*[= *Val*]]
#2: *Obj.MbrA.MbrB* [= *ValB* | *ArgsB*]
A **Member** object's syntax supports named arguments and contains these parts:

- *Obj*: Required. A variable to be assigned an object instance. *Obj* can be named the same as the **Member** class being instantiated. *Obj* can also be declared as the generic **Object** or as **Variant**, but this slows performance.

- VBIDE: Optional. The VB5 Extensibility object library containing the **Member** class.

- *IndexA*: Required. Used with the default **Item** method, *IndexA* is a numeric or **String** expression that specifies the ordinal position of a **VBComponent** object in a **VBComponents** collection. If *IndexA* is a **String** expression, it must evaluate to the **Name** property of a **VBComponent** object.

- *IndexB*: Required. Used with the default **Item** method, *IndexB* is a numeric or **String** expression that specifies the ordinal position of a **Member** object in a **Members** collection. If *IndexB* is a **String** expression, it must evaluate to the declared name of a **Member** object (that is, a public member of a code module).

- *Mbr*: Optional. A property of a **Member** object.

- *Val*: Optional. You use *Val* if *Mbr* is a property being set.

- *MbrA*: Required. A **Member** object's property that returns an object or collection.

- *MbrB*: Required. A member of the object or collection that is returned by *MbrA*.

- *ValB* |*ArgsB*: Optional. You use *ValB* if *MbrB* is a property being set or *ArgsB* if *MbrB* is a method being called.

M-M

MEMBERS

- Events: None at this time

- Methods: None at this time

- Properties: **Bindable, Browsable, Category, CodeLocation, Collection, DefaultBind, Description, DisplayBind, HelpContextID, Hidden, Name, PropertyPage, RequestEdit, Scope, StandardMethod, Static, Type, UIDefault, VBE**

COMMENTS

A **Member** object of a code module represents an identifier that has module-level scope and is a constant, variable, property, method, or event of that code module. You can access a **Member** object by:

- Calling the **Item** method of a **Members** collection.

- Using a **For...Each...Next** statement to loop through the items of a **Members** collection until you find the **Member** object you want.

Until you select an event procedure in a code module, write a general procedure in it, or make a general declaration, a code module does not contain any **Member** objects. A general declaration made with the **Declare** statement (for example, a Windows API function) is considered to be a member of a code module and is treated the same as a method.

EXAMPLE CODE

See the Help topic Member Object Example in ADDINEFS.HLP or the procedure DemoMemberObj in DEMOSYNT.VBP.

Members Collection/Property

A **Members** collection contains the **Member** objects that represent the members of a code module. The read-only **Members** property of a **CodeModule** object returns an object instance of the **Members** class.

INSTANTIATION

Dim *Obj* **As [VBIDE.]Members|Object|Variant**
Set *Obj* = **VBE.VBComponents[.Item]**(*IndexA*)**.CodeModule.Members**

USAGE

#1: *Obj*.**Mbr**
#2: *Obj* [.**Item**](*IndexB*)[.*MbrA* [= *ValA*]]
#3: *Obj*.**MbrB.MbrC**[= *ValC* | *ArgsC*]

The **Members** syntax supports named arguments and contains these parts:

- *Obj*: Required. A variable to be assigned an object instance. *Obj* can be named the same as the **Members** class being instantiated. *Obj* can also be declared as the generic **Object** or as **Variant**, but this slows performance.

- VBIDE: Optional. The VB5 Extensibility object library containing the **Members** class.

- *IndexA*: Required. Used with the default **Item** method, *IndexA* is a numeric or **String** expression that specifies the ordinal position of a **VBComponent** object in a **VBComponents** collection. If *IndexA* is a **String** expression, it must evaluate to the **Name** property of a **VBComponent** object.

- *Mbr*: Required. A property or method of a **Members** collection other than the **Item** method.

- *IndexB*: Required. Used with the default **Item** method, *IndexB* is a numeric or **String** expression that specifies the ordinal position of a **Member** object in a **Members** collection. If *IndexB* is a **String** expression, it must evaluate to the declared name of a **Member** object (that is, a public member of a code module).

- *MbrA*: Optional. A property of a **Member** object.

- *ValA*: Optional. You use *ValA* if *MbrA* is a property being set.

- *MbrB*: Required. A **Members** collection's property that returns an object.

- *MbrC*: Required. A member of the object that is returned by *MbrB*.

- *ValC | ArgsC*: Optional. You use *ValC* if *MbrC* is a property being set or *ArgsC* if *MbrC* is a method being called.

Members

- Events : None at this time

- Methods : **Item, _NewEnum** (Hidden)

- Properties : **Count, Parent, VBE**

Comments

Until you select an event procedure in a code module, write a general procedure in it, or make a general declaration, a code module's **Members** collection does not contain any **Member** objects. A **Member** object of a code module represents an identifier that has module-level scope and that is a constant, variable, property, method, or event of that code module.

You can access a **Member** object by first using the **Members** property to return a **Members** collection. Then you can apply that collection's **Item** method or use a **For...Each...Next** statement to loop through the items in that collection to find the member you want.

Example Code
See the Help topic Members Collection/Property Example in ADDINEFS.HLP or the procedure DemoMembersObj in DEMOSYNT.VBP.

Minor Property

Minor returns a **Long** containing the minor version number of the referenced class library. Read-only.

M-M

USAGE

Obj.**Minor**

The **Minor** property's syntax contains these parts:

- *Obj*: Required. An object expression that evaluates to a **Reference** object.

COMMENTS

The value of the **Minor** property of a **Reference** object corresponds to the minor version or release number. This can be set for a VB project on the Make tab of the Project Properties dialog box.

EXAMPLE CODE

See the Help topic Minor Property Example in ADDINEFS.HLP or the procedure DemoMinorPrp in DEMOSYNT.VBP.

Name Property

Name is a **String** that returns or sets the name used in code to identify an object. Read/write.

USAGE

Obj.**Name**[= *Val*]

The **Name** property's syntax contains these parts:

- *Obj*: Required. An object expression that evaluates to an **Application** (Hidden), **CodeModule**, **Component** (Hidden), **Member**, **Property**, **Reference**, **VBComponent**, **VBE**, or **VBProjects** object.

- *Val*: Optional. Only used when you set **Name**, *Val* is a **String** expression that specifies the name of a **CodeModule**, **VBProject**, or **VBComponent** object. **Name** is read-only for the other objects that have it as a member.

COMMENTS

The **Name** property setting applies to different objects in different ways:

- **CodeModule** object: Returns or sets the name of a code module and is always equivalent to the **Name** property setting of the code module's associated **VBComponent** object. **Name** is a **CodeModule** object's default member and, although it is hidden, you can access it. An error occurs if you try to set **Name** to a value already being used or to an invalid name.

- **Member** object: Returns the name of a member of a code module.

- **Property** object: Returns the name of the property as it appears in the Properties window. The setting of **Name** is used to index the **Properties** collection.

- **Reference** object: Returns the name used in code to identify a reference to a type library or project.

- **VBComponent** object: Returns or sets the name of a VB component and is always equivalent to the **Name** property setting of the component's associated **CodeModule** object. An error occurs if you try to set **Name** to a value already being used or an invalid name.

- **VBE** object: Returns the name of a **VBE** object, which is always Microsoft Visual Basic in VB5.

- **VBProject** object: Returns or sets the name of the specified project. An error occurs if you try to set **Name** to a value already being used or to an invalid name.

The default name for new objects is the type of object plus a unique integer. For example, the first new **Form** object is named Form1 and the third **TextBox** control you create on a form is named TextBox3. An object's **Name** property must start with a letter and can be a maximum of 40 characters. It can include numbers and underline (_) characters, but it can't include punctuation or spaces. Forms and modules can't have the same name as another public object, such as **Clipboard**, **Screen**, or **App**. Although the **Name** property setting can be a keyword, property name, or the name of another object, this can create conflicts in your code.

 Although you cannot directly set the **Name** property of a **Member** object, you can change it indirectly by changing its declaration statement. See the Example code for the **ItemRenamed** event to see how to do this.

EXAMPLE CODE
See the Help topic Name Property Example in ADDINEFS.HLP or the procedure DemoNamePrp in DEMOSYNT.VBP.

NumIndices Property

NumIndices returns an **Integer** that specifies the number of indices on the property returned by the **Property** object. Read-only.

USAGE
Obj.**NumIndices**

The **NumIndices** property's syntax contains these parts:

- *Obj*: Required. An object expression that evaluates to a **Property** object.

COMMENTS
The value of the **NumIndices** property can be an integer from 0 to 4. For most properties, **NumIndices** returns 0. Conventionally indexed properties return 1. Property arrays might return 2. If **NumIndices** returns a value greater than zero for a **Property** object, you need to use the **IndexedValue** property to set the value of that **Property** object.

EXAMPLE CODE
See the Help topic NumIndices Property Example in ADDINEFS.HLP or the procedure DemoNumIndicesPrp in DEMOSYNT.VBP.

Object Property

Object returns or sets the value of an object returned by a property. Read/write.

Usage

Obj.**Object** [= *Val*]

The **Object** property's syntax contains these parts:

- *Obj*: Required. An object expression that evaluates to an **AddIn** or **Property** object.

- *Val*: Optional. Only used when you set **Object**, *Val* is an object expression that evaluates to the kind of object required by a property.

Comments

If a property requires an object as its setting, you must use the **Object** property to return or set the value of that object. For example, to set a form's **Icon** property (which requires a **Picture** object), you can set the **Object** property of that form's **Properties** collection with the **LoadPicture** statement. See the Example code for a demonstration of how to do this.

 For some reason, setting the **Object** property while an add-in is running in debug mode can result in OLE Automation error -2147467259 (Method 'Object' of object 'Property' failed). This would occur with the Example code except that it aborts the procedure when running in debug mode. However, the Example code executes correctly when the demo add-in is run in normal mode.

Example Code

See the Help topic Object Property Example in ADDINEFS.HLP or the procedure DemoObjectPrp in DEMOSYNT.VBP.

OnAddInsUpdate Method

OnAddInsUpdate is a **Sub** that occurs automatically when changes to the VBADDIN.INI file are saved by the current instance of VB's IDE through the Add-In Manager dialog box.

Usage

Obj. **OnAddInsUpdate**(*Custom()*)

The **OnAddInsUpdate** method supports named arguments and contains these parts:

- *Obj*: Required. An object expression that evaluates to an **IDTExtensibility** object.

- *Custom()*: Required. An array of **Variant** expressions to hold user-defined data. If you use the **VarType** function on *Custom()*, it returns 8204 (**vbArray** + **vbVariant**). However, if you try to use the **LBound** function on *Custom()*, it results in trappable error 9 (Subscript out of range), which indicates that VB is passing *Custom()* an unsized array. This means that *Custom()* is not currently being used and is probably provided for future use by Microsoft's VB development team.

Comments

The **OnAddInsUpdate** method is created when you implement an **IDTExtensibility** object, with the statement

```
Implements IDTExtensibility
```

in the Declarations section of the **ClassModule** object that serves as the add-in's connection object. You can then select IDTExtensibility from the code module's Object drop-down box and OnAddInsUpdate from its Procedure drop-down box to create the **OnAddInsUpdate** method's argument template. You could change its *Custom()* argument's name, but this would be inconsistent with conventional VB Add-In programming practice.

Although **OnAddInsUpdate** is a method of an **IDTExtensibility** object, to the developer it behaves more like an event. There are three different scenarios that cause VB to call **OnAddInsUpdate**:

- That add-in's entry in VBADDIN.INI is set to "1" when the current instance of VB's IDE starts.

- The developer checks that add-in's item in the Add-In Manager dialog box's list and selects OK to save the change to VBADDIN.INI.

- The developer checks or unchecks another add-in item in the Add-In Manager dialog box's list and selects OK to save the change to VBADDIN.INI.

When any of these three scenarios occur, code in the add-in's **OnAddInsUpdate** method automatically executes, just as if it was an event procedure.

 VB's Help file incorrectly states that each of an **IDTExtensibility** object's four methods must contain at least one executable statement; instead, just a remark or comment will prevent the compiler from removing the method. Also, VB's Help file incorrectly and incompletely states that the **OnAddInsUpdate** method occurs automatically when changes to the VBADDIN.INI file are saved; instead, **OnAddInsUpdate** is called, as described in the Comments section.

Example Code

Because the **OnAddInsUpdate** method is called by VB itself, it is not possible to write the normal kind of Example code for it. See the code in DEMOSYNT.VBP. It typifies the kind of procedure that you would write for the **OnAddInsUpdate** method.

OnConnection Method

OnConnection is a **Sub** that occurs automatically when an add-in is connected to the current instance of VB's IDE and is started.

USAGE

Obj. **OnConnection**(**ByVal** *VBInst*, **ByVal** *ConnectMode*, **ByVal** *AddInInst*, *Custom()*)

The **OnConnection** method supports named arguments and contains these parts:

- *Obj*: Required. An object expression that evaluates to an **IDTExtensibility** object.

- *VBInst*: Required. An object representing the current instance of VB. The developer should immediately assign *VBInst* to a project-level variable declared as a **VBE** object.

- *ConnectMode*: Required. It is an intrinsic constant of the enumerated type **vbext_ConnectMode**, which specifies how an add-in is connected. See Settings for a list of these constants.

- *AddInInst*: Required. An **AddIn** object representing the instance of the add-in being connected. If *ConnectMode* is 2 - **vbext_cm_External**, *AddInInst* evaluates to **Nothing**.

- *Custom()*: Required. An array of **Variant** expressions to hold user-defined data. If you use the **VarType** function on *Custom()*, it returns 8204 (**vbArray** + **vbVariant**). However, if you try to use the **LBound** function on *Custom()*, it results in trappable error 9 (Subscript out of range), which indicates that VB is passing *Custom()* an unsized array. This means that *Custom()* is not currently being used and is probably provided for future use by Microsoft's VB development team.

SETTINGS

The settings for *ConnectMode* (**vbext_ConnectMode**) are:

- 0 - **vbext_cm_AfterStartup**: Add-in is connected after the initial Open Project dialog box is shown. This occurs when the developer checks an add-in item in the Add-In Manager dialog box or when an add-in's code sets another add-in's **Connect** property to **True**.

- 1 - **vbext_cm_Startup**: Add-in is connected before the initial Open Project dialog box is shown and while VB's splash screen is visible. This occurs when, upon startup, VB finds that an item in the Add-In Manager dialog box's list is checked and automatically connects that add-in.

- 2 - **vbext_cm_External**: Add-in is connected by another program or programmatically by calling **OnConnection** method from within add-in. This normally occurs when the developer clicks on the add-in's button on the Add-In toolbar.

COMMENTS

The **OnConnection** method is created when you implement an **IDTExtensibility** object, with the statement

```
Implements IDTExtensibility
```

in the Declarations section of the **ClassModule** object that serves as the add-in's connection object. You can then select IDTExtensibility from the code module's Object drop-down box to create the **OnConnection** method's template of arguments. You could change the argument names, but this would be inconsistent with conventional VB Add-In programming practice. However, you can change and shorten the declared types for the *ConnectMode* argument (**VBIDE.vbext_ConnectMode**) and *AddInInst* argument (**VBIDE.AddIn**) to just **vbext_ConnectMode** and **AddIn** respectively.

Although **OnConnection** is a method of an **IDTExtensibility** object, to the developer it behaves more like an event. See the Settings section for a list of the scenarios that cause VB to call the **OnConnection** method. While the **OnConnection** method's opening and closing statements are automatically implemented for you, you must write the code that comprises the procedure. The typical things you do with the **OnConnection** method's code are:

- Assign the *VBInst* argument's object to a project-level variable in a standard module in the Add-In's project.

- Check if the add-in is registered to be uses with the Add-In toolbar, and, if not, register it.

- Check if the VB Add-In Toolbar add-in is connected, and, if it is not, connect it and display the Add-In toolbar.

- Specify the VB menu to which the add-in's menu item is to be added (can be any of the 11 menus from File to Help) and then add it. Conventional add-in programming practice dictates that you add the menu item to the Add-Ins menu.

 You can programmatically call the **OnConnection** method from another method of an **IDTExtensibility** object (see the **OnDisconnection** method's code in the add-in titled *Demo VB5 Add-In Syntax*). However, this capability is of limited use and should be employed sparingly and carefully.

EXAMPLE CODE
Because the **OnConnection** method is called by VB itself, it is not possible to write the normal kind of Example code for it. See the code in DEMOSYNT.VBP. It typifies the kind of procedure that you would write for the **OnConnection** method.

0-0

OnDisconnection Method
OnDisconnection is a **Sub** that occurs automatically when an add-in is disconnected from the current instance of VB's IDE and is shut down.

USAGE
Obj. **OnDisconnection**(**ByVal** *RemoveMode, Custom()*)

The **OnDisconnection** method supports named arguments and contains these parts:

- *Obj*: Required. An object expression that evaluates to an **IDTExtensibility** object.

- *RemoveMode*: Required. It is an intrinsic constant of the enumerated type **vbext_DisconnectMode**, which specifies how an add-in is disconnected. See Settings for a list of these constants.

- *Custom()*: Required. An array of **Variant** expressions to hold user-defined data. If you use the **VarType** function on *Custom()*, it returns 8204 (**vbArray** + **vbVariant**). However, if you try to use the **LBound** function on *Custom()*, it results in trappable error 9 (Subscript out of range), which indicates that VB is passing *Custom( )* an unsized array. This means that *Custom( )* is not currently being used and is probably provided for future use by Microsoft's VB development team.

SETTINGS

The settings for *RemoveMode* (**vbext_DisconnectMode**) are:

- 0 - **vbext_dm_HostShutdown**: Add-in is disconnected when developer closes current instance of VB.

- 1 - **vbext_dm_UserClosed**: Add-in is disconnected when the developer unchecks its item in the Add-In Manager dialog box or when an add-in's code sets an add-in's **Connect** property to **False**.

COMMENTS

The **OnDisconnection** method is created when you implement an **IDTExtensibility** object, with the statement

```
Implements IDTExtensibility
```

in the Declarations section of the **ClassModule** object that serves as the add-in's connection object. You can then select IDTExtensibility from the code module's Object drop-down box and OnDisconnection from its Procedure drop-down box to create the **OnDisconnection** method's template of arguments. You could change the argument names, but this would be inconsistent with conventional VB Add-In programming practice. However, you can change and shorten the declared type for the *RemoveMode* argument (VBIDE.**vbext_DisconnectMode**) to **vbext_DisconnectMode**.

Although **OnDisconnection** is a method of an **IDTExtensibility** object, to the developer it behaves more like an event. See the Settings section for a list of scenarios that cause VB to call the **OnDisconnection** method. While the **OnDisconnection** method's opening and closing statements are automatically implemented for you, you must write the code that comprises the procedure. The typical things you do with the **OnDisconnection** method's code are:

- Remove the add-in menu item from the VB menu to which it is attached.

- Unload any form(s) displayed by the add-in.

- Free any system resources associated with objects used by the add-in.

- Write an entry to the Windows registry to remove the add-in's button from the Add-In toolbar (if the add-in has a button) the next time the developer starts VB.

If an in-process, DLL add-in is connected to a VB menu and you close the current instance of VB (that is, *RemoveMode* argument of **OnDisconnection** method is **vbext_dm_HostShutdown**), it is not necessary to do anything in the method's code. When VB shuts down, it also shuts down any in-process, DLL add-in. If you connect and start an add-in by clicking on its button on the Add-In toolbar and the add-in is not connected to a VB menu, the **OnDisconnection** method is not called when you shut down VB.

EXAMPLE CODE

Because the **OnDisconnection** method is called by VB itself, it is not possible to write the normal kind of Example code for it. See the code in DEMOSYNT.VBP. It typifies the kind of procedure that you would write for the **OnDisconnection** method.

OnStartupComplete Method

OnStartupComplete is a **Sub** that occurs automatically when the startup of the current instance of VB's IDE is complete and the add-in's entry in VBADDIN.INI is "1".

USAGE

Obj. **OnStartupComplete**(*Custom( )*)

The **OnStartupComplete** method supports named arguments and contains these parts:

- *Obj*: Required. An object expression that evaluates to an **IDTExtensibility** object.

- *Custom( )*: Required. An array of **Variant** expressions to hold user-defined data. If you use the **VarType** function on *Custom( )*, it returns 8204 (**vbArray** + **vbVariant**). However, if you try to use the **LBound** function on *Custom( )*, it results in trappable error 9 (Subscript out of range), which indicates that VB is passing *Custom( )* an unsized array. This means that *Custom( )* is not currently being used and is probably provided for future use by Microsoft's VB development team.

COMMENTS

The **OnStartupComplete** method is created when you implement an **IDTExtensibility** object, with the statement

```
Implements IDTExtensibility
```

in the Declarations section of the **ClassModule** object that serves as the add-in's connection object. You can then select IDTExtensibility from the code module's Object drop-down box and OnStartupComplete from its Procedure drop-down box to create the **OnStartupComplete** method's template of arguments. You could change its *Custom()* argument's name, but this would be inconsistent with conventional VB Add-In programming practice.

Although **OnStartupComplete** is a method of an **IDTExtensibility** object, to the developer it behaves more like an event. If an add-in's item in the Add-In Manager dialog box's list is checked when VB's IDE completes its startup, any code in the add-in's **OnStartupComplete** method automatically executes as if it were an event procedure. **OnStartupComplete** gives the developer a chance to recreate an add-in's state just as it was the last time VB was shut down.

While the **OnStartupComplete** method's opening and closing statements are automatically implemented for you, you must write the code that comprises the procedure yourself. The typical thing you do in the **OnStartupComplete** method's code is to read a Windows registry entry for the add-in to determine if one of the add-in's forms was displayed when VB was last shut down. If so, the method's code should redisplay the form.

O-O

EXAMPLE CODE

Because the **OnStartupComplete** method is called by VB itself, it is not possible to write the normal kind of Example code for it. See the code in DEMOSYNT.VBP. It typifies the kind of procedure that you would write for the **OnStartupComplete** method.

OpenSubKey Method (VBAI)

OpenSubKey is a **Function** that returns a **Long** handle to a subkey in the Windows registry. If the subkey does not exist, **OpenSubKey** creates it and then returns the handle.

USAGE

Obj.**OpenSubKey**(*HWnd, SubKey*) **As Long**

The **OpenSubKey** method's syntax supports named arguments and contains these parts:

- *Obj*: Required. An object expression that evaluates to a **Reg** object of the VBAI class library.

- *HWnd*: Required. A **Long** expression that is the handle to one of the Windows registry's six predefined keys or an open subkey. *HWnd* can be one of the intrinsic constants of the enumerated type **aiKeyType** (see the Settings section), a Windows API function constant that specifies a predefined key, or a handle returned by a previous call to **OpenSubKey**.

- *SubKey*: Required. A **String** expression that specifies the subkey to be opened or created/opened. If *SubKey* is a zero-length string (that is, "" or **vbNullString**), **OpenSubKey** opens the predefined key or subkey specified by *HWnd* and returns *HWnd*.

SETTINGS

The predefined key values for *HWnd* (**aiKeyType**) are:

- 0 - **aiKTClasses**: HKEY_CLASSES_ROOT key

- 1 - **aiKTCurUser**: HKEY_CURRENT_USER key

- 2 - **aiKTMachine**: HKEY_LOCAL_MACHINE key

- 3 - **aiKTUsers**: HKEY_USERS key

- 5 - **aiKTCurConfig**: HKEY_CURRENT_CONFIG key

- 6 - **aiKTDynData**: HKEY_DYN_DATA key

ERROR HANDLING

OpenSubKey returns 0 (**False**) upon failure.

COMMENTS

OpenSubKey is a proxy or wrapper method for the Windows API function **RegCreateKey**. You can use **OpenSubKey** to create several subkeys at once. For example, you can create a subkey four levels deep at the same time as **RegCreateKey** creates the three preceding subkeys by specifying a string like the following for *SubKey* - "subkey1\subkey2\subkey3\subkey4". In this example, the handle returned by **OpenSubKey** is to the fourth subkey.

After calling **OpenSubKey** to get a handle to a subkey, depending on the context, you could use that handle to call the **DelSubKey**, **DelValue**, **GetSubKeyName**, **GetSubKeysCount**, **GetValue**, **GetValueName**, **GetValuesCount**, or **SetValue** method of a **Reg** object. After you are done using the handle to a subkey, you should call the **CloseSubKey** method of a **Reg** object to release the handle and free system resources.

METHOD'S CODE

See the Help topic OpenSubKey Method in ADDINEFS.HLP or the **OpenSubKey** method's procedure in VBAI.VBP.

EXAMPLE CODE

See the Help topic OpenSubKey Method Example in ADDINEFS.HLP or the procedure DemoRegObj in DEMOSYNT.VBP.

PARENT PROPERTY

Parent returns an object or collection that contains another object or collection. Read-only.

USAGE

Obj.**Parent**

The **Parent** property's syntax contains these parts:

- *Obj*: Required. An object expression that evaluates to an **Addins**, **CodeModule**, **CodePanes**, **ContainedVBControls**, **Members**, **Properties**, **References**, **SelectedVBControls**, **VBComponents**, **VBControls**, **VBForm**, **VBProjects**, or **Windows** object.

COMMENTS

You use the **Parent** property to access the properties, methods, and controls of an object's parent object. Most objects in the Extensibility object model have either a **Parent** property or a **Collection** property. The **Collection** property is used if the parent object is a collection.

EXAMPLE CODE

See the Help topic Parent Property Example in ADDINEFS.HLP or the procedure DemoParentPrp in DEMOSYNT.VBP.

Paste Method

Paste is a **Sub** that pastes the contents of the **Clipboard** object onto a **VBForm** object.

USAGE

Obj.**Paste**

The **Paste** method's syntax contains these parts:

- *Obj*: Required. An object expression that evaluates to a **VBForm** object.

COMMENTS

To copy VB controls to the Clipboard, first call the **SelectAll** method or set the **InSelection** property of a **VBForm** object to select the **VBControl** objects you want to copy. Then call the **Copy** or **Cut** method of the **SelectedVBControls** collection to place the selected controls on the Clipboard. Before you call the **Paste** method, you should read the **CanPaste** property of a **VBForm** object. If it returns **True**, then call the **Paste** method.

O-P

Example Code

See the Help topic Paste Method Example in ADDINEFS.HLP or the procedure DemoPasteMet in DEMOSYNT.VBP.

ProcBodyLine, ProcCountLines Property

ProcBodyLine returns a **Long** containing the first line number of a procedure in a code module. Read-only. **ProcCountLines** returns a **Long** containing the number of lines in a procedure in a code module. Read-only.

Usage

Obj.**ProcBodyLine**(*ProcName*, *ProcKind*) **As Long**

Obj.**ProcCountLines**(*ProcName*, *ProcKind*) **As Long**

The **ProcBodyLine** and **ProcCountLines** properties' syntax contains these parts:

- *Obj*: Required. An object expression that evaluates to a **CodeModule** object.

- *ProcName*: Required. A **String** expression that specifies the name of the event, general or property procedure (for example, "Form_Load").

- *ProcKind*: Required. A constant or value that specifies the kind of procedure to locate. Because property procedures can have multiple representations in the module, you must specify the kind of procedure you want to locate. See Settings for the values of the kinds of procedures.

Settings

The *ProcKind* argument's possible values are:

- 0 - **vbext_pk_Proc**: A **Sub** or **Function** procedure.

- 1 - **vbext_pk_Let**: A **Property Let** procedure.

- 2 - **vbext_pk_Set**: A **Property Set** procedure.

- 3 - **vbext_pk_Get**: A **Property Get** procedure.

Comments

The first line of a procedure is the line on which its **Sub**, **Function**, or **Property** declaration statement appears. The first line number of a procedure in a code module can change as you add or delete procedures. If you want to work with the code in a specific procedure, you should always reread its first line number. The **CodeLocation** property of a **Member** object can also return the line number where a procedure is defined.

The **ProcCountLines** property returns the count of all blank or comment lines preceding the procedure declaration and, if the procedure is the last procedure in a code module, any blank lines following the procedure. The best way to view how many lines a procedure contains (including blanks) is to check Default To Full Module View on the Editor tab of the Options dialog box.

If you have just added a code module to a project and have not yet added code to an event procedure or opened the event procedure's code pane, trying to read **ProcBodyLine** or

ProcCountLines results in trappable error 35 (Sub or Function not defined) if you pass *ProcName* the event procedure's name.

 Although it is not documented in Visual Basic's Help file, **ProcBodyLine** does return a line number and **ProcCountLines** does return a line count for a **Function** or **Sub** declared in the Declarations section of a code module (for example, a Windows API function). However, the return value is meaningless because it is always 1.

EXAMPLE CODE

See the Help topics ProcBodyLine Property Example and ProcCountLines Property Example in ADDINEFS.HLP or the procedures DemoProcBodyLinePrp and DemoProcCountLinesPrp in DEMOSYNT.VBP.

ProcOfLine Property

ProcOfLine returns a **String** containing the name of the procedure that the specified line number is in. Read-only.

USAGE

Obj.**ProcOfLine**(*Line*, *ProcKind*) **As String**

The **ProcOfLine** property's syntax contains these parts:

* *Obj*: Required. An object expression that evaluates to a **CodeModule** object.

* *Line*: Required. A **Long** expression that specifies the line number to check.

* *ProcKind*: Required. Zero or any other numeric expression. Any numeric value passed to *ProcKind* is ignored by **ProcOfLine**.

COMMENTS

A line is within a procedure if it is a blank line or comment line preceding the procedure declaration and, if the procedure is the last procedure in a code module, a blank line or lines following the procedure. The best way to view how many lines a procedure contains (including blanks) is to check Default To Full Module View on the Editor tab of the Options dialog box. If you pass *Line* a number that is in the Declarations section or that does not exist in the code module, **ProcOfLine** returns a zero-length string (that is, "" or **vbNullString**).

 Visual Basic's Help file incorrectly states that the *ProcKind* argument of the **ProcOfLine** property has to be 0, 1, 2, or 3. Even if you pass **ProcKind** a string, **ProcOfLine** will not cause a trappable error; instead, it returns a zero-length string.

EXAMPLE CODE

See the Help topic ProcOfLine Property Example in ADDINEFS.HLP or the procedure DemoProcOfLinePrp in DEMOSYNT.VBP.

ProcStartLine Property

ProcStartLine returns a **Long** containing the line number at which a procedure begins in a code module. Read-only.

USAGE

Obj.**ProcStartLine**

The **ProcStartLine** property's syntax contains these parts:

- *Obj*: Required. An object expression that evaluates to a **CodeModule** object.

- *ProcName*: Required. A **String** expression that specifies the name of the event, general or property procedure (for example, "Form_Load").

- *ProcKind*: Required. A constant or value that specifies the kind of procedure to locate. Because property procedures can have multiple representations in the module, you must specify the kind of procedure you want to locate. See Settings for the values of the kinds of procedures.

SETTINGS

The *ProcKind* argument's possible values are:

- 0 - vbext_pk_Proc: A **Sub** or **Function** procedure.

- 1 - vbext_pk_Let: A **Property Let** procedure.

- 2 - vbext_pk_Set: A **Property Set** procedure.

- 3 - vbext_pk_Get: A **Property Get** procedure.

COMMENTS

A procedure starts at the first line below the **End Sub** statement of the preceding procedure. If it is the first procedure, the procedure starts at the end of the general Declarations section. The best way to view the line where a procedure starts is to check Default To Full Module View on the Editor tab of the Options dialog box.

The difference between the **ProcStartLine** property and the **ProcBodyLine** property is that **ProcStartLine** can return a line number for a comment or space immediately above the declaration statement of the procedure. **ProcBodyLine**, on the other hand, always returns the line number on which the procedure's **Sub**, **Function**, or **Property** declaration statement appears.

If you have just added a code module to a project and have not yet added code to an event procedure or opened the event procedure's code pane, **ProcStartLine** results in trappable error 35 (Sub or Function not defined) if you pass *ProcName* the event procedure's name.

 Although it is not documented in Visual Basic's Help file, **ProcStartLine** does return a line number for a **Function** or **Sub** declared in the Declarations section of a code module (for example, a Windows API function). However, the return value is meaningless because it is always 1.

P-P

EXAMPLE CODE

See the Help topic ProcStartLine Property Example in ADDINEFS.HLP or the procedure DemoProcStartLinePrp in DEMOSYNT.VBP.

ProgID Property

ProgID returns a **String** from the Windows registry that specifies the programmatic ID of an add-in or VB control. Read-only.

USAGE

Obj.**ProgID**

The **ProgID** property's syntax contains these parts:

*   *Obj*: Required. An object expression that evaluates to an **AddIn** or **VBControl** object.

COMMENTS

The programmatic ID string of an add-in (for example, "Chapter2.Connect") is made up of two parts. The part to the left of the dot delimiter is the add-in project's Project Name entry, which is made on the General tab of the Project Properties dialog box. The second part is the **Name** property of the **ClassModule** object that functions as the add-in. The first part of the programmatic ID string of a VB control is always "VB" and the second part is the class name of the control (for example, "CommandButton").

Because an add-in is an ActiveX component, you can use Visual Basic's **CreateObject** function and the add-in's programmatic ID to create an instance of the add-in. Then, in theory, you could reuse any of its public members without connecting it to Visual Basic's IDE in the normal manner for an add-in. Therefore, you should do one of two things:

*   Declare all members of public **ClassModule** objects in the add-in as **Private** or **Friend**.

*   Make sure any public members of public **ClassModule** objects in your add-in run correctly if they are reused from another application.

EXAMPLE CODE

See the Help topic ProgID Property Example in ADDINEFS.HLP or the procedure DemoProgIDPrp in DEMOSYNT.VBP.

Properties Collection/Property

A **Properties** collection contains all **Property** objects that represent the properties of an object. The read-only **Properties** property of a **VBComponent** or **VBControl** object returns an object instance of the **Properties** class.

INSTANTIATION

Dim *Obj* **As** [VBIDE.]**Properties|Object|Variant**
Set *Obj* = **VBE.ActiveVBProject.VBComponents**[.**Item**](*IndexA*).**Properties**
Set *Obj*=**VBE.ActiveVBProject.VBComponents**[.**Item**](*IndexA*).**Designer.VBControls**[.**Item**] (*IndexB*).**Properties**

Usage

#1: *Obj.Mbr*

#2: *Obj* [.**Item**] (*IndexC*) [.*MbrA* [= *ValA*]]

#3: *Obj.MbrB.MbrC* [= *ValC* | *ArgsC*]

The **Properties** syntax supports named arguments and contains these parts:

- *Obj*: Required. A variable to be assigned an object instance. *Obj* can be named the same as the **Properties** class being instantiated. *Obj* can also be declared as the generic **Object** or as **Variant** but this slows performance.

- VBIDE: Optional. The VB5 Extensibility object library containing the **Properties** class.

- *IndexA*: Required. Used with the default **Item** method, *IndexA* is a numeric or **String** expression that specifies the ordinal position of a **VBComponent** object in a **VBComponents** collection. If *IndexA* is a **String** expression, it must evaluate to the **Name** property of a **VBComponent** object.

- *IndexB*: Required. Used with the default **Item** method, *IndexB* is a numeric or **String** expression that specifies the ordinal position of a **VBControl** object in a **VBControls** collection. If *IndexB* is a **String** expression, it must evaluate to the **Name** property of the intrinsic or ActiveX control represented by a **VBControl** object.

- *Mbr*: Required. A member of a **Properties** collection other than the **Item** method.

- *IndexC*: Required. Used with the default **Item** method, *IndexC* is a numeric or **String** expression that specifies the ordinal position of a **Property** object in a **Properties** collection. If *IndexC* is a **String** expression, it must evaluate to the **Name** property of a **Property** object.

- *MbrA*: Optional. A member of a **Property** object.

- *ValA*: Optional. You use *ValA* if *MbrA* is a property being set.

- *MbrB*: Required. A **Properties** collection's property that returns an object.

- *MbrC*: Required. A member of the object that is returned by *MbrB*.

- *ValC* | *ArgsC*: Optional. You use *ValC* if *MbrC* is a property being set or *ArgsC* if *MbrC* is a method being called.

Members

- Events: None at this time

- Methods: **Item**

- Properties: **Count, Parent, VBE**

Comments

A **Properties** collection that contains **Property** objects includes all the properties of a VB component or control that can be accessed at design time in the Properties window. For every property listed in the Properties window, there is an object in a **Properties** collection. You can access a **Property** object by calling the **Item** method of a **Properties** collection or by using a **For...Each...Next** statement to loop through the items of a **Properties** collection until you find the **Property** object you want. You can use the **Count** property to return the number of **Property** objects in the collection.

EXAMPLE CODE
See the Help topic Properties Collection/Property Example in ADDINEFS.HLP or the procedure DemoPropertiesObj in DEMOSYNT.VBP.

Property Object
Property is an item in a **Properties** collection that represents a design-time property of a VB component or control.

INSTANTIATION
Dim *Obj* **As** [**VBIDE.**]**Property** | **Object** | **Variant**
Set *Obj* = **VBE.ActiveVBProject.VBComponents**[**.Item**](*IndexA*).**Properties**[**.Item**](*IndexC*)
Set *Obj*=**VBE.ActiveVBProject.VBComponents**[**.Item**](*IndexA*).**Designer.VBControls**[**.Item**]
(*IndexB*).**Properties**[**.Item**](*IndexC*)

USAGE
#1: *Obj*[.*Mbr*[= *Val*]]
#2: *Obj.MbrA.MbrB* [= *ValB* | *ArgsB*]

A **Property** object's syntax supports named arguments and contains these parts:

- *Obj*: Required. A variable to be assigned an object instance. *Obj* can be named the same as the **Property** class being instantiated. *Obj* can also be declared as the generic **Object** or as **Variant**, but this slows performance.

- VBIDE: Optional. The VB5 Extensibility object library containing the **Property** class.

- *IndexA*: Required. Used with the default **Item** method, *IndexA* is a numeric or **String** expression that specifies the ordinal position of a **VBComponent** object in a **VBComponents** collection. If *IndexA* is a **String** expression, it must evaluate to the **Name** property of a **VBComponent** object.

- *IndexB*: Required. Used with the default **Item** method, *IndexB* is a numeric or **String** expression that specifies the ordinal position of a **VBControl** object in a **VBControls** collection. If *IndexB* is a **String** expression, it must evaluate to the **Name** property of the intrinsic or ActiveX control represented by a **VBControl** object.

- *IndexC*: Required. Used with the default **Item** method, *IndexC* is a numeric or **String** expression that specifies the ordinal position of a **Property** object in a **Properties** collection. If *IndexC* is a **String** expression, it must evaluate to the **Name** property of a **Property** object.

- *Mbr*: Required. A member of a **Property** object.

- *Val*: Optional. You use *Val* if *Mbr* is a property being set.

P-P

- *MbrA*: Required. A **Property** object's property that returns an object or collection.

- *MbrB*: Required. A member of the object or collection that is returned by *MbrA*.

- *ValB|ArgsB*: Optional. You use *ValB* if *MbrB* is a property being set or *ArgsB* if *MbrB* is a method being called.

MEMBERS

- Events: None at this time

- Methods: None at this time

- Properties: **Collection, IndexedValue, Name, NumIndices, Object, Parent** (Hidden), **Value, VBE**

COMMENTS

A **Property** object is an item in a **Properties** collection that represents one of the design-time properties of a VB component or control. Each property listed in the Properties window of VB's IDE has a corresponding **Property** object. You can access a **Property** object by:

- Calling the **Item** method of a **Properties** collection.

- Using a **For...Each...Next** statement to loop through the items of a **Properties** collection until you find the **Property** object you want.

You can use the default **Value** property of a **Property** object to return or set the value of a property of a component or control. If the value returned by a **Property** object is an object, you must use the **Object** property to set the **Property** object to a new object. If a **Property** object represents a list (as indicated by its **NumIndices** setting), you must use the **IndexedValue** property to return or set the value of the property. **IndexedValue** is used only if the value of the **NumIndices** property is greater than zero.

EXAMPLE CODE

See the Help topic Property Object Example in ADDINEFS.HLP or the procedure DemoPropertyObj in DEMOSYNT.VBP.

PropertyPage Property

PropertyPage is a **String** that determines whether or not one of the standard property pages is associated with a **Member** object. Read/write.

USAGE

Obj.**PropertyPage**[= *Val*]

The **PropertyPage** property's syntax contains these parts:

- *Obj*: Required. An object expression that evaluates to a **Member** object.

- *Val*: Optional. Only used when you set **PropertyPage**, *Val* is a **String** expression that specifies the setting of the Use This Page In Property Browser drop-down box on the Procedure Attributes Advanced dialog box. The default setting is a zero-length string (that

P-P

is, "" or **vbNullString**) that signifies None. Other settings available are StandardColor, StandardFont, and StandardPicture.

COMMENTS

You only associate a standard property page with a public **Property** procedure when you are creating an ActiveX control and are working with the code module of a User Control VB component. You can use the Procedure Attributes Advanced dialog box, accessed from the Tools menu, to manually set this attribute for a public **Property** procedure (select one of the four items in the Use This Page In Property Browser drop-down box). You can also do this programmatically by setting the Property procedure's **Member** object's **PropertyPage** property to one of the available settings. When you save the User Control component that contains the **Property** procedure, VB writes the setting of **PropertyPage** to the ActiveX control's type library.

VB does not permit you to manually select an item in the Use This Page In Property Browser drop-down box for a member that is not a public **Property** procedure. Unfortunately, VB does permit an add-in to programmatically set **PropertyPage** for a non-property **Member** object without causing a trappable error. This can, under certain circumstances, crash the current instance of VB's IDE.

EXAMPLE CODE

See the Help topic PropertyPage Property Example in ADDINEFS.HLP or the procedure DemoPropertyPagePrp in DEMOSYNT.VBP.

Quit Method

P-Q

Quit is a **Sub** that automatically saves changes to any projects that are open in the current instance of VB's IDE and then terminates VB.

USAGE

Obj.**Quit**

The **Quit** method's syntax contains these parts:

*   *Obj*: Required. An object expression that evaluates to a **VBE** object.

COMMENTS

Calling the **Quit** method is equivalent to manually selecting File|Exit. However, the **Quit** method does not prompt you to save any changes to open projects. Instead it automatically saves all changes and closes VB's IDE. You can write code in the **RequestWriteFile** event procedure of a **FileControlEvents** object to intervene in this process and allow you to control which files are saved and which are not.

VB's Help file incorrectly states that the **Quit** method attempts to exit VB. Instead **Quit** always succeeds in exiting VB.

EXAMPLE CODE

See the Help topic Quit Method Example in ADDINEFS.HLP or the procedure DemoQuitMet in DEMOSYNT.VBP.

ReadOnlyMode Property

ReadOnlyMode returns an **Integer** or sets a numeric expression that determines how VB's IDE interacts with read-only files. Read/write.

USAGE

Obj.**ReadOnlyMode**[= *Val*]

The **ReadOnlyMode** property's syntax contains these parts:

- *Obj*: Required. An object expression that evaluates to a **VBE** object.

- *Val*: Optional. Only used when you set **ReadOnlyMode**, *Val* is an **Integer** expression that evaluates to 0 - Lenient (Default) or 1 - Strict. See Comments for a description of these settings.

COMMENTS

If **ReadOnlyMode** is set to 0 - Lenient, you can modify code, designers, and the project; however, you cannot save any of these changes back to disk if they affect read-only files.

If **ReadOnlyMode** is set to 1 - Strict, no changes can be saved to read-only files. In addition, for read-only project files, Project|Remove File and Project|Add File commands are available; however, trying to select these commands causes VB to display a read-only error message. For read-only code modules, trying to edit the code causes VB to display the message "Can't edit module." For read-only designers, controls cannot be added or removed, control positions are locked, property settings can't be changed, and custom Properties dialog boxes are disabled.

VB's Help file incorrectly states that 0 corresponds to Strict and 1 to Lenient for the **ReadOnlyMode** property's setting. Instead, it is the opposite, as described in Comments.

EXAMPLE CODE

See the Help topic ReadOnlyMode Property Example in ADDINEFS.HLP or the procedure DemoReadOnlyModePrp in DEMOSYNT.VBP.

ReadProperty Method

ReadProperty is a **Function** that returns a property's setting as a **String** from the specified user-defined section and key in a project's or component's file.

USAGE

#1: *Obj*.**ReadProperty**(*Section*, *Key*) **As String**
#2: *Obj*.**ReadProperty**(*Key*) **As String**

The **ReadProperty** method's syntax supports named arguments and contains these parts:

- *Obj*: Required. An object expression that evaluates to a **VB Component** or **VB Project** object.

- *Section*: Optional. Used only when *Obj* is a **VBProject** object, *Section* is a **String** expression that specifies the name of the section where *Key* is found.

- *Key*: Required. A **String** expression that specifies the name of the property whose setting is to be returned.

COMMENTS
To read a property's setting with the **ReadProperty** method, you must have first written its setting to a project's VBP file or a component's file with the **WriteProperty** method. If *Section* or *Key* doesn't exist in the file or is empty, calling **ReadProperty** results in trappable error 5 (Illegal function call). VB stores the setting of a property as an attribute. In the Example code, the setting for the **Picture** property is stored as Attribute VB_Ext_KEY = "Picture", "C:\VB5\GRAPHICS\ICONS\ELEMENTS\FIRE.ICO".

EXAMPLE CODE
See the Help topic ReadProperty Method Example in ADDINEFS.HLP or the procedure DemoReadPropertyMet in DEMOSYNT.VBP.

Reference Object
Reference is an item in a **References** collection. It represents a reference to a class library or a VB project.

INSTANTIATION
Dim *Obj* **As** [VBIDE.]**Reference|Object|Variant**
Set *Obj* = **VBE.References**[.**Item**](*Index*)

USAGE
#1: *Obj*[.*Mbr*]
#2: *Obj.MbrA.MbrB* [= *ValB* | *ArgsB*]

A **Reference** object's syntax supports named arguments and contains these parts:

- *Obj*: Required. A variable to be assigned an object instance. *Obj* can be named the same as the **Reference** class being instantiated. *Obj* can also be declared as the generic **Object** or as **Variant**, but this slows performance.

- VBIDE: Optional. The VB5 Extensibility object library containing the **Reference** class.

- *Index*: Required. Used with the default **Item** method, *Index* is a numeric or **String** expression that specifies the ordinal position of a **Reference** object in a **References** collection. If *Index* is a **String** expression, it must evaluate to the **Name** property of a **Reference** object.

- *Mbr*: Optional. A member of a **Reference** object.

- *MbrA*: Required. A **Reference** object's property that returns an object or collection.

- *MbrB*: Required. A member of the object or collection that is returned by *MbrA*.

- *ValB | ArgsB*: Optional. You use *ValB* if *MbrB* is a property being set or *ArgsB* if *MbrB* is a method being called.

MEMBERS

- Events: None at this time

- Methods: None at this time

- Properties: **BuiltIn, Collection, Description, FullPath, Guid, IsBroken, Major, Minor, Name, Type, VBE**

COMMENTS

To see a list of **Reference** objects while working within VB's IDE, select Project|References to display the References dialog box. The **References** collection that contains **Reference** objects is the same as the set of references selected in the References dialog box. When you check or uncheck an item in the References dialog box, VB adds a **Reference** object to or removes one from the **References** collection. You can access a **Reference** object by:

- Calling the **Item** method of a **References** collection.

- Using a **For...Each...Next** statement to loop through the items of a **References** collection until you find the **Reference** object you want.

You can use a **Reference** object to verify whether a reference is still valid; its **IsBroken** property returns **True** if the reference no longer points to a valid reference. Its **BuiltIn** property returns **True** if the reference is a default reference that can't be moved or removed. You can use its **Name** property to determine if the reference you want to add or remove is the correct one.

EXAMPLE CODE

See the Help topic Reference Object Example in ADDINEFS.HLP or the procedure DemoReferenceObj in DEMOSYNT.VBP.

References Collection/Property

A **References** collection contains all **Reference** objects that represent references to a class library or a VB project. The read-only **References** property of a **VBProject** object returns an object instance of the **References** class.

INSTANTIATION

Dim *Obj* **As** [VBIDE.]**References|Object|Variant**
Set *Obj* = **VBE.ActiveVBProject.References**

USAGE

#1: *Obj.Mbr*[*Args*]
#2: *Obj* [.**Item**](*Index*)[.*MbrA*]
#3: *Obj. MbrB.MbrC* [= *ValC* | *ArgsC*]

The **References** syntax supports named arguments and contains these parts:

- *Obj*: Required. A variable to be assigned an object instance. *Obj* can be named the same as the **References** class being instantiated. *Obj* can also be declared as the generic **Object** or as **Variant**, but this slows performance.

- VBIDE: Optional. The VB5 Extensibility object library containing the **References** class.

- *Mbr*: Required. A member of a **References** collection other than the **Item** method.

- *Args*: Optional. You use *Args* if *Mbr* is a method being called.

- *Index*: Required. Used with the default **Item** method, *Index* is a numeric or **String** expression that specifies the ordinal position of a **Reference** object in a **References** collection. If *Index* is a **String** expression, it must evaluate to the **Name** property of a **Reference** object.

- *MbrA*: Optional. A member of a **Reference** object.

- *MbrB*: Required. A **References** collection's property that returns a **VBE** object.

- *MbrC*: Required. A member of the object that is returned by *MbrB*.

- *ValC|ArgsC*: Optional. You use *ValC* if *MbrC* is a property being set or *ArgsC* if *MbrC* is a method being called.

MEMBERS

- Events: **ItemAdded, ItemRemoved**

- Methods: **AddFromFile, AddFromGuid, Item, Remove**

- Properties: **Count, Parent, VBE**

COMMENTS

The **References** collection that contains **Reference** objects is the same as the set of references selected in the References dialog box. When you check or uncheck an item in the References dialog box, VB adds a **Reference** object to or removes one from the **References** collection. You can access a **Reference** object by calling the **Item** method of a **References** collection or by using a **For...Each...Next** statement to loop through the items of a **References** collection until you find the **Reference** object you want.

You can add or remove a **Reference** object programmatically by calling the **AddFromFile**, **AddFromGuid**, or **Remove** method of the **References** collection. Adding or removing an item from the **References** collection causes VB to raise the **ItemAdded** or **ItemRemoved** event.

EXAMPLE CODE

See the Help topic References Collection/Property Example in ADDINEFS.HLP or the procedure DemoReferencesObj in DEMOSYNT.VBP.

ReferencesEvents Object/Property

A **ReferencesEvents** object represents the events raised by VB's IDE when a reference is added to or deleted from a project. The read-only **ReferencesEvents** property of an **Events** object returns a **ReferencesEvents** object.

Usage

#1: **Public WithEvents** *References* **As ReferencesEvents**
#2: **Set** *References* = **VBE.Events.ReferencesEvents**(*VBProjectObj*)

The **ReferencesEvents** syntax contains these parts:

- *References*: Required. A module-level object variable, in an add-in's **ClassModule** object, that is assigned the **ReferencesEvents** object returned by the **ReferencesEvents** property. *References* must be declared with the **Public** statement and the **WithEvents** keyword and may not be declared as the generic **Object** or as **Variant**.

- *VBProjectObj*: Required. An object expression that evaluates to a **VBProject** object whose reference-related events you want to monitor.

In Usage #1, **ReferencesEvents** is the object. In Usage #2, **ReferencesEvents** is a property of an **Events** object. This property returns a **ReferencesEvents** object.

Members

- Events: **ItemAdded, ItemRemoved**
- Methods: None at this time
- Properties: None at this time

Comments

A **ReferencesEvents** object allows an add-in to receive and react to reference-related events raised by VB's IDE. When more than one running add-in is receiving reference-related events, VB notifies the add-ins in the order in which they were connected.

To use a **ReferencesEvents** object, follow these steps in a **ClassModule** object in the add-in's project:

- Use the **Public** statement and the **WithEvents** keyword to declare an object variable that will respond to the reference-related events raised by VB. You do this in the Declarations section and the declaration statement adds a **ReferencesEvents** object, under the name of the object variable, to the class module's Object drop-down box. You can give this object variable any name you want, but it is most readable to name it *References*.

- Select References from the Object drop-down box of the class module and VB automatically creates the beginning and ending statements of the **ItemAdded** event procedure. Then, from the Procedure drop-down box, select the other reference-related events for which you want to create procedures.

- Write code in the various event procedures that will execute when VB raises their events.

- Make the add-in responsive to VB's reference-related events. You do this by using the **ReferencesEvents** property of an **Events** object to return a **ReferencesEvents** object that is assigned to *References*. You can write this assignment statement in the **OnConnection** method of an add-in's **IDTExtensibility** object; or, if you want more flexibility, you can

R-R

write it in a separate **ClassModule** object that exists solely to respond to add-in related events raised in VB's IDE. See the **ClassModule** object named VBEvents and the **ConnectTo** method declared as **Friend** in DEMOSYNT.VBP for a demonstration of how to do this.

The **ItemAdded** event of a **ReferencesEvents** object occurs after a reference is added to a project and the **ItemRemoved** event occurs after a reference is deleted from a project. The kinds of references that a **ReferencesEvents** object gives you control over are a type library reference (0 - **vbext_rk_TypeLib**) and a project reference (1 - **vbext_rk_Project**).

EXAMPLE CODE

See the Help topic ReferencesEvents Object/Property Example in ADDINEFS.HLP or the procedures DemoReferencesEventsObj and ConnectTo in DEMOSYNT.VBP.

Reg Object (VBAI)

A **Reg** object of the VBAI class library provides methods for an add-in to call that add, modify, and remove string entries from the Windows registry.

USAGE

Obj.Mbr Args, *[Arg]*

A **Reg** object's syntax supports named arguments and contains these parts:

- *Obj*: Required. An object expression that evaluates to a **Reg** object of the VBAI class library.

- *Mbr*: Required. A member of a **Reg** object.

- *Args*: Required. An argument or arguments of *Mbr*.

- *Arg*: Optional. An argument of *Mbr*. Only the **DelSubKey**, **GetValue**, and **SetValue** members have an optional argument.

MEMBERS

- Events: None at this time

- Methods: **CloseSubKey**, **DelSubKey**, **DelValue**, **GetSubKeyName**, **GetSubKeysCount**, **GetValue**, **GetValueName**, **GetValuesCount**, **OpenSubKey**, **SetValue**

- Properties: None at this time

COMMENTS

The wrapper methods of a **Reg** object enable an add-in to call these Windows API functions without having to declare them and without having to pass all of the arguments that they would require if they were called directly.

The **GetValue** and **SetValue** methods of a **Reg** object are designed to work only with string entries. If an add-in needs to read or write an entry to the registry that uses a data type other than **String**, it must call the **RegQueryValueEx** or **RegSetValueEx** Windows API function directly. Because most of the entries in the Windows registry are strings, the **GetValue** and **SetValue** methods of a **Reg** object will suffice in most situations.

R-R

The **GetValueName** and **GetValuesCount** methods of a **Reg** object work only under Windows 95 because the Windows API functions they use (**RegEnumValue** and **RegQueryInfoKey**) always fail when called under Windows NT4. This inability to successfully call **RegEnumValue** and **RegQueryInfoKey** under Windows NT4 is not documented in WIN32.HLP or API32.HLP.

EXAMPLE CODE

See the Help topic Reg Object Example in ADDINEFS.HLP or the procedure DemoRegObj in DEMOSYNT.VBP.

Reload Method

Reload is a **Sub** that reloads a VB component from disk, discarding any unsaved changes to the component in VB's IDE.

USAGE

Obj.**Reload**

The **Reload** method's syntax contains these parts:

- *Obj*: Required. An object expression that evaluates to a **VBComponent** object.

COMMENTS

Cursor position, code window, and form visibility are not affected by the **Reload** method. **Reload** also doesn't change the setting that indicates whether the project was edited since the last time it was saved.

EXAMPLE CODE

See the Help topic Reload Method Example in ADDINEFS.HLP or the procedure DemoReloadMet in DEMOSYNT.VBP.

Remove Method

R-R

Remove is a **Sub** that deletes an item from an add-in collection.

USAGE

Col.**Remove** *Obj*

The **Remove** method's syntax supports named arguments and contains these parts:

- *Col*: Required. An object expression that evaluates to a **ContainedVBControls**, **LinkedWindows**, **References**, **VBComponents**, **VBControls**, or **VBProjects** collection.

- *Obj*: Required. An object expression that evaluates to an object that is currently an item in *Col*.

COMMENTS

For a **LinkedWindows** collection, removing a window from the collection causes the removed window to become a floating window with its own linked window frame. This also has the effect of creating another **LinkedWindowsCollection**. If one **VBControl** object contains another **VBControl** object, removing the container control from its **VBControls** collection removes both controls. When you call the **Remove** method, VB raises the **ItemRemoved** event.

 VB's Help file incorrectly states that the **Remove** method's argument is a **Variant** expression that specifies the name or index in the collection of the item to be accessed. Instead it must be an object expression that evaluates to an item in one of the collections listed under *Col*.

EXAMPLE CODE
See the Help topic Remove Method Example in ADDINEFS.HLP or the procedure DemoRemoveMet in DEMOSYNT.VBP.

RemoveAddInFromToolbar Method

RemoveAddInFromToolbar is a **Sub** that deletes a button that references an add-in from the Add-In toolbar that will be displayed when the next instance of VB's IDE is started.

USAGE
Obj.**RemoveAddInFromToolbar** *sAddInName*

The **RemoveAddInFromToolbar** method's syntax supports named arguments and contains these parts:

- *Obj*: Required. An object expression that evaluates to a **Manager** object of the VB Add-In Toolbar ActiveX component (AITOOL.DLL).

- *sAddInName*: Required. A **String** expression that specifies the name of the add-in whose button is to be deleted. The value for *sAddInName* is listed in the Add-In Manager dialog box.

COMMENTS
You can call **RemoveAddInFromToolbar** from any VB application, not just an add-in. To call it, you must first instantiate the Manager class of the VB Add-In Toolbar ActiveX component. You can create a **Manager** object either by setting a reference to the ActiveX component and declaring an object variable **As New** AddInToolbar.Manager (early binding), or by declaring an object variable as **Object** and assigning it a reference to a **Manager** object with the **CreateObject** function (late binding). To add a button to the Add-In toolbar, call the **AddToAddInToolbar** method of a **Manager** object.

When you make changes to the Add-In toolbar with the Add/Remove Toolbar Items dialog box, the toolbar is refreshed as soon as you close the dialog box. When you call the **RemoveAddInFromToolbar** method, the Add-In toolbar is not refreshed until the next instance of VB's IDE is started. The **DelButton** method of an **AITBar** object compensates for this deficiency by adding a button and immediately refreshing the toolbar for the current instance of VB.

R-R

What the **RemoveAddInFromToolbar** method actually does is to write an entry of "0" to a subkey in the Windows registry. For example, to delete the button for the API Text Viewer add-in, it writes a "0" to the ShowOnToolbar entry of the subkey HKEY _CURRENT_USER\Software\Microsoft\Visual Basic\5.0\AddInToolbar\VB API Viewer.

EXAMPLE CODE

See the Help topic RemoveAddInFromToolbar Method Example in ADDINEFS.HLP or the procedure DemoManagerObj in DEMOSYNT.VBP.

ReplaceLine Method

ReplaceLine is a **Sub** that replaces an existing line of code with another line of code.

USAGE

Obj.**ReplaceLine** *Line, Code*

The **ReplaceLine** method's syntax supports named arguments and contains these parts:

- *Obj*: Required. An object expression that evaluates to a **CodeModule** object.

- *Line*: Required. A **Long** expression that specifies the line number of the code you want to replace.

- *Code*: Required. A **String** expression that contains the line of code you want to substitute for the existing line.

COMMENTS

The safest way to use the **ReplaceLine** method is to first read the line of code you want to replace with the **ProcOfLine** property. If it is the correct line, you can then apply **ReplaceLine**.

If you pass *Line* a number that does not exist in the code module, OLE Automation error -2,147,024,809 (Invalid procedure call or argument) occurs. This can happen for several different reasons:

- The line number is zero.

- The line number is too large.

- There is no code in the BAS or CLS module yet.

- You have just added a code module to a project and have not yet added code to an event procedure or opened the event procedure's code pane.

EXAMPLE CODE

See the Help topic ReplaceLine Method Example in ADDINEFS.HLP or the procedure DemoReplaceLineMet in DEMOSYNT.VBP.

RequestChangeFileName Event

RequestChangeFileName is raised by VB's IDE after you save a VB file with the File|Save 'Name' or File|Save Project command for a new file, with the File|Save 'Name' As or File|Save

Project As command for an existing file, with the File|Make 'Name' command, or programmatically with an add-in.

USAGE

*Obj*_**RequestChangeFileName**(**ByVal** *VBProject*, **ByVal** *FileType*, **ByVal** *NewName*, **ByVal** *OldName*, *Cancel*)

The **RequestChangeFileName** event's syntax contains these parts:

- *Obj*: An object expression that evaluates to a **FileControlEvents** object.

- *VBProject*: A **VBProject** object that specifies the name of the project for which the file's name was chnaged.

- *FileType*: An intrinsic constant of the enumerated type **vbext_FileType**, which specifies the type of file whose name was changed. See Details in the **FileControlEvents** object's topic for a list of these constants.

- *NewName*: A **String** expression that specifies the new path and name of the file.

- *OldName*: A **String** expression that specifies the old path and name of the file.

- *Cancel*: A **Boolean** expression that either prevents VB from (**True**) or allows VB to (**False**) continue raising **RequestChangeFileName** for subsequent add-ins connected to a **FileControlEvents** object.

COMMENTS

The **RequestChangeFileName** event occurs in all add-ins that are connected to a **FileControlEvents** object. To make an add-in responsive to a **RequestChangeFileName** event raised by VB, you first need to declare an object variable as a **FileControlEvents** object and assign it the object returned by the **FileControlEvents** property of an **Events** object. For detailed information about how to do this, see the **FileControlEvents** object's topic.

1) VB's Help file incorrectly states that **RequestChangeFileName** is a member of the **FileControl** object. Instead, it is a member of the **FileControlEvents** object (in VB4 it was the **FileControl** object). 2) VB's Help file incorrectly states that if you set the *Cancel* argument of the **RequestChangeFileName** event to **True**, VB cancels the renaming of the saved file within its project. Instead, **RequestChangeFileName** has no effect at all on VB and serves no obvious purpose. To cancel the renaming of the saved file, you must write code in the **RequestWriteFile** event procedure and set its *Cancel* argument to **True**.

EXAMPLE CODE

See the Help topic RequestChangeFileName Event Example in ADDINEFS.HLP or the procedure DemoRequestChangeFileNameEvt in DEMOSYNT.VBP.

RequestEdit Property

RequestEdit is a **Boolean** that returns or sets the RequestEdit attribute associated with a **Member** object. Read/write.

USAGE

Obj.**RequestEdit**[= *Val*]

The **RequestEdit** property's syntax contains these parts:

- *Obj*: Required. An object expression that evaluates to a **Member** object.

- *Val*: Optional. Only used when you set **RequestEdit**, *Val* is a **Boolean** expression that specifies whether Property Will Call CanPropertyChange Before Changing on the Procedure Attributes Advanced dialog box is checked for a member (**True**) or not (the default of **False**).

COMMENTS

You only set the **RequestEdit** property of a public **Property** procedure to **True** when you are creating an ActiveX control and are working with the code module of a User Control VB component. You would do this to specify that a property, which can be bound to a data source and which the user can change (for example, the **Text** property of a **TextBox** object), should call the **CanPropertyChange** method of the ActiveX control's **UserControl** object before its value is changed. Before you can set **RequestEdit**, however, you must first set **Bindable** to **True** for the public **Property** procedure.

You can use the Procedure Attributes Advanced dialog box, accessed from the Tools menu, to manually specify that a public **Property** procedure should call **CanPropertyChange** (check the Property Will Call CanPropertyChange Before Changing checkbox). You can also programmatically specify this attribute for a public **Property** procedure by setting its corresponding **Member** object's **RequestEdit** property to **True**. When you save the User Control component that contains the **Property** procedure, VB writes the setting of **RequestEdit** to the ActiveX control's type library.

VB does not permit you to manually set **RequestEdit** for a member that is not a public **Property** procedure. Unfortunately, VB does permit an add-in to programmatically set **RequestEdit** to **True** for a non-property **Member** object without causing a trappable error. This results in contradictory settings on the Procedure Attributes Advanced dialog box; that is, the Property Is Data Bound checkbox is unchecked but the Property Will Call CanPropertyChange Before Changing checkbox is checked. It can also, under certain circumstances, crash the current instance of VB's IDE.

EXAMPLE CODE

See the Help topic RequestEdit Property Example in ADDINEFS.HLP or the procedure DemoRequestEditPrp in DEMOSYNT.VBP.

RequestWriteFile Event

RequestWriteFile is raised by VB's IDE before you save a VB file with the File|Save 'Name' or File|Save Project command for a new file, with the File|Save 'Name' As or File|Save Project As command for an existing file, with the File|Make 'Name' command, or programmatically with an add-in.

USAGE

*Obj*_**RequestWriteFile**(**ByVal** *VBProject*, **ByVal** *FileName*, *Cancel*)

The **RequestChangeFileName** event's syntax contains these parts:

- *Obj*: An object expression that evaluates to a **FileControlEvents** object.

- *VBProject*: A **VBProject** object that specifies the name of the project for which the file is to be saved.

- *FileName*: A **String** expression that specifies the name of the file to be saved.

- *Cancel*: A **Boolean** expression. If *Cancel* is **True**, VB does not save the file to disk and does not raise the **RequestWriteFile** event for any subsequent add-ins connected to the **FileControlEvents** object. If *Cancel* is **False**, VB saves the file and continues to raise the **RequestWriteFile** event for subsequent add-ins connected to the **FileControlEvents** object.

COMMENTS

The **RequestWriteFile** event occurs once for each saved VB component. VB raises the **RequestWriteFile** event whether you save a component's file by manually selecting a File menu item or you save it programmatically through an add-in. You can write code in the **RequestWriteFile** event procedure to perform such tasks as preparing the file to be saved, logging information about the event, updating information about the file, backing up the file, and so on.

The **RequestWriteFile** event occurs in all add-ins that are connected to a **FileControlEvents** object. To make an add-in responsive to a **RequestWriteFile** event raised by VB, you first need to declare an object variable as a **FileControlEvents** object and assign it the object returned by the **FileControlEvents** property of an **Events** object. For detailed information about how to do this, see the **FileControlEvents** object's topic.

1) VB's Help file incorrectly states that **RequestWriteFile** is a member of the **FileControl** object. Instead, it is a member of the **FileControlEvents** object (in VB4 it was the **FileControl** object). 2) VB's Help incorrectly states that an add-in cannot prevent a file from being written to disk with the **RequestWriteFile** event procedure because the operation is complete. Instead, setting *Cancel* to **True** does prevent VB from saving the file to disk.

R-R

Example Code

See the Help topic RequestWriteFile Event Example in ADDINEFS.HLP or the procedure DemoRequestWriteFileEvt in DEMOSYNT.VBP.

SaveAs Method

SaveAs is a **Sub** or **Function** that saves a VB component or project's file under the same name or a new file name to a specified path.

Usage

#1: *Obj*.**SaveAs** *PathName*
#2: *Obj*.**SaveAs** *FileName*
#3: *Obj*.**SaveAs**(*NewFileName*)

The **SaveAs** method's syntax supports named arguments and contains these parts:

- *Obj*: Required. An object expression that evaluates to a **VBProjects** collection (usage #1), **VBProject** object (usage #2), or **VBComponent** object (usage #3).

- **ArgName**: Required. A **String** expression that specifies the path and name for the component or project file to be saved. If you use a named argument, each of the three implementations of the **SaveAs** method uses a different argument name.

Comments

If a new path name is given, it is used. Otherwise, the old path name is used. If you want to actually change the current path before calling the **SaveAs** method, set the **LastUsedPath** property. If a new file name is invalid or refers to a read-only file, an error occurs. When a form is saved, the name you use specifies the new name of the form file itself. The FRX file, if applicable, is saved automatically with an FRX extension. Successfully calling **SaveAs** causes the associated events from the **FileControlEvents** object to be raised.

Only when applied to a **VBComponent** object (usage #3), **SaveAs** is a **Function** that returns a **Boolean** that is **True** upon success or **False** upon failure. The fact that, depending upon the object it applies to, **SaveAs** is implemented either as a **Sub** or as a **Function** and that each of the three implementations uses a different argument name, is a good example of how not to write a class library.

Example Code

See the Help topic SaveAs Method Example in ADDINEFS.HLP or the procedure DemoSaveAsMet in DEMOSYNT.VBP.

Saved Property

Saved returns a **Boolean** that specifies whether a project has been edited since the last time it was saved (**False**) and needs to be saved or has not been edited (**True**) and does not need to be saved. Read-only.

Usage

Obj.**Saved**

The **Saved** property's syntax contains these parts:

- *Obj*: Required. An object expression that evaluates to a **VBProject** object.

Comments

The **SaveAs** method of a **VBProject** object causes the **Saved** property to return **True**. Setting the **IsDirty** property of a **VBProject** object to **False** also causes the **Saved** property to return **True**, while setting **IsDirty** to **True** causes the **Saved** property to return **False**. See the Example code for a demonstration of this.

 VB's Help file incorrectly states that **Saved** is read/write and that if you programmatically set the **Saved** property to **False**, the project is marked as if it were edited since the last time it was saved. Instead, **Saved** is read-only and cannot be set.

Example Code

See the Help topic Saved Property Example in ADDINEFS.HLP or the procedure DemoSavedPrp in DEMOSYNT.VBP.

Scope Property

Scope returns a **Long** that specifies whether a member is public, private, or friend in scope. Read-only.

Usage

Obj.**Scope**

The **Scope** property's syntax contains these parts:

- *Obj*: Required. An object expression that evaluates to a **Member** object.

Comments

Scope returns one of three possible intrinsic constants of the **vbext_Scope** enumerated type:

- 1 - **vbext_Private**: Member is available only from within module in which it is declared.

- 2 - **vbext_Public**: Member is available to all procedures in all modules within application. If VB component containing member is public **ClassModule** object in an ActiveX component, member is available to any application that can instantiate the member's class.

- 3 - **vbext_Friend**: Applies only to members of a **ClassModule** object declared with the **Friend** keyword. **Friend** makes a member visible throughout the application, but not to a controller of an instance of the class. **Friend** can only modify procedure names, not variables or types. **Friend** members don't appear in the type library of their class and can't be late-bound.

S-S

EXAMPLE CODE

See the Help topic Scope Property Example in ADDINEFS.HLP or the procedure DemoScopePrp in DEMOSYNT.VBP.

SelectAll Method

SelectAll is a **Function** that selects all the **VBControl** objects on a **VBForm** object and returns a **Long** specifying the number of selected controls.

USAGE

Obj.SelectAll

The **SelectAll** method's syntax contains these parts:

- *Obj*: Required. An object expression that evaluates to a **VBForm** object.

COMMENTS

To copy VB controls to the Clipboard, first call the **SelectAll** method or set the **InSelection** property of a **VBControl** object to select the controls you want to copy. Then call the **Copy** or **Cut** method of the **SelectedVBControls** collection to place the selected controls on the Clipboard. You should read the **CanPaste** property of a **VBForm** object before you call the **Paste** method. If it returns **True**, then call the **Paste** method.

EXAMPLE CODE

See the Help topic SelectAll Method Example in ADDINEFS.HLP or the procedure DemoSelectAllMet in DEMOSYNT.VBP.

SelectedVBComponent Property

SelectedVBComponent returns an object instance of a **VBComponent** class that is the selected component in VB's IDE. Read-only.

INSTANTIATION

Dim *Obj* **As** [VBIDE.]**VBComponent**|**Object**|**Variant**
Set *Obj* = **VBE.SelectedVBComponent**

USAGE

#1: *Obj*[.*Mbr*[= *Val* | *Arg*]]
#2: *Obj*.*MbrA*.*MbrB*[= *ValB* | *ArgsB*]

The **SelectedVBComponent** property's syntax supports named arguments and contains these parts:

- *Obj*: Required. A variable to be assigned an object instance. *Obj* can be named the same as the **VBComponent** class being instantiated. *Obj* can also be declared as the generic **Object** or as **Variant**, but this slows performance.

- VBIDE: Optional. The VB5 Extensibility object library containing the **VBComponent** class.

- *Mbr*: Optional. A member of a **VBComponent** object.

- *Val | Args*: Optional. You use *Val* if *Mbr* is a property being set or *Args* if *Mbr* is a method being called.

- *MbrA*: Required. A **VBComponent** object's property that returns an object or collection.

- *MbrB*: Required. A member of the object or collection that is returned by *MbrA*.

- *ValB | ArgsB*: Optional. You use *ValB* if *MbrB* is a property being set or *ArgsB* if *MbrB* is a method being called.

COMMENTS
The **SelectedVBComponent** property returns the selected component in the Project Explorer window. If the selected item in the Project Explorer window isn't a component (that is, it's a folder or project), **SelectedVBComponent** returns **Nothing**. **SelectedVBComponent** is read-only; to select another component, call the **Activate** method of a **VBComponent** object.

EXAMPLE CODE
See the Help topic SelectedVBComponent Property Example in ADDINEFS.HLP or the procedure DemoSelectedVBComponentPrp in DEMOSYNT.VBP.

SelectedVBControls Collection/Property

A **SelectedVBControls** collection contains the selected **VBControl** objects on a **VBForm** object. The read-only **SelectedVBControls** property of a **VBForm** object returns an object instance of the **SelectedVBControls** class.

INSTANTIATION
Dim *Obj* **As** [VBIDE.]**SelectedVBControls|Object|Variant**
Set *Obj*=**VBF.ActiveVBProject.VBComponents**[.**Item**]*(IndexA)*.**Designer.SelectedVBControls**

 In order to read the **SelectedVBControls** property, first use the **Designer** property of a **VBComponent** object to return a **VBForm** object. Then you can access the **SelectedVBControls** property to return a **SelectedVBControls** collection.

USAGE
#1: *Obj.Mbr*
#2: *Obj*[.**Item**]*(IndexB)*[.*MbrA*[*ArgsA*]]
#3: *Obj.MbrB.MbrC*[= *ValC | ArgsC*]

The **SelectedVBControls** syntax supports named arguments and contains these parts:

- *Obj*: Required. A variable to be assigned an object instance. *Obj* can be named the same as the **SelectedVBControls** class being instantiated. *Obj* can also be declared as the generic **Object** or as **Variant**, but this slows performance.

- VBIDE: Optional. The VB5 Extensibility object library containing the **SelectedVBControls** class.

S-S

- *IndexA*: Required. Used with the default **Item** method, *IndexA* is a numeric or **String** expression that specifies the ordinal position of a **VBComponent** object in a **VBComponents** collection. If *IndexA* is a **String** expression, it must evaluate to the **Name** property of a **VBComponent** object.

- *Mbr*: Required. A member of a **SelectedVBControls** collection other than the **Item** method.

- *IndexB*: Required. Used with the default **Item** method, *IndexB* is a numeric or **String** expression that specifies the ordinal position of a **VBControl** object in a **SelectedVBControls** collection. If *IndexB* is a **String** expression, it must evaluate to the **Name** property of the control represented by a **VBControl** object.

- *MbrA*: Optional. A member of a **VBControl** object.

- *ArgsA*: Optional. You use *ArgsA* if *MbrA* is a method being called.

- *MbrB*: Required. A **SelectedVBControls** collection's property that returns an object.

- *MbrC*: Required. A member of the object that is returned by *MbrB*.

- *ValC\ArgsC*: Optional. You use *ValC* if *MbrC* is a property being set or *ArgsC* if *MbrC* is a method being called.

MEMBERS

- Events: **ItemAdded, ItemRemoved**

- Methods: **Clear, Copy, Cut, Item**

- Properties: **Count, Parent, VBE**

COMMENTS

A **SelectedVBControls** collection that contains **VBControl** objects represents the selected intrinsic and ActiveX controls contained on a form. You use a **SelectedVBControls** collection to clear, copy, and cut selected controls on a form. You can access a selected **VBControl** object by calling the **Item** method of a **SelectedVBControls** collection or by using a **For...Each...Next** statement to loop through the items of a **SelectedVBControls** collection until you find the selected **VBControl** object you want.

Unlike most collections in the VBIDE class library, a **SelectedVBControls** collection does not have **Add** and **Remove** methods. Instead you use the **SelectAll** method of a **VBForm** object or the **InSelection** property (**True/False**) of a **VBControl** object to add items to and delete items from a **SelectedVBControls** collection. You use the **Count** property to return the number of **VBControls** objects in the collection.

Unlike most collections in the VBIDE class library, a **SelectedVBControls** collection is zero-based instead of one-based. This is a bug that Microsoft needs to fix. Until it is fixed, you must remember to offset the **Count** property of the **SelectedVBControls** collection by one, as demonstrated in the Example code.

EXAMPLE CODE

See the Help topic SelectedVBControls Collection/Property Example in ADDINEFS.HLP or the procedure DemoSelectedVBControlsObj in DEMOSYNT.VBP.

SelectedVBControlsEvents Object/Property

A **SelectedVBControlsEvents** object represents the events raised by VB's IDE when a control is added to or deleted from a set of selected controls on a form. The read-only **SelectedVBControlsEvents** property of an **Events** object returns a **SelectedVB ControlsEvents** object.

USAGE

#1: **Public WithEvents** *SelectedVBControls* **As SelectedVBControlsEvents**
#2: **Set** *SelectedVBControls* = **VBE.Events.SelectedVBControlsEvents(** *VBProjectObj*, *VBFormObj***)**

The **SelectedVBControlsEvents** syntax contains these parts:

- *SelectedVBControls*: Required. A module-level object variable in an add-in's **ClassModule** object that is assigned the **SelectedVBControlsEvents** object returned by the **SelectedVBControlsEvents** property. *SelectedVBControls* must be declared with the **Public** statement and the **WithEvents** keyword and may not be declared as the generic **Object** or as **Variant**.

- *VBProjectObj*: Required. An object expression that evaluates to a **VBProject** object whose selected controls-related events you want to monitor.

- *VBFormObj*: Required. An object expression that evaluates to a **VBForm** object whose selected controls-related events you want to monitor.

 In Usage #1, SelectedVBControlsEvents is the object. In Usage #2, SelectedVBControlsEvents is a property of an Events object. This property returns a SelectedVBControlsEvents object.

MEMBERS

- Events: **ItemAdded**, **ItemRemoved**

- Methods: None at this time

- Properties: None at this time

COMMENTS

A **SelectedVBControlsEvents** object allows an add-in to receive and react to selected controls-related events raised by VB's IDE. When more than one running add-in is receiving selected controls-related events, VB notifies the add-ins in the order in which they were connected.

To use a **SelectedVBControlsEvents** object, follow these steps in a **ClassModule** object in the add-in's project:

S-S

- Use the **Public** statement and the **WithEvents** keyword to declare an object variable that will respond to the selected controls-related events raised by VB. You do this in the Declarations section and the declaration statement adds a **SelectedVBControlsEvents** object, under the name of the object variable, to the class module's Object drop-down box. You can give this object variable any name you want, but it is most readable to name it *SelectedVBControls*.

- Select SelectedVBControls from the Object drop-down box of the class module and VB automatically creates the beginning and ending statements of the **ItemAdded** event procedure. Then, from the Procedure drop-down box, select the other selected controls-related events for which you want to create procedures.

- Write code in the various event procedures that will execute when VB raises their events.

- Make the add-in responsive to VB's selected controls-related events. You do this by using the **SelectedVBControlsEvents** property of an **Events** object to return a **SelectedVB ControlsEvents** object that is assigned to *SelectedVBControls*. You can write this assignment statement in the **OnConnection** method of an add-in's **IDTExtensibility** object; or, if you want more flexibility, you can write it in a separate **ClassModule** object that exists solely to respond to add-in related events raised in VB's IDE. See the **ClassModule** object named VBEvents and the **ConnectTo** method declared as **Friend** in DEMOSYNT.VBP for a demonstration of how to do this.

The two events of a **SelectedVBControlsEvents** object are raised for any selected intrinsic or ActiveX control. **ItemAdded** occurs after a control is added to a set of selected controls on a project's form, and **ItemRemoved** occurs after a control is deleted from a set of selected controls on a project's form.

EXAMPLE CODE

See the Help topic SelectedVBControlsEvents Object/Property Example in ADDINEFS.HLP or the procedures DemoSelectedVBControlsEventsObj and ConnectTo in DEMOSYNT.VBP.

SetFocus Method

SetFocus is a **Sub** that moves the focus to the specified window.

USAGE

Obj.SetFocus

The **SetFocus** method's syntax contains these parts:

- *Obj*: Required. An object expression that evaluates to a **Window** object.

COMMENTS

If you apply **SetFocus** to a window that is minimized, it restores the window to its previous state. If you apply **SetFocus** to a window that is not visible or that is closed, no trappable error occurs.

 Do not confuse the **SetFocus** method of the VBIDE class library with the SetFocus method of the VB class library.

Example Code

See the Help topic SetFocus Method Example in ADDINEFS.HLP or the procedure DemoSetFocusMet in DEMOSYNT.VBP.

SetSelection Method

SetSelection is a **Sub** that selects text in a code pane.

Usage

Obj.**SetSelection** *StartLine, StartCol, EndLine, EndCol*

The **SetSelection** method's syntax supports named arguments and contains these parts:

- *Obj*: Required. An object expression that evaluates to a **CodePane** object.

- *StartLine*: Required. A numeric expression that specifies the first line of the selection.

- *StartCol*: Required. A numeric expression that specifies the first column of the selection.

- *EndLine*: Required. A numeric expression that specifies the last line of the selection

- *EndCol*: Required. A numeric expression that specifies the last column of the selection.

Comments

None of the arguments of the **SetSelection** method can be zero or a negative number. If you want to select an entire single line, set *StartLine* and *EndLine* to the same value and *EndCol* to some arbitrarily large number. To determine the position of the selected text in a code pane, call the **GetSelection** method of a **CodePane** object.

Example Code

See the Help topic SetSelection Method Example in ADDINEFS.HLP or the procedure DemoSetSelectionMet in DEMOSYNT.VBP.

SetValue Method (VBAI)

SetValue is a **Function** that writes a subkey's value and its string entry to the Windows registry and returns **True**.

Usage

Obj.**SetValue**(*HWndSubKey, Entry,* [*ValName* = ""]) **As String**

The **SetValue** method's syntax supports named arguments and contains these parts:

- *Obj*: Required. An object expression that evaluates to a **Reg** object of the VBAI class library.

- *HWndSubKey*: Required. A **Long** expression that is the handle to an open subkey. You can get *HWndSubKey* by calling the **OpenSubKey** method of a **Reg** object.

- *Entry*: Required. A **String** expression that specifies the entry to be written to a value of the subkey.

S-S

- *ValName*: Optional. A **String** expression that specifies the name of a value of the subkey. If *ValName* is not passed, it defaults to a zero-length string (that is, "" or **vbNullString**) and an entry is written to the default value of the subkey.

ERROR HANDLING

SetValue returns **False** upon failure.

COMMENTS

SetValue is a proxy or wrapper method for a simplified version of the Windows API function **RegSetValueEx**. **SetValue** is only intended to write a string entry to a subkey's value. To write an entry other than a **String** data type, you must declare and call **RegSetValueEx** directly. Entry lengths are limited by available memory. Long entries (more than 2,048 bytes) should be stored as files with the file names stored in the registry. **SetValue** does not release the handle of the subkey after it writes the entry. You should do this and free system resources by calling the **CloseSubKey** method of a **Reg** object.

METHOD'S CODE

See the Help topic SetValue Method in ADDINEFS.HLP or the **SetValue** method's procedure in VBAI.VBP.

EXAMPLE CODE

See the Help topic SetValue Method Example in ADDINEFS.HLP or the procedure DemoRegObj in DEMOSYNT.VBP.

Show Method

Show is a **Sub** that displays a VB component's code pane.

USAGE

Obj.**Show**

The **Show** method's syntax contains these parts:

- *Obj*: Required. An object expression that evaluates to a **CodePane** object.

COMMENTS

Calling the **Show** method is the programmatic equivalent of selecting a component's item in the Project Explorer window, right-clicking on the item, and selecting View Code from the shortcut menu. There is no **Close** method or **Visible** property for a **CodePane** object. To close a code pane after you have called **Show** to display it, you must return the code pane's **Window** object and then call that **Window** object's **Close** method or set its **Visible** property to **False**. See the Example code for a demonstration of how to do this.

EXAMPLE CODE

See the Help topic Show Method Example in ADDINEFS.HLP or the procedure DemoShowMet in DEMOSYNT.VBP.

Show Method (VBAI)

Show is a **Function** that displays the VB Add-In toolbar on the main window of the current instance of VB's IDE and returns **True**.

USAGE

Obj.**Show**(*VBE, ProgID*) As **Boolean**

The **Show** method's syntax supports named arguments and contains these parts:

- *Obj*: Required. An object expression that evaluates to an **AITBar** object of the VBAI class library.

- *VBE*: Required. An object expression that evaluates to a **VBE** object of the VBIDE class library.

- *ProgID*: Required. A **String** expression that specifies the programmatic ID of the add-in that is calling the **Show** method. The programmatic IDs of all registered add-ins are listed in VBADDIN.INI. If *ProgID* is set to "AddInToolbar.Connect" (that is, the VB Add-In Toolbar add-in itself) or to a nonexistent programmatic ID, **Show** fails.

ERROR HANDLING

Show returns **False** upon failure.

COMMENTS

It is possible to display the Add-In toolbar on VB's main window by simply setting the **Connect** property of the toolbar's **AddIn** object to **True**. Unfortunately, this does not cause VB to check the toolbar's item in the Add-In Manager dialog box's list. As a result, the next time an instance of VB runs, the toolbar reverts back to its previous status and is hidden. **Show** prevents this from happening and keeps the setting of the toolbar's item in the Add-In Manager dialog box's list synchronized with its **Connect** property setting. If the Add-In toolbar is already displayed, the **Show** method fails.

 Encapsulation Violation **Show** runs a separate thread in a **Timer** object (tmrAIMgrDlgBox) on a hidden **Form** object (frmTimer) in the VBAI class library that, after **Show** opens the Add-In Manager dialog box, finds the dialog box's window, checks the VB Add-In Toolbar item, and closes the dialog box. This **Timer** thread executes while drawing of the desktop window is suspended and, as a result, these actions are not visible to the developer. Although this technique violates the encapsulation of an **AITBar** object, it is necessary because the Add-In Manager dialog box is displayed modally and cannot be closed programmatically except by a separate thread.

METHOD'S CODE

See the Help topic Show Method (AITBar) in ADDINEFS.HLP or the **Show** method's procedure in VBAI.VBP.

EXAMPLE CODE

See the Help topic Show Method Example (AITBar) in ADDINEFS.HLP or the procedure DemoAITBarObj in DEMOSYNT.VBP.

ShowMsg Method (VBAI)

ShowMsg is a **Function** that creates an enhanced message box that can display a Help topic by keyword instead of context number and as a popup instead of a jump. **ShowMsg** returns an **Integer** that is the number of the chosen button.

Usage

Obj.**ShowMsg**(*Prompt*, [*Buttons*], [*Title* = "ShowMsg Method"], [*HelpFile*, *Context*], [*HWndOwner*], [*Popup* = **False**]) **As Integer**

The **ShowMsg** method's syntax supports named arguments and contains these parts:

- *Obj*: Required. An object expression that evaluates to a **Util** object of the VBAI class library.

- *Prompt*: Required. A **String** expression that is the message displayed in the dialog box. The maximum length of *Prompt* is approximately 1,024 characters, depending on the width of the characters used. If *Prompt* consists of more than one line, you can separate the lines using a carriage return character (**vbCr**).

- *Buttons*: Optional. A numeric expression that is the sum of values specifying the number and type of buttons to display, the icon style to use, the identity of the default button, and the modality of the message box. See the Help topic for VB's **MsgBox** function for a list of the possible values of *Buttons*. The Help topic's list of settings for *Buttons* fails to mention that a value of 262144 (the Windows API function constant MB_TOPMOST or &H40000) displays the message box window on top of all other windows. If omitted, the default value for *Buttons* is 0 (that is, **vbOKOnly** + **vbDefaultButton1**).

- *Title*: Optional. A **String** expression that specifies the caption displayed in the title bar of the message box. If omitted, the default value of "ShowMsg Method" is placed in the title bar.

- *HelpFile*: Optional. A **String** expression that specifies the path and name of the Help file to use to provide context-sensitive Help for the message box. If *HelpFile* is provided, *Context* must also be provided and a Help button is displayed on the message box.

- *Context*: Optional. A numeric or **String** expression that specifies the Help topic to be displayed when the developer presses F1 or chooses the Help button. If *Context* is a number, the topic is identified by its context ID number. If *Context* is a string, the topic is identified by its keyword. If *Context* is provided, *HelpFile* must also be provided and a Help button is displayed on the message box.

- *HWndOwner*: Optional. A **Long** expression that specifies the handle of a VB **Form** object that is the owner of the modal message box. If *HWndOwner* is not provided, the message box is not modal and the client application should hide its active form before calling **ShowMsg**.

- *Popup*: Optional. A **Boolean** expression that specifies the Help topic is displayed as a popup (**True**) or as a jump (the default of **False**). If *Popup* is provided, *HelpFile* and *Context* must also be provided and a Help button is displayed on the message box.

VB's Help file incorrectly states that the **vbSystemModal** setting of *Buttons* causes all applications to be suspended until the user responds to the message box. Instead, it only causes the message box window to be displayed on top of all other windows. 32-bit Windows does not support the creation of a system-modal window.

RETURNS

A value from 1 to 7 that specifies the button chosen. See the Help topic for VB's **MsgBox** function for a list of the intrinsic constants returned by **ShowMsg**.

ERROR HANDLING

ShowMsg returns 0 (**False**) upon failure.

COMMENTS

When both the *HelpFile* and *Context* arguments are provided, the user can choose the Help command button or press F1 to view the Help topic associated with the context ID number or keyword. Choosing the Help command button never closes the dialog box. The dialog box is not closed and no value is returned until the user chooses one of the other command buttons. If the message box displays a Cancel, Abort, or No command button, pressing the Esc key has the same effect as choosing one of those command buttons.

The **ShowMsg** method is able to display a Help topic by keyword or as a popup because it uses the Windows API function **MessageBoxIndirect** to display the message box. As a result, the message box is not automatically displayed as modal.

Encapsulation Violation. To display a Help topic using **Message-BoxIndirect** requires that a callback be made from the API function's procedure to the address of a procedure in the VBAI class library. Because VB's **AddressOf** function, which enables a callback to be made, can only point to a procedure in a standard module, a **Util** object must violate encapsulation in this regard.

METHOD'S CODE

See the Help topic ShowMsg Method in ADDINEFS.HLP or the **ShowMsg** method's procedure in VBAI.VBP.

EXAMPLE CODE

See the Help topic ShowMsg Method Example in ADDINEFS.HLP or the procedure DemoShowMsgMet in DEMOSYNT.VBP.

StandardMethod Property

StandardMethod returns a **Long** or sets a numeric expression that specifies the DispID or procedure number of a member. Read/write.

Usage

Obj.StandardMethod[= *Val*]

The **StandardMethod** property's syntax contains these parts:

- *Obj*: Required. An object expression that evaluates to a **Member** object.

- *Val*: Optional. Only used when you set **StandardMethod**, *Val* is a numeric expression that identifies a member in a type library.

Comments

You normally only use the **StandardMethod** property when you are creating an ActiveX control and are working with the code module of a User Control VB component. Some members of an ActiveX control are important enough to have special DispID numbers, which are defined by the ActiveX specification. These standard member IDs are used by some programs and system functions to access standard properties of the control.

You can use the Procedure Attributes Advanced dialog box, accessed from the Tools menu, to manually assign a DispID number to a member (select an item from the Procedure ID drop-down box or enter the number). You can also programmatically assign a DispID number by setting its corresponding **Member** object's **StandardMethod** property to the number. When you compile the project, VB stores the DispID number in the ActiveX control's type library. If you do not use the **StandardMethod** property to assign a DispID number, VB automatically assigns one. A member of an ActiveX control can have only one DispID number, and no other member of the control can have the same number. For a complete list of standard DispID numbers, consult the ActiveX specification.

DispID numbers are used when you early bind a client application to an ActiveX component by setting a reference to the component and instantiating one of its classes with the **Dim As New** statement. When early binding is in effect, VB can look up the DispID number of a member in its type library and determine at compile time what object the member belongs to. Early binding reduces the time required to set or return a property value or call a method of an ActiveX component.

 The only way to programmatically specify a particular property as the default property of an ActiveX component is to set the **StandardMethod** property of that property's **Member** object to zero. This has the same effect as manually selecting (Default) from the Procedure ID drop-down box on the Procedure Attributes Advanced dialog box. Once you have specified a default property, you no longer have to explicitly refer to it in your code when you return or set its value.

Example Code

See the Help topic StandardMethod Property Example in ADDINEFS.HLP or the procedure DemoStandardMethodPrp in DEMOSYNT.VBP.

StartMode Property

StartMode returns a **Long** or sets a constant or value that specifies the startup mode of a VB project. Read/write.

USAGE

Obj.StartMode[= *Val*]

The **StartMode** property's syntax contains these parts:

- *Obj*: Required. An object expression that evaluates to a **VBProject** collection.

- *Val*: Optional. Only used when you set **StartMode**, *Val* is a constant or value that can be either 0 - **vbext_psm_StandAlone** (startup mode is standalone executable) or 1 - **vbext_psm_OleServer** (startup mode is ActiveX component).

COMMENTS

The setting of **StartMode** corresponds to the setting of the two Start Mode option buttons on the Component tab of the Project Properties dialog box. These two option buttons are only enabled for manual access if the project is an ActiveX EXE project. If the project compiles a non-ActiveX EXE, DLL, or OCX project, then the two option buttons are disabled. The default settings for **StartMode** for the four kinds of projects are listed in Table D.5.

You should only change the default **StartMode** setting for an ActiveX EXE project. If you programmatically set **StartMode** to 1 - **vbext_psm_OleServer** for a non-ActiveX, standard EXE project, VB checks the ActiveX Component option button but leaves both option buttons disabled and ignores the setting when you compile the project. Similarly, if you programmatically set **StartMode** to 0 - **vbext_psm_StandAlone** for a DLL or ActiveX control project, VB checks the Standalone option button but leaves both option buttons disabled and ignores the setting at compile time.

 VB's Help file incorrectly states that **StartMode** can return or set three values (RunMode, BreakMode, and DesignMode). Instead, **StartMode** only returns two possible values (0 or 1).

Table D.5   Default settings for **StartMode** property.

Type Of Project	Default Setting
0 - vbext_pt_StandardExe	0 - vbext_psm_StandAlone
1 - vbext_pt_ActiveXExe	1 - vbext_psm_OleServer
2 - vbext_pt_ActiveXDll	1 - vbext_psm_OleServer
3 - vbext_pt_ActiveXControl	1 - vbext_psm_OleServer

S-S

EXAMPLE CODE

See the Help topic StartMode Property Example in ADDINEFS.HLP or the procedure DemoStartModePrp in DEMOSYNT.VBP.

StartProject Property

StartProject returns or sets a **Variant** that represents the project that will be started when you select Run|Start or press the F5 key. Read/write.

USAGE

Obj.**StartProject**[= *Val*]

The **StartProject** property's syntax contains these parts:

- *Obj*: Required. An object expression that evaluates to a **VBProjects** collection.

- *Val*: Optional. Only used when you set **StartProject**, *Val* is a **Variant** expression that must evaluate to a **VBProject** object that represents the project you want to start.

COMMENTS

When you programmatically set the **StartProject** property and run the project, you will want to ensure that the **StartUpObject** property of a **VBComponents** collection has also been set. If **StartUpObject** has not been set when you start the project, VB will display the Project Properties dialog box with the focus on the General tab's Startup Object drop-down box. This forces you to manually set a startup object. The Extensibility Object model provides no way to programmatically start a project, but you can use a **SendKeys** statement to do this, as demonstrated in the Example code.

 The Object Browser incorrectly states that **StartProject** returns or sets a **VBProject** object. Instead, it returns or sets a **Variant** that evaluates to a **VBProject** object.

EXAMPLE CODE

See the Help topic StartProject Property Example in ADDINEFS.HLP or the procedure DemoStartProjectPrp in DEMOSYNT.VBP.

S-S

StartUpObject Property

StartUpObject returns or sets a **Variant** that specifies the startup component for the project. Read/write.

USAGE

Obj.**StartUpObject**[= *Val*]

The **StartUpObject** property's syntax contains these parts:

- *Obj*: Required. An object expression that evaluates to a **VBComponents** collection.

- *Val*: Optional. Only used when you set **StartUpObject**, *Val* is a **Variant** expression that can either evaluate to a **VBComponent** object or to a constant or value as specified in Settings.

SETTINGS

The *Val* argument's possible values other than a **VBComponent** object are:

- 0 - **vbext_so_SubMain**: Startup object is the **Sub** procedure Main.

- 1 - **vbext_so_None**: There is no startup object.

COMMENTS

You will want to ensure that **StartUpObject** has been set before you programmatically call the **MakeCompiledFile** method of a **VBProject** object. If **StartUpObject** has not been set, VB will display the Project Properties dialog box with the focus on the General tab's Startup Object drop-down box; this forces you to manually set a startup object before the add-in's code can execute the **MakeCompiledFile** method.

The Object Browser incorrectly states that the **StartUpObject** property is read-only. Instead, it is read/write.

EXAMPLE CODE

See the Help topic StartUpObject Property Example in ADDINEFS.HLP or the procedure DemoStartUpObjectPrp in DEMOSYNT.VBP.

Static Property

Static returns a **Boolean** that specifies whether a member of a code module is declared with the **Static** keyword (**True**) or not (**False**). Read-only.

USAGE

Obj.**Static**

The **Static** property's syntax contains these parts:

- *Obj*: Required. An object expression that evaluates to a **Member** object.

COMMENTS

Static can only be **True** for a member of a code module that is a method or property procedure (that is, the member's **Type** property returns 1 - **vbext_mt_Method** or 2 - **vbext_mt_Property**). If **Static** is **True**, the member procedure's local variables are preserved between calls. The **Static** attribute doesn't affect variables that are declared outside the member's procedure, even if they are used in the procedure.

S-S

EXAMPLE CODE

See the Help topic Static Property Example in ADDINEFS.HLP or the procedure DemoStaticPrp in DEMOSYNT.VBP.

TemplatePath Property

TemplatePath returns a **String** that specifies the fully qualified path on which VB stores the template files. Read-only.

USAGE

*Obj.*TemplatePath

The **TemplatePath** property's syntax contains these parts:

- *Obj*: Required. An object expression that evaluates to a **VBE** object.

COMMENTS

When VB5 installs itself, it creates a \TEMPLATE subdirectory in which it places its various template files.

EXAMPLE CODE

See the Help topic TemplatePath Property Example in ADDINEFS.HLP or the procedure DemoTemplatePathPrp in DEMOSYNT.VBP.

Top Property

Top returns a **Long** or sets a numeric expression that specifies the position of the top side of a window in VB's IDE. Read/write.

USAGE

*Obj.*Top[= *Val*]

The **Top** property's syntax contains these parts:

- *Obj*: Required. An object expression that evaluates to a **Window** object.

- *Val*: Optional. Only used when you set **Top**, *Val* is a numeric expression that specifies in pixels the position of the top edge of a VB IDE window.

COMMENTS

There is a difference between the **Top** property of a VB IDE designer **Window** object (specified in pixels) and the **Top** property of a VB **Form** object (specified in twips). The value returned by the **Top** property of a **Window** object depends on whether or not the window is linked or docked. If the window is linked, the value of **Top** is actually for the frame window to which it is linked. If the window is not linked, the value of **Top** is for the window itself.

Setting the **Top** property of a linked window has no effect. You can set the **Top** property of any VB IDE window to a value so small or so large that the window is positioned entirely off the screen. See the Example code for a demonstration of this effect on VB's main window.

 1) VB's Help file and the Object Browser incorrectly state that the **Top** property of a **Window** object is specified in twips. Instead, it is specified in pixels. 2) VB's Help file incorrectly states that **Top** returns a **Single**. Instead, it returns a **Long**.

Example Code

See the Help topic Top Property Example in ADDINEFS.HLP or the procedure DemoTopPrp in DEMOSYNT.VBP.

TopLine Property

TopLine returns a **Long** or sets a numeric expression that specifies the line number of the line at the top of the code pane or sets the line showing at the top of the code pane. Read/write.

Usage

*Obj.***TopLine**[= *Val*]

The **TopLine** property's syntax contains these parts:

- *Obj*: Required. An object expression that evaluates to a **CodePane** object.

- *Val*: Optional. Only used when you set **TopLine**, *Val* is a numeric expression that sets the line showing at the top of the code pane.

Comments

You use the **TopLine** property to return or set the line showing at the top of the code pane. For example, if you want line 25 to be the first line showing in a code pane, set **TopLine** to 25. The **TopLine** setting must be a positive number. If **TopLine** is set to a value greater than the actual number of lines in the code pane, the setting will be the last line in the code pane.

Example Code

See the Help topic TopLine Property Example in ADDINEFS.HLP or the procedure DemoTopLinePrp in DEMOSYNT.VBP.

Type Property

Type returns a **Long** that specifies the kind of **Member, Reference, VBComponent, VBProject,** or **Window** object that you are working with. Read-only.

Usage

*Obj.***Type**

The **Type** property's syntax contains these parts:

- *Obj*: Required. An object expression that evaluates to a **Member, Reference, VBComponent, VBProject,** or **Window** object.

Settings

The **Type** property returns these settings for a **Member** object:

- 1 - **vbext_mt_Method**: Method (that is, a **Function** procedure, **Sub** procedure, or a general declaration made with the **Declare** statement)

- 2 - **vbext_mt_Property**: Property (that is, a **Property Get, Let,** or **Set** procedure)

- 3 - **vbext_mt_Variable**: Variable (but not a general declaration of a user-defined data type)

T-T

- 4 - **vbext_mt_Event:** Event (that is, a general declaration made with the **Event** statement)

- 5 - **vbext_mt_Const:** Constant (that is, a general declaration made with the **Const** statement; an enumerated type is not considered a member)

The **Type** property returns these settings for a **Reference** object:

- 0 - **vbext_rk_TypeLib:** Type/class library

- 1 - **vbext_rk_Project:** Project

The **Type** property returns these settings for a **VBComponent** object:

- 1 - **vbext_ct_StdModule:** Standard module

- 2 - **vbext_ct_ClassModule: ClassModule** object

- 3 - **vbext_ct_MSForm:** Microsoft form

- 4 - **vbext_ct_ResFile:** Resource file

- 5 - **vbext_ct_VBForm: Form** object

- 6 - **vbext_ct_VBMDIForm: MDIForm** object

- 7 - **vbext_ct_PropPage: PropertyPage** object

- 8 - **vbext_ct_UserControl: UserControl** object

- 9 - **vbext_ct_DocObject: UserDocument** object

- 10 - **vbext_ct_RelatedDocument: RelatedDocument** object

- 100 - **vbext_ct_Document: Document** object

The **Type** property returns these settings for a **VBProject** object:

- 0 - **vbext_pt_StandardExe:** Standard executable

- 1 - **vbext_pt_ActiveXExe:** ActiveX executable

- 2 - **vbext_pt_ActiveXDll:** ActiveX DLL

- 3 - **vbext_pt_ActiveXControl:** ActiveX control

The **Type** property returns these settings for a **Window** object:

- 0 - **vbext_wt_CodeWindow:** Code

- 1 - **vbext_wt_Designer:** Designer (Form, MDI form, Property page, User control, User document form, or ActiveX designer)

- 2 - **vbext_wt_Browser:** Object Browser

- 3 - **vbext_wt_Watch:** Watch

- 4 - **vbext_wt_Locals:** Locals

- 5 - **vbext_wt_Immediate:** Immediate

- 6 - **vbext_wt_ProjectWindow**: Project

- 7 - **vbext_wt_PropertyWindow**: Locals

- 8 - **vbext_wt_Find**: Find

- 9 - **vbext_wt_FindReplace**: Replace

- 11 - **vbext_wt_LinkedWindowFrame**: Linked window frame

- 12 - **vbext_wt_MainWindow**: Main window (only gets returned from the **MainWindow** property of a **VBE** object and is not an object in a **Windows** collection)

- 13 - **vbext_wt_Preview**: Form Layout

- 14 - **vbext_wt_ColorPalette**: Color palette (no caption on it)

- 15 - **vbext_wt_ToolWindow**: Toolbox (no caption on it)

COMMENTS

Use the **Type** setting of a **Window** object to find a specific IDE window (for example, the Properties window). Use the **Type** setting of a **VBComponent** object to find a specific kind of component in the Project window (for example, a **ClassModule** object). Then you can use the component's **Name** property to find a specific instance of the component and its **Activate** method to display it.

1) VB's Help file incorrectly states that the **Type** property can return a **String** value specifying the kind of object. Instead, **Type** can only return a **Long** that is one of the intrinsic constants listed earlier. 2) VB's Help file incorrectly states the values that **Type** can return for a **Member** object. Instead, the values listed earlier (and in the Object Browser) are correct. 3) VB's Help file fails to list certain values that **Type** can return for a Window object (13 - **vbext_wt_Preview**, 14 - **vbext_wt_ColorPalette** and 15 -**vbext_wt_ToolWindow**). 4) The Object Browser incorrectly states that **Type** returns 10 - **vbext_wt_Toolbox** for the Toolbox window. Instead, it returns 15 - **vbext_wt_ToolWindow** for the Toolbox window.

EXAMPLE CODE

See the Help topic Type Property Example in ADDINEFS.HLP or the procedure DemoTypePrp in DEMOSYNT.VBP.

UIDefault Property

UIDefault is a **Boolean** that returns or sets the User Interface Default attribute associated with a **Member** object. Read/write.

USAGE

Obj.**UIDefault**[= *Val*]

T-U

The **UIDefault** property's syntax contains these parts:

- *Obj*: Required. An object expression that evaluates to a **Member** object.

- *Val*: Optional. Only used when you set **UIDefault**, *Val* is a **Boolean** expression that specifies whether User Interface Default on the Procedure Attributes Advanced dialog box is checked for a member (**True**) or not (the default of **False**).

COMMENTS

You only set the User Interface Default attribute of a public **Property** procedure to **True** when you are creating an ActiveX control and are working with the code module of a User Control VB component. You can use the Procedure Attributes Advanced dialog box, accessed from the Tools menu, to manually set the User Interface Default attribute for a public **Property** procedure (check the User Interface Default checkbox). You can also do this programmatically by setting the Property procedure's **Member** object's **UIDefault** property to **True**.

Setting **UIDefault** to **True** for a **Property** procedure's **Member** object results in that property being highlighted in the Properties window when you first place the ActiveX control on a container object. You can only have one User Interface Default property per control. When you save the User Control component that contains the **Property** procedure, VB writes the setting of **UIDefault** to the ActiveX control's type library.

VB does not permit you to manually set User Interface Default for a member that is not a public **Property** procedure. Unfortunately, VB does permit an add-in to programmatically set **UIDefault** to **True** for a non-property **Member** object without causing a trappable error. This results in contradictory settings on the Procedure Attributes Advanced dialog box; that is, the User Interface Default checkbox is checked but disabled. It can also, under certain circumstances, crash the current instance of VB's IDE.

EXAMPLE CODE

See the Help topic UIDefault Property Example in ADDINEFS.HLP or the procedure DemoUIDefaultPrp in DEMOSYNT.VBP.

Update Method

Update is a **Sub** that refreshes an **Addins** collection from the Windows registry just as if you had opened VB's Add-In Manager dialog box.

USAGE

Obj.**Update**

The **Update** method's syntax contains these parts:

- *Obj*: Required. An object expression that evaluates to an **Addins** collection.

COMMENTS

The **Update** method reads the entries in the Windows registry related to add-ins and, if a new add-in has been added to the registry, refreshes the **Addins** collection for the current instance of VB to reflect the addition. Unfortunately, the **Update** method fails to refresh the **Addins** collection if an add-in has been deleted from the registry. In the case of a deletion, the only way to refresh the **Addins** collection is to start another instance of VB.

Calling the **Update** method is not required to reflect a change you make to an item in the Add-In Manager dialog box's list because, in this case, VB itself automatically refreshes the **Addins** collection. However, if you programmatically change an add-in's entry in the VBADDIN.INI file by calling the Windows API function **WritePrivateProfileString**, neither the **Update** method nor VB can react to such a change. Instead you must start another instance of VB's IDE to refresh the **Addins** collection.

One place where you should always have a statement that calls the **Update** method is in the procedure for the **OnAddinsUpdate** method of the **IDTExtensibility** object. In addition, you can call the **Update** method from any other routine where it is appropriate to do so; for example, you would want to do so after programmatically compiling and registering a new add-in project. See the Example code for a demonstration of how to do this.

VB Books Online, in the topic titled *Connecting Or Disconnecting Add-Ins*, makes several incorrect statements about the **Update** method of an **Addins** collection and the **Connect** property of an **AddIn** object. 1) It states that you can set **Connect** to 1; instead, **Connect** is a **Boolean** that is either **True** (-1) or **False** (0). 2) It states that after you set **Connect**, you must call **Update** to alert VB to connect the add-in; instead, VB automatically connects the add-in. 3) It states that calling **Update** forces VB to read VBADDIN.INI and react to any changes made to its entries. Instead, **Update** reads the Windows registry and has nothing to do with VBADDIN.INI.

EXAMPLE CODE

See the Help topic Update Method Example in ADDINEFS.HLP or the procedure DemoUpdateMet in DEMOSYNT.VBP.

Util Object (VBAI)

A **Util** object of the VBAI class library provides methods for an add-in to call to perform miscellaneous tasks.

USAGE

Obj.Mbr Args

A **Util** object's syntax supports named arguments and contains these parts:

- *Obj*: Required. An object expression that evaluates to a **Util** object of the VBAI class library.

- *Mbr*: Required. A member of a **Util** object.

- *Args*: Required. An argument or arguments of *Mbr*. Only the **IsWinNT** member has no arguments. All other members of a **Util** object have at least one required argument.

U-U

MEMBERS

- Events: None at this time

- Methods: **Connect, GetDesc, IsBeingDebugged, IsFormDisplayed, IsWinNT, ShowMsg**

- Properties: None at this time

COMMENTS

To programmatically check or uncheck an add-in's item in the Add-In Manager dialog box, call the **Connect** method. To read an add-in's **Description** setting from the Windows registry, call the **GetDesc** method. To find out if an add-in is being run in debug mode or if an add-in's form is already displayed, call the **IsBeingDebugged** or the **IsFormDisplayed** method. To find out if the operating system is Windows NT, call the **IsWinNT** method. To show a message box that can display a Help topic by keyword instead of context number and as a popup instead of a jump, call the **ShowMsg** method.

EXAMPLE CODE

See the Help topic Util Object Example in ADDINEFS.HLP or the procedures in DEMOSYNT.VBP that demonstrate the individual methods of the **Util** object.

Value Property

Value returns or sets a **Variant** that specifies the value of a property. Read/write.

USAGE

Obj.**Value**[= *Val*]

The **Value** property's syntax contains these parts:

- *Obj*: Required. An object expression that evaluates to a **Property** object.

- *Val*: Optional. Only used when you set **Value**, *Val* is a **Variant** expression that must evaluate to the subtype required by a given property.

COMMENTS

The **Value** property is the default property for the **Property** object. Because **Value** returns a **Variant**, you can access or set almost any property. The one situation where **Value** does not work is when a property takes an object reference as its value; in that case, you must return or set the property with the **Object** property. To access a property like **List**, which takes an array, use the **IndexedValue** property.

If the property that a **Property** object represents is read/write, the **Value** property is read/write. If the property is read-only, attempting to set **Value** causes an error. If the property is write-only, attempting to return **Value** causes an error.

 The Object Browser incorrectly states that **Value** returns or sets the value of an object. Instead, VB's Help file is correct when it states that **Value** returns or sets the value of a property.

J-V

EXAMPLE CODE
See the Help topic Value Property Example in ADDINEFS.HLP or the procedure
DemoValuePrp in DEMOSYNT.VBP.

VBComponent Object
VBComponent is an item in a **VBComponents** collection and represents a component, such
as a class module, standard module, or form module, contained in a project.

INSTANTIATION
Dim *Obj* **As** [VBIDE.]**VBComponent|Object|Variant**
Set *Obj* = **VBE.ActiveVBProject.VBComponents**[**.Item**](*Index*)

USAGE
#1: *Obj*[.*Mbr*[= *Val* | *Args*]]
#2: *Obj.MbrA.MbrB* [= *ValB* | *ArgsB*]

A **VBComponent** object's syntax supports named arguments and contains these parts:

- *Obj*: Required. A variable to be assigned an object instance. *Obj* can be named the same as the **VBComponent** class being instantiated. *Obj* can also be declared as the generic **Object** or as **Variant**, but this slows performance.

- VBIDE: Optional. The VB5 Extensibility object library containing the **VBComponent** class.

- *Index*: Required. Used with the default **Item** method, *Index* is a numeric or **String** expression that specifies the ordinal position of a **VBComponent** object in a **VBComponents** collection. If *Index* is a **String** expression, it must evaluate to the **Name** property of a **VBComponent** object.

- *Mbr*: Required. A member of a **VBComponent** object.

- *Val* | *Args*: Optional. You use *Val* if *Mbr* is a property being set or *Args* if *Mbr* is a method being called.

- *MbrA*: Required. A member of the object or collection that is returned by *MbrA*.

- *MbrB*: Required. A member of a **VBComponent** object.

- *ValB* | *ArgsB*: Optional. You use *ValB* if *MbrB* is a property being set or *ArgsB* if *MbrB* is a method being called.

MEMBERS

- Events: None at this time

- Methods: **Activate, DesignerWindow, InsertFile, ReadProperty, Reload, SaveAs, WriteProperty**

V-V

- Properties: CodeModule, Collection, Description, Designer, DesignerID, FileCount, FileNames, HasOpenDesigner, HelpContextID, IconState, IsDirty, Names, Properties, Type, VBE

COMMENTS

A VB project can contain eight kinds of VB components:

- Forms (.FRM extension)

- Basic modules (.BAS extension)

- Class modules (.CLS extension)

- User controls (.CTL extension)

- Property pages (.PAG extension)

- User document forms (.DOB extension)

- ActiveX designers (.DSR extension)

- Related documents (.RES or other extension)

You can access a **VBComponent** object by:

- Calling the **Item** method of a **VBComponents** collection.

- Using a **For...Each...Next** statement to loop through the items of a **VBComponents** collection until you find the **VBComponent** object you want.

You can use the **Type** property to find out what kind of component a **VBComponent** object refers to. Use the **CodeModule** property to access a component's code or the **DesignerWindow** method to access the component's designer window.

EXAMPLE CODE

See the Help topic VBComponent Object Example in ADDINEFS.HLP or the procedure DemoVBComponentObj in DEMOSYNT.VBP.

VBComponents Collection/Property

A **VBComponents** collection contains the **VBComponent** objects in a project. The read-only **VBComponents** property of a **VBProject** object returns an object instance of the **VBComponents** class.

INSTANTIATION

Dim *Obj* **As** [VBIDE.]**VBComponents**|**Object**|**Variant**
Set *Obj* = **VBE.ActiveVBProject.VBComponents**

USAGE

#1: *Obj.Mbr*
#2: *Obj*[.**Item**](*Index*)[.*MbrA* [= *ValA* | *ArgsA*]]
#3: *Obj.MbrB.MbrC* [= *ValC* | *ArgsC*]

The **VBComponents** syntax supports named arguments and contains these parts:

- *Obj*: Required. A variable to be assigned an object instance. *Obj* can be named the same as the **VBComponents** class being instantiated. *Obj* can also be declared as the generic **Object** or as **Variant** but this slows performance.

- VBIDE: Optional. The VB5 Extensibility object library containing the **VBComponents** class.

- *Mbr*: Required. A member of a **VBComponents** collection other than the **Item** method.

- *Index*: Required. Used with the default **Item** method, *Index* is a numeric or **String** expression that specifies the ordinal position of a **VBComponent** object in a **VBComponents** collection. If *Index* is a **String** expression, it must evaluate to the **Name** property of a **VBComponent** object.

- *MbrA*: Optional. A member of a **VBComponent** object.

- *ValA\ArgsA*: Optional. You use *ValA* if *MbrA* is a property being set or *ArgsA* if *MbrA* is a method being called.

- *MbrB*: Required. A **VBComponents** collection's property that returns an object.

- *MbrC*: Required. A member of the object that is returned by *MbrB*.

- *ValC\ArgsC*: Optional. You use *ValC* if *MbrC* is a property being set or *ArgsC* if *MbrC* is a method being called.

MEMBERS

- Events: **ItemActivated, ItemAdded, ItemReloaded, ItemRemoved, ItemRenamed, ItemSelected**

- Methods: **Add, AddCustom, AddFile, AddFromTemplate, Item, Remove**

- Properties: **Count, Parent, StartUpObject, VBE**

COMMENTS

A **VBComponents** collection that contains **VBComponent** objects represents the components contained in a project. You use a **VBComponents** collection to access, add, or remove components in a project. You can access a **VBComponent** object by calling the **Item** method of a **VBComponents** collection or by using a **For...Each...Next** statement to loop through the items of a **VBComponents** collection until you find the **VBComponent** object you want. You can use the **Count** property to return the number of **VBComponent** objects in the collection.

EXAMPLE CODE

See the Help topic VBComponents Collection/Property Example in ADDINEFS.HLP or the procedure DemoVBComponentsObj in DEMOSYNT.VBP.

VBComponentsEvents Object/Property

A **VBComponentsEvents** object represents all events raised by VB's IDE when a VB component is activated, added, reloaded, deleted, renamed, or selected. The read-only **VBComponentsEvents** property of an **Events** object returns a **VBComponentsEvents** object.

USAGE

#1: **Public WithEvents** *VBComponents* **As VBComponentsEvents**
#2: **Set** *VBComponents* = **VBE.Events.VBComponentsEvents**(*VBProjectObj*)

The **VBComponentsEvents** syntax contains these parts:

- *VBComponents*: Required. A module-level object variable, in an add-in's **ClassModule** object, that is assigned the **VBComponentsEvents** object returned by the **VBComponentsEvents** property. *VBComponents* must be declared with the **Public** statement and the **WithEvents** keyword and may not be declared as the generic **Object** or as **Variant**.

- *VBProjectObj*: Required. An object expression that evaluates to a **VBProject** object whose component-related events you want to monitor.

 In Usage #1, **VBComponentsEvents** is the object. In Usage #2, **VBComponentsEvents** is a property of an **Events** object. This property returns a **VBComponentsEvents** object.

MEMBERS

- Events: **ItemActivated, ItemAdded, ItemReloaded, ItemRemoved, ItemRenamed, ItemSelected**

- Methods: None at this time

- Properties: None at this time

COMMENTS

A **VBComponentsEvents** object allows an add-in to receive and react to VB component-related events raised by VB's IDE. When more than one running add-in is receiving component-related events, VB notifies the add-ins in the order in which they were connected.

To use a **VBComponentsEvents** object, follow these steps in a **ClassModule** object in the add-in's project:

- Use the **Public** statement and the **WithEvents** keyword to declare an object variable that will respond to the file component-related events raised by VB. You do this in the Declarations section and the declaration statement adds a **VBComponentsEvents** object, under the name of the object variable, to the class module's Object drop-down box. You can give this object variable any name you want, but it is most readable to name it *VBComponents*.

- Select VBComponents from the Object drop-down box of the class module and VB automatically creates the beginning and ending statements of the **ItemActivated** event procedure. Then, from the Procedure drop-down box, select the other component-related events for which you want to create procedures.

 V-V

- Write code in the various event procedures that will execute when VB raises their events.

- Make the add-in responsive to VB's file component-related events. You do this by using the **VBComponentsEvents** property of an **Events** object to return a **VBComponentsEvents** object that is assigned to *VBComponents*. You can write this assignment statement in the **OnConnection** method of an add-in's **IDTExtensibility** object; or, if you want more flexibility, you can write it in a separate **ClassModule** object that exists solely to respond to add-in related events raised in VB's IDE. See the **ClassModule** object named VBEvents and the **ConnectTo** method declared as **Friend** in DEMOSYNT.VBP for a demonstration of how to do this.

DETAILS
The events of a **VBComponentsEvents** object are listed in Table D.6. The kinds of components that a **VBComponentsEvents** object gives you control over are listed in Table D.7.

EXAMPLE CODE
See the Help topic VBComponentsEvents Object/Property Example in ADDINEFS.HLP or the procedures DemoVBComponentsEventsObj and ConnectTo in DEMOSYNT.VBP.

VBControl Object
VBControl is an item in a **VBControls** collection that represents an intrinsic VB or an ActiveX control on a **VBForm** object in VB's IDE.

INSTANTIATION
Dim *Obj* **As** [VBIDE.]**VBControl|Object|Variant**
Set*Obj*=**VBE.ActiveVBProject.VBComponents**[**.Item**](*IndexA*)**.Designer.VBControls** [**.Item**](*IndexB*)

USAGE
#1: *Obj.Mbr*[*Args*]
#2: *Obj.MbrA.MbrB*[= *ValB*| *ArgsB*]

Table D.6   VBComponentsEvents object's events.

Event	Description
ItemActivated	Occurs after a component is activated
ItemAdded	Occurs after a component is added to a project
ItemReloaded	Occurs after a component is reloaded into a project
ItemRemoved	Occurs after a component is deleted from a project
ItemRenamed	Occurs after a component is renamed
ItemSelected	Occurs after a component is selected

V-V

Table D.7   Kinds of components for which VB raises events.

Value/Constant	Description
1 - vbext_ct_StdModule	Standard module
2 - vbext_ct_ClassModule	ClassModule object
3 - vbext_ct_MSForm	Microsoft form
4 - vbext_ct_ResFile	Resource file
5 - vbext_ct_VBForm	Form object
6 - vbext_ct_VBMDIForm	MDIForm object
7 - vbext_ct_PropPage	PropertyPage object
8 - vbext_ct_UserControl	UserControl object
9 - vbext_ct_DocObject	UserDocument object
10 - vbext_ct_RelatedDocument	RelatedDocument object
100 - vbext_ct_Document	Document object

A **VBControl** object's syntax supports named arguments and contains these parts:

- *Obj*: Required. A variable to be assigned an object instance. *Obj* can be named the same as the **VBControl** class being instantiated. *Obj* can also be declared as the generic **Object** or as **Variant**, but this slows performance.

- VBIDE: Optional. The VB5 Extensibility object library containing the **VBControl** class.

- *IndexA*: Required. Used with the default **Item** method, *IndexA* is a numeric or **String** expression that specifies the ordinal position of a **VBComponent** object in a **VBComponents** collection. If *IndexA* is a **String** expression, it must evaluate to the **Name** property of a **VBComponent** object.

- *IndexB*: Required. Used with the default **Item** method, *IndexB* is a numeric or **String** expression that specifies the ordinal position of a **VBControl** object in a **VBControls** collection. If *IndexB* is a **String** expression, it must evaluate to the **Name** property of the control represented by a **VBControl** object.

- *Mbr*: Required. A member of a **VBControl** object.

- *Args*: Optional. You use *Args* if *Mbr* is a method being called.

- *MbrA*: Required. A **VBControl** object's property that returns an object or collection.

- *MbrB*: Required. A member of the object or collection that is returned by *MbrA*.

- *ValB | ArgsB*: Optional. You use *ValB* if *MbrB* is a property being set or *ArgsB* if *MbrB* is a method being called.

MEMBERS

- Events: None at this time

- Methods: **ZOrder**

- Properties: **ClassName, Collection, ContainedVBControls, Container, ControlObject, ControlType, InSelection, ProgID, Properties, VBE**

COMMENTS

A **VBControl** object is an item in a **VBControls** collection that represents an intrinsic VB or an ActiveX control contained on a **VBForm** object in a project. You can access a **VBControl** object by:

- Calling the **Item** method of a **VBControls** collection.

- Using a **For...Each...Next** statement to loop through the items of a **VBControls** collection until you find the **VBControl** object you want.

You can use the **ClassName** property to find out what kind of control you are working with or the **Container** property to return the **VBForm** or **VBControl** object that contains a control. The **InSelection** property returns **True** if a control is selected and the **ZOrder** method places a specified control at the front or back of the z-order within its graphical level.

To programmatically access the design-time properties of a control that are displayed in the Properties window, you can use the **Properties** property of a **VBControl** object to return its **Properties** collection. You can then access any items in the **Properties** collection by either the item's numeric index or the item's **Name** property. See the Example code for a demonstration of how to do this.

EXAMPLE CODE

See the Help topic VBControl Object Example in ADDINEFS.HLP or the procedure DemoVBControlObj in DEMOSYNT.VBP.

VBControls Collection/Property

A **VBControls** collection contains the **VBControl** objects on a **VBForm** object. The read-only **VBControls** property of a **VBForm** object returns an object instance of the **VBControls** class.

INSTANTIATION

Dim *Obj* **As** [VBIDE.]VBControls|Object|Variant
Set *Obj* = VBE.ActiveVBProject.VBComponents[.Item](*IndexA*).Designer.VBControls

In order to read the **VBControls** property, first use the **Designer** property of a **VBComponent** object to return a **VBForm** object. Then you can access the **VBControls** property to return a **VBControls** collection.

V-V

Usage

#1: *Obj.Mbr*

#2: *Obj*[.**Item**](*IndexB*)[.*MbrA*[*ArgsA*]]

#3: *Obj.MbrB.MbrC*[= *ValC* | *ArgsC*]

The **VBControls** syntax supports named arguments and contains these parts:

- *Obj*: Required. A variable to be assigned an object instance. *Obj* can be named the same as the **VBControls** class being instantiated. *Obj* can also be declared as the generic **Object** or as **Variant** but this slows performance.

- VBIDE: Optional. The VB5 Extensibility object library containing the **VBControls** class.

- *IndexA*: Required. Used with the default **Item** method, *IndexA* is a numeric or **String** expression that specifies the ordinal position of a **VBComponent** object in a **VBComponents** collection. If *IndexA* is a **String** expression, it must evaluate to the **Name** property of a **VBComponent** object.

- *Mbr*: Required. A member of a **VBControls** collection other than the **Item** method.

- *IndexB*: Required. Used with the default **Item** method, *IndexB* is a numeric or **String** expression that specifies the ordinal position of a **VBControl** object in a **VBControls** collection. If *IndexB* is a **String** expression, it must evaluate to the **Name** property of the control represented by a **VBControl** object.

- *MbrA*: Optional. A member of a **VBControl** object.

- *ArgsA*: Optional. You use *ArgsA* if *MbrA* is a method being called.

- *MbrB*: Required. A **VBControls** collection's property that returns an object.

- *MbrC*: Required. A member of the object that is returned by *MbrB*.

- *ValC* | *ArgsC*: Optional. You use *ValC* if *MbrC* is a property being set or *ArgsC* if *MbrC* is a method being called.

Members

- Events: **ItemAdded, ItemRemoved, ItemRenamed**

- Methods: **Add, Item, Remove**

- Properties: **Count, Parent, VBE**

Comments

A **VBControls** collection that contains **VBControl** objects represents the intrinsic and ActiveX controls contained on a form. You use a **VBControls** collection to add controls to or delete them from a form. You can access a **VBControl** object by calling the **Item** method of a **VBControls** collection or by using a **For...Each...Next** statement to loop through the items of a **VBControls** collection until you find the **VBControl** object you want. You can use the **Count** property to return the number of **VBControl** objects in the collection.

Example Code

See the Help topic VBControls Collection/Property Example in ADDINEFS.HLP or the procedure DemoVBControlsObj in DEMOSYNT.VBP.

VBControlsEvents Object/Property

A **VBControlsEvents** object represents the events raised by VB's IDE after a control is added to or deleted from a form or after it is renamed. The read-only **VBControlsEvents** property of an **Events** object returns a **VBControlsEvents** object.

Usage

#1: **Public WithEvents** *VBControls* **As VBControlsEvents**
#2: **Set** *VBControls* = **VBE.Events.VBControlsEvents**(*VBProjectObj*, *VBFormObj*)

The **VBControlsEvents** syntax contains these parts:

- *VBControls*: Required. A module-level object variable, in an add-in's **ClassModule** object, that is assigned the **VBControlsEvents** object returned by the **VBControlsEvents** property. *VBControls* must be declared with the **Public** statement and the **WithEvents** keyword and may not be declared as the generic **Object** or as **Variant**.

- *VBProjectObj*: Required. An object expression that evaluates to a **VBProject** object whose controls-related events you want to monitor.

- *VBFormObj*: Required. An object expression that evaluates to a **VBForm** object whose controls-related events you want to monitor.

 In Usage #1, **VBControlsEvents** is the object. In Usage #2, **VBControlsEvents** is a property of an **Events** object. This property returns a **VBControlsEvents** object.

Members

- Events: **ItemAdded, ItemRemoved, ItemRenamed**

- Methods: None at this time

- Properties: None at this time

Comments

A **VBControlsEvents** object allows an add-in to receive and react to controls-related events raised by VB's IDE. When more than one running add-in is receiving controls-related events, VB notifies the add-ins in the order in which they were connected.

To use a **VBControlsEvents** object, follow these steps in a **ClassModule** object in the add-in's project:

- Use the **Public** statement and the **WithEvents** keyword to declare an object variable that will respond to the controls-related events raised by VB. You do this in the Declarations section and the declaration statement adds a **VBControlsEvents** object, under the name of

V-V

the object variable, to the class module's Object drop-down box. You can give this object variable any name you want, but it is most readable to name it *VBControls*.

- Select VBControls from the Object drop-down box of the class module and VB automatically creates the beginning and ending statements of the **ItemAdded** event procedure. Then, from the Procedure drop-down box, select the other controls-related events for which you want to create procedures.

- Write code in the various event procedures that will execute when VB raises their events.

- Make the add-in responsive to VB's controls-related events. You do this by using the **VBControlsEvents** property of an **Events** object to return a **VBControlsEvents** object that is assigned to *VBControls*. You can write this assignment statement in the **OnConnection** method of an add-in's **IDTExtensibility** object; or, if you want more flexibility, you can write it in a separate **ClassModule** object that exists solely to respond to add-in related events raised in VB's IDE. See the **ClassModule** object named VBEvents and the **ConnectTo** method declared as **Friend** in DEMOSYNT.VBP for a demonstration of how to do this.

The three events of a **VBControlsEvents** object are raised for any intrinsic or ActiveX control that is not part of a selected set of controls. The **ItemAdded** event occurs after a control is added to a project's form and the **ItemRemoved** event occurs after a control is deleted from a project's form. The **ItemRenamed** event occurs after a control is renamed.

EXAMPLE CODE
See the Help topic VBControlsEvents Object/Property Example in ADDINEFS.HLP or the procedures DemoVBControlsEventsObj and ConnectTo in DEMOSYNT.VBP.

VBE Object/Property

VBE is the root object that represents the current instance of VB's IDE and that contains all other objects and collections in the VBIDE class library. The read-only **VBE** property of various objects and collections returns an object instance of the **VBE** class.

INSTANTIATION
Dim|Private|Public *Obj* **As VBE|Object|Variant**
Set *Obj* = *VBInst*

USAGE
#1: *Obj.Mbr* [= *Val*]
#2: *Obj.MbrA.MbrB* [= *ValB* | *ArgsB*]
#3: *ObjExp*.**VBE**.*Mbr* [= *Val*]
#4: *ObjExp*.**VBE**.*MbrA.MbrB* [= *ValB* | *ArgsB*]

A **VBE** object's syntax supports named arguments and contains these parts:

- *Obj*: Required. A module-level or project-level object variable to be assigned an object instance. *Obj* can be named the same as the **VBE** class being instantiated. *Obj* is declared in the Declarations section of the **ClassModule** object that serves as the add-in or in a standard module. *Obj* can also be declared as the generic **Object** or as **Variant**, but this slows performance.

- *VBInst*: Required. An object expression that is the first argument of the **OnConnection** method of an **IDTExtensibility** object. *VBInst* must be declared **ByVal** and as **Object**. When an add-in is connected, VB passes to *VBInst* an object representing the current instance of the IDE. You then assign this object reference to the module-level or project-level object variable *Obj*.

- *Mbr*: Optional. A member of a **VBE** object.

- *Val*: Optional. You use *Val* if *Mbr* is a property being set.

- *MbrA*: Required. A **VBE** object's property that returns an object or collection.

- *MbrB*: Required. A member of the object or collection that is returned by *MbrA*.

- *ValB | ArgsB*: Optional. You use *ValB* if *MbrB* is a property being set or *ArgsB* if *MbrB* is a method being called.

- *ObjExp*: Required. An object expression that evaluates to an object or collection that has the **VBE** property as a member. *ObjExp* can be an **AddIn**, **Addins**, **CodeModule**, **CodePane**, **CodePanes**, **ContainedVBControls**, **LinkedWindows**, **Member**, **Members**, **Properties**, **Property**, **Reference**, **References**, **SelectedVBControls**, **VBComponent**, **VBComponents**, **VBControl**, **VBControls**, **VBForm**, **VBNewProjects**, **VBProject**, **VBProjects**, **Window**, or **Windows** object.

Members

- Events: None at this time

- Methods: **LoadProject** (Hidden), **Quit**

- Properties: **ActiveCodePane**, **ActiveProject** (Hidden), **ActiveVBProject**, **ActiveWindow**, **AddInMenu** (Hidden), **Addins**, **Application** (Hidden), **CodePanes**, **CommandBars**, **DisplayModel**, **Events**, **FileControl** (Hidden), **FullName**, **LastUsedPath**, **MainWindow**, **Name**, **Parent** (Hidden), **ReadOnly**, **SelectedVBComponent**, **TemplatePath**, **VBProjects**, **Version**, **Windows**

Comments

A **VBE** object is instantiated when an add-in is connected to the current instance of VB's IDE. It is passed in to the add-in's code through the *VBInst* argument of the **OnConnection** method of **IDTExtensibility**. You then use the **Set** statement to assign *VBInst* to object variables in all code modules that need to access the other objects and collections of the Extensibility Object model. An add-in's code can only access the functionality of the Extensibility object library through a **VBE** object.

When you start a new instance of VB and an add-in is connected to it, another **VBE** object is created. The same add-in, with the same **Form** object, can be run simultaneously under several instances of VB. A **VBE** object replaces an **Application** object used in VB4's VBEXT32.OLB Add-In type library. **Application** is a hidden member of VB5's Extensibility Object model.

 To make your add-in code more readable and consistent with the Extensibility object library's terminology displayed by the Object Browser, give the object variable that is assigned the instance of the **VBE** class the name *VBE*.

V-V

EXAMPLE CODE

See the Help topic VBE Object Example in ADDINEFS.HLP or the procedure DemoVBEObj in DEMOSYNT.VBP.

VBForm Object

VBForm represents an object, returned by the **Designer** property of a **VBComponent** object, that enables you to access the design characteristics of a component.

INSTANTIATION

Dim *Obj* **As** [VBIDE.]**VBForm|Object|Variant**
Set *Obj* = **VBE.ActiveVBProject.VBComponents[.Item]**(*Index*).**Designer**

USAGE

#1: *Obj.Mbr*
#2: *Obj.MbrA.MbrB* [= *ValB* | *ArgsB*]

A **VBForm** object's syntax supports named arguments and contains these parts:

- *Obj*: Required. A variable to be assigned an object instance. *Obj* can be named the same as the **VBForm** class being instantiated. *Obj* can also be declared as the generic **Object** or as **Variant**, but this slows performance.

- VBIDE: Optional. The VB5 Extensibility object library containing the **VBForm** class.

- *Index*: Required. Used with the default **Item** method, *Index* is a numeric or **String** expression that specifies the ordinal position of a **VBComponent** object in a **VBComponents** collection. If *Index* is a **String** expression, it must evaluate to the **Name** property of a **VBComponent** object.

- *Mbr*: Required. A member of a **VBForm** object.

- *MbrA*: Required. A **VBForm** object's property that returns an object or collection.

- *MbrB*: Required. A member of the object or collection that is returned by *MbrA*.

- *ValB* | *ArgsB*: Optional. You use *ValB* if *MbrB* is a property being set or *ArgsB* if *MbrB* is a method being called.

MEMBERS

- Events: None at this time

- Methods: **Paste, SelectAll**

- Properties: **CanPaste, ContainedVBControls, Parent, SelectedVBControls, VBControls, VBE**

COMMENTS

A designer provides a visual design window in VB's IDE to create new classes visually. VB4 provided only a designer for forms. The Professional and Enterprise editions of VB5 also implement designers for user controls, property pages, user document forms, and active

V-V

designers. A **VBForm** object can represent any one of these five kinds of designers and can only be instantiated by returning the **Designer** property of a **VBComponent** object. **Designer** returns **Nothing** if a **VBComponent** object doesn't have a designer (for example, a standard module).

The main purpose of a **VBForm** object is to enable you to access and manipulate the controls contained by a designer. You can use the **ContainedVBControls**, **SelectedVBControls**, and **VBControls** properties of a **VBForm** object to return their respective collection objects. You can call the **Paste** and **SelectAll** methods to change the composition of these control collection objects.

1) VB's Object Browser incorrectly states that a **VBForm** object represents a form in a project. Instead, it represents a designer. 2) VB's Help file incorrectly states that **VBForm** returns a component in a project. Instead, it represents a designer returned by the **Designer** property of a **VBComponent** object. 3) VB's Help file incorrectly states that the **ClassName** property, which is a member of a **VBControl** object, determines the default value of a **VBForm** object. Instead, the **ClassName** property has nothing to do with a **VBForm** object.

EXAMPLE CODE

See the Help topic VBForm Object Example in ADDINEFS.HLP or the procedure DemoVBFormObj in DEMOSYNT.VBP.

VBProject Object

VBProject is an item in a **VBProjects** collection and represents an open project in VB's IDE.

INSTANTIATION

Dim *Obj* **As** [VBIDE.]**VBProject**|**Object**|**Variant**
Set *Obj* = **VBE.VBProjects**[.**Item**](*Index*)
Set *Obj* = **VBE.ActiveVBProject**

USAGE

#1: *Obj* [.*Mbr* [= *Val* | *Args*]]
#2: *Obj.MbrA.MbrB* [= *ValB* | *ArgsB*]

A **VBProject** object's syntax supports named arguments and contains these parts:

- *Obj*: Required. A variable to be assigned an object instance. *Obj* can be named the same as the **VBProject** class being instantiated. *Obj* can also be declared as the generic **Object** or as **Variant**, but this slows performance.

- VBIDE: Optional. The VB5 Extensibility object library containing the **VBProject** class.

- *Index*: Required. Used with the default **Item** method, *Index* is a numeric or **String** expression that specifies the ordinal position of a **VBProject** object in a **VBProjects** collection. If *Index* is a **String** expression, it must evaluate to the **Name** property of a **VBProject** object.

- *Mbr*: Required. A member of a **VBProject** object.

V-V

- *Val\Args*: Optional. You use *Val* if *Mbr* is a property being set or *Args* if *Mbr* is a method being called.

- *MbrA*: Required. A **VBProject** object's property that returns an object or collection.

- *MbrB*: Required. A member of the object or collection that is returned by *MbrA*.

- *ValB\ArgsB*: Optional. You use *ValB* if *MbrB* is a property being set or *ArgsB* if *MbrB* is a method being called.

MEMBERS

- Events: None at this time

- Methods: **AddToolboxProgID, MakeCompiledFile, ReadProperty, SaveAs, WriteProperty**

- Properties: **BuildFileName, Collection, CompatibleOleServer, Description, FileName, HelpContextID, HelpFile, IconState, IsDirty, Name, References, Saved, StartMode, Type, VBComponents, VBE**

COMMENTS

You can access a **VBProject** object by:

- Calling the **Item** method of a **VBProjects** collection.

- Returning the **ActiveVBProject** property of a **VBE** object.

- Using a **For...Each...Next** statement to loop through the items of a **VBProjects** collection until you find the **VBProject** object you want.

You can use the **VBProject** object to set properties for a project, to access the **VBComponents** and **References** collections, and to save a project's files or compile them into an EXE or DLL file.

EXAMPLE CODE

See the Help topic VBProject Object Example in ADDINEFS.HLP or the procedure DemoVBProjectObj in DEMOSYNT.VBP.

VBProjects Collection/Property

A **VBProjects** collection contains the **VBProject** objects open in VB's IDE. The read-only **VBProjects** property of a **VBE** object returns an object instance of the **VBProjects** class.

INSTANTIATION

Dim *Obj* **As [VBIDE.]VBProjects|Object|Variant**
Set *Obj* = **VBE.VBProjects**

USAGE

#1: *Obj.Mbr*
#2: *Obj*[**.Item**](*Index*)[.*MbrA*[= *ValA*| *ArgsA*]]
#3: *Obj.MbrB.MbrC*[= *ValC*| *ArgsC*]

The **VBProjects** syntax supports named arguments and contains these parts:

- *Obj*: Required. A variable to be assigned an object instance. *Obj* can be named the same as the **VBProjects** class being instantiated. *Obj* can also be declared as the generic **Object** or as **Variant**, but this slows performance.

- VBIDE: Optional. The VB5 Extensibility object library containing the **VBProjects** class.

- *Mbr*: Required. A member of a **VBProjects** collection other than the **Item** method.

- *Index*: Required. Used with the default **Item** method, *Index* is a numeric or **String** expression that specifies the ordinal position of a **VBProject** object in a **VBProjects** collection. If *Index* is a **String** expression, it must evaluate to the **Name** property of a **VBProject** object.

- *MbrA*: Optional. A member of a **VBProject** object.

- *ValA* | *ArgsA*: Optional. You use *ValA* if *MbrA* is a property being set or *ArgsA* if *MbrA* is a method being called.

- *MbrB*: Required. A **VBProjects** collection's property that returns a **VBE** object.

- *MbrC*: Required. A member of the **VBE** object that is returned by *MbrB*.

- *ValC* | *ArgsC*: Optional. You use *ValC* if *MbrC* is a property being set or *ArgsC* if *MbrC* is a method being called.

MEMBERS

- Events: **ItemActivated, ItemAdded, ItemRemoved, ItemRenamed**

- Methods: **Add, AddFromFile, AddFromTemplate, FileName, Item, Remove, SaveAs**

- Properties: **Count, IconState, Parent, StartProject, VBE**

COMMENTS

A **VBProjects** collection that contains **VBProject** objects represents all the projects that are open in VB's development environment. You use a **VBProjects** collection to access, add, or remove projects from VB's IDE. You can access a **VBProject** object by calling the **Item** method of a **VBProjects** collection or by using a **For...Each...Next** statement to loop through the items of a **VBProjects** collection until you find the **VBProject** object you want. You can use the **Count** property to return the number of **VBProject** objects in the collection.

EXAMPLE CODE

See the Help topic VBProjects Collection/Property Example in ADDINEFS.HLP or the procedure DemoVBProjectsObj in DEMOSYNT.VBP.

VBProjectsEvents Object/Property

A **VBProjectsEvents** object represents all events raised by VB's IDE when a VB project is activated, added, deleted, or renamed. The read-only **VBProjectsEvents** property of an **Events** object returns a **VBProjectsEvents** object.

Usage

#1: **Public WithEvents** *VBProjects* **As VBProjectsEvents**
#2: **Set** *VBProjects* = **VBE.Events.VBProjectsEvents**

The **VBProjectsEvents** syntax contains these parts:

- *VBProjects*: Required. A module-level object variable, in an add-in's **ClassModule** object, that is assigned the **VBProjectsEvents** object returned by the **VBProjectsEvents** property. *VBProjects* must be declared with the **Public** statement and the **WithEvents** keyword and may not be declared as the generic **Object** or as **Variant**.

 In Usage #1, **VBProjectsEvents** is the object. In Usage #2, **VBProjectsEvents** is a property of an **Events** object. This property returns a **VBProjectsEvents** object.

Members

- Events: **ItemActivated, ItemAdded, ItemRemoved, ItemRenamed**

- Methods: None at this time

- Properties: None at this time

Comments

A **VBProjectsEvents** object allows an add-in to receive and react to project-related events raised by VB's IDE. When more than one running add-in is receiving project-related events, VB notifies the add-ins in the order in which they were connected.

To use a **VBProjectsEvents** object, follow these steps in a **ClassModule** object in the add-in's project:

- Use the **Public** statement and the **WithEvents** keyword to declare an object variable that will respond to the project-related events raised by VB. You do this in the Declarations section and the declaration statement adds a **VBProjectsEvents** object, under the name of the object variable, to the class module's Object drop-down box. You can give this object variable any name you want, but it is most readable to name it *VBProjects*.

- Select VBProjects from the Object drop-down box of the class module and VB automatically creates the beginning and ending statements of the **ItemActivated** event procedure. Then, from the Procedure drop-down box, select the other project-related events for which you want to create procedures.

- Write code in the various event procedures that will execute when VB raises their events.

- Make the add-in responsive to VB's project-related events. You do this by using the **VBProjectsEvents** property of an **Events** object to return a **VBProjectsEvents** object that is assigned to *VBProjects*. You can write this assignment statement in the **OnConnection** method of an add-in's **IDTExtensibility** object; or, if you want more flexibility, you can write it in a separate **ClassModule** object that exists solely to respond to add-in related events raised in VB's IDE. See the **ClassModule** object named VBEvents and the **ConnectTo** method declared as **Friend** in DEMOSYNT.VBP for a demonstration of how to do this.

DETAILS

The events of a **VBProjectsEvents** object are listed in Table D.8. The kinds of projects that a **VBProjectsEvents** object gives you control over are listed in Table D.9.

EXAMPLE CODE

See the Help topic VBProjectsEvents Object/Property Example in ADDINEFS.HLP or the procedures DemoVBProjectsEventsObj and ConnectTo in DEMOSYNT.VBP.

Version Property

Version returns a **String** that specifies the version of Visual Basic for Applications that the application is using. Read-only.

USAGE

Obj.Version

The **Version** property's syntax contains these parts:

- *Obj*: Required. An object expression that evaluates to a **VBE** object.

COMMENTS

The **Version** property setting is a string beginning with one or two digits, a period, and two digits; the rest of the string is undefined and may contain text or numbers.

EXAMPLE CODE

See the Help topic Version Property Example in ADDINEFS.HLP or the procedure DemoVersionPrp in DEMOSYNT.VBP.

Table D.8   VBProjectsEvents object's events.

Event	Description
ItemActivated	Occurs after a project is activated
ItemAdded	Occurs after a project is added to VB's IDE
ItemRemoved	Occurs after a project is deleted from VB's IDE
ItemRenamed	Occurs after a project is renamed

Table D.9   Kinds of projects for which VB raises events.

Value/Constant	Description
0 - vbext_pt_StandardExe	Standard executable
1 - vbext_pt_ActiveXExe	ActiveX executable
2 - vbext_pt_ActiveXDll	ActiveX DLL
3 - vbext_pt_ActiveXControl	ActiveX control

V-V

Visible Property

Visible returns or sets a **Boolean** that specifies the visibility of a **Window** object. Read/write.

Usage

*Obj.*Visible [= *Val*]

The **Visible** property's syntax contains these parts:

- *Obj*: Required. An object expression that evaluates to a **Window** object.

- *Val*: Optional. Only used when you set **Visible,** *Val* is a **Boolean** expression that specifies that the window is visible (the default of **True**) or that the window is hidden (**False**).

Comments

Applying the **Close** method to a **Window** object has the same effect as setting its **Visible** property to **False.** There is no **Open** or **Show** method that you can use after applying the **Close** method to a window; instead, you must set its **Visible** property to **True** to see the window again.

 VB's Help file incorrectly states that the **Visible** property applies to a **CodePane** object. Instead, it applies only to a **Window** object.

Example Code

See the Help topic Visible Property Example in ADDINEFS.HLP or the procedure DemoVisiblePrp in DEMOSYNT.VBP.

Width Property

Width returns a **Long** or sets a numeric expression that specifies the width of a window in VB's IDE. Read/write.

Usage

*Obj.*Width[= *Val*]

The **Width** property's syntax contains these parts:

- *Obj*: Required. An object expression that evaluates to a **Window** object.

- *Val*: Optional. Only used when you set **Width,** *Val* is a numeric expression that specifies in pixels the width of a VB IDE window.

Comments

 There is a difference between the **Width** property of a VB IDE designer **Window** object (specified in pixels) and the **Width** property of a VB **Form** object (specified in twips). The value returned by the **Width** property of a **Window** object depends on whether or not the window is linked or docked. If the window is linked, the value of **Width** is actually for the frame window to which it is linked. If the window is not linked, the value of **Width** is for the window itself.

If you set the width of a VB IDE window to a value greater than the width of the **Screen** object, VB adjusts the window's width to that of a maximized **Form** object plus four pixels. Setting the **Width** property of a linked window has no effect.

1) VB's Help file and the Object Browser incorrectly state that the **Width** property of a **Window** object is specified in twips. Instead, it is specified in pixels. 2) VB's Help file incorrectly states that **Width** returns a **Single**. Instead, it returns a **Long**.

EXAMPLE CODE
See the Help topic Width Property Example in ADDINEFS.HLP or the procedure DemoWidthPrp in DEMOSYNT.VBP.

Window Object/Property

Window is an item in a **Windows** collection and represents a window in VB's IDE. The read-only **Window** property of a **CodePane** object returns an object instance of the **Window** class.

INSTANTIATION
Dim *Obj* As [VBIDE.]Window|Object|Variant
Set *Obj* = **VBE.Windows**[.**Item**](*IndexA*)
Set *Obj* = **VBE.ActiveWindow**
Set *Obj*=**VBE.ActiveVBProject.VBComponents**[.**Item**](*IndexB*).**CodeModule**.
CodePane.Window

USAGE
#1: *Obj*[.*Mbr*[= *Val*]]
#2: *Obj*.*MbrA*.*MbrB*[= *ValB* | *ArgsB*]

A **Window** object's syntax supports named arguments and contains these parts:

- *Obj*: Required. A variable to be assigned an object instance. *Obj* can be named the same as the **Window** class being instantiated. *Obj* can also be declared as the generic **Object** or as **Variant**, but this slows performance.

- VBIDE: Optional. The VB5 Extensibility object library containing the **Window** class.

- *IndexA*: Required. Used with the default **Item** method, *IndexA* is a numeric or **String** expression that specifies the ordinal position of a **Window** object in a **Windows** collection. If *IndexA* is a **String** expression, it must evaluate to the **Caption** property of a **Window** object.

- *IndexB*: Required. Used with the default **Item** method, *IndexB* is a numeric or **String** expression that specifies the ordinal position of a **VBComponent** object in a **VBComponents** collection. If *IndexB* is a **String** expression, it must evaluate to the **Name** property of a **VBComponent** object.

- *Mbr*: Required. A member of a **Window** object.

- *Val*: Optional. You use *Val* if *Mbr* is a property being set.

- *MbrA*: Required. A **Window** object's property that returns an object or collection.

- *MbrB*: Required. A member of the object or collection that is returned by *MbrA*.

- *ValB* | *ArgsB*: Optional. You use *ValB* if *MbrB* is a property being set or *ArgsB* if *MbrB* is a method being called.

MEMBERS

- Events: None at this time

- Methods: **Close, SetFocus**

- Properties: **Caption, Collection, Height, HWnd** (Hidden), **Left, LinkedWindowFrame, LinkedWindows, Top, Type, VBE, Visible, Width, WindowState**

COMMENTS

You can access a **Window** object by:

- Calling the **Item** method of a **Windows** collection.

- Returning the **ActiveWindow** property of a **VBE** object.

- Returning the **Window** property of a **CodePane** object.

- Using a **For...Each...Next** statement to loop through the items of a **Windows** collection until you find the **Window** object you want.

You can read the **Caption, Type,** or **WindowState** properties of **Window** to determine which item in a **Windows** collection you are working with. To hide a window, apply the **Close** method or set the **Visible** property to **False**. To show a window, apply the **SetFocus** method or set the **Visible** property to **True**. Set the **Left** and **Top** properties to position a window or the **Height** and **Width** properties to size it.

1) VB's Help file and the Object Browser incorrectly state that the **Left, Top, Height,** and **Width** properties of a **Window** object are specified in twips. Instead, they are specified in pixels. 2) VB's Help file incorrectly states that the **Left, Top, Height,** and **Width** properties return a **Single**. Instead, they return a **Long**.

EXAMPLE CODE

See the Help topic Window Object Example in ADDINEFS.HLP or the procedure DemoWindowObj in DEMOSYNT.VBP.

Windows Collection/Property

A **Windows** collection contains all **Window** objects that represent open or permanent windows in VB's IDE. The read-only **Windows** property of a **VBE** object returns an object instance of the **Windows** class.

INSTANTIATION

Dim *Obj* As [VBIDE.]Windows|Object|Variant
Set *Obj* = VBE.Windows

USAGE

#1: *Obj.Mbr*
#2: *Obj*[.**Item**](*Index*)[.*MbrA*[= *ValA*]]
#3: *Obj.MbrB.MbrC*[= *ValC* | *ArgsC*]

The **Windows** syntax supports named arguments and contains these parts:

- *Obj*: Required. A variable to be assigned an object instance. *Obj* can be named the same as the **Windows** class being instantiated. *Obj* can also be declared as the generic **Object** or as **Variant**, but this slows performance.

- VBIDE: Optional. The VB5 Extensibility object library containing the **Windows** class.

- *Mbr*: Required. A member of a **Windows** collection other than the **Item** method.

- *Index*: Required. Used with the default **Item** method, *Index* is a numeric or **String** expression that specifies the ordinal position of a **Window** object in a **Windows** collection. If *Index* is a **String** expression, it must evaluate to the **Caption** property of a **Window** object.

- *MbrA*: Optional. A member of a **Window** object.

- *ValA*: Optional. You use *ValA* if *MbrA* is a property being set.

- *MbrB*: Required. A **Windows** collection's property that returns a **VBE** object.

- *MbrC*: Required. A member of the **VBE** object that is returned by *MbrB*.

- *ValC* | *ArgsC*: Optional. You use *ValC* if *MbrC* is a property being set or *ArgsC* if *MbrC* is a method being called.

MEMBERS

- Events: None at this time

- Methods: **CreateToolWindow, Item**

- Properties: **Count, Parent, VBE**

COMMENTS

A **Windows** collection has a fixed set of permanent IDE windows that are always available in the collection, such as the Project window, the Properties window, and so on. Closing a permanent window does not remove the corresponding **Window** object from a **Windows** collection, but results in the window not being visible.

A **Windows** collection also has a variable set of windows that represent all open code module windows and designer windows. Opening a code or designer window adds a new member to a **Windows** collection. Closing a code or designer window removes a member from a **Windows** collection.

EXAMPLE CODE

See the Help topic Windows Collection/Property Example in ADDINEFS.HLP or the procedure DemoWindowsObj in DEMOSYNT.VBP.

WindowState Property

WindowState returns a **Long** or sets a numeric expression that specifies the visual state of a
window at run time. Read/write.

USAGE

Obj.**WindowState** [= *Val*]

The **WindowState** property's syntax contains these parts:

*   *Obj* : Required. An object expression that evaluates to a **Window** object.

*   *Val* : Optional. Only used when you set **WindowState**, *Val* is a numeric expression that
    specifies the state of a **Window** object, as described in Settings.

SETTINGS

The **WindowState** property returns or sets these values:

*   0 - **vbext_ws_Normal**: Normal (default)

*   1 - **vbext_ws_Minimize**: Minimized (minimized to an icon)

*   2 - **vbext_ws_Maximize**: Maximized (enlarged to maximum size)

COMMENTS

If a **Window** object's **Visible** property is set to **False**, its **WindowState** property returns
vbext_ws_Normal. However, setting an invisible window's **WindowState** property to
vbext_ws_Normal makes the window visible.

If you try to minimize or maximize a permanent IDE window that does not support such a
setting (for example, Project or Properties), no trappable error occurs and the window simply
receives the focus. Because they are assigned the same values, you could use the VBRUN type
library's intrinsic constants **vbNormal**, **vbMinimized**, and **vbMaximized** instead of the VBIDE
constants listed in Settings.

VB's Help file incorrectly states that two of the intrinsic constants for
WindowState are **vbext_ws_Min** and **vbext_ws_Max**. Instead, they are as
listed in Settings.

EXAMPLE CODE

See the Help topic WindowState Property Example in ADDINEFS.HLP or the procedure
DemoWindowStatePrp in DEMOSYNT.VBP.

WriteProperty Method

WriteProperty is a **Sub** that saves a property's setting as a **String** to the specified user-defined section and key in a project's or component's file.

USAGE

#1: *Obj*.**WriteProperty** *Section, Key, Value*
#2: *Obj*.**WriteProperty** *Key, Value*

The **WriteProperty** method's syntax supports named arguments and contains these parts:

- *Obj*: Required. An object expression that evaluates to an object that has **WriteProperty** as a member.

- *Section*: Optional. Used only when *Obj* is a **VBProject** object, *Section* is a **String** expression that specifies the name of the section where *Key* is found.

- *Key*: Required. A **String** expression that specifies the name of the property whose setting is to be written.

- *Value*: Required. A **String** expression that specifies the setting of the property to be written.

COMMENTS

After you call **WriteProperty** to save a property's setting to a project's VBP file or a component's file, you can read its stored value by calling the **ReadProperty** method. In the Example code, the setting for the **Picture** property is stored as Attribute VB_Ext_KEY = "Picture", "C:\VB5\GRAPHICS\ICONS\ELEMENTS\FIRE.ICO".

EXAMPLE CODE

See the Help topic WriteProperty Method Example in ADDINEFS.HLP or the procedure DemoWritePropertyMet in DEMOSYNT.VBP.

ZOrder Method

ZOrder is a **Function** that places a control object at the front or back of the z-order within its graphical level and returns a **VBControl** object that represents the placed control.

USAGE

Obj.**ZOrder**(*Position*)

The **ZOrder** method's syntax supports named arguments and contains these parts:

- *Obj*: Required. An object expression that evaluates to a **VBControl** object.

- *Position*: Required. A numeric expression that specifies the position of *Obj* relative to other instances of the same object. If *Position* is 0 - **vbBringToFront**, *Obj* is positioned at the front of the z-order. If *Position* is 1 - **vbSendToBack**, *Obj* is positioned at the back of the z-order.

W-

COMMENTS

Calling the **ZOrder** method programmatically is the same as setting the z-order of control objects by manually selecting the Format|Order|Bring To Front or Format|Order|Send To Back commands. Do not confuse the **ZOrder** method of the **VBControl** object with the **ZOrder** method that applies to most of VB's controls. The former is only called by an add-in at design time while the latter is called by an application at runtime.

Three graphical layers are associated with forms and controls. The back layer is the drawing space where the results of the graphics methods are displayed. Next is the middle layer where graphical objects and **Label** controls are displayed. The front layer is where all nongraphical controls like **CommandButton**, **CheckBox**, or **ListBox** are displayed. Anything contained in a layer closer to the front covers anything contained in the layer(s) behind it. **ZOrder** arranges objects only within the layer where the object is displayed.

 VB's Help file incorrectly states that you can manually set the z-order of a control by selecting the Edit|Bring To Front or Edit|Send To Back commands. Instead, in VB5 you must select the Format|Order|Bring To Front or Format|Order|Send To Back commands.

EXAMPLE CODE

See the Help topic ZOrder Method Example in ADDINEFS.HLP or the procedure DemoZOrderMet in DEMOSYNT.VBP.

INDEX

V

Value property, 157
Variables, scoping locally, 28-29
VB components. *See also* projects.
  ActiveX designer modules, 138
  definition, 137
  designer-related members, 140-141
  file manipulation, 141-144
  file types, 137
  forms, 140-141
  non-designer accessor properties, 140
  property pages, 140-141
  startup modules, 139
  user controls, 140-141
  user documents, 140-141
  VB-created modules, adding, 138
VB controls, 146-147
  container controls, 148
  types, 148
  ZOrder method, 148
VB IDE window captions, changing, 243-246
VB tool window, creating, 127-128
VB Toolbox
  adding ActiveX controls, 134
  adding embedded components, 134
  deleting components, 135
VB (Visual Basic), shutting down, 109
VB4 Application object, 105-106
VBAI class library
  methods, 58-60
  size, 57
VBComponent object automation, 192-193
VBComponents collection, 137
VBComponentsEvents accessor property, 180
VBComponentsEvents object, 17, 181
VBControls collection, 145-146
VBControlsEvents accessor property, 180
VBControlsEvents object
  event-related objects, 181
  IDTExtensibility object, 17
  naming, 18
VBE, declaring as Public, 27-28
VBE argument, 92
VBEvents class procedures, 26-27

vbext_cm_AfterStartup argument
  code example, 80-81
  definition, 79
vbext_cm_External argument, 79
vbext_cm_Startup argument, 79
vbext_mt_Const member object, 168
vbext_mt_Event member object, 168
vbext_mt_Method member object, 168
vbext_mt_Property member object, 168
vbext_mt_Variable member object, 168
VBForm object, 145-146
VBProject object automation, 192
VBProjects collection
  Add method, 120-121
  AddFromFile method, 121-122
  AddFromTemplate method, 121-122
  IconState property, 120, 124
  projects
    adding, 120-121
    assigning as different status, 120
    file status, returning, 124
    removing, 123
    saving, 122
    starting automatically, 124-125
  Remove method, 123
  SaveAs method, 122
  StartProject property, 120, 124
VBProjects property, 108
VBProjectsEvents accessor property, 180
VBProjectsEvents object, 17, 181
Version compatibility property, setting, 44
Version property, 108
Visual designers, 140-141
  manipulating, 145-146

W

Windows. *See also* Windows collection.
  linked, positioning, 126
  VB main, 108
  window type, returning, 126
Windows collection
  Caption property, 126
  Close property, 126
  Height property, 126
  Left property, 126

Got Bugs in Your Access/VB Apps?